GRILLAERT

LIFE, HEALTH, AND ANNUITY REINSURANCE

John E. Tiller, Jr., FSA
Denise Fagerberg, FSA

ACTEX Publications, Inc.
Winsted and Avon, Connecticut

Requests for permission should be addressed to
    ACTEX Publications
    P.O. Box 974
    Winsted, CT 06098

Manufactured in the United States of America

10 9 8 7 6 5 4 3 2 1

Cover Design by MUF

Library of Congress Cataloging-in-Publication Data

Tiller, John E.
    Life and health reinsurance / John E. Tiller, Denise E. Fagerberg.
        p.   cm.
    Includes bibliographical references and index.
    ISBN 0-936031-06-9
    1. Reinsurance--United States. 2. Insurance, Life--United States.
    3. Insurance, Health--United States. I. Fagerberg, Denise E.
    II. Title.
    HG8083. T55   1990
    368.3'0122--dc20   90-44071
                                                          CIP

ISBN: 0-936031-06-9

Introduction

The reinsurance mechanism is critical to the smooth and efficient functioning of the primary life and health insurance market. Yet, the insurance literature that is focused on this specialized field is sparse. This book fills the current gap in the literature by providing a comprehensive survey of reinsurance concepts, products and practices.

The book is comprehensive. The text defines basic reinsurance terms, describes traditional reinsurance products, introduces contemporary uses of reinsurance, discusses treaty wording and administrative practices, and summarizes current practices in the legal, regulatory and accounting environment.

The book will be useful to students and experienced practitioners alike regarding historical and generally accepted practices within the life and health reinsurance industry.

A basic introduction to life, health and annuity reinsurance has been overdue for some time. As an individual who has enjoyed both a personal and professional involvement with the world of reinsurance for most of my business career, it is a pleasure to thank the authors for their contribution.

William K. Tyler, FSA
Lincoln National Life Insurance Company

Preface

This book was written to provide, in one source, the life and health insurance industry with both basic and advanced information regarding the various aspects of reinsurance. Since new applications for reinsurance are still being introduced, an exhaustive list of legitimate uses would be impossible. However, the principles of reinsurance remain relatively constant. This book documents the basic principles which the authors believe apply to life, health, and annuity reinsurance, as well as the widely used applications and practices. Some examples and applications of these principles regarding specific products or features are included to enhance the reader's understanding.

This book is intended to be a reference for both experts and novices involved in either ceding or assuming reinsurance. In analyzing a specific reinsurance need or agreement, the reader should be aware that a seemingly infinite number of legitimate variations of reinsurance are possible in practice. It is this diversity which creates the intellectual richness of the field.

The reader is assumed to have a basic knowledge of individual life, health, and annuity products and practices. The book takes the reader from the very basic definitions and uses of reinsurance to very advanced applications. While both authors are

Fellows of the Society of Actuaries, an actuarial background is not necessary for understanding the concepts presented in the book except for the discussions of pricing and retention limit determination in Chapters Eight and Nine.

The book is intended primarily for United States and Canadian audiences, but the basic principles apply internationally. Considerations specific to international reinsurance transactions are discussed in Chapter Eighteen.

The book is arranged in four parts. Part One, consisting of Chapters One through Five, addresses the basic terminology of life, health, and annuity reinsurance and builds to working models of the more popular plans of reinsurance, including the coinsurance hybrids. It is recommended that all readers review these chapters, at least for vocabulary and general understanding.

Chapter One introduces many of the basic reinsurance terms and presents a discussion of the uses of reinsurance, the various classifications of reinsurance, the classifications of reinsurers, and the operational effects of reinsurance.

Chapter Two is devoted to a detailed discussion of automatic reinsurance. The normal requirements for automatic reinsurance, the methods of determining the amounts of automatic reinsurance, and the methods of allocating automatic reinsurance are covered.

Underwriting and facultative reinsurance considerations are presented in Chapter Three. The uses of facultative reinsurance are discussed as well as the considerations in developing a facultative program.

Chapter Four discusses traditional reinsurance and addresses the operation, uses, and characteristics of coinsurance, modified coinsurance, and yearly renewable term reinsurance. A simplistic model is developed to illustrate the effects of each plan on, and differences in results for, both the ceding and the assuming companies.

Financial reinsurance is discussed in Chapter Five. Models are used to illustrate the effects of coinsurance, modified coinsurance, funds withheld coinsurance, funds withheld modified coinsurance, and combinations of coinsurance and modified coinsurance. These models have evolved over a number of years and have been tested in seminars and lectures as well as in written formats.

By studying the models in Chapters Four and Five, the reader can gain an understanding of the various plans of reinsurance, including both similarities and differences. This understanding should be helpful in designing a reinsurance program to fit the needs of a particular situation.

Part Two is comprised of Chapters Six through Nine and deals with the administrative and functional considerations of reinsurance.

Chapter Six addresses the document known as the reinsurance treaty or reinsurance agreement. The normal terms and provisions contained in a typical treaty are reviewed.

Chapter Seven discusses reinsurance administration for both ceding and assuming companies. Typical procedures and functional responsibilities for both individual cession and self-administered reinsurance are described.

Chapter Eight deals with management of reinsurance by the ceding company. Four basic approaches for setting retention limits are described. Methods of evaluating the financial and nonfinancial aspects of reinsurance proposals are discussed, as well as certain considerations for managing facultative, financial, and inforce reinsurance. Many systems and methods exist for pricing individual life insurance products; it would be impractical, if not impossible, to document all of these. This chapter has been designed to assist the reader in identifying the considerations necessary to reflect reinsurance in the pricing of the ceding company's products.

Assuming company considerations are discussed in Chapter Nine. As in Chapter Eight, the reader is assumed to have an understanding of the principles of pricing individual life insurance products. The principles of reinsurance pricing are the same as for direct products, although the risks, guarantees, and benefits may be different. This chapter discusses many of the special considerations which arise in pricing reinsurance. The discussions of reinsurance pricing, experience refund formulas, bonuses, and chargebacks, in particular, will also be of interest to ceding company personnel involved in soliciting and evaluating reinsurance proposals or in administering and reporting ceded reinsurance.

Part Three, which includes Chapters Ten through Fourteen, covers regulatory, accounting, and tax considerations for companies operating in the United States. The reader is assumed to have an understanding of the basic principles of insurance regulation, statutory and GAAP accounting, and federal taxation of life insurance companies. These chapters are designed to build upon that knowledge through a discussion and application of those principles to the special requirements of reinsurance.

These chapters address the most fluid areas of the topic since changes occur almost continuously. While the reader is urged to do independent research regarding current guidelines when reviewing or designing a reinsurance agreement, the underlying premises and considerations should remain as discussed in these chapters. Material in these chapters was current as of August 1990.

Chapter Ten addresses the regulatory environment and the special concerns of regulators in various states in the United States. A major concern surrounds risk transfer analysis and requirements. It is almost impossible to separate any discussion of the regulatory issues from those of insolvency in Chapter Eleven and those of statutory accounting in Chapter Twelve.

Chapter Eleven is devoted to an examination of insolvency and its effect on the operation of a reinsurance treaty. This is especially important to those involved in long-term reinsurance commitments.

Statutory accounting in the United States is the subject of Chapter Twelve. Although modifications and refinements in reporting requirements and standards typically occur annually, the principles remain relatively unchanged.

GAAP accounting is discussed in Chapter Thirteen. While the details are also subject to modification by the accounting profession, this chapter documents the considerations unique to reinsurance transactions.

Chapter Fourteen addresses basic tax implications and principles, both state and federal, as they apply to reinsurance transactions. The bulk of this chapter is devoted to United States federal income taxation and its influence and effect on reinsurance agreements.

Part Four of the book is made up of Chapters Fifteen through Twenty-two and describes certain special topics and applications.

Chapter Fifteen covers aspects of nonproportional reinsurance: stop loss, catastrophe, and spread loss. While not as well known as the plans of reinsurance discussed earlier, these types of reinsurance are common in the field of health reinsurance and may even play a key role in the management of life insurance operations.

Chapter Sixteen discusses the unique aspects of assumption reinsurance, including the effects on policyholders, the financial effects on both the ceding company and the assuming company, and strategic considerations.

Chapter Seventeen deals with the captive reinsurance company concept. Business, financial, regulatory, and tax considerations involving agent-owned reinsurance companies and credit captive companies are discussed.

Reinsurance transactions involving United States life insurance companies and companies domiciled in Canada, the United Kingdom, Australia, Continental Europe, Japan, and offshore locations are reviewed in Chapter Eighteen. The basic principles of international reinsurance are also discussed.

Chapters Nineteen through Twenty-two address the reinsurance of specific insurance products or features. These chapters provide discussion of some of the special considerations which might be involved in reinsuring these products, applying the principles discussed in the previous chapters.

Chapter Nineteen reviews considerations specific to the reinsurance of accident and health insurance. Chapter Twenty discusses the reinsurance of annuities, and Chapter Twenty-one addresses other lines of insurance, such as credit and group, and certain products, benefits, and provisions which require special consideration for reinsurance. Chapter Twenty-two covers the treatment of deficiency reserves, dividend options, conversions, and reissues and changes, and discusses reinsurance with affiliates and the role of insurance intermediaries.

Fairview, Texas
August, 1990

John E. Tiller, Jr.
Denise Fagerberg

Acknowledgments

This book was made possible by the efforts of a number of people, whose contributions we gratefully acknowledge. These include many people with whom we have had discussions regarding reinsurance over the past sixteen years or so. It is impossible to remember all such conversations, but we thank all of these people just the same. Of course, the work experience provided by our employers, both past and present, and our clients was a major opportunity to increase our understanding of reinsurance.

In the same vein, we acknowledge the contributions of the many people whose books, papers, study notes, journal articles, and meeting discussions contributed to our knowledge of the reinsurance topic. In this regard, there is a wealth of information to be found in the *Transactions* and the *Record* of the Society of Actuaries, and we recommend this material to the interested reader.

Part of our early reinsurance education resulted from our preparation for the Society of Actuaries examination on that topic. We would like to acknowledge the authors of the various examination study notes, especially the late John C. Wooddy, FSA.

Many individuals were involved in the manuscript reviews leading to the publication of this book, and we wish to thank all of them. If we have left anyone out, please accept our sincere apologies.

Specific chapters of the first draft of the manuscript were reviewed by the following persons: John E. Bailey, FSA, Northwestern Mutual Life Insurance Company; Cecil D. Bykerk, FSA, Mutual of Omaha Insurance Company; Sue Ann Collins, FSA, Tillinghast / Towers Perrin; Deborah A. Gero, FSA, Tillinghast / Towers Perrin; Robert P. Johnson, FSA, Atrium Corporation; Donald C. Kiefer, FSA, Northwestern Mutual Life Insurance Company; Denis W. Loring, FSA, Equitable Life Assurance Society; Richard S. Miller, FSA, Tillinghast / Towers Perrin; Thomas W. Reese, FSA, Tillinghast / Towers Perrin; Irwin T. Vanderhoof, FSA, I.T. Vanderhoof Consulting; Diane Wallace, FSA, D.B. Wallace Company; Michael R. Winn, FSA, Lewis & Ellis Inc.; A. Greig Woodring, FSA, General American Life Insurance Company; James W. Ylvisaker, FSA, Cologne Life Reinsurance Company; and Melville J. Young, FSA, Tillinghast / Towers Perrin.

In addition to these selected chapter reviewers, the first draft was reviewed in its entirety by the following persons: David M. Holland, FSA, Munich American Reassurance Company; Peter B. Patterson, FSA, Mercantile & General Reinsurance Company; Jack M. Turnquist, FSA, Totidem Verbis; William K. Tyler, FSA, Lincoln National Life Insurance Company; and William W. Zeilman, FSA, Life Reassurance Corporation of America.

Several draft versions following the initial review were used as study notes by the Society of Actuaries Education and Examination program for their Course I-550 exam. In connection with this, valuable editorial improvements were made by Bruce D. Moore, FSA, Prudential Insurance Company of America, and his contribution is gratefully acknowledged.

The final draft was again submitted for a complete review by Cecil Bykerk, and by review teams at Lincoln National (headed by Bill Tyler, and including Mike Higgins, Larsh Rothert, and Jim Schibley), Mercantile & General (headed by Pete Patterson, and including Steve Abba, Bill Caulfield-Browne, Bill Hazlewood, Martin Kirr, Renate Nellich, Leo Penney, and Bob Tiessen), and Munich American (headed by Craig M. Baldwin, FSA, and including David Bruggeman, Maureen Fuller, Bob Orean, and Becky Underwood).

Other contributions to the final text for which we are extremely grateful include the following: Dave Holland for providing us with the updates of NAIC proceedings and with general encouragement; Robert Kaufman of Creative Strategies and Ardian Gill, FSA, and Kirk Roeser, FSA, of Gill and Roeser, Inc. for providing us with a basic glossary of reinsurance terms upon which the glossary included in this text is based; Darlene M. Cox, American United Life Insurance Company, for providing the reporting and auditing guidelines developed by the Reinsurance Section of the Society of Actuaries, reproduced as Appendix B and Appendix C; and Lincoln National Life Insurance Company for providing the sample reinsurance treaty reproduced as Appendix A.

Jim Schibley of Lincoln National deserves special thanks for his time in discussing legal and regulatory points of reinsurance with us.

Special thanks is also due to Bill Tyler of Lincoln National for writing the Introduction to the text, in addition to his valuable contributions to the manuscript review.

Certain individuals also provided us with specific information or made themselves available to discuss technical points. These include Diane Wallace, FSA, of D. B. Wallace Company; Richard S. Miller, FSA, and Melville Young, FSA, of Tillinghast / Towers Perrin; William E. Simms, Shigeko Kagawa, and Phillip Kruse of Transamerica Occidental Life Insurance Company; Richard N. O'Brien; Gordon Dowsley of Crown Life Insurance Company; LeRoy H. Christenson, FSA, of American United Life Insurance Company; Carolyn Cobb of the American Council of Life Insurance; and Sheldon D. Summers, FSA, and John O. Montgomery, FSA, of the California Department of Insurance.

We also wish to acknowledge the contributions of Tillinghast / Towers Perrin. Not only did the management and our colleagues show much encouragement throughout the project, but the firm also provided typists for much of the book.

We would like to express our appreciation to the people at ACTEX Publications, who took the project from manuscript form to a finished textbook. The principal persons involved in this phase of the project were Dick London, FSA, managing editor, Marilyn J. Baleshiski, format and layout editor, and Marlene F. Lundbeck, the graphic artist who designed the text's cover.

Finally, our very, very special thanks go to our friend, Jack M. Turnquist, FSA, of Totidem Verbis in Dallas for his technical review and assistance in topic selection, organization, and expression. Without Jack's contributions, this work would be of less value, although probably shorter. Nor should we forget Jack's wife Edith who opened her home to us while we worked with Jack.

J.T. & D.F.

Contents

PART TWO
ADMINISTRATIVE AND FUNCTIONAL
CONSIDERATIONS

PART THREE
REGULATORY, ACCOUNTING, AND
TAX CONSIDERATIONS

PART FOUR
SPECIAL TOPICS AND APPLICATIONS

About the Authors

To ELIZABETH ELAINE and VICTORIA JO,
our other collaborations,
and to KATHERINE MARIE and MARY ELIZABETH.

Perhaps some day the Tiller girls will be able to use this book
to help answer the age-old question facing all actuarial
offspring: "What do your parents do?"

Basic Terminology of Life, Health, and Annuity Reinsurance

Part One

1 | Introduction

In the simplest terms, reinsurance refers to insurance purchased by an insurance company to cover all or part of certain risks on insurance policies issued by that company. Reinsurance is the process whereby one insurance company, referred to as the reinsurer, for a consideration, agrees to indemnify another insurance company, referred to as the ceding company or the reinsured, against all or part of a loss which the ceding company may incur under certain policies of insurance which it has issued. The fundamental principle of reinsurance is that a transfer of risk occurs. The risk transferred can be either a single risk, or any combination of the risks on the underlying policies.

This book is concerned only with reinsurance risks transferred on individual and group life, health, and annuity policies.[1] The risks transferred under a reinsurance arrangement on these policies may include mortality, morbidity, lapse or surrender, expense, and investment performance. Depending on the terms of the reinsurance arrangement, the reinsurer's participation in any one of these risks can vary from none to total.

---

[1]For information on reinsurance for property and casualty coverages, see Strain [15].

3

In this chapter, many of the basic terms used are introduced and defined. The uses of reinsurance, classifications of reinsurance, classifications of reinsurers, and the operational effects of reinsurance are discussed.

USES OF REINSURANCE

Reinsurance is one of the major risk management tools available to insurance companies, providing these companies with protection against adverse fluctuations in experience. Reinsurance is also a powerful financial planning tool. It can be used to increase or decrease the statutory earnings and surplus for either the ceding company or the reinsurer in any given year. The most common reasons why an insurance company would purchase or sell reinsurance are discussed below.

Mortality/Morbidity Risk Transfer

Perhaps the most common reason for an insurance company to purchase reinsurance is to enable that company to issue a policy on a single life for an amount in excess of the limit which it considers to be prudent. This predetermined limit is called the retention limit. If there is no retention limit, or if the limit is set at too high a level, a company could face insolvency if it experienced a number of large claims over a short period of time. The retention limit is normally set at a level which will enable the company to use reinsurance as a tool to smooth out fluctuations in statutory earnings and surplus which could result from variations in the claim frequency and volume.

Lapse or Surrender Risk Transfer

Generally, an insurance company cedes business to cover excessive mortality or morbidity risks but, on occasion, a company may cede reinsurance to cover the risk of excessive lapses or surrenders. The lapse or surrender risk is the greatest on products with large first year surplus strain, particularly on products where the first year commission or the sum of first year commission and the first year cash value exceeds the first year premium. Products with steeply increasing premiums and products with heavy policy loan activity also are prone to high lapses or surrenders.

Investment Risk Transfer

In some cases, the ceding company may reinsure a block of business in order to take advantage of the reinsurer's investment facilities or otherwise shift part of the investment risk to the reinsurer. Historically, this course of action has rarely been taken. It may be used when the reinsurer has access to particular investments which are not available to the ceding company or when the ceding company wishes to avoid a high concentration of assets arising from a single product or from a single large policy, such as an annuity.

New Business Financing

A common use of reinsurance is to finance the acquisition of new business. In certain circumstances, the acquisition costs and reserve requirements associated with the writing of new business may be such that a successful sales effort would depress statutory earnings to the point of possible impairment of the company's statutory capital and surplus position. In this situation, the insurance company may seek a reinsurer willing to share the burden of the acquisition costs. In most cases, the sharing of acquisition costs will be in proportion to the mortality or morbidity risk sharing. In some instances, where permitted by state regulations, the reinsurer may actually cover a proportionately larger amount of the first year surplus strain, increasing its expected profit margins in later years to recover its additional investment.

Underwriting Assistance

An insurer may seek reinsurance for underwriting needs. In the early days of reinsurance, all business subject to reinsurance was underwritten by the reinsurers and the reinsurers were the underwriting experts. Many insurance companies today use an underwriting manual developed by a reinsurer, and the reinsurer may provide training for the insurer's underwriters.

The availability of an experienced reinsurance underwriter provides the insurer's underwriter the opportunity to have a difficult case reviewed, to seek a second opinion, or to obtain a more competitive rating. The reinsurer, which typically sees a greater number of large or complicated risks, often makes more aggressive underwriting decisions than a ceding company due to more advanced underwriting knowledge and techniques and because it has a wider spread of these risks. Competitive pressure among reinsurers may also lead to more aggressive underwriting decisions.

The reinsurer may be willing to reinsure all or a large portion of a difficult case, enabling the insurance company to place the case for its agent. An insurance company may maintain an underwriting relationship with several reinsurers in order to offer its agents the best possible underwriting service on difficult cases. In fact, several reinsurers may share the risk on a given policy.

Gaining Product Expertise

An insurance company entering a new line of business or embarking in otherwise unfamiliar territory, may form a partnership arrangement with a reinsurer because of the reinsurer's expertise in this particular area. The ceding company may receive assistance from the reinsurer in product development. In some cases, the ceding company may utilize the reinsurer's administration systems for a fee or in exchange for ceding the reinsurance on the product. Typically, such an arrangement lasts for only a short period of time until the insurer has gained sufficient experience to administer the business itself.

Divesting a Product Line

An insurance company may cede reinsurance in order to exit from a certain product line or geographic area. It may choose to cede the business by the means of an assumption reinsurance agreement,[2] or through indemnity reinsurance.

Fronting

In some reinsurance transactions, the ceding company is "fronting" for another company, that is, issuing insurance policies to specified applicants at the request of another company, then reinsuring all or substantially all of the risks on the insurance to the other company. The ceding company receives a fee or portion of the profits on the business it has issued for the reinsurer. Fronting may be used in the circumstance of a company desiring to do business in a certain jurisdiction where it is not yet licensed. In order to secure business in that jurisdiction, the company finds an appropriately licensed company willing to write the insurance on its

---

[2]See Chapter 16, Assumption Reinsurance.

own policy forms and reinsure it. The reinsurer, in this circumstance, may perform the actual policy administration and underwrite the policies as well.

Several states have very specific regulations regarding fronting. Quality of service and certainty of benefit payments to policyholders are of primary concern to regulators as they have no jurisdiction over unlicensed insurers.[3]

Increasing Ceding Company Sales and Profits

While there is a cost to reinsurance, there are advantages for a company to write business and cede the excess risk. Some of the most common advantages are discussed below.

(1) Because reinsurers normally have lower issue and administrative expenses,[4] reinsurance frequently can be purchased at a relatively low marginal cost to the ceding company. Within reason, the insurance company can cede a large portion of the risks on an insurance policy and still maintain an acceptable level of profit on the total policy. A small profit is generally considered superior to no profit at all.

(2) The company's agency force can write business with the company which might otherwise be placed with competitors having higher retention limits. This increases the insurance company's sales and enables the agents to earn more commissions with one company, encouraging loyalty. Reinsurance allows smaller companies to compete with companies having larger retention limits.

(3) The insurance company's underwriters can gain valuable experience in underwriting larger amounts of insurance which will be useful when retention limits are increased. This would not be possible if all large policies were declined.

(4) If the reinsurance treaty contains a recapture provision, the company may increase its retention limit at some future point and recapture amounts on previously issued policies up to the new retention limit, subject to the terms

---

[3]See Chapter 10, Reinsurance Regulations.

[4]For a discussion of reinsurance expenses, see Chapter 9, Managing Assumed Reinsurance.

of the contract.[5] This might allow the company to generate more future profits from currently reinsured policies.

Surplus Planning and Management

On occasion, an insurance company may have a need for increased
statutory surplus. A temporary provision of increased surplus is
frequently referred to as surplus relief. Surplus relief can be
provided in a number of ways, including the use of surplus relief
reinsurance. In a surplus relief transaction,[6] the ceding company's
statutory earnings and surplus are increased in the year in which
the relief is provided. The amount of the relief is repaid to the
reinsurer out of future statutory earnings.

There are several reasons why a company might wish to
increase its surplus position. These include the following:

(1) The company has been overly successful in issuing new
      policies with resultant acquisition expenses reducing its
      surplus below prudent or required levels.
(2) The company must increase its surplus in order to obtain
      a license in a new jurisdiction.
(3) The company's surplus may have been temporarily re-
      duced because of poor mortality, morbidity, or surrender
      experience.
(4) The company desires to improve or maintain its rating
      with A.M. Best, Moody, Standard and Poor, or other
      insurance company rating agencies in order to increase
      agent, policyholder, or stockholder confidence in the
      company, or to permit it to market in certain situations.
(5) The company wishes to meet certain shareholder dividend
      or debt service objectives.

Tax Planning

Historically, reinsurance has had powerful applications in tax
planning[7] for both ceding companies and reinsurers. Some
examples of these applications are discussed below.

---

[5]See Chapter 6, The Reinsurance Treaty.

[6]For a discussion of surplus relief, see Chapter 5, Financial Reinsurance.

[7]See Chapter 14, Tax Effects of Reinsurance.

(1) A company may wish to assume life insurance or cede health insurance in order to maintain or secure life insurance company status for federal income tax purposes. Conversely, it may cede life insurance or accept health insurance in order to secure or retain a non-life insurance company status for federal income tax purposes.

(2) A company may wish to cede insurance and use the increased statutory earnings in order to utilize expiring tax loss carry-forwards. The company can use reinsurance to change the timing of taxable income for federal income tax purposes.

The federal tax laws and regulations are complex and constantly changing, so use of reinsurance to assist in tax planning requires considerable expertise.

Increasing Reinsurer's Profit

As with directly issued insurance and annuity contracts, insurance companies accept reinsurance anticipating a profit. There are several ways in which a company can participate in the reinsurance marketplace; these are discussed later in this chapter.

Increasing Reinsurer's Inforce

Some companies may assume reinsurance in order to increase the size of the company. A company may do this to take advantage of under-utilized administrative capacities, to develop a larger base of policies over which to spread administrative or overhead expenses, or to augment inforce when direct sales do not meet business plans.

Limiting Catastrophic Claims

When a jet airliner crashes or a hotel burns, an insurance company may incur claims on two, three, or more individuals. While multiple claims from a single event is not a common occurrence, when it does occur it can have a dramatic effect on a company's earnings. Multiple deaths from a single event will affect both large companies and small companies. Because of this, many companies purchase catastrophic insurance coverage, or "cat cover."[8]

Catastrophic coverage generally provides for the reinsurer to pay claims in excess of a certain limit, subject to a minimum

---

[8]See Chapter 15, Nonproportional Reinsurance.

number of claims and subject to a maximum amount of reinsurance per event. Coverage is usually limited to accidental deaths due to catastrophes such as plane crashes or earthquakes and does not include deaths due to epidemics, wars, insurrections, or natural causes. This coverage often excludes specific concentrations of lives such as sports teams, airline personnel, and other organizations or groups which would involve a large single conveyance transportation exposure. Coverage for these concentrated risk groups may sometimes be obtained from domestic or foreign syndicates and pools.

Limiting Total Claims

While the major purpose of retention limits is to help smooth out fluctuations in earnings caused by large individual claims, some insurers, particularly smaller ones, are concerned with fluctuations caused by excessive claims in any one year. In order to provide protection against this risk, some companies obtain stop loss reinsurance coverage.[9] A stop loss program provides for the reinsurer to reimburse the company for all, or a specified percentage of retained claims in excess of a specified amount up to a defined maximum. This specified amount, referred to as the attachment point, is usually expressed as a percentage of the expected claims. The contract usually limits the amount of any claim to be included in the stop loss calculation to the company's retained portion of the claim. Claims from all causes generally are covered under a stop loss agreement.

CLASSIFICATIONS OF REINSURANCE

In this section the different ways in which reinsurance may be classified or distinguished are discussed, and several new terms are introduced.

Ceded/Assumed/Retroceded

Ceding refers to the transfer of an insurance risk from the company which originally issued the policy, called the ceding company or the reinsured, to another insurance company, called the reinsurer. The unit of insurance which is passed to the reinsurer is known as the

---

[9] *Ibid.*

cession. In most traditional individual life, health, and annuity reinsurance arrangements, a cession is defined in terms of the individual policy. However, a cession may cover a block of policies.

Assuming refers to the acceptance of an insurance risk from the ceding company by the reinsurer. The reinsurer may also be referred to as the assuming company.

The reinsurer is not obligated to retain all risks which it has assumed. It may decide to retrocede to another company all or some portions of the risks it has assumed. The company that accepts the retroceded risks is known as the retrocessionaire. The individual unit of insurance in this situation, known as the retrocession, is usually defined in terms of an individual policy.

Indemnity/Assumption

Reinsurance arrangements are defined by written agreements commonly referred to as reinsurance treaties. These agreements identify the risks being transferred, define the manner in which the risks are to be transferred, and describe the basic administrative and accounting procedures which both parties follow.

A reinsurance agreement may be written on either an indemnity or assumption basis. The differences between these two types of transactions lie in the relationship among the owners of the insurance policies, the ceding company, and the reinsurer.

Under indemnity reinsurance, the policyholders have no contractual relationship with the reinsurance company, and in fact, the policyholders rarely have any knowledge of the reinsurance agreement. The policyholders remit premium payments to the insurance company that issued the policy and look to that company for the payment of benefits. The ceding company remits the reinsurance premium to the reinsurer and looks to the reinsurer for reimbursement on claims for ceded policies. Should the reinsurer fail to meet its obligations to the ceding company, the ceding company still has full liability to the policyholder. A recapture provision in the reinsurance contract, allowing the ceding company to regain all or a portion of its liabilities under the policies reinsured upon the occurrence of some specified conditions, is a common feature of indemnity reinsurance treaties, but is not mandatory.

Assumption reinsurance is the permanent transfer of insurance liabilities from one company to another.[10] Under assumption

---

[10]See Chapter 16, Assumption Reinsurance.

reinsurance, the assumption reinsurer assumes the position formerly occupied by the company which originally issued the insurance. The exact manner in which this is done will vary with state regulatory requirements. In most situations, the policyholders are given assumption certificates by the assumption reinsurer and the original insurance company ceases to have any contractual obligation to the policyholders. The policyholders, from the date of assumption forward, remit premium payments to the assumption reinsurer and look to the assumption reinsurer for payment of benefits. Because assumption reinsurance involves a permanent transfer of risk, the accounting treatment and income tax effect of the transaction may differ from the treatment given to indemnity reinsurance.

Assumption reinsurance is less common than indemnity reinsurance. Unless otherwise specified in this book, reinsurance will refer to indemnity reinsurance and special reference will be made to assumption reinsurance and assumption reinsurers where applicable.

Proportional/Nonproportional

Reinsurance may be conducted on either a proportional or a nonproportional basis. If business is ceded on a proportional basis, the portion of the benefit for which the reinsurer is responsible is defined at the time of the cession by a formula relating to the ceding company's retention limits. As an example, a company issues a $400,000 annually renewable term insurance policy and reinsures the amount in excess of its $100,000 retention. In this situation, the company retains 25% of the risk in all years.

There are other methods of determining the proportion of reinsurance ceded, and the proportion may vary by policy duration. In each case, however, the proportion by duration is fixed at issue by some formula and is dependent upon the parameters for that policy only.[11]

Proportional reinsurance is conducted using traditional coinsurance, modified coinsurance, and yearly renewable term plans of reinsurance.[12]

When nonproportional reinsurance is used, the amount for which the reinsurer is liable is not fixed in advance. Rather, the

---

[11]See Chapter 4, Traditional Reinsurance.

[12]*Ibid.*

amount of reinsurance benefit is dependent on the amount of claims incurred during the contract period. The primary nonproportional plans of reinsurance are stop loss and catastrophe. When stop loss coverage is purchased, the company only collects on a claim if total claims exceed a defined attachment point. If a company purchases catastrophe coverage, it collects only if multiple deaths occur from a single covered event.[13]

Automatic/Facultative

A reinsurance treaty may allow business to be ceded on either an automatic or facultative basis. An automatic reinsurance treaty provides that the ceding company is allowed to cede risks issued in excess of its retention limit, subject to certain specific criteria, to a specific reinsurer at a predetermined cost without submitting underwriting papers to the reinsurer for approval.[14]

A facultative reinsurance treaty provides that a reinsurer must approve each individual risk before it has any liability.[15] Variations include the conditional automatic treaty where the reinsurer provides an underwriting service to the ceding company and the facultative obligatory treaty where the reinsurer can decline a risk only when it has previously retained its full retention on the individual involved.

Excess/Quota Share

An excess treaty covers risks ceded in accordance with a scheduled system of retention limits. The retention limits usually vary by age and underwriting classification of the insured.

Alternatively, the reinsurance treaty may provide that a fixed percentage of each risk will be ceded. This is known as quota share reinsurance.

Experience Rated/Non-Experience Rated

At one time, most reinsurance treaties were written on an experience rated or refund basis, that is, the ceding company was permitted to share in a portion of any profits realized on the

---

[13]For a further discussion of stop loss and catastrophic reinsurance, see Chapter 15, Nonproportional Reinsurance.

[14]See Chapter 2, Automatic Reinsurance.

[15]See Chapter 3, Facultative Reinsurance and Underwriting.

reinsurance. Premiums on experience refund treaties are higher than the premiums on comparable non-refund treaties. This provides the reinsurer with an additional margin for fluctuation. In today's market, most reinsurers and ceding companies prefer the use of non-refund treaties.

Traditional/Financial

Two basic classifications of reinsurance are defined in this book: traditional and financial. Traditional reinsurance refers to reinsurance arrangements where the primary purpose is the transfer of risks.[16] Financial reinsurance refers to reinsurance arrangements where the primary purpose is the achievement of a specific business objective such as increasing statutory surplus, reducing taxes, or acquiring blocks of business.[17] While financial reinsurance involves risk transfer, the risk transfer is secondary to the business purpose. The distinction between traditional and financial reinsurance may not be immediately obvious in the treaty itself but it will dictate many of the terms of the agreement. These differences will be discussed throughout this book.

CLASSIFICATIONS OF REINSURERS

Insurance companies may assume reinsurance for a number of different reasons. Their degree of involvement ranges from an occasional reinsurance transaction to a full-time commitment of all resources. The various classifications of reinsurers are described in this section. A reinsurer may fall into more than one classification.

Professional Reinsurer

All companies that assume reinsurance do so with the expectation of earning a profit. In this book, the term *professional reinsurers* refers to those companies that actively seek to assume reinsurance as a major line of business or as their only line of business. A distinguishing feature of professional reinsurers is a sales staff dedicated to reinsurance activities. Professional life reinsurers also have specialized actuarial and accounting departments to meet the special needs of the reinsurance line. Most professional reinsurers

---

[16]See Chapter 4, Traditional Reinsurance.

[17]See Chapter 5, Financial Reinsurance.

offer the full range of reinsurance plans and services including traditional and financial reinsurance, and automatic and facultative reinsurance. However, a few reinsurers specialize in facultative or financial reinsurance while others provide such treaties only as an accommodation to clients with automatic treaties.

Occasional Reinsurer

The term occasional reinsurer is used to refer to a company that does not actively seek reinsurance in the general market, but participates in certain reinsurance pools. Many companies participate in two large government sponsored pools: Federal Employees' Group Life Insurance (FEGLI) and Servicemens' Group Life Insurance (SGLI). These pools offer very low exposure to risk and require little administrative effort. Their development may, in fact, be more political than based upon the satisfaction of a need.

Reinsurers sometimes offer selected clients reciprocity in their own retrocession pools in exchange for participation in the client's automatic reinsurance. The retrocession pool is made up from the reinsurer's assumed business. The amount of reciprocity reinsurance typically is proportional to the amount ceded the reinsurer, but the ratio of ceded to accepted volume is subject to negotiation.

These reciprocity arrangements traditionally were profitable to the retrocessionaires until the overall poor persistency experienced by the insurance industry in the late 1970's and early 1980's. Also, many reinsurers find they can no longer afford to retrocede reinsurance assumed on competitive coinsurance rates unless competitive YRT rates are used in the pools. Consequently, reciprocity is less frequently used today.

Special Purpose Reinsurer

Some insurance companies actively seek to acquire blocks of business. This is often done to utilize excess administrative capabilities or to increase the inforce insurance base for the purpose of spreading overhead and other expenses. Most companies in this reinsurance market tend to specialize in one type of business. In most of these situations, assumption reinsurance would be used.

Financial Reinsurer

A few insurance companies specialize in providing financial reinsurance. Most companies in this market have excess surplus available for investment. In order to participate in this market, a company must have a staff knowledgeable in the areas of tax and financial planning. Most financial reinsurance requires relatively little administrative effort when compared to traditional reinsurance since most of the administration is usually done by the ceding company. Companies operating only in the financial reinsurance market may maintain a small sales staff to seek out clients but, more often, work with a professional, full service reinsurer in the capacity of a retrocessionaire or with an insurance consultant, reinsurance intermediary, or some combination of these.

Retrocessionaire

Some companies act only as professional retrocessionaires serving professional reinsurers. As discussed earlier, some companies have participated in reciprocal pools with professional reinsurers. However, because of the highly competitive coinsurance market-place, reinsurers frequently must retrocede assumed business on more competitive and, therefore, less profitable terms. Professional retrocessionaires are those companies that are willing and able to assume risks from professional reinsurers at competitive rates. Because of the nature of the business, a professional retroces-sionaire does not need a sales staff or a large administrative staff. The underwriting function, however, is very important to the professional retrocessionaire because it is involved in a large portion of jumbo policies.

Pool Participant

Prior to about 1980, there were a few special reinsurance pools, each involving a group of three to ten nonprofessional reinsurers that would cede a portion of their risks to the pool and, in return, assume a proportion of the risks contained in the pool. These pools were operated on an experience rated basis and were, in essence, a sort of spread loss coverage.[18] The primary purpose of these pools was to smooth out mortality fluctuations at no long term cost to any participant; under the terms of the pool agreement, a company was usually required to remain in the pool until its experience account was positive.

---

[18]See Chapter 15, Nonproportional Reinsurance.

These pools were established by companies whose overall mortality and underwriting characteristics were perceived to be homogeneous. When companies began to generate larger volumes of reinsurance and commercial reinsurance costs became very competitive, pools could no longer easily be kept in balance. While pools continued to exist for many products, the members came to look to commercial reinsurance for the large volume plans, such as term insurance.

Joint Venture Reinsurer

Sometimes a life insurance company may have a particular expertise in a given product area which it can market to other insurance companies utilizing a joint venture approach. In such an arrangement, the insurance company with the expertise forms an informal partnership with an inexperienced insurance company and assists it in developing a particular insurance product. In return for the assistance, the company agrees to cede to the other company some portion of the risk on the policies it writes using the new products. The reinsurer may allow the ceding company to use its administrative systems for a fee until the ceding company can develop its own.

Joint ventures tend to be more common in situations involving difficult or new products, such as disability income and variable life.

Captive Reinsurer

A substantial volume of reinsurance is ceded to captive reinsurers.[19] These are companies formed and controlled by a separate entity in order to assume business from a specific source, usually of a related nature. In the credit insurance arena, many credit captive insurance companies have been formed to reinsure business produced by a particular credit insurance agent such as an automobile dealership. Banks, savings and loans, and other financial institutions often form captive insurance companies in order to assume insurance coverages written on their customers.

In the past few years, some life insurance companies have assisted their agents in forming captive insurance companies. The insurance company cedes a portion of the business written by the agents to the agent-owned company in order that the agents may share in the overall profitability of the business which they write.

---

[19]See Chapter 17, Captive Reinsurance.

Companies expect that by giving the agents a stake in the future profitability of the business, the agents will be stimulated to produce a higher quality book of business.

Affiliate Reinsurer

It is common for reinsurance transactions to occur among affiliated insurance companies. The affiliated companies may have a reinsurance pool in which all companies participate, or a subsidiary may cede part or all of its reinsurance to its parent or to a larger affiliate. Reinsurance pools of affiliated companies may have spread loss characteristics or they may be traditional risk transfer arrangements. Reinsurance among affiliates is frequently financially motivated.

Syndicate Member

There are certain syndicates of professional reinsurers in North America and Europe which provide speciality reinsurance such as accidental death and health coverage and also stop loss and catastrophe protection. Syndicates usually have dedicated staffs to handle marketing, underwriting, administration, and claims.

EFFECTS OF REINSURANCE ON COMPANY OPERATIONS

Reinsurance affects many areas of an insurance company's operations. The major areas are accounting, regulation, taxation, underwriting, administration, and pricing. Some of the key issues are summarized briefly below.

Regulation and Compliance

Reinsurance is less regulated than individual insurance because the perceived need is not as great since the insureds are not parties to the reinsurance treaties, and the insurance companies, which are parties to the treaties, are considered to be sophisticated. In most states, reinsurance treaties do not need approval of the insurance department. However, it is important to determine that reinsurance treaties comply with all existing regulations,[20] particularly in the areas of reserve credits and insolvency.

---

[20]See Chapter 10, Reinsurance Regulations.

Accounting

Reinsurance transactions generally have an effect on the statutory balance sheet and summary of operations.[21] An insurance company must determine when it is appropriate to take reserve credit on reinsurance ceded. This determination should be addressed when the reinsurance treaty is drafted.

Procedures must be communicated to the accounting department, in order that proper recognition is given to reinsurance premiums, allowances and claims.

Companies that prepare financial statements in accordance with Generally Accepted Accounting Principles (GAAP) must apply these principles to all reinsurance transactions. For traditional reinsurance, appropriate GAAP treatment is fairly well defined. However, in the area of financial reinsurance, the appropriate GAAP treatment is less well defined and subject to greater latitude. Special treatments or different methods are frequently used to arrive at a common result.[22]

Pricing and Profitability

The cost of reinsurance will affect the overall profitability of a life insurance company and should be reflected in pricing. The actuarial department should be involved in the analysis of reinsurance proposals and in evaluating the overall reinsurance program. This periodic evaluation will normally include a retention limit study.[23]

Valuation and Actuarial Opinion

In the United States, the role of valuation actuary is becoming increasingly important. The valuation actuary's review of the insurance company's liabilities is very important and calls for a detailed study of all components of these values. All reinsurance reserves, reserve credits, and receivable and payable items must be carefully evaluated.[24]

---

[21]See Chapter 12, Statutory Accounting for Reinsurance.

[22]See Chapter 13, GAAP Accounting for Reinsurance.

[23]See Chapter 8, Managing Ceded Reinsurance.

[24]See Chapter 12, Statutory Accounting for Reinsurance.

Administration

The proper administration of reinsurance is necessary to ensure that all policies requiring reinsurance are ceded and that the reinsurance coverage on these policies is maintained throughout their life. Today, many companies have taken on more of the administrative responsibility for reinsurance using self-administered programs.[25] Valuation actuary considerations have also increased the ceding company awareness of the need to establish sound administrative procedures.

Underwriting

An insurance company's underwriting philosophy and facultative reinsurance program are closely related.[26]   A company uses facultative reinsurance for many reasons and may have relationships with several reinsurers for different purposes. The insurance company underwriter may have daily contact with the reinsurer's underwriter and may develop a longstanding relationship.

---

[25]See Chapter 7, Reinsurance Administration.

[26]See Chapter 3, Underwriting and Facultative Reinsurance.

2 | Automatic Reinsurance

The basic distinctions between automatic and facultative reinsurance were discussed in Chapter 1. This chapter is devoted to a more detailed discussion of automatic reinsurance. Chapter 3 provides a corresponding discussion of facultative reinsurance.

Originally all reinsurance was facultative, with individual underwriting evaluation and terms for each risk. As underwriting standards and insurance company practices became more defined, automatic reinsurance was developed. An automatic agreement allows reinsurance to be placed with a specific reinsurer with reliance upon the ceding company's selection criteria. This saves companies both time and expense and avoids unnecessary duplication of effort.

Automatic reinsurance is a contractual arrangement[1] whereby an insurance company is allowed to cede insurance issued in amounts over its retention limit, subject to certain criteria, to a specific reinsurer at a predetermined cost without submitting underwriting papers. The reinsurer is obligated to accept all policies which meet the criteria for automatic cession and the ceding company is obligated to cede all such policies. An exception is usually made permitting the ceding company to use the facultative underwriting facilities of that or another reinsurer.

---

[1]See Chapter 6, The Reinsurance Treaty.

21

Automatic reinsurance is a form of proportional reinsurance, that is, the portion of each policy which is reinsured is determined in advance according to a formula stated in the treaty. Historically, the formula would result in a proportional sharing of the risk throughout the life of the individual policy, subject to recapture. Today, however, it is not uncommon for the proportion of reinsurance to diminish as the net amount at risk decreases.

Automatic reinsurance may be ceded on an excess basis using a schedule of retention limits stated in terms of an amount of insurance, or it may be ceded on a quota share basis where the retention is stated in terms of a percentage of the risk.

REQUIREMENTS FOR AUTOMATIC REINSURANCE

An automatic reinsurance treaty contains several requirements[2] which each policy must meet before it qualifies for automatic cession. These requirements are usually designed so that the majority of policies requiring reinsurance can be ceded automatically. Certain of these requirements concern the amount of risk that the ceding company must retain, and places limits on the maximum amount of automatic reinsurance that can be ceded on a life as well as a limit on the maximum amount of insurance inforce on the life. Other requirements cover underwriting and issue rules, residence, and plan of insurance to assure the reinsurer that the business it is receiving meets the standards anticipated in its pricing. When all automatic requirements are met, the ceding company can bind the reinsurer for the coverage and the reinsurer is said to be bound. The typical requirements are discussed below.

Full Retention

One of the most critical requirements for automatic reinsurance is that the ceding company keep its full retention at issue on any policy ceded under the treaty.[3] This indicates that the ceding

---

[2]Requirements typically included in an automatic life reinsurance treaty are discussed in this chapter. Requirements peculiar to accident and health reinsurance and annuity reinsurance are discussed in Chapters 19 and 20, respectively.

[3]Requirements for maintaining retention subsequent to issue are discussed in Chapter 6, The Reinsurance Treaty.

company has evaluated the risk and is willing to accept it under its own underwriting terms. This does not necessarily mean that the risk must be standard, as many companies include substandard risks in their automatic reinsurance. Without this condition, the ceding company would be free to select against the reinsurer as it pleased, holding a smaller or no retention on poorer risks.

The term *full retention* refers to the established retention schedule of the company. All companies have a schedule of retention limits. Many companies have scheduled a lesser retention for the lower and higher issue ages and for the higher substandard ratings where the risks are perceived to be greater or where the number of risks is small. While this approach for grading retention limits is widely accepted in practice, it may not be justifiable in theory.[4] Retention limits may vary by product, by source of business, or by line of business. Retention limits on accidental death coverage or waiver of premium may differ from the basic limits. These scheduled variations in retention limits do not violate the full retention rule. A violation occurs when the actual amount retained deviates from the established schedule.

The retention limit may be expressed as a flat amount of coverage, such as $250,000 per life. In a pool or quota share situation where the company cedes a percentage of all risks, the retention condition is met if the ceding company keeps its stated percentage of the coverage issued, subject to a maximum amount per life.

The full retention requirement applies to all policies issued on any one life by the ceding company. For example, if a company has filled its retention on a given life due to previously issued policies, a new policy may qualify for automatic reinsurance even if no portion of the risk on this policy is retained by the company, provided the other conditions are met. In most of these instances, the reinsurer requires that the rating class of the risk not have deteriorated since the last underwriting.

As an example, assume that ABC Life Insurance Company receives an application for $400,000 on the life of John Doe, age 35. Further assume that ABC Life has the right to cede automatically up to $400,000 of coverage per life to its reinsurer using the retention schedule shown on page 24.

If there is no other insurance inforce with ABC Life on John Doe and he is classified as a standard risk, ABC Life could

---

[4]See Chapter 8, Managing Ceded Reinsurance.

automatically cede the $300,000 in excess of its retention. If John Doe already has $100,000 of life insurance inforce with ABC Life, ABC could cede the entire $400,000 of insurance.

ABC LIFE INSURANCE COMPANY
INDIVIDUAL LIFE RETENTION SCHEDULE

Issue Age	Standard Through 200% Extra Mortality	Over 200% Extra Mortality
0 - 18	$ 50,000	$ 25,000
19 - 65	100,000	50,000
65 +	50,000	25,000

The retention limit requirement applies at the time of policy issue. Under certain conditions, the ceding company may have the right to take out additional reinsurance at a later time. Additional reinsurance might be necessitated for financial reinsurance purposes or to permit the sale of a block of business. However, some treaties specifically prohibit the placement of any additional reinsurance on policies covered by that treaty.

Companies periodically revise their retention schedules. The retention in effect at the date of the current coverage is applicable regardless of any amounts of reinsurance which may have been placed on the same life.

In filling the new retention, all insurance currently inforce on the life must be considered.

Minimum Cession

Many reinsurance treaties provide that, to qualify for automatic coverage, the cession must be for an amount in excess of a stated minimum. The purpose of this provision is to avoid the inordinate expense associated with administering very small cessions.

Binding Limit

The binding limit, or automatic capacity, is an important element of the automatic reinsurance formula. This is the amount of risk on a given life which the ceding company can cede automatically to the reinsurer and which the reinsurer must accept if all other conditions for automatic reinsurance are met. For purposes of determining the amount of risk when applying this limit, any amounts of insurance previously issued on the life by the ceding company that are currently reinsured with the reinsurer are added to the amounts to be ceded under the current cession. The binding limit may be stated either as a multiple of the ceding company's retention or as an amount of insurance. It may be restricted at certain issue ages or substandard ratings. Even though the binding limit for the reinsurer is not exceeded, a life having extensive insurance coverage with other carriers might not qualify for automatic coverage as the result of the operation of the jumbo limit, described in the next section.

The binding limit is determined by the ceding company's underwriting ability, its retention limit, and its needs. A company with inexperienced underwriters will usually have a lower binding limit than a company with experienced underwriters, even if the first company has a higher retention limit. A company which writes large policies with great frequency may find it more convenient and desirable to have a higher binding limit than a company where large policies are rarely encountered. In most situations, both the reinsurer and the ceding company would like the binding limit set at a level such that the majority of the policies requiring reinsurance can be ceded automatically. This lowers the administrative cost for both companies and allows the ceding company to issue policies more quickly. Higher binding limits also provide the reinsurer with more reinsurance by eliminating the need to compete with other carriers for facultative business on the larger policies.

The advantages of a higher binding limit must be balanced with the reinsurer's desire to review the larger cases which may need specialized underwriting, and must also be coordinated with the reinsurer's retention and retrocession arrangements. On a very large case, the reinsurer will want to check its own retention on the insured before accepting the risk, since it may need to make special retrocession arrangements.

Prior to the late 1970's, binding limits of two, three, or four times the ceding company's retention were quite common. The multiple tended to decrease as the retention limit increased. Years of high inflation and plummeting term insurance rates led to increasingly larger issue amounts. This caused insurance companies to seek higher binding limits to lower administrative costs and to shorten the time needed to issue a policy. Today, some companies have binding limits of several million dollars in excess of their retention limits. Such high limits are no longer as unusual as they once were since reinsurers have responded to competitive pressure and improved underwriting techniques. Today, binding limits are typically four to six times the retention, although much higher multiples are sometimes encountered.

If the sum of the amount applied for and the amount already inforce in the ceding company exceed the sum of the ceding company's retention limit and binding limit, the automatic feature is not allowed and the case must be submitted facultatively. Exceptions to this practice may be granted by the treaty.

In the previous example, assume ABC Life has a binding limit of $400,000 above its $100,000 retention, so it is able to reinsure automatically up to $400,000 on the life of John Doe. If John Doe previously had more than $100,000 of insurance inforce with ABC Life, resulting in more than $500,000 of insurance in total, ABC Life would not be able to cede this case automatically, and would be required to submit its underwriting papers for facultative review by the reinsurer.

Jumbo Limit

In order to qualify for automatic reinsurance, most companies require that the total amounts of insurance inforce and applied for in all companies on the individual life not exceed a specified amount, called the jumbo limit. Some reinsurers do not include amounts of insurance applied for with other companies in this definition. The jumbo limit is usually in the range of $5,000,000 to $15,000,000.

The purpose of the jumbo limit is to allow the reinsurer to check its retention and capacity on the life in question. When amounts of insurance approach these levels it is probable that the reinsurer may already have filled all or part of its retention on the life and would be required to retrocede all excess amounts to several other carriers. Since this is difficult and costly, the reinsurer may decline to participate or may accept the risk only at a higher premium.

The jumbo limit is also used by the reinsurer to ensure that it can participate in the risk-acceptance decisions regarding large amounts as it normally has more expertise in financial underwriting analysis and other problems associated with large policies. The reinsurer may also use the jumbo limit as a means to ensure its retrocessionaires of consistent quality in the underwriting of risks.

Participation Limit

A reinsurer may decline to participate in the reinsurance on a given life if the total coverage inforce and applied for exceeds a specified maximum called its participation limit. If the participation limit is exceeded, the reinsurer will not accept any coverage, even on a facultative basis, irrespective of whether it currently has any reinsurance coverage on the life.

Participation limits may be used with individual life insurance risks but are most commonly applied to benefits such as accidental death and disability income. The limit may vary by line of business or type of benefit.

Facultative Exclusion

Another important requirement for automatically ceding reinsurance is that the ceding company must not have previously tried to reinsure the case facultatively. Automatic coverage is based on an agreement that the ceding company will cede to the reinsurer all business which fits a certain definition and the reinsurer will accept this business with no further conditions.

Most treaties will not allow the ceding company to submit a case which qualifies for automatic cession to another reinsurer for review and retain any automatic coverage rights. When the ceding company submits the case to another reinsurer, it is deemed to be voluntarily waiving its automatic privilege, and the automatic reinsurer is no longer bound by the terms of the agreement relative to that case.

This requirement protects the automatic reinsurer from anti-selection. Clearly, applications that the ceding company was unable to place facultatively represent an unfavorable class. The automatic reinsurer would be placed in an unfair position if such risks were subsequently placed with it on an automatic basis even if the ceding company is holding its normal retention. This requirement helps to maintain the partnership and good faith aspects of a reinsurance relationship.

This requirement also protects the reinsurer in the event of a claim arising prior to policy issue, facultative acceptance, or rejection of the application. Normally, the automatic reinsurer would be responsible for a defined portion of a claim under the coverage provided by the life insurance policy's conditional receipt. If a case is sent out facultatively, the automatic reinsurer is freed from this obligation unless there is specific coverage afforded by the treaty. Such special coverage is granted only in exceptional circumstances and subject to very clear, extensive rules on coverage and administration of applications, underwriting, and claims.

Normal Underwriting

Reinsurance treaties require that normal new business underwriting standards be applied to each cession. It is critical that the reinsurer be aware of the underwriting standards being applied to new issues and that these standards be consistently applied in all cases. Because the reinsurer has relied on the underwriting standards in setting the price for the automatic reinsurance, any deviation from these standards could adversely affect the reinsurer's profitability.

The definition of normal underwriting standards varies by treaty. In some instances it may include guaranteed or simplified issue for certain designated plans of insurance or markets. Where limited underwriting is included, the requirements, such as minimum group participation levels, are usually contained in the treaty.

A problem arises when an external replacement is involved or when underwriting standards are waived for business reasons such as in multiple life sales situations. Occasional deviations from normal underwriting standards may be handled on a facultative basis, or, if many such risks are encountered, a separate automatic agreement may be prepared.

Replacements and Continuations

Another requirement concerns insurance coverage resulting from the internal replacement or continuation of a policy from one policy form to another where normal new business underwriting is not used or where the normal first year commissions are not paid. The widespread use of formal internal replacement programs has caused several reinsurers to address specifically the requirements related to replacements in the treaty.

The traditional requirement covering a continuation is that the new policy remain with the original reinsurer on terms appropriate for the original issue age and current duration of the original policy. For example, if an insurance policy issued four years ago to a man aged 35 and currently reinsured on a YRT basis is rewritten as a different plan of insurance without new full evidence of insurability and with a lesser first year commission, the original reinsurer would charge a YRT premium on the second policy appropriate for an issue age 35 in the fifth duration, not that appropriate for a new issue at age 39. The requirement is based on the fact that neither party can unilaterally terminate inforce reinsurance coverage. Moving coverage to another reinsurer on a continuation is considered a unilateral termination.

A reinsurer will deny coverage if the continuation rules are not followed and the ceding company places the continued policy with it as if normal underwriting and issue rules had been applied because its requirements for automatic reinsurance have been violated. In this event, the ceding company would have no reinsurance coverage at time of claim.

The ceding company must be aware of the reinsurance cost implications of continuations. As stated, the cost of such reinsurance will typically be based upon the current duration of the original policy. This cost will normally be higher than the normal reinsurance cost for new issues. Therefore, in contemplating any replacement, conversion, or continuation program, the ceding company must take into account the appropriate cost of reinsurance in establishing the terms, conditions, and charges for these program.

If the ceding company wishes to involve a new reinsurer on a continuation, the ceding company should negotiate rules with both reinsurers. A reputable reinsurer would not replace another reinsurer on a given risk without obtaining the first reinsurer's written permission. This practice is not merely a courtesy, it also clearly establishes the liability on the policy. Without this agreement, all three parties may be involved in a disputed settlement at time of claim.

Residence

In some instances, a treaty may require that the life reinsured be a resident of the United States, Canada, or some other specific region. There frequently are problems encountered with the insuring of foreign risks, including the inability to obtain reliable medical data and claim information and the exposure to less predictable mortality.

Legal Authorization

Reinsurers frequently require that the reinsurance be generated from policies written in territories where the ceding company is legally authorized to do business. In addition, there may be a requirement that the policies are written in conformity with applicable regulations.

Plan of Insurance

Prior to the mid-1970's, it was common for one reinsurance agreement to apply to all plans of insurance. Today, it is more typical for a reinsurance agreement to apply to one or a restricted number of plans of insurance.

Other Restrictions

Other restrictions may be contained in the reinsurance treaty. Certain aviation risks are sometimes excluded from automatic reinsurance coverage. A reinsurance treaty might also exclude all business from a certain source, or be written so as to include only business from certain sources.

DETERMINING THE AMOUNT OF AUTOMATIC REINSURANCE

When an application meets the requirements for automatic reinsurance, the amount of coverage to be reinsured must be determined. The two approaches used to determine the amount ceded are the excess and the quota share bases.

Excess

When reinsurance is ceded on an excess basis, the ceding company reinsures amounts in excess of those specified its retention schedule. The retention schedule may be the normal schedule for the company, a special schedule for the product, or a facultative retention schedule.

Quota Share

A quota share arrangement is a form of reinsurance where the ceding company states its retention in terms of a level percentage of the risk on each policy issued up to its maximum retention. If the reinsurance is shared by more than one reinsurer, each receives a specified percentage.

The quota share arrangement will result in more reinsurance being ceded on a given block of business than under the excess arrangement, as a portion of each policy issued is reinsured rather than only a portion of those policies which have amounts in excess of the retention limit.

Probably the most common use of a quota share arrangement is in those situations where the ceding company expects to write a substantial number of policies needing reinsurance. This may be because of large amounts per life, or because significant surplus strain is expected and the ceding company needs financial assistance. In this case, one or more reinsurers are employed and self-administration is typically utilized. This results in a predetermined equitable sharing of risks and strain among reinsurers and fairly simple administration.

Another use of a quota share arrangement is for a joint venture. These arrangements are usually created when the ceding company is entering a new product line or market where it lacks the experience to make its normal commitment. The ceding company will seek a more experienced company to assist it in entering the market and compensates the company by ceding it a portion of the business.

Quota share arrangements are also used in situations where it would be inconvenient or impossible to identify individually amounts reinsured in excess of a certain limits. Examples of this include group life insurance or accidental death benefits. It is also the most convenient method to provide surplus relief on a block of inforce policies as the ceding company can simply apply a level percentage to its premiums, claims, and reserves to determine the reinsurer's share with appropriate adjustment for previously reinsured amounts.

A quota share arrangement is typically used only in conjunction with coinsurance or modified coinsurance since a basic purpose is to simplify administration by using percentage of premiums, reserves, and claims for reinsurance. The use with yearly renewable term would require the calculating of individual net amounts at risk and yearly renewable term premiums.

While quota share agreements are almost always automatic in nature, facultative arrangements are possible. For example, a company with a significant new marketing opportunity might seek a quota share reinsurer to provide both financial depth and underwriting capacity. In this instance, the arrangement would technically be facultative, but if the reinsurer turned the application down, it is unlikely the ceding company would look further.

In the previous example, ABC Life might have chosen to enter into a quota share arrangement because of the strain involved in this particular product. Under this arrangement, if ABC Life had chosen to retain 10% of each risk up to its normal retention and split the reinsurance evenly between XYZ Re and 123 Re, it would retain $40,000 of the insurance issued on John Doe and cede $180,000 to XYZ Re and $180,000 to 123 Re.

USING MULTIPLE AUTOMATIC TREATIES

It is not uncommon for a ceding company to reinsure a product on an automatic basis with more than one reinsurer in order to increase its facultative outlets, reduce its dependence on one reinsurer, increase its automatic capacity, or because it perceives that the practice will result in a more competitive situation, and therefore, in better price or service. However, a company will rarely use more than three or four reinsurers on any product as it is not cost-efficient for the ceding company or for the reinsurers. An insurance company may have different reinsurers for different products.

Splitting and allocating business among reinsurers must be done in a systematic manner so that all reinsurers believe they are receiving a fair cross-section of risks. Several methods which may be used to divide automatic insurance among reinsurers are described below.

Alphabet Split

The most common method of dividing individual cession automatic reinsurance among reinsurers is the alphabet split. Under this method, reinsurers are assigned a portion of the alphabet and automatically receive reinsurance based on the first letter of the insured's last name. In the previous example, if ABC Life reinsures all business for surnames beginning with letters A through K with XYZ Re and for all surnames beginning with L through Z with 123 Re, XYZ Re would automatically receive the $300,000 of reinsurance to be ceded on John Doe's life.

Joint life and joint and last survivor policies present a special problem if the insureds have different surnames. The treaties must be clear regarding how the reinsurers are to be assigned in such cases. It might be desirable to place all coverages arising from a given policy with the same reinsurer. Any clear and fair rule, such as following the established alphabet split using the surname of the oldest insured, would be acceptable.

Based on typical distribution of U.S. surnames, the A to K, L to Z split should result in approximately equal shares. An A to G, H to O, and P to Z division should result in an appropriate three way division. An A to D, E to K, L to R, and S to Z should result in each reinsurer receiving about one-fourth of the reinsurance. Actual splits can vary with the individual company's markets and experience.

Pooling

Automatic reinsurance may be ceded through a pooling arrangement. Under this method each reinsurer receives a certain percentage of the reinsurance on each life reinsured. The portion of reinsurance going to each reinsurer need not be the same. From the prior example, ABC Life may form a reinsurance pool and cede 75% of each risk to XYZ Re and 25% to 123 Re. In this situation, XYZ Re would automatically receive $225,000 of the reinsurance on John Doe, with 123 Re receiving the remaining $75,000.

The ceding company may choose to use the pooling method in order to obtain a larger automatic binding capacity, since the mortality fluctuation risk is spread more evenly among the reinsurers in a pool. A larger binding limit may reduce the ceding company's administrative and reinsurance costs as well as reduce the turnaround time involved in submitting facultative papers. However, reinsurers typically will not agree to a new total binding limit significantly larger than the normal binding limit for the company.

Pools are usually used only when the ceding company is administering the pool itself in some automated manner. If traditional individual cession administration is used, the ceding company's paperwork is increased as a result of the number of cession cards required on each policy. In a pool, it is usually important that all reinsurers have identical terms, except for percentage shares. This facilitates the reinsurance administration and simplifies claim settlement. Some minor terms may differ, allowing for the idiosyncrasies of the various reinsurers.

In some situations, a pool may have a "lead reinsurer." This company may take the lead in pricing, facultative underwriting, establishing and reviewing administrative procedures, claim settlement, or any additional matters agreed upon by the ceding company and the pool participants. Sometimes, the lead reinsurer may have more favorable terms or a larger share of the reinsurance. Lead reinsurers are not common in life insurance, but are frequently used in nonproportional, accident and health, and property and casualty reinsurance.

Layering

Under a layering arrangement, an insurance company will cede all amounts in excess of its retention up to a given limit to one reinsurer then cede the excess over this limit up to a second limit to a second reinsurer. The first reinsurer will normally receive the majority of the reinsurance as it receives the first reinsurance on all risks, but there are exceptions if the first layer is relatively narrow.

Layering was created in order extend a company's total binding authority and to introduce a new reinsurer into the program. The first layer of coverage was normally defined by the ceding company's binding limit with the first reinsurer. A second reinsurer, wishing to build a relationship with the ceding company, might agree to accept automatically business in excess of this binding limit up to another limit.

Sometimes, the second excess arrangements involve an alphabet split and a flip-flop or switch. Under a flip-flop arrangement, the first reinsurer receives the first excess of reinsurance on one portion of the alphabet, while the second reinsurer receives the second excess, and the relationships flip-flop or switch on the other portion of the alphabet, with the second reinsurer receiving the first layer. The reinsurance under a flip-flop arrangement can be divided among the reinsurers more equally if the traditional alphabet split method is used to determine the point where the flip-flop occurs.

A layered arrangement complicates the ceding company's administration as two cessions are required on the policies issued for amounts in excess of the first layer. Layering is probably the method least favored by reinsurers. As second, third and even fourth layers of coverage are secured, the reinsurers in all levels may find the overall quality of the business declining since the ceding company is underwriting the large cases alone. Layering has become less popular as administrative procedures have been simplified and automatic limits raised.

Issue Age

On occasion, companies have split reinsurance by issue ages, having determined the cost difference by age between reinsurers to be significant. Reinsurers normally look carefully at such arrangements before agreeing to them. It is not uncommon for a reinsurer to provide a quote which will produce gains at some ages and losses at others. Obviously, the reinsurance of lives only at those ages where losses or small profits are expected is not wise.

Agent

Reinsurance may also be divided based on the writing agent. While this method is used primarily for credit reinsurance or reinsurance involving agent-owned companies, it may be used in other situations.

Other Methods

Any reasonable method may be used to allocate reinsurance. A few companies have allocated reinsurance based on state of residence. One company has traditionally split its reinsurance based on the policyholder's residence being east or west of the Missouri River. Even and odd years of birth may also be employed. In certain cases, reinsurance has been split by smoker status. As with splitting reinsurers by issue age, splitting reinsurers by smoker status may enable the ceding company to achieve a better cost, but reinsurers may be reluctant to agree if the reinsurer's pricing contemplated one class subsidizing another.

EFFECTING AUTOMATIC REINSURANCE

If the application from the ceding company meets the automatic cession criteria, the reinsurance treaty will define the notification procedure. If more than one reinsurer is involved, the treaty will define how the reinsurer is chosen for a given policy, or how the reinsurance is to be divided among the reinsurers.

The type of notification required depends on the type of policy being reinsured and the type of administration being used. If individual cession administration is used, the ceding company merely notifies the reinsurer when the application for insurance is processed by sending an automatic cession card. This card contains the information necessary to allow the reinsurer to set up its records. Today, the cession card is sometimes sent in a computer readable form rather than on paper and this approach is expected to become more common.

If the ceding company is performing the basic administrative functions under a self-administered reinsurance arrangement,[5] the reinsurer will only receive a listing containing this information for all new cessions occurring during a defined period, usually monthly or quarterly.

The reinsurer normally does not receive a copy of the application or underwriting papers on an automatic cession although the reinsurer has the right to inspect the ceding company's records. Sometimes the reinsurer routinely requests to review papers, or to receive copies of all or some underwriting files to determine if underwriting standards are being maintained. Other reinsurers may do this as part of an audit process, or not at all. The procedure may depend upon the ceding company and its relationship with the reinsurer.

AUTOMATIC REINSURANCE CONSIDERATIONS

Automatic excess reinsurance is a very popular method because it is time and cost efficient for both parties. Because the terms and conditions are outlined in advance in the reinsurance treaty, the ceding company does not need to go through the process of finding a reinsurer separately for each and every policy which exceeds its retention. This saves the ceding company much time and administrative expense, and allows it to issue the majority of its policies on a timely basis. If the reinsurance is to be shared among two or more reinsurers, the ceding company can usually negotiate uniform terms and conditions with minor exceptions. Uniformity in pricing terms is more difficult to achieve on a facultative basis.

The reinsurer anticipates receiving quality business because the ceding company is retaining its full retention. It does not have to compete on underwriting decisions with other reinsurers which saves each reinsurer time as well as the expense of underwriting.

Automatic reinsurance is the only effective way to handle quota share reinsurance due to the large volume of policies normally involved.

---

[5]See Chapter 7, Reinsurance Administration.

Underwriting and Facultative
3 | Reinsurance

Facultative reinsurance is an arrangement whereby the ceding company submits its underwriting file on an application to the reinsurer for the reinsurer's decision. The reinsurance underwriter, after reviewing all the data he has requested, makes a decision as to the appropriate mortality assessment on the individual. The range of possible decisions includes standard, substandard, defer decision to a later date, and decline or reject. The underwriter's decision is also known as the action or the offer. The ceding company typically is given a certain time period, such as 60, 90, or 120 days, to accept a reinsurer's offer in writing.

Acceptance is usually accomplished by sending an individual cession card or notice of acceptance. If the offer is not specifically accepted or declined by the ceding company within that period, it is deemed to be withdrawn by the reinsurer. Some reinsurers automatically send notification of withdrawal of the offer to minimize administrative errors and legal exposure.

Facultative reinsurance is utilized when a cession does not meet the requirements for automatic reinsurance, or when the ceding company voluntarily requests that the reinsurer underwrite an application. The ceding company may make such a request in order to reduce its exposure on a questionable risk or to allow the reinsurer to make a decision regarding a questionable impairment. Facultative reinsurance is a form of proportional reinsurance as the amount of reinsurance on each policy is determined at the time it is ceded.

A key point regarding facultative reinsurance is that the terms of the cession and the choice of reinsurer are negotiated separately for each policy. General terms may apply under a given facultative treaty, but specific terms can vary for each policy. Facultative risks can have a full retention by the ceding company, no retention, or any mutually agreed upon split of the risks.

CEDING COMPANY USES OF FACULTATIVE REINSURANCE

A ceding company may submit an application for facultative underwriting in order to obtain excess capacity, underwriting assistance, or a competitive underwriting rating. Facultative applications are frequently employed with experimental under-writing programs. In each situation, it is expected the reinsurer will participate in the reinsurance if its terms are acceptable to the ceding company. These uses are more fully discussed below.

Excess Capacity

A ceding company must submit for facultative reinsurance any application that does not qualify for automatic reinsurance because the amount exceeds its binding limit or jumbo limit.

Depending on the terms of the automatic treaty, the ceding company may be under no contractual obligation to submit the application to the reinsurer that otherwise would be required to accept the case on an automatic basis had the application been for an amount within the binding limit. Under the terms of some automatic treaties, the ceding company could be required to submit facultative applications to the automatic reinsurer first.

Even if the automatic treaty does not limit the ceding company, it may choose to submit a standard case only to the carrier that qualifies for the automatic reinsurance because it is less costly to submit an application to only one reinsurer. However, if the company is involved in a substandard shopping program, it may be under some obligation to submit clean or standard cases to all the reinsurers to "sweeten the pot" by allowing the reinsurers an equal chance at more preferred business.

Underwriting Assistance

An insurance company may seek facultative reinsurance to get a second opinion or underwriting assistance on difficult cases. Reinsurance underwriters see impaired and questionable risks with far more frequency than traditional life insurance company underwriters. If there is a large amount of previous reinsurance inforce on a particular case, the reinsurance underwriter may be familiar with the insured or have additional information on the case. Care must be taken to respect the confidentiality of records.

If an insured has had very complex financial dealings, perhaps involving large amounts of insurance already in force, the ceding company may send the application out for facultative review to reinsurers whose underwriters are more experienced in dealing with financial underwriting.

Reasons for seeking underwriting assistance may be quite varied. The primary reason is concern over multiple or complicated medical impairments. Applications for large amounts of insurance or requiring complex financial underwriting often lead to facultative submissions, even if the reinsurance could be placed automatically. On occasion, an underwriter simply feels uncomfortable with an application and submits the case facultatively, stating that his company will keep no retention.

In the case of second opinion submissions, the amount applied for may even be within the ceding company's retention. Depending upon the ceding company's and the reinsurer's decisions, the ceding company might cede some, none, or all of the risk.

A ceding company will sometimes submit a case to the reinsurer as a courtesy. While the ceding company's underwriter could be comfortable with his decision, he could recognize an area of concern and allow the reinsurer to make its own decision to agree with him. In this case, the ceding company would keep its retention and the reinsurer could decide to accept no reinsurance on that policy.

A reinsurer provides underwriting assistance for several reasons. To begin with, it expects to make a profit if the case is placed with it. In the case of automatic treaty clients, the reinsurer would prefer to review questionable cases itself than to have them ceded automatically and possibly erode assumed profit margins. Reinsurers also provide this service in an attempt to minimize the need for their automatic treaty clients to establish relationships with other reinsurers.

Shopping for Competitive Underwriting Ratings

Ceding companies frequently submit cases facultatively in order to get the most competitive ratings, a practice known as shopping. The ceding company searching for the best underwriting rating will send a particular application to a number of reinsurers, typically three or four, but in some instances the number of reinsurers may be significantly greater. Usually each reinsurer will know which reinsurers are included in the program and what criteria will be used for submissions and acceptance before it agrees to participate.

The ceding company generally accepts the best offer received from the first reinsurer to make that offer. Sometimes the case will be split among equally competitive reinsurers. "Best" may refer to either the lowest underwriting rating or the lowest overall cost, depending on the sophistication and objectives of the ceding company.

The ceding company may retain little or none of the risk. Some companies base their participation decision on the level of competitiveness of the reinsurer's decision. One company established rules that if the best reinsurance decision matched its own, it would keep its full retention. If the reinsurance decision was one table[1] lower, it would reduce its retention by 25%, if two tables, 50%, and if three tables, 75%. If the reinsurance decision was four or more tables lower, it would retain nothing.

While the insurer usually will issue the policy at the reinsurer's rating, some insurers will issue at one table rating higher than that quoted by the reinsurers. This may be done to cover the administrative costs of shopping, or for other economic reasons. Generally, the reinsurer would want the right to approve such actions.

Some direct writing companies view extensive shopping programs as a valuable service to agents, enabling their agents to place difficult cases through them at a better rating than their underwriting would allow. This supposedly results in improved agent morale and loyalty as well as lower premiums and a psychological advantage to the policyholder. Shopping can also add to the ceding company's profit as long as it adjusts its retention in accordance with its perception of the adequacy of the reinsurer's rating.

---

[1]A table, as referred to in this book means an underwriting rating equivalent to 25% extra mortality. Thus, a Table 2 case would have expected mortality equal to 150% of standard.

As an example, suppose ABC Life's underwriters find that the proposed insured has an abnormal EKG which would normally result in a substandard table rating based on their underwriting manual. The agent, however, feels he cannot place the case with a substandard rating, so the underwriter sends the case to several reinsurers to determine if any of them will accept the case on a standard basis. XYZ Re, which specializes in abnormal EKG's and has a good relationship with ABC Life, offers to take the case on a standard basis. Because ABC Life's underwriting manual would have required a rating, it allows XYZ Re to reinsure the entire amount.

The primary disadvantage of shopping is the increased costs and the potential for decreased profit margins. When a case is submitted facultatively, all underwriting papers must be sent to the reinsurer. This is a costly process. These costs include not only those for supplies, telephone and facsimile transmission, and express delivery, but also for significant clerical and underwriting time.

Shopping for a more competitive risk rating may subject the ceding company to reduced profit margins as the result of higher mortality costs in relation to the premium received on the retained portion of the risk. Companies frequently control this by reducing retention on shopped cases, sometimes retaining nothing.

Reinsurance premiums on shopped facultative business are often higher than those on other sorts of facultative business. This is because of the higher costs associated with extra mortality in a facultative shopping program and the higher underwriting costs per case placed.

Shopping programs may inhibit the development of the issuing company's underwriting staff since typically the most difficult cases are sent to the reinsurers, leaving the underwriters little opportunity to gain real experience with these cases. Shopping may cause agents to lose confidence in the issuing company's underwriters, believing that the underwriters cannot handle the more difficult impairments. Instead of alleviating pressure on the underwriter, a shopping program may actually add some pressure as agents lobby to have cases shopped even though such cases would normally not qualify for facultative treatment. Agents have even been known to ask for a specific reinsurer's underwriting action.

Shopping was very popular starting in the mid 1970's, as facultative underwriting moved from being an accommodation to automatic clients to becoming a "loss leader" or "door opener." Facultative reinsurance has often been viewed as a stepping stone to an automatic arrangement; that is, the reinsurer could use a facultative arrangement to prove itself to the client in the hope of being included in the automatic reinsurance arrangements.

As more companies in the late 1970's and early 1980's entered the reinsurance market, the facultative market became highly competitive. These companies used competitive facultative underwriting to gain a market share.

Many competitive shopping programs of the early 1980's produced very poor mortality and persistency results. Procedures have since become more stringent. Some reinsurers have curtailed participation in larger shopping programs where single risks are submitted to more than four reinsurers. Some reinsurers will not participate if the placement ratio[2] of the ceding company drops below a certain level because of the high costs associated with these programs. It is also not unusual to require the ceding company to retain a minimum portion of the risk, for example, 10%.

Today, as a result of the adverse experience and the high costs involved, facultative underwriting is seldom used as a "door opener." Rather, many reinsurers offer it only as a service to their automatic treaty clients.

FACULTATIVE REINSURANCE CONSIDERATIONS: THE CEDING COMPANY

In developing a facultative reinsurance program, the ceding company must weigh the costs versus the benefits of any such program. Facultative reinsurance has higher costs associated with it than automatic reinsurance even if the reinsurance terms are the same. The ceding company must first underwrite the case which necessitates obtaining all the necessary examinations, tests, and reports. It then turns this file over to the reinsurers. The reinsurance underwriter reviews the case and makes an offer. If the case has been sent to more than one reinsurer, and more than one offer is received, the direct writing company must compare the offers and determine which to accept, if any. While the use of

---

[2]A placement ratio is the ratio of the number of paid cessions from a given ceding company to the number of risks submitted to the reinsurer for evaluation.

facsimile machines may allow the insurance company to receive facultative offers on the same day that the files are submitted, it is not uncommon for several days to elapse before the company receives an acceptable offer. It is, of course, necessary to have reinsurance in place before a policy is issued or the ceding company may find itself on the entire risk without reinsurance.

The amount of reinsurance ceded on a facultative basis will vary among ceding companies based on each company's perception of the advantages and disadvantages of facultative reinsurance.

Advantages

Some of the advantages of facultative reinsurance to the ceding company include the following:

(1) It allows the ceding company to issue policies in excess of its binding limits, providing more profit potential and better service to its agents. This also permits the company to compete with larger insurance companies with higher retentions or binding limits.

(2) It may allow a ceding company to issue a policy it would otherwise not be able to issue due to a noncompetitive rating based on its own underwriting manual as compared to that of the reinsurer. The reinsurer may allow the ceding company to retain something less than its normal retention in this instance.

(3) The ceding company can use the reinsurer's underwriting expertise on difficult cases rather than be committed to using internal resources.

Disadvantages

While there are clear advantages to the use of facultative reinsurance in a reinsurance program, there are several disadvantages to the ceding company. These include the following:

(1) Facultative submissions are a time consuming process. The company could possibly lose the case in a competitive situation if the other company involved does not need to submit the case facultatively or if it has a quicker response from its reinsurers.

(2) Conditional receipt coverage is usually lost in the facultative process unless the ceding company is able to negotiate

special coverage. Any claim incurred under the conditional receipt prior to securing a facultative offer could be quite costly.

(3) Submitting a case facultatively is more expensive as the underwriting files must be submitted to each facultative reinsurer. Since facultative cases frequently involve large amounts of insurance or unusual impairments, it would not be unusual for the underwriting file to contain several hundred pages. Because of the time element, these files are usually sent via a facsimile machine or express mail to each reinsurer. Obviously, the more reinsurers involved, the more costly this becomes. An individual reinsurer may require additional reports which would add to the expense and the time required.

(4) For self-administered pool business, facultative cessions may be a burden because they require special handling. There may be special retention limits and reinsurance rates which vary by reinsurer for facultative cessions. Usually, only one reinsurer may accept a particular facultative risk, not the entire pool. These factors add complexity to the reinsurance administrative system and, if not considered initially, may be quite difficult to address later.

(5) The field force may lose confidence in the company's underwriters, believing they cannot handle the more difficult impairments or are too conservative when they follow the company's underwriting standards. This may cause agents to push for more shopping, adding pressure on the underwriters to submit cases for shopping that do not meet normal rules.

(6) Mortality ratios may rise if the ceding company maintains a retention on facultative policies because of competitive underwriting by the reinsurer reducing the rating on the portion retained.

(7) Facultative reinsurance premiums are usually higher than automatic reinsurance premiums, increasing costs.

REINSURER USES OF FACULTATIVE REINSURANCE

All professional reinsurers provide facultative reinsurance coverage. Before the creation of automatic reinsurance, facultative reinsurance was the only coverage available. Today, reinsurers have different philosophies regarding facultative reinsurance and, therefore, may offer it for the following different purposes.

Quality Control

Facultative reinsurance may be used as a quality control device by the reinsurer. The reinsurer would set a binding limit for each automatic treaty to allow it to review larger applications prior to accepting them. This would enable the reinsurer to control the quality of the business it accepts at these levels.

Primary Business Source

For some reinsurers, facultative reinsurance is the primary business source. These companies have built a longstanding reputation on underwriting knowledge. Ceding companies seek them out because of this expertise. These companies participate on a facultative only basis in many reinsurance programs. More recently, even these companies have sought automatic business.

Accommodation to Automatic Clients

Some reinsurers focus on automatic reinsurance and offer facultative coverage only as an accommodation to automatic clients. An automatic reinsurance carrier almost always provides facultative reinsurance for its automatic clients. Normally it wants to be in position to provide reinsurance capacity on the large applications which are in excess of the ceding company's binding or jumbo limit. In most instances, these applications fall into the standard rating class and represent profitable business.

A reinsurer which uses facultative reinsurance only as an accommodation to automatic clients will seldom participate as a facultative-only reinsurer because it believes it cannot compete on a profitable basis.

Experimental Underwriting Programs

Experimental underwriting programs have been important in the development of the modern life insurance industry. Prior to World War II, there was very little mortality data on impaired insured lives since very few insurance companies had any significant experience and there was no central source to pool data from among these several companies. Since then, reinsurers have been instrumental in initiating formal experimental underwriting programs covering important impairments such as diabetes and coronary heart disease.

A reinsurer has an advantage in developing such programs because it can readily pool the experience of several companies in order to broaden its database and increase the statistical significance of the results. These programs have allowed companies to study carefully the mortality under these impairments and have helped in the development of modern underwriting manuals.

In order to develop an experimental underwriting program today, a company must avail itself of all the most modern clinical information concerning the impairments to be studied, use this information to develop an appropriate rating which is low enough to attract business but high enough to avoid loss, and monitor the mortality results carefully and move quickly to make adjustments when they appear necessary. The successful programs of the past have generally involved only a few impairments which were often highly rated or considered uninsurable. Today's experimental underwriting programs may involve a larger number of impairments and less highly rated risks.

It must be remembered that experimental underwriting programs are research programs and, as such, are quite involved. The underwriting rules must remain flexible and should be set so that as many risks as possible are insured in order to facilitate the gathering of significant data while the premium level must be set so as to minimize the potential for loss. Establishing a reserve to cover extra claims is a good budgeting and control technique. Experimental programs established by reinsurers are often reinsured on a quota share basis in order to spread the risks. The ceding company would also be notified that a certain action was an experimental decision so it could make an informal decision about its own retention. Ceding companies may be allowed to lower their normal retention or even retain nothing if they participate in an experimental program established by a reinsurer.

Automatic Reinsurance Marketing Tool

Many reinsurers use their underwriting expertise as a marketing tool for automatic coverage. As a marketing tool, the reinsurer may supply the ceding company with an underwriting manual which it developed, and may provide training services for ceding company underwriters.

Facultative reinsurance has often been viewed as a stepping stone to an automatic reinsurance agreement. The reinsurer would use a facultative arrangement to prove itself to the client in the hope of being added to the next automatic treaty.

In the early 1980's, competition for automatic reinsurance became very intense and spread into the facultative market. Some reinsurers made quotes on facultative shopping programs as a loss leader to attract new automatic clients and to increase market share. Poor results ended this practice.

REINSURER CONSIDERATIONS

Beyond the use of facultative reinsurance as a marketing tool and a quality control device, all facultative reinsurers must be concerned about the relationship of underwriting action, underwriting expense, additional mortality, and price. Balancing these items can be very difficult, but it is important because any given risk is generally ceded to the reinsurer with the lowest overall cost to the ceding company. These considerations are discussed below.

Underwriting Action

Reinsurers have different underwriting specialities and philosophies. Some may specialize in specific impairments or in financial under-writing. Since underwriting is not an exact science, underwriting action will vary by company and, to an extent, by underwriter within a company.

Cost Control

The reinsurer's ultimate cost is related to the placement ratio for any facultative client. Placement ratios vary by client and are related to the number of reinsurers participating in the program. Low placement ratios are undesirable because of the high cost per cession. A low placement ratio is also indicative of anti-selection. A placement ratio less than the ratio expected due to the proportion of reinsurers involved indicates that the reinsurer is not receiving its appropriate share of all business. A low placement ratio, even if it is equal to the expected placement ratio, increases the chance of anti-selection because so few cases are being placed.

The reinsurer's underwriting expenses per application will differ from those of the ceding company for a number of reasons.

For a given degree of underwriting complexity, the reinsurance underwriter may review more cases in a day than his ceding company counterpart because reinsurance underwriters generally are better trained, are more experienced, and have fewer administrative distractions. Also, the ceding company builds the underwriting file and pays for the tests. However, it is the placement ratio that effects the ultimate per cession costs of reinsurance underwriting. The reinsurer must determine an acceptable placement ratio level in its pricing structure, and a reinsurer may decline to participate in a program where the placement ratio is below its limit.

Additional Mortality

It is more difficult to predict facultative mortality than automatic mortality. A basic problem is that deviations in quotes are not balanced. In any rating category, an insurer can normally expect a range of risks, with some lives being better and some being worse than the assumed average for the catagory. In a competitive facultative situation, the actual average may shift to the higher than expected mortality side, since the better risks in each category are more likely to be given a lower rating by some other reinsurer.

If a case is being submitted to several reinsurers, a competitive quote is more likely to be placed than a noncompetitive quote. Also, a ceding company is likely to capitalize on any underwriting error made in its favor by a reinsurer. Therefore, deviations will not balance and a disproportionately larger number of aggressive decisions will be accepted.

Facultative Pricing

It is very difficult to relate underwriting action to pricing. Aggressive underwriting leads to higher mortality costs. If the pricing mortality assumption is less than the mortality that the underwriting action will produce, the reinsurer will lose by placing these cases. Coordinating pricing and underwriting requires good communications between underwriters and actuaries and careful monitoring of results.

Because of the difficulties involved in pricing facultative reinsurance there is more diversity in the costs of facultative reinsurance to the ceding company. The ceding company can usually expect to cede facultative reinsurance to its automatic reinsurer at the same premium or allowances as its automatic business as an accommodation. However, if placement ratios are low or the automatic price is extremely competitive, the automatic reinsurers may charge a higher price for facultative coverage. A reinsurer may also look at a ceding company's mix of automatic and facultative business in determining its facultative price. The greater the proportion of facultative, the greater the need for higher facultative prices.

A facultative only outlet may sometimes follow the automatic reinsurance terms for competitive reasons. However, if placement ratios are not adequate, if the reinsurer feels it is not getting an opportunity to review the better cases, or if the ceding company uses more aggressive underwriting, the reinsurer may charge a higher price.

FACULTATIVE REINSURANCE VARIATIONS

Two variations of facultative reinsurance are facultative obligatory and conditional automatic. These are special arrangements which have elements of both facultative and automatic reinsurance. Another variation, the facultative pool, is sometimes used as a time and cost savings device.

Facultative Obligatory

On rare occasion, a company may have a facultative obligatory arrangement with the reinsurer. Under such an arrangement, the ceding company has no obligation to cede a particular risk to the reinsurer, but the reinsurer is obligated to accept any risks using the ceding company's underwriting evaluation, within certain limits. Generally, the reinsurer may refuse the risk only if its retention has already been filled on the risk from other policies. This privilege is usually granted only to ceding companies in which the reinsurer has absolute trust as to both integrity and underwriting skill. This form of reinsurance is rarely used today.

Conditional Automatic

In a conditional automatic situation, an insurance company has a contractual relationship with a reinsurer such that the insurer must cede policies to the reinsurer which fulfill certain criteria. However, the reinsurer underwrites each case and retains the right to refuse to issue those risks which it finds uninsurable by its own standards.

Conditional automatic reinsurance is generally used only in situations where the ceding company does not have underwriters of its own and relies on the reinsurer to underwrite all applications. It may also be used when the ceding company has underwriters, but the company is not a member of the Medical Information Bureau.[3] Such an agreement allows the ceding company access to valuable information in exchange for ceding a portion of the risk to the reinsurer.

Facultative Pools

In order to reduce the time and expense involved in facultative underwriting, a few companies have formed facultative reinsurance pools. In a facultative pool, a wheel may be used whereby the reinsurers take turns underwriting the cases or the ceding company may underwrite the cases using a previously agreed upon underwriting manual. The reinsurers share in all cases placed in the pool. The ceding company may also participate in the pool or it may hold no retention.

A facultative reinsurance pool would be formed as a time and cost savings device. For example, if three reinsurers participated on an equal basis, each reinsurer would only have to underwrite a third of the cases and would have a placement ratio equal to the insurer's direct placement ratio, thus reducing its costs.

Valuable time can be saved since the ceding company will not have to wait for responses from several reinsurers. If the ceding company is responsible for underwriting, then there is a larger savings in both time and expense. The reinsurer's expense savings are likely to be reflected in lower reinsurance premiums.

In order to have a successful reinsurance pool, the reinsurers must have compatible, or at least clearly understood, underwriting philosophies. The rules for selecting policies for the pool must be clear and easy to follow. Normally, highly substandard lives or large amounts of insurance will not be placed in the pool. The pool might be limited to those lives which the ceding company would rate through Table 4, or perhaps Table 8,

---

[3]Members of the Medical Information Bureau (MIB) submit coded underwriting information on applicants to the MIB and receive coded information concerning impairments from the MIB regarding new applicants. The insurance company must independently verify this information, but it is regarded as a very useful underwriting tool.

and issued for amounts less than $1,000,000. If the ceding company performs all the risk evaluation, the rules for evaluating the risks must be carefully defined. In the event the ceding company performs the risk evaluation, the underwriting actions should be audited periodically.

The use of facultative reinsurance pools is limited. The ceding company must be able to generate enough business to produce a significant cost savings to interest reinsurers.

4 | Traditional Reinsurance

Reinsurance has many uses, but these can be divided largely into two basic categories, each with its own marketplace and participants. For the purposes of this book, reference will be made to these two basic reinsurance markets as traditional and financial.

The traditional reinsurance market encompasses reinsurance which exists for mortality, morbidity, investment, or persistency risk sharing, involving newly issued[1] life, health and annuity policies. This chapter is devoted to individual life insurance but the basic principles apply to other products. Traditional reinsurance can be issued on automatic or facultative bases, and can be proportional or nonproportional. This chapter describes the operation and characteristics of each of the traditional, proportional reinsurance plans, including the procedure used to calculate

---

[1]While some of the same general considerations applicable to the reinsurance of newly issued policies may apply to the reinsurance of inforce blocks of business, the later is generally restricted to financial reinsurance transactions or the sale or transfer of business using assumption reinsurance. See Chapter 5, Financial Reinsurance, and Chapter 16, Assumption Reinsurance, for further discussion of these considerations.

the reinsurance premiums and allowances and the principal uses and considerations for each plan.

To illustrate the financial effect of each plan of reinsurance on the ceding company and the reinsurer, a simple one-policy model is developed for comparative purposes.

COMPARATIVE MODEL

For the purpose of illustration of the effect and differences of the traditional reinsurance plans in this chapter, a simplistic model is developed. It is assumed that ABC Life Insurance Company issues a $400,000 nonsmoker whole life policy on the life of John Doe, a nonsmoking male age 35. ABC Life retains $100,000 of the risk according to its normal retention schedule and cedes the balance to XYZ Re. ABC Life and XYZ Re each have $500 of surplus on hand on January 1 of the calendar year. XYZ Re has issue expenses of $30 per cession and maintenance expenses of $15 per cession.[2]

Assumptions

For ease of presentation, the following simplifying assumptions and approaches are utilized:

(1) Investment income is assumed to be earned only on assets present at the beginning of the calendar year and not on cash flows.
(2) Policy premiums are assumed to be paid on an annual basis, eliminating the need for deferred premium calculations.
(3) No deaths or surrenders are assumed, since the illustration is based on a single life insurance policy.
(4) Federal income tax effects are ignored.
(5) All calculated amounts are rounded to the nearest dollar.

The principal assumptions are summarized on the following page.

---

[2] A reinsurer usually has lower issue expenses because it has no underwriting costs on automatic reinsurance and no agency development expenses. Its maintenance expenses are lower because it does not have to perform the same degree of policyholder service and agent service as the ceding company, and accounting functions are simpler.

POLICY ASSUMPTIONS

Insured:	John Doe
Issue Age:	35 age near birthday
Underwriting Class:	Standard nonsmoker
Issue Date:	7/1/XX
Plan of Insurance:	Whole Life
Face Amount:	$400,000
Premium Rate/1000:	$10
Annual Policy Fee:	$25
Reserve Basis:	1980 CSO NS, ANB, 5.5% CRVM
Cash Value Basis:	1980 CSO NS, ANB, 7% MIN
Mean Reserves/1000:	
Year 1:	$0.80
Year 2:	$8.56
Commissions:	
Year 1:	90%
Year 2:	10%
Premium Tax:	2.5%
Expenses:	
Underwriting and Issue:	$350 per policy
Maintenance:	$25 per policy

COMPANY AND REINSURANCE ASSUMPTIONS

	ABC Life	XYZ Re
Initial Surplus:	$500	$500
Investment Rate of Return:	10%	10%
Retention Limit:	$100,000	$2,000,000
Reinsurance Expenses:		
Issue:	(included in	$30
Maintenance:	policy expenses)	$15

Illustrations Before Reinsurance

In order to provide a base for comparative purposes, statutory
financial statements for both companies are developed before any
reinsurance occurs. Tables 4.1A and 4.1B show the Gains from
Operations and Balance Sheets, respectively, for the first calendar
year, and Tables 4.2A and 4.2B for the second calendar year.

TABLE 11A

STATUTORY FINANCIAL STATEMENTS
BEFORE REINSURANCE – YEAR 1

GAIN FROM OPERATIONS

	ABC LIFE	XYZ RE
Revenue:		
Premiums:		
Gross	$ 4,025	$ 0
Ceded	0	0
Net	$ 4,025	$ 0
Investment Income:		
Surplus	$ 50	$ 50
Reserves	0	0
Total	$ 50	$ 0
Reinsurance Allowances	$ 0	$ 0
Mod-co Adjustment	0	0
TOTAL REVENUE	$ 4,075	$ 50
Benefits:		
Claims	$ 0	$ 0
Surrenders	0	0
Reserve Increase:		
Gross	$ 320	$ 0
Ceded	0	0
Net	$ 320	$ 0
Mod-co Adjustment	0	0
TOTAL BENEFITS	$ 320	$ 0
Expenses:		
Commissions	$ 3,622	$ 0
Acquisition	350	0
Maintenance	25	0
Premium Tax	101	0
TOTAL EXPENSES	$ 4,098	$ 0
GAIN FROM OPERATIONS	$ (343)	$ 50

TABLE 4.1B

STATUTORY FINANCIAL STATEMENTS
BEFORE REINSURANCE - YEAR 1

BALANCE SHEET

	ABC LIFE	XYZ RE
Assets		
Invested Assets	$ 477	$ 550
TOTAL ASSETS	$ 477	$ 550
Liabilities and Capital		
Policy Reserves:		
Gross	$ 320	$ 0
Ceded	0	0
Net	$ 320	$ 0
TOTAL LIABILITIES	$ 320	$ 0
Surplus	$ 157	$ 550
TOTAL CAPITAL	$ 157	$ 550
TOTAL LIABILITIES AND CAPITAL	$ 477	$ 550

TABLE 4.2A

STATUTORY FINANCIAL STATEMENTS
BEFORE REINSURANCE – YEAR 2

GAIN FROM OPERATIONS

	ABC LIFE	XYZ RE
Revenue:		
Premiums:		
Gross	$ 4,025	$ 0
Ceded	0	0
Net	$ 4,025	$ 0
Investment Income:		
Surplus	$ 16	$ 55
Reserves	32	0
Total	$ 48	$ 55
Reinsurance Allowances	0	0
Mod-co Adjustment	0	0
TOTAL REVENUE	$ 4,073	$ 55
Benefits:		
Claims	$ 0	$ 0
Surrenders	0	0
Reserve Increase:		
Gross	$ 3,104	$ 0
Ceded	0	0
Net	$ 3,104	$ 0
Mod-co Adjustment	0	0
TOTAL BENEFITS	$ 3,104	$ 0
Expenses:		
Commissions	$ 402	$ 0
Acquisition	0	0
Maintenance	25	0
Premium Tax	101	0
TOTAL EXPENSES	$ 528	$ 0
GAIN FROM OPERATIONS	$ 441	$ 55

TABLE 4.2B

STATUTORY FINANCIAL STATEMENTS
BEFORE REINSURANCE – YEAR 2

BALANCE SHEET

	ABC LIFE	XYZ RE
Assets		
Invested Assets	$ 4,022	$ 605
TOTAL ASSETS	$ 4,022	$ 605
Liabilities and Capital		
Policy Reserves:		
Gross	$ 3,424	$ 0
Ceded	0	0
Net	$ 3,424	$ 0
TOTAL LIABILITIES	$ 3,424	$ 0
Surplus	$ 598	$ 605
TOTAL CAPITAL	$ 598	$ 605
TOTAL LIABILITIES AND CAPITAL	$ 4,022	$ 605

PLANS OF TRADITIONAL REINSURANCE

The primary proportional reinsurance plans in the traditional market are yearly renewable term, frequently referred to as YRT; coinsurance, sometimes referred to as full coinsurance; and modified coinsurance, frequently referred to as mod-co. These three plans are discussed in detail and their relative effects on the financial statements of ABC Life and XYZ Re are illustrated.

Yearly Renewable Term Insurance

Yearly renewable term or risk premium reinsurance (RPR) is a plan of reinsurance for which the premium rates are not directly related to the premium rates of the original plan of insurance. Under YRT reinsurance, the ceding company reinsures the mortality or morbidity risk only. The amount reinsured in any one year is not based on the face amount of the policy, but rather on the net amount at risk. The ceding company retains responsibility for establishing the policy reserves and the payment of all surrender values, dividends, commissions, and expenses involved in issuing and maintaining the policy. Yearly renewable term reinsurance is considered to be simpler to administer than either coinsurance or modified coinsurance and is usually less expensive, given the same experience assumptions.

Net Amount at Risk Calculation. The net amount at risk in any policy year is usually defined as the face amount of the policy less the terminal reserve and this amount is actually calculated for most YRT cessions. In some instances, however, simplifying assumptions are made to facilitate its calculation. The most common ones are discussed below:

Level Term Policies. For level term plans of less than twenty years, reserves are generally minimal and, consequently, are usually ignored for reinsurance purposes. The net amount at risk in all years is taken to be the reinsured face amount.

For level term policies of twenty years or longer, the first year net amount at risk is the reinsurance face amount. In years two through ten, the net amount at risk is usually determined by using the tenth year cash value. The cash value is used because it is available from the policy form and the reserve might not be. The tenth year cash value divided by nine is the assumed annual decrease in the net amount at risk in years two through ten. In years eleven through twenty, the net amount at risk is determined by a straight line interpolation between the face amount less the tenth year cash value and the face amount less the twentieth year cash value. A similar approach is used for each successive ten year period.

For example, assume that ABC Life issues a 100,000 term to 65 policy. The tenth year cash value for issue age 35 is $36.00 per thousand and the twentieth year cash value is $76.00 per thousand.

In the first year, the net amount at risk is $100,000. One-ninth of the tenth year cash value on is $400. In the second year, the net amount at risk is $99,600; in the third year, $99,200, and so on, until the tenth year when the net amount at risk is $96,400. The difference between the tenth and twentieth year cash values is $4,000, one-tenth of the difference is $400. The net amount at risk is, therefore, reduced by $400 each year from year ten to year twenty. The difference between the twentieth year cash value and the cash value at age 65 is ($7,600). In each of the last ten years, the net amount at risk is increased $760.

Decreasing Term Policies. The net amount at risk under decreasing term policies is usually agreed upon in advance based on a formula or table of values. This is particularly useful if decreases occur monthly or if the coverage was designed for use with adjustable interest rate mortgages. A common method is to use the initial reinsurance face amount as the net amount at risk in the first policy year. In years two through ten, the annual reduction in the net amount at risk is one-ninth of the difference between the tenth year death benefit and the first year value. In years eleven through twenty, the net amount at risk is decreased by one-tenth of the difference between the tenth and twentieth year death benefits.

For example, assume ABC Life reinsured a $100,000 thirty year decreasing term policy with a tenth year death benefit of $93,000 and a twentieth year death benefit of $68,800. The first year net amount at risk is $100,000. The second year net amount at risk is $99,222; in the third year $98,444; and so on, reducing $778 each year. In years eleven through twenty, the annual reduction is $2,420. In the final ten years, the annual reduction is $6,880.

Permanent Policies. The most common simplifying method for calculating the net amount at risk is to assume that the initial terminal reserve is zero so that the initial net amount at risk is equal to the face amount reinsured. For years two through ten, the net amount at risk is reduced annually by one-ninth of the tenth year cash values. For years eleven through twenty, the net amount at risk is reduced each year by one-tenth of the difference between the tenth and twentieth year cash values. This is repeated for each subsequent ten year period. This is analogous to the method used for level term policies.

Universal Life. The principal for net amount at risk calculations is the same as for permanent plans. However, the variable amounts of cash value and face amounts create administrative problems.

The amounts can be recalculated as frequently as the ceding company and reinsurer deem necessary. Because of this complexity, self administration or some form of computerized administration is frequently used for universal life and other interest sensitive products.

Retention Determination. Once the net amount at risk is calculated, it is important to determine the amount of the risk to be retained. There are four methods commonly used:

Pro Rata. This is the original proportional method. Under this method the ceding company retains a constant percentage of the net amount at risk. Typically this is calculated as the ratio of original face amount ceded to total original face amount of the policy.

For example, if ABC Life issues a $1,000,000 whole life policy and cedes $900,000, on the pro rata method it would always reinsure 90% of the policy. If the tenth year terminal reserve is $55,000, the net amount at risk reinsured in the tenth year is 90% of $945,000, or $850,500.

Under the pro rata method, the amount retained will drop below the ceding company's retention limit if the net amount at risk decreases. The pro rata method is the preferred method for reinsuring decreasing term policies as it assures that the policies will be reinsured for the entire term period, although it can result in very small amounts of reinsurance in later policy durations. This method can be used for all plans of insurance.

Level or Constant Retention.   Under the level or constant retention method, the company retains a fixed amount of the net amount at risk.   The entire decrease in net amount at risk is allocated to the reinsured portion. Because the net amount at risk is generally a decreasing amount, the amount reinsured under this method will decrease each year more rapidly than under the pro rata method and the reinsurer eventually may have no risk on the policy. While the amount of risk borne by the ceding company and the reinsurer are not in the same proportion each year, this is still referred to as proportional reinsurance because the net amount at risk can still be determined in advance.

If in the previous example of the $1,000,000 whole life policy, ABC Life keeps a level $100,000 retention, the first year net amount at risk reinsured is $900,000, and the tenth year net amount at risk reinsured is $845,000, the total net amount at risk less $100,000. This value is $5,500 less than that obtained using the pro rata method above. This difference is equal to the tenth year terminal reserve on the original retention.

Constant Risk Reinsured.   This is a relatively rare method under which the reinsurance is a constant amount and the ceding company absorbs the reduction.   Under this method the amount retained decreases as the reserves increase under the entire policy. In the example of the $1,000,000 whole life policy, ABC Life would always reinsure $900,000, or the entire net amount at risk under the original policy, if less.   In the tenth year, the net amount is $945,000, and ABC Life would only retain $45,000.

Formula Retention.   Under this method, the net amount at risk and retention are determined by an initially agreed upon formula. This method is often used in the case of decreasing term policies.

Premium Scales. YRT reinsurance rates are usually specific for a given age, duration, and sex.   If the plan reinsured distinguishes premiums between smokers and nonsmokers or uses preferred risk discounts, these distinctions are usually reflected in the reinsurance YRT premium scale. Normally, a select period of five, ten, fifteen, or even twenty years is used, with fifteen years being the most common today.   The select rate structure is used to reflect expected mortality experience for underwritten lives and provides the ceding company with lower reinsurance costs in the early years.

In some cases, there is no first year premium. The so called "zero first year premium" scale is used to assist the company in reducing its surplus strain on new issues. Sometimes a production bonus or negative first year premium is used to further reduce the surplus strain for the ceding company. A persistency bonus is employed infrequently to reward good experience and is usually paid on thirteen month experience. The reinsurer may charge a cession fee for YRT reinsurance to cover maintenance expenses.[3]

Reinsurers may have several YRT scales available. The scales may vary by the anticipated production of the account, the anticipated average size, the anticipated experience, or the type of products reinsured. If a large volume of production is expected on a particular plan of insurance or if there are special product considerations, the reinsurer may develop a YRT scale specifically for the product. These scales are often designed and stated in coinsurance terms, that is the reinsurance premiums are stated in terms of percentages of the basic plan premium. This approach is commonly used for interest sensitive products where the reinsurance premiums can be stated in terms of a percentage of the cost of insurance rates for the policy. This may simplify the ceding company's administration.

Prior to the mid-1970's most YRT scales were experience rated. On an experience rated basis, the reinsurer would return a portion of the excess of premiums received over benefits paid. Experience refund scales were usually 10%-20% higher than non-refund YRT scales. Today, most YRT rate scales are not experience rated.

Traditionally, reinsurance YRT scales guaranteed in the reinsurance treaty are equal to the valuation net premiums. These rates are usually far in excess of the actual YRT rates in use. The non-guaranteed or indeterminate premium[4] approach has been used to allow the reinsurer to avoid establishing deficiency reserves on assumed YRT reinsurance. While the reinsurer has the contractual right to raise rates to the guaranteed level, it is usually understood by the parties that there is no intention to do so. However, the fact that the reinsurer can raise rates should not be ignored. This approach is similar to that used by most insurance companies on direct issues of certain term and other indeterminate premium products.

---

[3] Cession fees are relatively rare today, but are used in this book to illustrate principles of reinsurance and to demonstrate some of the variety of reinsurance terms available.

[4] Indeterminate premium policies provide that the insurance company may change premiums, subject to a guaranteed maximum premium, under conditions outlined in the policy.

Most reinsurance YRT rate scales are calculated on a policy year basis, but calendar year YRT rate scales are also in use. Calendar year YRT rate scales are most frequently used with some sort of simplified administrative procedures.   Since terminal reserves on the one year term coverage are zero, calendar year scales allow the reinsurer to avoid the necessity of setting up any reserve at the end of the year.

Premium Calculation

The reinsurance premium for a specific policy year on a given YRT cession is equal to the reinsurance YRT rate per $1,000 appropriate for the policyholder's age, sex, policy year, and smoker status times the number of thousands of net amount at risk reinsured. Adjustments for substandard rating are made as necessary, and the cession fee, if any, is then added. Premiums are generally paid on an annual basis, although modal premiums are sometimes used.

In the case of a substandard table rating, the YRT reinsurance premium is increased to reflect the table rating. The substandard extra premium may take the form of a separate scale or a multiple of the basic YRT premium scale.   There is no uniformity in the manner in which substandard table premiums are calculated when distinct smoker and nonsmoker YRT rates are being used.   Some reinsurers use the traditional multiple of the nonsmoker or smoker YRT rate for table ratings. Other reinsurers have introduced special substandard rate scales which do not distinguish between smoking habits, thus avoiding the double discounting which occurs when a multiple of a nonsmoker table is used as a substandard rate and the double surcharging when a multiple smoker table is used on a substandard life. Substandard charges may be waived after a period of years if the ceding company also removes the rating on the underlying policy.

Temporary or flat permanent extra ratings are typically co-insured. Frequently, unsophisticated allowances are granted; that is, the allowances are not individually priced. For ratings extending for more than five years, allowances of 75% to 85% for the first year and 10% to 15% renewal are typical. For ratings of five years or less, allowances of 10% to 15% in each year are typical.

Reinsurance premiums for ancillary benefits such as waiver of premium, guaranteed insurability options, payor death and disability, and monthly income are generally coinsured, again using standard allowances such as 75% to 85% first year and 10% to 15% renewal.

Accidental death benefits are usually reinsured on a YRT basis with a rate which rarely varies by age or duration. Term life insurance riders would generally be reinsured using the same YRT rates used for the base policy. Administration is often on a bulk basis.

Uses of Yearly Renewable Term

Yearly renewable term reinsurance is generally used for reinsuring traditional whole life products. It is also frequently used in reinsuring interest sensitive products. In this situation, a special zero first year scale is usually developed. Special YRT rates scales may also be developed for use with specific products. In this case, the YRT rate scale is developed to match the slope of the term premium scale, with the YRT rates stated in terms of percentages of the base term rates. In essence, YRT is being used to emulate coinsurance in these situations. Yearly renewable term is also used in reinsuring certain disability income benefits. Annuities cannot be reinsured on a YRT basis.

Other Considerations

Yearly renewable term reinsurance is used to transfer only the mortality or morbidity risks involved in an insurance policy. Because YRT reinsurance involves only limited investment risk, no cash surrender risk, and little or no surplus strain, the reinsurers will usually have a lower profit objective for YRT reinsurance. Therefore, it is usually obtainable at a lower cost than either coinsurance or mod-co. For products with fixed benefits, the net amount at risk and retention schedules can be determined in advance and the administration of such contracts is fairly straight-forward. For products with flexible benefits such as interest sensitive products where the cash value can grow quite rapidly, the administration is usually handled by the ceding company. One YRT premium scale is usually applicable to all amounts of insurance issued on a given product, where under coinsurance or mod-co, premiums and allowances may vary by size of the ceded policy. Also, under YRT the reinsurer need not be concerned with policy loans, cash surrenders, or the payment of policy dividends.

Assuming annual premiums are paid, the reserve credit is equal to the one year term insurance reserves being held by the reinsurer. The ceding company need only adjust the reinsurer's values to account for items in transit. Yearly renewable term reinsurance does not provide relief for deficiency reserves.

In fact, little surplus relief is available because one year term reserves are generally quite small. If the company needs help with the initial surplus strain and wants to use YRT reinsurance, it may negotiate a zero first year scale. If more relief is needed, it may negotiate production bonuses or a negative first year premium. These, of course, add to the cost of the reinsurance in later years.

When a reinsured policy goes on a nonforfeiture status, the appropriate YRT premium must continue to be paid. In the case of extended term or reduced paid up insurance, the reinsurance amount must be adjusted to reflect both the new death benefit and the new net amount of risk pattern. The original YRT premium scale[5] is usually continued based upon the original terms at issue.[6]

YRT Reinsurance Illustrations. In the illustrative example, assume ABC Life has an automatic YRT reinsurance treaty with XYZ Re utilizing assumptions shown below.

YRT ASSUMPTIONS

Amount Reinsured: $300,000

YRT Premiums/1000:
     Year 1: $0.65
     Year 2: $0.77

Annual Cession Fee: $15.00

YRT Reserve Basis: 1980 CSO NS, ANB, 5.5%

YRT Mean Reserves/1000:
     Year 1: $0.80
     Year 2: $0.84

Mean reserves per $1,000 of net amount at risk are $.5(1000 \cdot c_x)$ because the YRT rates are not guaranteed.

---

[5]In some treaties, a "loaded" YRT premium scale is specified for use with extended term insurance.

[6]This concept of maintaining the original issue age, duration, sex, underwriting status, and smoker status is known as using "point-in-scale" YRT premium rates.

First Year Results. The first year YRT rate premium for John Doe's issue age and nonsmoker status is $.65 per $1,000 of coverage with a $15 cession fee. ABC Life would remit a premium of $210 to XYZ Re. The premium tax on the $210 reinsurance premium is $5. The net payment to XYZ Re is $205, but the $210 premium is normally paid by the ceding company at issue and the $5 premium tax reimbursement from the reinsurer is paid early in the next calendar year but would be accrued at the end of the year. At the end of the first calendar year, the total policy reserve is $320. The YRT reserve on the ceded portion is $240. ABC Life is left with a net reserve of $80. Tables 4.3A and 4.3B show the statutory Gains From Operations and Balance Sheets, respectively, for the first year of the YRT transaction for ABC Life and XYZ Re.

ABC Life's net loss in the first year has been reduced to $308, a reduction in loss of $35 from that shown in Table 4.1A. This $35 is equal to the difference between the reinsurance premium and the sum of the reinsurance reserve credit and the premium tax reimbursement, shown as the reinsurance allowance. XYZ Re now has a net loss of $30 for the year, some $80 less earnings than in the pre-reinsurance scenario. This is equal to the $30 difference between the reinsurance premium and the reinsurance reserve it has assumed, plus $45 of issue and maintenance expenses and $5 of premium tax reimbursement which it incurred on the ceded policy.

In comparing the Gains from Operations of Table 4.1A with those of Table 4.3A, it should be noted that the sum of the gains for the two companies is the same, except for the additional $45 expense ($30 acquisition and $15 maintenance) incurred by XYZ Re in handling the reinsurance. In particular, it should be noted that the total of the premiums and reserves for the two companies remains constant. While correct in principle, this constant sum principle will not always be maintained for reasons to be discussed subsequently.

A comparison of the Balance Sheets of Table 4.1B to those of Table 4.3B shows that ABC Life's invested assets have been reduced by $205, representing the reinsurance premium less premium tax reimbursement, while XYZ Re's invested assets have increased by the $210 of YRT premiums less $50 of expenses.

TABLE 3A

STATUTORY FINANCIAL STATEMENTS
YRT – YEAR 1

GAIN FROM OPERATIONS

	ABC LIFE	XYZ RE
Revenue:		
Premiums:		
Gross	$ 4,025	$ 210
Ceded	210	0
Net	$ 3,815	$ 210
Investment Income:		
Surplus	$ 50	$ 50
Reserves	0	0
Total	$ 50	$ 50
Reinsurance Allowances	5	0
Mod-co Adjustment	0	0
TOTAL REVENUE	$ 3,870	$ 260
Benefits:		
Claims	$ 0	$ 0
Surrenders	0	0
Reserve Increase:		
Gross	$ 320	$ 240
Ceded	240	0
Net	$ 80	$ 240
Mod-co Adjustment	0	0
TOTAL BENEFITS	$ 80	$ 240
Expenses:		
Commissions	$ 3,622	$ 0
Acquisition	350	30
Maintenance	25	15
Premium Tax	101	5
TOTAL EXPENSES	$ 4,098	$ 50
GAIN FROM OPERATIONS	$ (308)	$ (30)

TABLE 3B

STATUTORY FINANCIAL STATEMENTS
YRT – YEAR 1

BALANCE SHEET

	ABC LIFE	XYZ RE
Assets		
Invested Assets	$ 272	$ 710
TOTAL ASSETS	$ 272	$ 710
Liabilities and Capital		
Policy Reserves:		
Gross	$ 320	$ 240
Ceded	240	0
Net	$ 80	$ 240
TOTAL LIABILITIES	$ 80	$ 240
Surplus	$ 192	$ 470
TOTAL CAPITAL	$ 192	$ 470
TOTAL LIABILITIES AND CAPITAL	$ 272	$ 710

Second Year Results. Assuming a traditional proportional sharing in the net amount at risk, the death benefit reinsured in the second year is $297,300 because the net amount at risk to the nearer dollar is $991 per thousand, and 300 units are reinsured.

The YRT premium for the second year is $244. This is calculated as .77 per $1,000 times 297.3 plus the $15 cession fee. The reinsurance allowance for premium tax is $6.

The reserve credit is calculated based upon the amount at risk ceded. Assuming that $.5(1000 \cdot c_{36})$ is $.84, the correct reserve credit is 297.3 times $.84, or $250.

Tables 4.4A and 4.4B show the effect of the YRT transaction in the second calendar year. The YRT premium increases to $244. The YRT reserve at the end of the calendar year is $250, an increase of $10 over the previous year. XYZ Re now shows a net gain of $284 while ABC Life has a net gain of $192. The combined net gain for both companies of $476 is less than the corresponding combined net gain of $496 without reinsurance shown in Table 4.2B. The $20 difference in net gain is attributable to $15 of maintenance expense incurred by XYZ Re and the $5 of lost investment income on XYZ Re's surplus due to its increased expenses in the first year.

It is important to note that in this, and in each of the reinsurance examples, total liabilities for both companies remain unchanged while the total of the assets of both companies decrease only to the extent that the reinsurer incurs issue and maintenance expenses. Because of these increased expenses, the total of the investment incomes is also decreased. The combined surplus of both companies is decreased by the cumulative amount of these additional expenses and lost investment income.

Coinsurance

Under a coinsurance arrangement, reinsurance coverage ceded to the reinsurer on an individual policy is essentially in the same form as that of the policy issued. The reinsurer receives its proportionate share of the gross premium from the ceding company. The reinsurer provides a reimbursement to the ceding company in recognition of the commissions and other out-of-pocket expenses incurred on the ceded portion. This reimbursement is called the expense allowance. The allowance may or may not cover all of the expenses and commissions incurred by the ceding company, and timing of the payments would only coincidentally match the timing

TABLE 4.4A

STATUTORY FINANCIAL STATEMENTS
YRT – YEAR 2

GAIN FROM OPERATIONS

	ABC LIFE	XYZ RE
Revenue:		
Premiums:		
Gross	$ 4,025	$ 244
Ceded	244	0
Net	$ 3,781	$ 244
Investment Income:		
Surplus	$ 19	$ 47
Reserves	8	24
Total	$ 27	$ 71
Reinsurance Allowances	6	0
Mod-co Adjustment	0	0
TOTAL REVENUE	$ 3,814	$ 315
Benefits:		
Claims	$ 0	$ 0
Surrenders	0	0
Reserve Increase:		
Gross	$ 3,104	$ 10
Ceded	10	0
Net	$ 3,094	$ 10
Mod-co Adjustment	0	0
TOTAL BENEFITS	$ 3,094	$ 10
Expenses:		
Commissions	$ 402	$ 0
Acquisition	0	0
Maintenance	25	15
Premium Tax	101	6
TOTAL EXPENSES	$ 528	$ 21
GAIN FROM OPERATIONS	$ 192	$ 284

TABLE 4.4B

STATUTORY FINANCIAL STATEMENTS
YRT – YEAR 2

BALANCE SHEET

	ABC LIFE	XYZ RE
Assets		
Invested Assets	$ 3,558	$ 1,004
TOTAL ASSETS	$ 3,558	$ 1,004
Liabilities and Capital		
Policy Reserves:		
Gross	$ 3,424	$ 250
Ceded	250	0
Net	$ 3,174	$ 250
TOTAL LIABILITIES	$ 3,174	$ 250
Surplus	$ 384	$ 754
TOTAL CAPITAL	$ 384	$ 754
TOTAL LIABILITIES AND CAPITAL	$ 3,558	$ 1,004

of the expenditures. Occasionally, the allowance may exceed the commission and expenses of the ceding company, providing an additional element of profit.

In a coinsurance arrangement, the reinsurer establishes its proportionate share of the policy reserves. It shares proportionately in the risk of loss due to excessive mortality or morbidity, lapses, and cash surrenders, and in the investment risks inherent in the contract. The reinsurer also shares in the surplus drain of new issue, the proportion being a function of the relation of the first year expense allowance to the acquisition expense of the reinsurer. While several methods of determining the retention may be used, a level retention method is almost always used for coinsurance.

Coinsurance Premiums and Allowances. In most cases, the reinsurance premium used for coinsurance is proportionate to the gross premium paid by the policyholder. Many modern insurance products feature "banded" premiums; that is, the gross premium rate will vary with the face amount of the policy to reflect decreasing per thousand administrative expenses and improved mortality as additional underwriting is used. There are three common methods used to determine reinsurance premiums and allowances for banded policies.

(1) Perhaps the most common method is to base the reinsurance premium on the gross premium rate charged the policyholder and to use a common set of allowances for all bands of banded policies. This method is probably the simplest to understand and to use.

(2) The second method is to base the reinsurance premium on the gross premium rate charged the policyholder and vary the coinsurance allowances by the policy band. This method is less desirable than the first because it complicates the administration, but it is sometimes necessary for the reinsurer to have consistent margins for all policy bands. This usually leads to an equitable cost to the ceding company on all bands as well.

(3) The third method is to base the reinsurance premium on a specified band of premium rates regardless of the size of the policy. Typically, the reinsurance premium would be based on the premium rate for the highest policy band so that the reinsurance premium for the reinsured portion

will never exceed the premium received by the insurance company for that amount. One set of allowances is then used for all sizes, resulting in a common net reinsurance premium rate (reinsurance premium rate less allowance) for all policy sizes. This can simplify the administration but is most commonly used in competitive situations. It results in an additional margin on reinsurance for the ceding company on policies written on the lower bands.

Most insurance policies also utilize a policy fee to help cover the insurance company's maintenance expenses. In most circumstances, the reinsurer will allow the ceding company to retain the entire policy fee to offset its expenses and no cession fee is charged. On some occasions, especially for quota share coinsurance agreements, the policy fee will also be coinsured.

Most modern insurance products also recognize a difference between smoker and nonsmoker mortality in the premium structures. Some products may also add a preferred risk category. The coinsurance premiums will usually follow these underwriting classifications, with the reinsurance premium based on the gross premium rate, subject to the banding considerations discussed above. The coinsurance allowances will generally vary by the smoker/nonsmoker/preferred risk classifications since the reinsurer's mortality, morbidity, and persistency assumptions will seldom exactly parallel the ceding company's assumptions.

Coinsurance allowances frequently vary by age if the ceding company's commission scale varies by age. The reinsurer may also vary the allowances by age in order to maintain reasonably consistent profits by age where the reinsurer's mortality, morbidity, and persistency assumptions do not parallel the ceding company's assumptions.

Coinsurance allowances may also vary be sex, but this situation is encountered infrequently.

Some traditional coinsurance agreements are experience rated, providing for the periodic determination of experience refunds. The refund is generally expressed as a proportion of any gain, where the gain is based on a formula reflecting premiums, benefits, allowances, interest, and changes in reserves for the period. Because the ceding company would share only in profits and not in losses, the reinsurance premiums net of allowances on an experience rated basis are higher than similar net reinsurance premiums for a non-refund agreement. Today, most traditional coinsurance is on a non-experience rated basis.

In the early years of coinsurance, allowances would rarely equal or exceed 100% in the first policy year. At various points in history, such as the late 1970's and early 1980's, many reinsurers routinely offered first year allowances in excess of 100% of the first year premium. This was done to alleviate surplus strain and because of competitive pressures. The granting of allowances, which, together with cash values, exceed 100% of premium in the first year subjects the reinsurer to an added risk of loss from lapse or surrender. To counteract this, reinsurers will sometimes include a chargeback provision in the treaty. In general, a chargeback provision requires the return of the excess of allowances and cash values paid over premiums received to the reinsurer in the event of an early policy termination.

Occasionally, a reinsurer may reward a ceding company for high production or good persistency by means of a bonus. These bonuses may be stated in terms of a percentage of premium or as an amount per $1000. However, since persistency and production are difficult to monitor, such bonuses are rarely employed.

Many modern insurance products also feature indeterminate or non-guaranteed premiums. Coinsurance premiums and allowances are generally based on the current premium being charged on these products. The reinsurer would retain the right to recalculate coinsurance premiums and allowances should the premium charged for the product ever be changed.

Coinsurance Premium and Allowance Calculations. Under coinsurance, reinsurance allowances are uniquely developed for the product involved. Premiums generally are paid to the reinsurer on an annual basis regardless of the mode of payment received by the ceding company.

Substandard extras are somewhat complicated in their administration. Allowances will usually vary according to type of extra and the period of time to which they apply.

Permanent table extra premiums are normally coinsured with the same allowances as the base policy. Flat extra premiums which apply for more than five years may use a more generalized allowance, such as 75% to 85% in the first year and 10% to 15% renewal. Temporary extra premiums which apply for five years or less may have allowances of 10% to 15% in all years.

The reinsurance of a term rider attached to the base policy should theoretically have allowances unique for that rider, but sometimes, for the sake of simplicity, the base plan's allowances are used.

Ancillary benefits such as waiver of premium, guaranteed insurability options, payor death and disability, and monthly income are coinsured using generalized allowances such as 75% to 85% first year and 10% to 15% in renewal years. Generally, accidental death benefits are reinsured using a flat YRT rate per thousand.

In the illustrative example, assume that the whole life product has five bands: $10,000 to $99,999, $100,000 to $249,999, $250,000 to $499,999, $500,000 to $999,999, and $1 million and over. Assume that the appropriate standard basic rate for John Doe is $10 per $1000 plus a policy fee of $25. XYZ Re has offered ABC Life the following allowances:

Policy Year	Expense Allowance
1	100.0%
2-10	15.0%
Over 10	7.5%

It will allow ABC Life to retain the entire policy fee. It will also reimburse ABC Life for its premium tax of 2.5% on the ceded portion of the premium.

The ceded premium is $3,000. The initial expense allowance is 100% of the ceded premium, or a reimbursement of $3,000. The premium tax reimbursement is $75. For this illustration, this will be added to the allowance for the ceding company, even though the timing of payments differ.

In the second policy year, the reinsurance premium will again be $3,000. The expense allowance is 15% of $3,000 or $450. The premium tax reimbursement remains $75, making the total of allowance and premium taxes $525.

Had XYZ Re agreed to base the allowances on the $1 million band premium where the premium was only $8 per $1,000, the premium calculation would have been modified. The reinsurance premium would have become $8 times 300 or $2,400. The premium tax reimbursement would have been calculated on this lower amount for a total of $60. In the first policy year the allowance would have been 100% of $2,400. In the second policy year the allowance would have been 15% of $2,400 or $360. The total of allowances and premium taxes would then have been $2,460 in the first year and $420 in the second year.

Uses of Coinsurance. Coinsurance is applicable to any type of insurance: life, disability, medical, or annuity. For life insurance, coinsurance is most commonly used today for reinsuring term products since they have little or no cash value buildup and, therefore, minimal investment risk. However, coinsurance is used with cash value products if there is a desire to pass strain or investment risk to the reinsurer.

Other Considerations. While it was stated earlier that under a coinsurance arrangement, the reinsurer shares in the operating results of the basic plan, there are certain common exceptions. In a participating policy, the reinsurer will usually decline to participate in the dividends paid on the policies. This is because the common dividend formulas cover not only the underlying mortality and morbidity experience of the plan but also include the company's investment and expense results and profit criteria. Most importantly, dividend formulas would include the experience on all business, not just the segment reinsured. The result on retained and reinsured business may differ dramatically, but dividend results would tend to reflect the results on retained business.

If a large portion of a block of participating policies is ceded without reinsurer dividend participation, the ceding company may have a problem because it is not holding the assets underlying the reserves and therefore is not receiving the investment benefits. However, coinsurance allowances without dividend participation will be larger than coinsurance allowances which include dividend participation and this increase in the allowance is intended to offset the dividends. Sometimes reinsurers agree to participate in a current dividend scale, but not in any revisions to it. Participation in subsequent revisions may be subject to future negotiations. When the reinsurer participates in the dividends, the dividend is actually an additional allowance.

Reinsurers rarely participate in policy loans under coinsurance. Policy loans would represent an additional risk to the reinsurer as well as an additional administrative problem. It is not inconceivable that the total of all policy loans on a block which is largely reinsured could exceed the retained assets.

Because the ceding company is assessed premium taxes on the entire premium collected and not just on the retained portion, it is common practice for the reinsurer to reimburse the ceding company in some manner. In some cases, the reinsurer will make provisions for premium tax reimbursement in determining the overall expense allowance structure. The ceding company would be responsible for any increases in premium taxes and no special accounting would be made. In other cases, the reinsurer will provide for an exact premium tax reimbursement. Any increases or decreases in the premium tax rate would then be passed on to the reinsurer. Other agreements may call for premium tax reimbursement on a fixed percentage or some other mutually agreed upon basis.

Policies on nonforfeiture status can present a special reinsurance problem. If the insured elects the reduced paid up insurance option, the amount of reinsurance is proportionately adjusted to reflect the reduced amount, and no further premiums are received. If the extended term option is elected, the reinsurer will provide extended term insurance for the appropriate duration, and, again, no further premiums are received. In some instances, especially if the benefit is small, the reinsurer may pay the surrender value to the ceding company at the time the nonforfeiture option is elected and have no further liability.

Because the reinsurer does not normally participate in policy loans, if a policy goes on the automatic premium loan option, the reinsurer will continue to receive its premium and pay the normal allowances.

If the reinsurer is admitted or licensed in the ceding company's state of domicile, the ceding company is permitted to reduce its required reserve for the risks reinsured through a reinsurance ceded reserve credit. If the reinsurer is not admitted or licensed in the ceding company's state of domicile, it may be subject to special requirements[7] before the ceding company can take a credit. Coinsurance will pass the basic policy reserves as well as all policy deficiency reserves to the reinsurer on the ceded risk. The calculation and treatment of the reserve credit is under scrutiny by industry and regulatory groups at this time.[8] While the details of the credits may change, the basic principles remain as stated above.

The administration of coinsurance is relatively complex since it involves not only the calculations of premiums and payment of death benefits but also the calculation of expense allowances and reserves and the payments of cash surrenders.[9]

---

[7]See Chapter 10, Reinsurance Regulations.

[8]*Ibid.*

[9]See Chapter 7, Reinsurance Administration.

Coinsurance Illustrations. In the illustrative example of ABC Life, assume that ABC Life enters into a coinsurance treaty with XYZ Re using the following allowances:

Policy Year	Expense Allowance
1	100.0%
2-10	15.0%
Over 10	7.5%

XYZ Re has also agreed to reimburse for premium tax. In this case, the premium tax rate is 2.5%

First Year Results. Tables 4.5A and 4.5B show the results of the coinsurance for the first year. ABC Life shows ceded premium of $3,000, leaving a net retained premium of $1,025. It has received a reinsurance expense allowance, including the premium tax reimbursement, of $3,075 from XYZ Re. Its reserve increase has been reduced to $80 due to the reinsurance reserve credit it is allowed on the ceded business. Its expenses remain unchanged from the other examples. It now has a loss in the first year of $28 as compared to a loss of $343 without reinsurance and a loss of $308 with YRT. The difference in the net losses between the results with no reinsurance and with coinsurance is $315. This is equal to the reinsurance premium less the expense allowance, premium tax reimbursement, and the reinsurance reserve credit. The difference of $280 in the gains between the YRT and coinsurance situation is attributable to lower net reinsurance premium (premiums less allowance) and the higher premium tax reimbursement. The reserve credits are the same.[10]

In the case of XYZ Re, it now has $3,000 of premium and a $240 reserve increase. Its total expenses have risen to $3,120 because of the coinsurance expense allowance and the higher premium tax reimbursement. XYZ Re has a net loss of $310 in the first year under the coinsurance arrangement as opposed to a $50 gain without reinsurance and a $30 loss with YRT. The difference between the net loss with coinsurance and net gain without reinsurance is equal to sum of the reserve increase, the premium tax reimbursement, and the additional expenses incurred in the

---

[10]In this illustration, the YRT and coinsurance mean reserves are the same in the first year because the base plan is a whole life plan with CRVM reserves. Obviously, not all plans will have a first year mean reserve equal to $.5(1000c_x)$, the YRT reserve.

TABLE 4.5A

STATUTORY FINANCIAL STATEMENTS
COINSURANCE – YEAR 1

GAIN FROM OPERATIONS

	ABC LIFE	XYZ RE
Revenue:		
Premiums:		
Gross	$ 4,025	$ 3,000
Ceded	3,000	0
Net	$ 1,025	$ 3,000
Investment Income:		
Surplus	$ 50	$ 50
Reserves	0	0
Total	$ 50	$ 50
Reinsurance Allowances	$ 3,075	$ 0
Mod-co Adjustment	0	0
TOTAL REVENUE	$ 4,150	$ 3,050
Benefits:		
Claims	$ 0	$ 0
Surrenders	0	0
Reserve Increase:		
Gross	$ 320	$ 240
Ceded	240	0
Net	$ 80	$ 240
Mod-co Adjustment	0	0
TOTAL BENEFITS	$ 80	$ 240
Expenses:		
Commissions	$ 3,622	$ 3,000
Acquisition	350	30
Maintenance	25	15
Premium Tax	101	75
TOTAL EXPENSES	$ 4,098	$ 3,120
GAIN FROM OPERATIONS	$ (28)	$ (310)

TABLE 4.5B

STATUTORY FINANCIAL STATEMENTS
COINSURANCE – YEAR 1

BALANCE SHEET

	ABC LIFE	XYZ RE
Assets		
Invested Assets	$ 552	$ 430
TOTAL ASSETS	$ 552	$ 430
Liabilities and Capital		
Policy Reserves:		
Gross	$ 320	$ 240
Ceded	240	0
Net	$ 80	$ 240
TOTAL LIABILITIES	$ 80	$ 240
Surplus	$ 472	$ 190
TOTAL CAPITAL	$ 472	$ 190
TOTAL LIABILITIES AND CAPITAL	$ 552	$ 430

reinsurance transaction. The difference in the results for coinsurance and YRT lies in the expense allowance and the higher premium tax reimbursement, offset in part by the higher premium.

At the end of the first calendar year, ABC Life has $472 of surplus while XYZ Re has $190 of surplus. The combined surplus of both companies in the coinsurance illustration is $45 less than the combined surplus without reinsurance because of the additional expenses incurred at XYZ Re. It is equal to the combined surplus in the YRT illustration.

The combined assets of the two companies are also $45 less than the combined assets of the two companies with no reinsurance and equal to the combined assets of the two companies in the YRT illustration. The total reserve liability of both companies is the same in all illustrations. It is important to note that liabilities did not disappear, and that assets and surplus were not created by the reinsurance transactions.

Second Year Results. In Tables 4.6A and 4.6B, the accounting results for the second calendar year of the coinsurance transaction are shown. The retained gross premium net of ceded premium remains $1,025 for ABC Life. Its reinsurance allowance, including premium tax reimbursement, is $525. The total reserve on the policy is now $3,424, resulting in a reserve increase of $3,104. The ceded reserve is $2,568, resulting in ceded reserve increase of $2,328, leaving ABC Life with a net reserve increase of $776. ABC Life's other expenses remain unchanged. ABC Life now has a net gain of $301 as opposed to a gain of $441 without reinsurance and $192 with YRT.

XYZ Re has received $3,000 of premium and has a $2,328 reserve increase, with a net gain of $175. This compares to the $55 net gain without reinsurance and a net gain of $284 with YRT.

ABC Life's net surplus has grown to $773 and XYZ Re's has increased to $365. The combined surplus for both companies is $65 less than the combined surplus for both companies with no reinsurance. The $65 is equal to the $45 expenses incurred in the first year of the reinsurance transaction by XYZ Re plus the $5 of lost investment income resulting from those additional expenses and the $15 maintenance expense incurred by XYZ Re in the second year. Combined assets for both companies have also been reduced by this amount from that shown in the no reinsurance illustration. Combined surplus and assets in the coinsurance illustration are equal to the combined total of assets and surplus in the YRT illustration. Combined policy reserves are equal in all three illustrations.

TABLE 4.6A

STATUTORY FINANCIAL STATEMENTS
COINSURANCE – YEAR 2

GAIN FROM OPERATIONS

	ABC LIFE	XYZ RE
Revenue:		
Premiums:		
Gross	$ 4,025	$ 3,000
Ceded	3,000	0
Net	$ 1,025	$ 3,000
Investment Income:		
Surplus	$ 47	$ 19
Reserves	8	24
Total	$ 55	$ 43
Reinsurance Allowances	525	0
Mod-co Adjustment	0	0
TOTAL REVENUE	$ 1,605	$ 3,043
Benefits:		
Claims	$ 0	$ 0
Surrenders	0	0
Reserve Increase:		
Gross	$ 3,104	$ 2,328
Ceded	2,328	0
Net	$ 776	$ 2,328
Mod-co Adjustment	0	0
TOTAL BENEFITS	$ 776	$ 2,328
Expenses:		
Commissions	$ 402	$ 450
Acquisition	0	0
Maintenance	25	15
Premium Tax	101	75
TOTAL EXPENSES	$ 528	$ 540
GAIN FROM OPERATIONS	$ 301	$ 175

TABLE 4.6B

STATUTORY FINANCIAL STATEMENTS
COINSURANCE – YEAR 1

BALANCE SHEET

	ABC LIFE	XYZ RE
Assets		
Invested Assets	$ 1,629	$ 2,933
TOTAL ASSETS	$ 1,629	$ 2,933
Liabilities and Capital		
Policy Reserves:		
Gross	$ 3,424	$ 2,568
Ceded	2,568	0
Net	$ 856	$ 2,568
TOTAL LIABILITIES	$ 856	$ 2,568
Surplus	$ 773	$ 365
TOTAL CAPITAL	$ 773	$ 365
TOTAL LIABILITIES AND CAPITAL	$ 1,629	$ 2,933

Modified Coinsurance

Modified coinsurance differs from coinsurance in that the reserve on the ceded portion of the policy is an obligation of, and held by, the ceding company, rather than the reinsurer. As in coinsurance, the reinsurer receives its portion of the gross premium on all policies ceded on a mod-co basis and reimburses the ceding company for its commissions and related expenses by means of an expense allowance. Mod-co, like coinsurance, transfers surplus strain on the reinsured portion of new issues to the reinsurer as well as a proportional share of the risk of loss from lapse, surrender, and death.

Assets equal to the reserve are provided to, and become the property of, the ceding company through the mod-co reserve adjustment, discussed subsequently in this section. These assets, and therefore the investment risk, are retained by the ceding company, unless special considerations are made in the formula for the interest element in the mod-co reserve adjustment. From an economic viewpoint, mod-co may be compared to coinsurance where the assets supporting the reserves represent a directed investment back to the ceding company. The reinsurer credits interest to the ceding company through the mod-co reserve adjustment.

Origins of Mod-co. The first use of mod-co is unclear. One explanation is that mod-co was originally created to satisfy reinsurance problems experienced by New York companies which were not allowed to take credit for reserves on policies reinsured to companies not licensed to do business in New York. Another explanation is that mod-co was developed for ceding companies that believed they could realize a better investment return on the assets underlying the reserves than the reinsurer would assume in its pricing.

Mod-co Premiums and Allowances. The premium and expense allowance considerations for mod-co are similar to those for coinsurance. The mod-co reinsurance premium is generally proportional to the gross annual premium of the policy ceded with the proper consideration for banding; smoker, nonsmoker and preferred risk classifications; indeterminate premiums; and the policy fee. Allowances follow the same pattern as in coinsurance; any differences in allowances between mod-co and coinsurance on a particular plan of insurance would arise from different tax implications or differences in the investment income assumption of the reinsurer on coinsurance and the interest rate used in the mod-co reserve adjustment.

Mod-co Premium and Allowance Calculations. The premium and allowance calculations for mod-co are also similar to those for coinsurance. The treatment of substandard extra premiums is also the same. Term riders attached to the base policy may be reinsured using modified coinsurance or coinsurance at the discretion of the ceding company and the reinsurer. Ancillary benefits such as waiver of premium benefits may be reinsured using either modified coinsurance or coinsurance, but are usually coinsured. Generally, accidental death benefits are reinsured using a flat YRT rate.

Mod-co Reserve Adjustment. Under a mod-co treaty, the reinsurer receives its proportionate share of the gross premium as in coinsurance, but the ceding company maintains the entire reserve on the reinsured policies. In order for the ceding company to do this, the reinsurer returns the increase in statutory reserves for the ceded portion to the ceding company. This is done through a mechanism know as the modified coinsurance reserve adjustment, or simply the mod-co adjustment. The mod-co reserve adjustment is equal to:

> The ending policy reserves, less
> the beginning policy reserves, less
> interest on the beginning policy reserves.

If the result is positive, the reinsurer pays that amount to the ceding company. If the result is negative, the ceding company pays the reinsurer. The calculation is normally done on a calendar year basis, but it may be done more frequently. The reserves referred to in the above formula are, of course, the proportionate share of the statutory reserves which are held for annual statement purposes.

The interest rate used to determine the interest credited on the beginning reserves held by the ceding company is known as the mod-co interest rate. It is a very important element in determining the overall cost of modified coinsurance. The method for determining the mod-co interest rate is defined in the treaty. The interest rate could be defined in terms of the ceding company's portfolio rate, its rate of return on new money, or an outside index. Sometimes a fixed rate is used. If the mod-co interest rate is equal to the ceding company's rate of return on the assets underlying the reserves, the result to the ceding company would be the same as if coinsurance had been used. The same would be true relative to the reinsurer if the mod-co interest rate equaled the reinsurer's rate of return.

Except in rare instances, the reinsurer does not participate in any capital gains and losses on the assets of the ceding company. Depending upon the actual performance, this can work to the advantage or disadvantage of either party. In general, the reinsurer is believed to have less investment risk under mod-co because it has no direct exposure to default or disintermediation risk. However, reinsurers usually prefer to manage their own assets and not to assume a credit risk by transferring the assets to another party.

If the ceding company believes it can secure significant capital gains, then it would prefer mod-co to coinsurance. Under coinsurance, the reinsurer retains all capital gains and losses on the assets underlying the reserves on the business ceded to it. Of course, under coinsurance, the reinsurer assumes the asset default risk while under mod-co the ceding company has this risk.

Uses of Mod-co. Modified coinsurance is used primarily in reinsuring products which develop cash values. This allows the ceding company to retain the assets for investment purposes while still obtaining the surplus relief aspects of coinsurance. This has a particular advantage for participating products or for interest sensitive products where the interest element in the dividend or cash value formula plays a major role.

Mod-co was popular when the ceding company desired to maintain tax basis reserves calculated in accordance with Section 818(c)(2)[11] of the Life Insurance Company Income Tax Act of 1959 for all policies on the block reinsured.

The 818(c)(2) reserves were an approximate revaluation of reserves maintained on a modified reserve basis to a net level basis.

In the early 1980's, many companies used modified coinsurance to reinsure vast amounts of individual life products in order to reduce federal income taxes. This tax reduction was accomplished by transforming investment income to underwriting income, moving investment income out of the ceding company through the mod-co reserve adjustment and returning it through the experience refund formula as underwriting gain.[12]

---

[11]See Chapter 14, Tax Effects of Reinsurance.

[12]*Ibid.*

Other Considerations. Mod-co eliminates some of the problems of coinsurance. Because the ceding company maintains the policy reserves, there is no question about reserve credits. The use of mod-co eliminates the problem of participation in policy loans by the reinsurer as the ceding company holds the assets. Mod-co also allows the ceding company more control over investments. This is important in developing dividend scales and in matching assets and liabilities. In addition, mod-co allows the ceding company to maintain a higher level of assets and, therefore, attain a higher comparative asset ranking than would coinsurance. While the dividend participation concerns still remain, the magnitude of the participation requirement is greatly diminished.

The main drawback to the use of mod-co is that it is more complicated to administer than coinsurance because of the reserve adjustment calculation.

Mod-co Illustrations. For the purpose of illustrating the effect of modified coinsurance on ABC Life and XYZ Re, it is assumed that XYZ Re has granted the same allowances as were used in the coinsurance example. It is further assumed that the mod-co interest rate is equal to the portfolio rate of 10% earned by both companies. Given these two conditions, the statutory net income and surplus for both companies are unchanged from those coinsurance example.

First year Results. Tables 4.7A and 4.7B show the Statutory Gains from Operations and Balance Sheets for the first year of the modified coinsurance transaction.

ABC Life shows the same ceded premium and reinsurance allowances as in the coinsurance illustration from Table 4.5A. Now, however, ABC Life has an additional revenue item called mod-co adjustment. The first year mod-co adjustment is calculated as follows.

ABC LIFE
MOD-CO RESERVE ADJUSTMENT - YEAR 1

Ending Policy Reserves:		$240
Less: Beginning Policy Reserves	$-0-	
Interest on Beginning Policy Reserves	-0-	(-0-)
Mod-co Adjustment:		$240

TABLE 4.7A

STATUTORY FINANCIAL STATEMENTS
MODIFIED COINSURANCE – YEAR 1

GAIN FROM OPERATIONS

	ABC LIFE	XYZ RE
Revenue:		
Premiums:		
Gross	$ 4,025	$ 3,000
Ceded	3,000	0
Net	$ 1,025	$ 3,000
Investment Income:		
Surplus	$ 50	$ 50
Reserves	0	0
Total	$ 50	$ 50
Reinsurance Allowances	$ 3,075	$ 0
Mod-co Adjustment	240	0
TOTAL REVENUE	$ 4,390	$ 3,050
Benefits:		
Claims	$ 0	$ 0
Surrenders	0	0
Reserve Increase:		
Gross	$ 320	$ 0
Ceded	0	0
Net	$ 320	$ 0
Mod-co Adjustment	0	240
TOTAL BENEFITS	$ 320	$ 240
Expenses:		
Commissions	$ 3,622	$ 3,000
Acquisition	350	30
Maintenance	25	15
Premium Tax	101	75
TOTAL EXPENSES	$ 4,098	$ 3,120
GAIN FROM OPERATIONS	$ (28)	$ (310)

TABLE 4.7B

STATUTORY FINANCIAL STATEMENTS
MODIFIED COINSURANCE – YEAR 1

BALANCE SHEET

	ABC LIFE	XYZ RE
Assets		
Invested Assets	$ 792	$ 190
TOTAL ASSETS	$ 792	$ 190
Liabilities and Capital		
Policy Reserves:		
Gross	$ 320	$ 0
Ceded	0	0
Net	$ 320	$ 0
TOTAL LIABILITIES	320	0
Surplus	$ 472	$ 190
TOTAL CAPITAL	$ 472	$ 190
TOTAL LIABILITIES AND CAPITAL	$ 792	$ 190

ABC Life now has the entire reserve increase reflected in its gain from operations, and an additional income item representing the mod-co adjustment. Its expenses remain unchanged. ABC Life has a net loss of $28, identical to that in the coinsurance illustration.

XYZ Re receives its $3,000 of premium, just as it did in the coinsurance example. However, in this case, it has no reserve increase as it is not holding any reserve on this policy. It has an additional benefit item for the mod-co adjustment of $240. Its expenses remain unchanged, and it has a net loss in the first year of $310, again identical to its financial position under the coinsurance transaction.

The Statutory Balance Sheet shows that the surplus of ABC Life has been reduced to $472 and that of XYZ Re has been reduced to $190. These values are identical to those for the coinsurance illustration. ABC Life shows all $320 of the policy reserves on its statutory balance sheet and holds assets of $792. XYZ Re's assets equal its surplus because it has no liabilities; it has paid the mod-co reserve increase in cash. Combined assets for both companies are the same as in the coinsurance illustration. The assets have been redistributed to reflect the fact that ABC Life is maintaining the entire reserve.

Second Year Results. Tables 4.8A and 4.8B show the Statutory Gains from Operations and Balance Sheets resulting from modified coinsurance in the second year. The second year mod-co adjustment is developed as follows:

ABC LIFE
MOD-CO RESERVE ADJUSTMENT - YEAR 2

Ending Policy Reserves:		$2,568
Less: Beginning Policy Reserves	$240	
Interest on Beginning Policy Reserves	24	(264)
Mod-co Adjustment:		$2,304

This mod-co adjustment appears as a revenue item for ABC Life and as a benefit item for XYZ Re.

Investment income has been redistributed between the two companies. Since the mod-co interest rate is equal to the investment income rate, ABC Life's investment income has increased by

TABLE 4.8A

STATUTORY FINANCIAL STATEMENTS
MODIFIED COINSURANCE – YEAR 2

GAIN FROM OPERATIONS

	ABC LIFE	XYZ RE
Revenue:		
Premiums:		
Gross	$ 4,025	$ 3,000
Ceded	3,000	0
Net	$ 1,025	$ 3,000
Investment Income:		
Surplus	$ 47	$ 19
Reserves	32	0
Total	$ 79	$ 19
Reinsurance Allowances	$ 525	$ 0
Mod-co Adjustment	2,304	0
TOTAL REVENUE	$ 3,933	$ 3,019
Benefits:		
Claims	$ 0	$ 0
Surrenders	0	0
Reserve Increase:		
Gross	$ 3,104	$ 0
Ceded	0	0
Net	$ 3,104	$ 0
Mod-co Adjustment	0	2,304
TOTAL BENEFITS	$ 3,104	$ 2,304
Expenses:		
Commissions	$ 402	$ 450
Acquisition	0	0
Maintenance	25	15
Premium Tax	101	75
TOTAL EXPENSES	$ 528	$ 540
GAIN FROM OPERATIONS	$ 301	$ 175

TABLE 43B

STATUTORY FINANCIAL STATEMENTS
MODIFIED COINSURANCE – YEAR 1

BALANCE SHEET

	ABC LIFE	XYZ RE
Assets		
Invested Assets	$ 4,197	$ 365
TOTAL ASSETS	$ 4,197	$ 365
Liabilities and Capital		
Policy Reserves:		
Gross	$ 3,424	$ 0
Ceded	0	0
Net	$ 3,424	$ 0
TOTAL LIABILITIES	$ 3,424	$ 0
Surplus	$ 773	$ 365
TOTAL CAPITAL	$ 773	$ 365
TOTAL LIABILITIES AND CAPITAL	$ 4,197	$ 365

an amount equal to the mod-co interest while XYZ Re's investment income has decreased by the same amount.

As ABC Life is holding the entire reserve on this policy, it reflects the entire reserve increase of $3,104 in determining its gain from operations. The benefits and expenses remain unchanged, so ABC Life has a net income of $301 and XYZ Re has a net income of $175. The net incomes are again identical to the net incomes in the coinsurance illustration for both companies.

Had the treaty called for a different mod-co interest rate, the results would have been different and would no longer equal those for the coinsurance illustration. For example, if that mod-co interest rate had been 7.5%, the mod-co adjustment would have been $2,310; ABC's gain would have been $307 and that of XYZ Re $169. Note that the total of the earnings did not change, only the allocation.

The Statutory Balance Sheet shows the statutory surplus has increased by the amount of the net income for both companies. The statutory reserves on the entire block are carried on ABC Life's balance sheet. The combined assets for both companies are equal to the combined assets for both companies in the coinsurance illustration. The assets of ABC Life are higher than in the case of coinsurance because it is holding the entire reserve.

Financial
5 | Reinsurance

Reinsurance is a versatile tool for financial planning. In this chapter, the terminology, uses, and mechanics of financial reinsurance are discussed. To illustrate the financial effect of each plan of reinsurance on the ceding company and the reinsurer, a simple annuity model is developed for comparative purposes. The basic plans of financial reinsurance are defined and illustrated. A brief discussion of regulation, taxation, and security considerations is also included.

USES OF FINANCIAL REINSURANCE

Financial reinsurance is useful for several purposes. The most common uses are surplus relief, strategic business planning, and tax planning.

Surplus Relief

The most common use of financial reinsurance is to provide the ceding company with assets or reserve credits in order to improve its current statutory earnings and surplus position. This process is

95

commonly referred to as surplus relief. Surplus relief creates an increase in statutory earnings for the ceding company in the year in which the relief is given and a corresponding reduction in the statutory earnings of the reinsurer. If the business reinsured produces adequate future gains, the reinsurer recovers all of its investment plus a profit. The ceding company's earnings in future years are decreased by the same amount that the reinsurer's earnings are increased.

In surplus relief, the reinsurer commits cash or other assets to, or assumes liabilities of, the ceding company. Surplus relief differs from a loan in that the repayment of the relief is tied to the future cash flow or statutory earnings on the block reinsured and is not guaranteed as to timing or ultimate recovery.

Because the reinsurer is repaid from the future earnings, it is important to the reinsurer that the value of future statutory earnings of the reinsured block exceed the amount of surplus relief granted by an adequate margin. The risk or profit charge assessed by the reinsurer on a surplus relief agreement tends to be significantly less than what would be expected if the reinsurer were to underwrite fully and accept the risk on the same block of business in the traditional market. Since it expects less profit, the reinsurer usually looks for additional security in this type of transfer.

The value of future earnings is in part attributed to a redundancy in statutory reserves. The amount of redundancy is estimated by an analysis such as a gross premium valuation or an actuarial appraisal. In most surplus relief situations, the present value of the cash flows and the reserves released on the block reinsured significantly exceeds the amount of surplus relief granted. The excess profits are returned to the ceding company by paying experience rating refunds or allowing termination of the treaty once the surplus relief and charges have been recovered.

Tax Planning

Reinsurance can be used in tax planning[1], although not to the extent it once was. In the most common tax planning application, a company cedes reinsurance, creating a taxable gain, which is used to offset current or carryforward tax losses. This is especially useful if a company has expiring tax loss carryforwards.

---

[1]See Chapter 14, Tax Effects of Reinsurance.

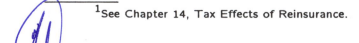

Any resulting statutory gain to the ceding company represents a corresponding loss to the reinsurer. Consequently, this type of reinsurance often resembles surplus relief, although the transfers are more commonly permanent. As in the case of surplus relief, the reinsurer recovers its initial statutory loss through the future statutory earnings on the reinsured block. A company might also assume reinsurance to create a loss in order to offset other taxable gains. The ceding company usually has the right to terminate the reinsurance rather than pay the ongoing cost of the reinsurance once the initial gain has been repaid.

A company may cede health insurance or assume life insurance in order to qualify as a life insurance company for tax purposes. It may also cede life insurance or assume health insurance in order to qualify as a non-life insurance company if it considers this to be advantageous.

Strategic Business Planning

A company may wish to acquire reinsurance for a number of business related purposes. Reinsurance may be used to increase future profits, utilize excess administrative capacity, or assist the company in entering a new market. Conversely, a company may cede or sell reinsurance to exit a certain market. Reinsurance may also be used as part of the financing in a leveraged buy-out.

In most instances, reinsurance for business planning purposes is of a permanent nature and specific provision for recapture is not usually included in the treaty. Assumption reinsurance is commonly used for this purpose.

TERMINOLOGY

The remainder of this chapter will focus on financial reinsurance which provides the ceding company with a gain in the first year of the transaction to fill a temporary or permanent financial need. Many of the commonly used reinsurance terms take on special meanings in financial reinsurance transactions. These terms are discussed below.

Initial Reinsurance Premium or Consideration

When reinsuring a block of inforce business on some form of coinsurance, the initial premium or consideration is typically the policy reserve, but it may be higher or lower. In subsequent accounting periods the reinsurance premium on any form of coinsurance is usually the gross premium paid on the policies reinsured. Allowances are used to adjust the effective amount of renewal premium.

Allowances

Allowances refer to the amounts paid by or allowed by the reinsurer to the ceding company. In financial reinsurance, the initial allowance provides the gain in the first year of the transaction. It may be stated as a percentage of the initial premium, as an amount per unit of coverage, or as a flat amount per transaction. In renewal years, allowances may be paid to provide for the ceding company's commission and maintenance expenses and to adjust the expected results to a mutually agreed upon level.

For example, allowances may be set at a level above the ceding company's commission and expense level to allow the ceding company a continuing profit from the business. Alternatively, lower allowances may be used to give the reinsurer some additional profit margin. In general, higher initial allowances should lead to lower renewal allowances and vice versa. Of course, the higher the allowances, the longer the period before the reinsurer recoups its initial strain.

Risk Charge

The term *risk charge*[2] refers to the portion of the reinsurance premium which the reinsurer retains for providing the reinsurance. The risk charge is normally stated in terms of the amount of the outstanding surplus or gain. The amount of the risk charge depends on the nature of the risks assumed, the size of the transaction, the reinsurer's profit objectives, the market conditions at the time, the ceding company's stability, tax considerations, company relationships, and the reinsurer's expenses for analysis, administration or intermediaries. Historic risk charges have varied between 1% and 5% of the outstanding surplus relief each year. The risk charge is negotiable on each treaty.

---

[2]The risk charge is also known by other names, such as risk and profit charge or expense and risk charge.

Experience Refund

Most financial reinsurance transactions provide for an experience refund. An experience refund is a mechanism used to identify and return some portion of the statutory earnings on the reinsured business to the ceding company. In the financial reinsurance area, experience refunds typically are not paid to the ceding company until the initial allowance has been recovered by the reinsurer from the statutory earnings on the reinsured business.

The payment of negative experience refunds, that is, payments by the ceding company to the reinsurer for poor experience, is uncommon. Treaty provisions creating such refunds will usually result in a disqualification of statutory reserve credits for the reinsurance transaction.[3] However, the use of loss deficit carry forwards or the requirement of the repayment of accumulated losses prior to recapture is not prohibited as long as the reinsurer is not allowed to terminate the agreement unilaterally forcing the ceding company into a loss position. Options in the agreement which permit the ceding company unilateral authority to terminate the treaty and pay the reinsurer for any accumulated losses are allowed.

Outstanding Surplus Account

All or a defined portion of any statutory gains on the business reinsured, after provision for the risk charge, experience refund, and interest accumulated on the outstanding initial allowance, are used to repay the initial allowance. In order to track this repayment, the reinsurer will establish an outstanding surplus account or outstanding initial allowance account for each treaty. Most financial reinsurance treaties preclude termination or recapture while the reinsurer's accumulated results are in a deficit position. Conversely, most such arrangements may be terminated by the ceding company after the accumulated surplus relief has been repaid.

There is no guarantee that gains will develop in renewal years. To the extent gains are achieved, the risk charge is paid and the surplus account is reduced. To the extent losses result, such losses are added to the accumulated surplus account. Losses are generally accumulated with interest, especially if the reinsurer paid the initial allowance in cash.

---

[3]See Chapter 10, Reinsurance Regulations.

The periodic risk charge may be paid as due or may be paid only to the extent that there are profits from the reinsurance, with any unpaid amounts carried forward. The first practice is utilized less frequently today because of regulatory concerns.

COMPARATIVE MODEL

In order to better understand how the various plans of financial reinsurance will affect the ceding company and the reinsurer, a simple illustration has been constructed using a single premium deferred annuity. The values used for premiums, reserves, investment income, and commissions have been arbitrarily chosen to simplify the illustrations and are not meant to be representative of an actual product. The risk charge and experience refund factors have also been arbitrarily chosen and should not be construed to represent those found in actual practice. A number of minor items which might affect the annual statement have been ignored for the sake of simplicity.

The single premium deferred annuity product was chosen to avoid renewal premium flows and to highlight the financial result from the reinsurance transaction. In practice, such annuities are often used for financial reinsurance. Since the persistency on these products is usually very high and the reserves are large, single premium deferred annuities are capable of supporting large initial allowances. The administration is relatively simple since there are no renewal premiums, and the mortality risk is small. Any other type of insurance product could have been illustrated.

Assumptions

It is assumed that ABC Life sells $1,000 of single premium deferred annuities. It pays its agents $100 of commissions. Its reserves on December 31 are $1,000. ABC Life is assumed to have no other assets or surplus in order to emphasize the marginal affect of the transaction. It is assumed that XYZ Re has $100 of free surplus available for the reinsurance transaction. As ABC Life is administering the reinsurance, XYZ Re's expenses are minimal and will not be considered. Both ABC Life and XYZ Re earn 10% on invested assets held at the beginning of each year but not on the cash flows. Taxes and maintenance expenses are ignored in order to highlight the reinsurance transaction.

To show the effect of claims, benefits of $5 are assumed to be incurred in the second calendar year. It is assumed that the second year reserve increase on the remaining contracts is $70.

Illustrations before Reinsurance

Tables 5.1A and 5.1B show the statutory Gains from Operations and Balance Sheets for ABC Life and XYZ Re for the year the annuities were issued before any reinsurance transaction. This shows ABC Life with $1,000 of premiums, $1,000 of reserves, and $100 of commissions and expenses for a gain of $(100). ABC Life, therefore, has $900 of invested assets and $1,000 of reserve liabilities, leaving it with a surplus for this particular transaction of $(100). XYZ Re's statutory balance sheet shows $100 of surplus.

Tables 5.2A and 5.2B show the results for the second calendar year had ABC Life had sufficient surplus from other sources to cover the $100 of strain and had not, therefore, entered into any sort of reinsurance arrangement. The negative $10 investment income on surplus demonstrates that ABC Life has to support the reserves on the plan.

Table 5.2A shows that ABC Life now has net income in the second year of $15 while XYZ Re has net income of $10 from the investment income on its surplus. Table 5.2B shows ABC Life's invested assets have grown to $985, its reserves to $1,070, and its surplus is now $(85). XYZ Re's assets and surplus have grown to $110 as the result of investment income.

PLANS OF FINANCIAL REINSURANCE

In addition to the three basic reinsurance plans, financial reinsurance utilizes certain hybrid plans. This section defines and illustrates the financial reinsurance use of the three basic plans as well as the following three hybrid plans: funds withheld coinsurance, funds withheld mod-co, and partially modified coinsurance.

Yearly Renewable Term Insurance

Under the YRT plan of reinsurance the reinsurer holds reserves appropriate for a yearly renewable term product. In the case of a whole life product, the amount of the credit can be quite small in relationship to the basic product reserves, especially in renewal years. Because YRT reserves are relatively small, YRT does not

TABLE 5.1A

STATUTORY FINANCIAL STATEMENTS
BEFORE REINSURANCE – YEAR 1

GAIN FROM OPERATIONS

	ABC LIFE	XYZ RE
Revenue:		
Premiums:		
Gross	$ 1,000	$ 0
Ceded	0	0
Net	$ 1,000	$ 0
Investment Income:		
Surplus	$ 0	$ 0
Reserves	0	0
Total	$ 0	$ 0
Reinsurance Allowances	$ 0	$ 0
Mod-co Adjustment	0	0
TOTAL REVENUE	$ 1,000	$ 0
Benefits:		
Claims and Surrenders		
Gross	$ 0	$ 0
Ceded	0	0
Net	$ 0	$ 0
Reserve Increase:		
Gross	$ 1,000	$ 0
Ceded	0	0
Net	$ 1,000	$ 0
Experience Refund	0	0
Mod-co Adjustment	0	0
TOTAL BENEFITS	$ 1,000	$ 0
Expenses:		
Expenses and Commissions	$ 100	$ 0
TOTAL EXPENSES	$ 100	$ 0
GAIN FROM OPERATIONS	$ (100)	$ 0

TABLE 5.1B

STATUTORY FINANCIAL STATEMENTS
BEFORE REINSURANCE – YEAR 1

BALANCE SHEET

	ABC LIFE	XYZ RE
Assets		
Invested Assets	$ 900	$ 100
Accounts Receivable	0	0
TOTAL ASSETS	$ 900	$ 100
Liabilities and Capital		
Policy Reserves:		
Gross	$ 1,000	$ 0
Ceded	0	0
Net	$ 1,000	$ 0
Accounts Payable	0	0
TOTAL LIABILITIES	$ 1,000	$ 0
Surplus	$ (100)	$ 100
TOTAL CAPITAL	$ (100)	$ 100
TOTAL LIABILITIES AND CAPITAL	$ 900	$ 100

TABLE 5.2A

STATUTORY FINANCIAL STATEMENTS
BEFORE REINSURANCE – YEAR 2

GAIN FROM OPERATIONS

	ABC LIFE	XYZ RE
Revenue:		
Premiums:		
Gross	$ 0	$ 0
Ceded	0	0
Net	$ 0	$ 0
Investment Income:		
Surplus	$ (10)	$ 10
Reserves	100	0
Total	$ 90	$ 10
Reinsurance Allowances	$ 0	$ 0
Mod-co Adjustment	0	0
TOTAL REVENUE	$ 90	$ 10
Benefits:		
Claims and Surrenders		
Gross	$ 5	$ 0
Ceded	0	0
Net	$ 5	$ 0
Reserve Increase:		
Gross	$ 70	$ 0
Ceded	0	0
Net	$ 70	$ 0
Experience Refund	0	0
Mod-co Adjustment	0	0
TOTAL BENEFITS	$ 75	$ 0
Expenses:		
Expenses and Commissions	$ 0	$ 0
TOTAL EXPENSES	$ 0	$ 0
GAIN FROM OPERATIONS	$ 15	$ 10

TABLE 5.2B

STATUTORY FINANCIAL STATEMENTS
BEFORE REINSURANCE – YEAR 2

BALANCE SHEET

	ABC LIFE	XYZ RE
Assets		
Invested Assets	$ 985	$ 110
Accounts Receivable	0	0
TOTAL ASSETS	$ 985	$ 110
Liabilities and Capital		
Policy Reserves:		
Gross	$ 1,070	$ 0
Ceded	0	0
Net	$ 1,070	$ 0
Accounts Payable	0	0
TOTAL LIABILITIES	$ 1,070	$ 0
Surplus	$ (85)	$ 110
TOTAL CAPITAL	$ (85)	$ 110
TOTAL LIABILITIES AND CAPITAL	$ 985	$ 110

provide any significant relief to the ceding company unless the product being reinsured is also of the YRT form. The gain is provided by a first year allowance or a negative first year premium.

The reinsurer assesses the ceding company a risk charge to cover the risks assumed, the use of its surplus, its expenses incurred, and a provision for profit. An experience refund may be used to return any excess profits to the ceding company. The reinsurer tracks the repayment of the initial allowance through a special account.

Uses of YRT. The most common use of the YRT plan for financial reinsurance would be with an interest sensitive life product where the reinsurer did not wish to become involved in the accumulation element of the basic contract. It could also be used with any form of whole life insurance when the reinsurer did not wish to become involved in the investment risks.

If a term product is being reinsured, YRT reinsurance could be used. Under these circumstances, the reinsurer might create a special YRT rate scale expressing the rates as percentages of the underlying term policy premium rates. In this instance, there would be little difference between the use of coinsurance or YRT. Yearly Renewable Term reinsurance is also used for health policies but it is not suitable for annuities.

In surplus relief situations, YRT is most effective if it is based on a premium scale which features no first year premium, or if it provides a bonus per unit of production with higher renewal rates. The higher renewal rates are needed to recoup the initial strain. A chargeback may be applied for lapses within a certain period.

YRT reinsurance could be used in circumstances where the ceding company wanted to minimize asset transfer. If an inforce block of business is involved, the initial premium on a coinsurance basis would be the outstanding policy reserves. For many companies, this may be a sizable sum of money. The initial YRT premium would normally be considerably less than the reserves on a mature block of whole life policies.

Advantages. The use of YRT reinsurance will limit the reinsurer's investment and lapse risk since there is no reserve or cash value buildup. This could be particularly useful if the initial policy reserves are large and the reinsurer does not have the facilities to manage adequately the assets it would receive in a coinsurance transaction.

Yearly renewable term reinsurance may have a lower ongoing cost than any form of coinsurance if the risks are limited to mortality and morbidity.

Disadvantages. The low cost of YRT reinsurance limits the amount of possible future profits, thereby limiting the amount of the initial allowance or bonus which the reinsurer can provide. Because of the limitations in the initial allowance, the use of YRT reinsurance is limited in financial reinsurance applications.

Another drawback of using YRT in financial reinsurance is that it is relatively difficult to administer compared to other forms of reinsurance. Financial reinsurance is most commonly administered on a simplified basis. Yearly renewable term does not lend itself to this type of administration. The reinsurance premium is calculated as a product of the YRT rate times the net amount of risk, and this calculation must be made for each policy. As will be discussed later, the administration of any form of coinsurance, if reinsured on a quota share basis, is relatively simple for a ceding company to perform.

Because of the drawbacks of YRT reinsurance, it rarely is used in financial reinsurance applications and will not be illustrated here. If it is used, it is normally used in conjunction with a form of coinsurance.

Coinsurance

Under a typical coinsurance arrangement involving inforce insurance, the initial reinsurance premium is equal to the reserve and the reinsurer pays the ceding company an allowance which provides the initial gain. In subsequent years, the allowance generally covers the ceding company's maintenance and commission expenses.

An alternative treatment is to set the initial premium equal to the initial reserves less the desired gain of the ceding company. Renewal premiums could also be defined without reference to the policy gross premium and specific expense allowances. This particular treatment will not be used in this book, but the net economic effect is the same if the reduction in premium is equal to the allowance to be granted.

The reinsurance premiums net of allowances in subsequent years are used by the reinsurer to fund reserve increases, to pay claims, to cover its administration costs, and to provide a margin for adverse deviations.   The reinsurer also includes a charge to reimburse it for the investment made in the first year of the contract.

In the traditional coinsurance market, pricing is done using the same techniques that the ceding company actuary used in developing the original product.   Today's traditional coinsurance market is highly competitive.   As a consequence, coinsurance allowances frequently have little provision for deviation in experience results.   The immediate benefits of larger allowances are considered preferable to the alternative of experience refunds by most ceding companies.

In the financial reinsurance market, pricing is not so precise.   It is generally anticipated that future profits will be more than sufficient to repay the surplus relief together with the risk charges.   Accordingly, most financial coinsurance treaties provide an experience rating feature whereby the reinsurer returns some or all of these excess profits to the ceding company.   At some predetermined interval, an accounting is made of all reinsurance premiums received, claims and allowances paid, risk charges, interest earned, and the reserve increase for the period.   The reinsurer may refund to the ceding company a portion of the profits in excess of any loss carry forwards or amounts used to repay the initial investment as experience unfolds, or it may use the entire earnings to repay its investment.

During the life of an arrangement, the reinsurer will generally keep a record of the repayment of the initial allowance in an outstanding surplus account.   Once the balance of this account reaches zero, the reinsurance is generally terminated as there is little need for ongoing reinsurance coverage. The treaty may sometimes provide that reinsurance may be terminated before the relief is entirely repaid if the ceding company is able to transfer funds equal to the amount of outstanding relief to the reinsurer. Upon termination of the reinsurance, the assets equal to the reserves held by the reinsurer are returned to the ceding company.

Coinsurance can be used with any insurance product: life, health, or annuity.   It works as well on term insurance as it does on interest sensitive life and annuity products.

Advantages.   When an inforce block of business is being reinsured, pure coinsurance is probably the simplest to administer if a quota share method is used.   Once previously reinsured amounts have been identified and removed, the quota share percentage can be applied to all premiums, claims, surrenders, and reserves. Under this method, the ceding company can easily provide the reinsurer with the information necessary for preparation of its statutory financial statements. From a regulatory viewpoint, pure coinsurance is probably the cleanest form of reinsurance because there are fewer questions regarding risk transfer in coinsurance.

Disadvantages. The chief disadvantage of coinsurance is the asset transfer. The ceding company must transfer control of the assets equal to the reserves to the reinsurer. In the case of the reinsurance of an inforce block, this may represent a significant portion of the assets of the ceding company. In the case of an interest sensitive or participating product, the ceding company may have to give the reinsurer control of or veto power over the dividend or interest rate determination. This could be a distinct disadvantage in competitive situations.

Another disadvantage is that it requires the reinsurer to manage the assets, subjecting it to additional investment risk which some reinsurers might find undesirable. Also, if the reinsurance is terminated, the reinsurer must transfer assets in an amount equal to the reserves to the ceding company. There is always a risk that capital gains or losses in an asset transfer may result in unfavorable statutory or tax consequences.

If the reinsurer is not licensed or admitted in the ceding company's state of domicile, the ceding company may be unable to take credit in its statutory annual statement for the reserves being held by the reinsurer unless the reinsurer provides some specific form of security acceptable to the state. This could be expensive and burdensome. Failure to secure the right to a reserve offset would defeat the surplus relief. In fact, if the desired reserve credit were greater than the intended surplus relief, the surplus position would be worsened.

Coinsurance also subjects the ceding company to an additional insolvency risk. Should the reinsurer become insolvent, the ceding company may be unable to obtain full reimbursement for benefits reinsured and, on termination, may not receive the full amount of policy reserves.

Coinsurance Illustrations. If ABC Life did not have at least $100 of available surplus in the first year, it would need reinsurance. Assume that ABC Life enters into a coinsurance treaty with XYZ Re on December 31, reinsuring 100% of this block of business, and

XYZ Re grants ABC Life an allowance equal to 10% of the premium.

First Year Results.   Tables 5.3A and 5.3B show the first year results of the coinsurance transaction.

ABC Life has ceded $1,000 of premium to XYZ Re, leaving it with a net premium of $0. The $100 of reinsurance allowances from XYZ Re gives ABC Life a total revenue of $100. This $100 is used to offset the $100 of commissions and expenses incurred in issuing the policies. This leaves ABC Life with a gain of $0. XYZ Re now has $1,000 of accepted premium and a $1,000 of reserve increase. Its commissions are $100, leaving it with a gain of $(100).

The statutory Balance Sheet for ABC Life shows that it has neither assets nor net retained reserves after the transactions. XYZ Re has $1,000 of invested assets, $1,000 of reserves, and no surplus. When the coinsurance illustrations are compared to those for no reinsurance in Tables 5.1A and 5.1B, it can be seen that the net income, invested assets, policy reserves, and surplus have merely been redistributed between the two companies. The transaction does not create any new invested assets, surplus, or liabilities.

XYZ Re prepares a reinsurance report. The report summarizes the transaction and indicates the net amount of funds to be transferred. The reinsurance report below shows that ABC Life owes XYZ Re $900, which is the premium net of allowances. This amount is paid in cash.

ABC LIFE
REINSURANCE REPORT – YEAR 1

Ceded Premium:			$1,000
Less:	Allowances	$100	
	Benefits	–0–	
	Mod-co Adjustment	–0–	
	Experience Refund	–0–	(100)
Total Due XYZ Re:			$ 900

TABLE 5.3A

STATUTORY FINANCIAL STATEMENTS
COINSURANCE – YEAR 1

GAIN FROM OPERATIONS

	ABC LIFE	XYZ RE
Revenue:		
Premiums:		
Gross	$ 1,000	$ 1,000
Ceded	1,000	0
Net	$ 0	$ 1,000
Investment Income:		
Surplus	$ 0	$ 0
Reserves	0	0
Total	$ 0	$ 0
Reinsurance Allowances	$ 100	$ 0
Mod-co Adjustment	0	0
TOTAL REVENUE	$ 100	$ 1,000
Benefits:		
Claims and Surrenders		
Gross	$ 0	$ 0
Ceded	0	0
Net	$ 0	$ 0
Reserve Increase:		
Gross	$ 1,000	$ 1,000
Ceded	1,000	0
Net	$ 0	$ 1,000
Experience Refund	0	0
Mod-co Adjustment	0	0
TOTAL BENEFITS	$ 0	$ 1,000
Expenses:		
Expenses and Commissions	$ 100	$ 100
TOTAL EXPENSES	$ 100	$ 100
GAIN FROM OPERATIONS	$ 0	$ (100)

TABLE 5.3B

STATUTORY FINANCIAL STATEMENTS
COINSURANCE – YEAR 1

BALANCE SHEET

	ABC LIFE	XYZ RE
Assets		
Invested Assets	$ 0	$ 1,000
Accounts Receivable	0	0
TOTAL ASSETS	$ 0	$ 1,000
Liabilities and Capital		
Policy Reserves:		
Gross	$ 1,000	$ 1,000
Ceded	1,000	0
Net	$ 0	$ 1,000
Accounts Payable	0	0
TOTAL LIABILITIES	$ 0	$ 1,000
Surplus	$ 0	$ 0
TOTAL CAPITAL	$ 0	$ 0
TOTAL LIABILITIES AND CAPITAL	$ 0	$ 1,000

For internal purposes, XYZ Re sets up an outstanding surplus account to track the funds advanced to ABC Life. The beginning balance in the account is $100.

ABC LIFE
OUTSTANDING SURPLUS ACCOUNT
END OF YEAR 1

Beginning Balance:		$ –0–
Plus:	Statutory Gain	(100)
Less:	Investment Income on Surplus $ –0–	
	Risk Charge –0–	(–0–)
Ending Balance:		$ (100)

Second Year Results. In the second year of the reinsurance transaction, shown in Tables 5.4A and 5.4B, XYZ Re earns $100 of investment income on its $1,000 of assets. For the purpose of this illustration, XYZ Re agreed to allow ABC Life to share in a portion of the profits, so it pays ABC Life an experience refund of $1. The experience refund has been included in the illustration to demonstrate its effect. Normally, an experience refund would not be paid until the outstanding surplus account has been repaid.

XYZ Re also reimburses ABC Life for 100% of the $5 of benefits paid. XYZ Re is responsible for the entire reserve increase of $70. At the end of the second year, XYZ Re now has a gain of $24 while ABC Life has a gain of $1 from the experience refund.

The statutory Balance Sheet for ABC Life shows that is has assets of $1 and surplus of $1. XYZ Re has assets of $1,094, reserves of $1,070, and surplus of $24. When the statutory Gains from Operations and Balance Sheets for the second year of the coinsurance transactions are compared to the corresponding values in the no reinsurance example, it can be seen that, again, the total income, assets, liabilities, and surplus have merely been redistributed between the companies; nothing has been created.

The reinsurance report for the second year of the coinsurance transaction shown below indicates that XYZ Re has paid ABC Life a total of $6, $5 for benefit reimbursements and $1 of experience refund.

TABLE 5.4A

STATUTORY FINANCIAL STATEMENTS
COINSURANCE – YEAR 2

GAIN FROM OPERATIONS

	ABC LIFE	XYZ RE
Revenue:		
Premiums:		
Gross	$ 0	$ 0
Ceded	0	0
Net	$ 0	$ 0
Investment Income:		
Surplus	$ 0	$ 0
Reserves	0	100
Total	$ 0	$ 100
Reinsurance Allowances	$ 0	$ 0
Mod-co Adjustment	0	0
Misc. (Experience Refund)	1	0
TOTAL REVENUE	$ 1	$ 100
Benefits:		
Claims and Surrenders		
Gross	$ 5	$ 5
Ceded	5	0
Net	$ 0	$ 5
Reserve Increase:		
Gross	$ 70	$ 70
Ceded	70	0
Net	$ 0	$ 70
Experience Refund	0	1
Mod-co Adjustment	0	0
TOTAL BENEFITS	$ 0	$ 76
Expenses:		
Expenses and Commissions	$ 0	$ 0
TOTAL EXPENSES	$ 0	$ 0
GAIN FROM OPERATIONS	$ 1	$ 24

TABLE 54B

STATUTORY FINANCIAL STATEMENTS
COINSURANCE – YEAR 2

BALANCE SHEET

	ABC LIFE	XYZ RE
Assets		
Invested Assets	$ 1	$ 1,094
Accounts Receivable	0	0
TOTAL ASSETS	$ 1	$ 1,094
Liabilities and Capital		
Policy Reserves:		
Gross	$ 1,070	$ 1,070
Ceded	1,070	0
Net	$ 0	$ 1,070
Accounts Payable	0	0
TOTAL LIABILITIES	$ 0	$ 1,070
Surplus	1	24
TOTAL CAPITAL	$ 1	$ 24
TOTAL LIABILITIES AND CAPITAL	$ 1	$ 1,094

ABC LIFE
REINSURANCE REPORT – YEAR 2

Ceded Premium:				$ –0–
Less:	Allowances	$ –0–		
	Benefits	5		
	Mod-co Adjustment	–0–		
	Experience Refund	1		(6)
Total Due XYZ Re:				$ (6)

At the close of the year, XYZ Re updates its outstanding surplus account for ABC Life. XYZ Re's risk charge is assumed to be 3% of the outstanding surplus account at the beginning of the year. The beginning balance is reduced by the statutory gain from operations less the investment income it would have earned on the surplus had no transaction taken place and less a risk charge of $3. The ending balance is now $89.

ABC LIFE
OUTSTANDING SURPLUS ACCOUNT
END OF YEAR 2

Beginning Balance:			$ (100)
Plus:	Statutory Gain		24
Less:	Investment Income on Surplus	$ 10	
	Risk Charge	3	(13)
Ending Balance:			$ (89)

XYZ Re's entire gains did not go to reduce the outstanding surplus account. Of the $24 gain, $10 was allowed to XYZ Re for investment income it would have had without this transaction. Of the remaining $14 of income attributable to it entering into the reinsurance agreement, $3 is XYZ Re's return for providing the reinsurance, leaving $11 to reduce the outstanding surplus account.

Modified Coinsurance

Modified coinsurance has been a particularly popular method of providing financial reinsurance since the ceding company maintains the reserves and the assets in support of these reserves. As in a coinsurance arrangement, there is a proportionate sharing of premiums, benefits, and reserve increases. Under the typical financial reinsurance arrangement involving modified coinsurance on an existing block of policies, the premium in the initial transaction will be equal to the reserves on the portion of the policies reinsured. The renewal premiums will typically be equal to the gross premiums on the portion of the policies reinsured. The reinsurer will pay the ceding company an allowance. If a first year gain is desired, it will be provided through the initial allowance. In renewal years, the allowance will help cover ceding company expenses.

The reinsurer uses the premium which it retains to pay claims and reinsurance expenses, to fund the reserve increase, and to repay any surplus committed to the agreement. Generally, it is anticipated that there will be a gain at the end of each accounting period. The reinsurer may allow the ceding company to participate in this gain through the use of an experience refund formula. As in the coinsurance example, the experience refund is generally calculated for each accounting period as the premiums received less allowances, claims, reserve increase, and a risk charge, less any repayment of the outstanding surplus relief. In most contracts, an experience refund is not paid unless the reinsurer's surplus account is positive.

As in the coinsurance case, the reinsurer also maintains a scorecard account for the outstanding surplus relief. This scorecard is tallied at the end of every accounting period. When the balance of the surplus account is zero, the ceding company may terminate the treaty.

The mod-co reserve adjustment is the same as that discussed in Chapter 4. If the initial transaction involves a block of inforce policies, the initial mod-co adjustment is equal to the policy reserves at the inception of the contract.

Advantages. Like coinsurance, mod-co is applicable to all plans of insurance. The major advantage of mod-co to the ceding company is that it avoids the necessity of liquidating or transferring ownership of assets to the reinsurer when an inforce block of business is involved. It is considered superior to coinsurance if a participating block or a block of interest sensitive products is being reinsured, as it allows the ceding company to retain control of the investment policy for the block of business.

The use of mod-co also eliminates the reserve credit problem found in coinsurance if the reinsurer is not licensed in the ceding company's state of domicile. Under mod-co, the reinsurer may deduct the entire reserve increase for federal income tax purposes, as it has paid the amount to the ceding company, even if the reserve does not otherwise qualify as a tax deductible item.[4]

The reinsurer may prefer the use of mod-co to avoid the necessity of managing assets. This might be particularly significant in the case of an occasional or speciality reinsurer that does not have a special staff dedicated to the administration of reinsurance investments.

Disadvantages. The main disadvantage of mod-co is that it is more complicated to administer than coinsurance because of the mod-co adjustment. Special transactions are required in the case of surrenders and death.

Transfer of assets back to the reinsurer in the event of treaty termination can create exposure to capital losses for the ceding company, just as transfer of the initial mod-co adjustment to the ceding company can create problems for the reinsurer.

If the reinsurer has genuine doubts about the solvency of the ceding company during the projected life of a financial reinsurance arrangement, the reinsurer will generally prefer coinsurance. Coinsurance will allow it to maintain control of the assets. In the case of the ceding company insolvency, the reinsurer might look to offset claims by the amount of the policy reserves if it held the assets supporting the reserves.

Mod-co Illustrations. For illustrative purposes, it is assumed that ABC Life enters into a mod-co reinsurance agreement with XYZ Re on essentially the same terms as the previously illustrated coinsurance agreement using a 10% mod-co interest rate.

First Year Results. Tables 5.5A and 5.5B show the statutory Gains from Operations and the Balance Sheets for the first year under this arrangement.

---

[4]On the other hand, the ceding company will have taxable income and no tax deductible reserve increase to match with it.

TABLE 5.5A

STATUTORY FINANCIAL STATEMENTS
MODIFIED COINSURANCE – YEAR 1

GAIN FROM OPERATIONS

	ABC LIFE	XYZ RE
Revenue:		
Premiums:		
Gross	$ 1,000	$ 1,000
Ceded	1,000	0
Net	$ 0	$ 1,000
Investment Income:		
Surplus	$ 0	$ 0
Reserves	0	0
Total	$ 0	$ 0
Reinsurance Allowances	$ 100	$ 0
Mod-co Adjustment	1,000	0
Misc. (Experience Refund)	0	0
TOTAL REVENUE	$ 1,100	$ 1,000
Benefits:		
Claims and Surrenders		
Gross	$ 0	$ 0
Ceded	0	0
Net	$ 0	$ 0
Reserve Increase:		
Gross	$ 1,000	$ 0
Ceded	0	0
Net	$ 1,000	$ 0
Experience Refund	0	0
Mod-co Adjustment	0	1,000
TOTAL BENEFITS	$ 1,000	$ 1,000
Expenses:		
Expenses and Commissions	$ 100	$ 100
TOTAL EXPENSES	$ 100	$ 100
GAIN FROM OPERATIONS	$ 0	$ (100)

TABLE 5.5B

STATUTORY FINANCIAL STATEMENTS
MODIFIED COINSURANCE – YEAR 1

BALANCE SHEET

	ABC LIFE	XYZ RE
Assets		
Invested Assets	$ 1,000	$ 0
Accounts Receivable	0	0
TOTAL ASSETS	$ 1,000	$ 0
Liabilities and Capital		
Policy Reserves:		
Gross	$ 1,000	$ 0
Ceded	0	0
Net	$ 1,000	$ 0
Accounts Payable	0	0
TOTAL LIABILITIES	$ 1,000	$ 0
Surplus	1,000	0
TOTAL CAPITAL	$ 0	$ 0
TOTAL LIABILITIES AND CAPITAL	$ 1,000	$ 0

As in the coinsurance example shown in Table 5.3, ABC Life shows a ceded premium of $1,000 and $100 of reinsurance allowances. However, it now has received a mod-co adjustment as a revenue item in the amount of $1,000, and it carries the entire $1,000 reserve increase in its income statement as a benefit. XYZ Re shows $1,000 of accepted premium and $1,000 mod-co adjustment to reflect the initial reserve increase. The statutory balance sheet shows that ABC Life now has $1,000 of assets and liabilities while XYZ Re has none. With respect to assets and liabilities, this is the exact opposite of the coinsurance example of Table 5.3. Earnings, however, are the same for the coinsurance example. Again, no invested assets, liabilities, or surplus have been created.

The reinsurance report prepared for the initial transaction shows the $1,000 of ceded premium less the allowances of $100 and the mod-co adjustment of $1,000. In this case, XYZ Re pays ABC Life $100. This compares to the $900 payment made by ABC Life to XYZ Re at the inception of the coinsurance treaty.

ABC LIFE
REINSURANCE REPORT – YEAR 1

Ceded Premium:			$1,000
Less:	Allowances	$ 100	
	Benefits	–0–	
	Mod-co Adjustment	1,000	
	Experience Refund	–0–	(1,100)
Total Due XYZ Re:			$ (100)

As in the coinsurance example, XYZ Re creates a special outstanding surplus account for this treaty. At the inception of the treaty, the outstanding surplus account indicates that XYZ Re has advanced $100 to ABC Life.

ABC LIFE
OUTSTANDING SURPLUS ACCOUNT
END OF YEAR 1

Beginning Balance:			$ –0–
Plus:	Statutory Gain		(100)
Less:	Investment Income on Surplus	$ –0–	
	Risk Charge	–0–	(–0–)
Ending Balance:			$ (100)

Second Year Results. In the second year of the mod-co transaction, the mod-co reserve adjustment must first be calculated. This calculation was not shown for the first year as the transaction was made on December 31. Assuming a mod-co interest rate of 10%, the calculation is as follows:

ABC LIFE
MOD-CO RESERVE ADJUSTMENT - YEAR 2

Ending Policy Reserves:		$1,070
Less: Beginning Policy Reserves	$1,000	
Interest on Beginning Policy Reserve	100	(1,100)
Mod-co Adjustment:		$ (30)

The calculation indicates that ABC Life owes $30 to XYZ Re. This occurs because the interest element in the adjustment plus the reserves released by termination exceeded the reserve increase for the remaining policies. The mod-co adjustment is reflected in the statutory Gains from Operations shown in Table 5.6A.

As ABC Life held all of the assets involved in the transaction, it has earned $100 of investment income. As in the coinsurance example, it has earned a $1 experience refund. It shows the entire $70 reserve increase as a benefit. It also shows that XYZ Re has reimbursed it for the claims incurred. ABC Life's statutory Gain from Operations also shows that it has paid XYZ Re a $30 mod-co adjustment. As a result, ABC Life has a gain of $1 while XYZ Re has a gain of $24, just as in the coinsurance example. This occurs because the mod-co interest rate is equal to the investment income interest rate for both companies. The statutory Balance Sheet for ABC indicates that it has $1,071 of assets, $1,070 of liabilities, and $1 of surplus. XYZ Re has assets and surplus of $24 and no reserve liabilities.

The reinsurance report prepared for the second year of the transaction shows the $5 of benefits and $1 experience refund netted against the mod-co adjustment of $30. In this case, ABC Life pays XYZ Re $24.

TABLE 5.6A

STATUTORY FINANCIAL STATEMENTS
MODIFIED COINSURANCE – YEAR 2

GAIN FROM OPERATIONS

	ABC LIFE		XYZ RE	
Revenue:				
Premiums:				
Gross	$	0	$	0
Ceded		0		0
Net	$	0	$	0
Investment Income:				
Surplus	$	0	$	0
Reserves		100		0
Total	$	100	$	0
Reinsurance Allowances	$	0	$	0
Mod-co Adjustment		0		30
Misc. (Experience Refund)		1		0
TOTAL REVENUE	$	101	$	30
Benefits:				
Claims and Surrenders				
Gross	$	5	$	5
Ceded		5		0
Net	$	0	$	5
Reserve Increase:				
Gross	$	70	$	0
Ceded		0		0
Net	$	70	$	0
Experience Refund		0		1
Mod-co Adjustment		30		0
TOTAL BENEFITS	$	100	$	6
Expenses:				
Expenses and Commissions	$	0	$	0
TOTAL EXPENSES	$	0	$	0
GAIN FROM OPERATIONS	$	1	$	24

TABLE 5.6B

STATUTORY FINANCIAL STATEMENTS
MODIFIED COINSURANCE – YEAR 2

BALANCE SHEET

	ABC LIFE	XYZ RE
Assets		
Invested Assets	$ 1,071	$ 24
Accounts Receivable	0	0
TOTAL ASSETS	$ 1,071	$ 24
Liabilities and Capital		
Policy Reserves:		
Gross	$ 1,070	$ 0
Ceded	0	0
Net	$ 1,070	$ 0
Accounts Payable	0	0
TOTAL LIABILITIES	$ 1,070	$ 0
Surplus	1	24
TOTAL CAPITAL	1	24
TOTAL LIABILITIES AND CAPITAL	$ 1,071	$ 24

ABC LIFE
REINSURANCE REPORT – YEAR 2

Ceded Premium:			$ –0–
Less:	Allowances	$ –0–	
	Benefits	5	
	Mod-co Adjustment	(30)	
	Experience Refund	1	24
Total Due XYZ Re:			$ 24

After the financial statement is prepared, XYZ Re updates its outstanding surplus account for the ABC Life treaty. It reduces the beginning balance by its statutory gain attributed to this account less investment income attributed to the amount financed and less the risk charge on the amount advanced of $3. This again results in an ending balance of $89. These amounts are equal to those of the coinsurance transaction, as the same interest rates were used.

ABC LIFE
OUTSTANDING SURPLUS ACCOUNT
END OF YEAR 2

Beginning Balance:			$ (100)
Plus:	Statutory Gain		24
Less:	Investment Income on Surplus	$ 10	
	Risk Charge	3	(13)
Ending Balance:			$ (89)

Funds Withheld Coinsurance

Funds withheld coinsurance looks like regular coinsurance in many ways. The reinsurer follows the ceding company's plan values and calculations of the premiums, allowances, experience refunds, and risk charges are all similar. When looking at the initial statutory gain from operations, it is impossible to tell the difference between coinsurance and funds withheld coinsurance. In order to see the difference between the two, the statutory balance sheet and reinsurance reports must be examined.

The only difference between coinsurance and funds withheld coinsurance is that in the initial funds withheld coinsurance transaction, the reinsurer retains the allowance and the ceding company retains the initial premium. If the allowance exceeds the initial premium, the reinsurer would set up an accounts payable item while the ceding company would have an accounts receivable asset. Should the initial premium exceed the allowance, the reverse would be true.

In subsequent accounting periods, the net balance of the funds withheld will increase or decrease as profit emerges, surplus is repaid, and the reserves increase or decrease. Until the net balance of the funds withheld reaches zero, no cash will change hands other than the reinsurer's risk charge. Since the ceding company is maintaining the assets underlying the reserves while the reinsurer holds the reserves on its financial statements, an interest adjustment much like the mod-co interest adjustment is made.

Advantages. The major advantage of funds withheld coinsurance is that no cash changes hands in the initial transaction and cash flow is minimized throughout the life of the treaty. This is particularly advantageous to the company with the net accounts payable item.

The use of funds withheld coinsurance also lessens the ceding company's insolvency risk should the reinsurer become insolvent. The ceding company, which has retained the assets underlying the reserves, is in a better position than it is under the regular coinsurance arrangement.

Use of funds withheld coinsurance will also lessen the risk to the reinsurer should the ceding company become insolvent as compared to a mod-co transaction. In the event of the ceding company's insolvency, the reinsurer may be able to use the amount it owes the ceding company for the allowance to offset any monies owed it by the ceding company.

Funds withheld coinsurance is also a legitimate alternative to mod-co if the funds stay with the ceding company. If the reinsurer is nonadmitted, the ceding company can still take reserve credit up to the amount of funds it is holding.

Disadvantages. The major drawback of funds withheld coinsurance is that it is more complicated than regular coinsurance. The receivables and payables must be tracked carefully. An interest adjustment must be made for the company with the net accounts receivable to reflect any foregone investment income.

Like coinsurance, funds withheld coinsurance may still result in a reserve credit problem for the ceding company if the reinsurer is not licensed or admitted in its state of domicile and the funds being withheld are with the reinsurer. However, the problem is alleviated somewhat because the ceding company is holding the assets behind the reserves.

Funds Withheld Coinsurance Illustrations. Assume ABC Life enters into a funds withheld coinsurance agreement using the same terms as previously.

First Year Results. Tables 5.7A and 5.7B illustrate the financial effect in the first year of a funds withheld coinsurance arrangement involving ABC Life and XYZ Re. In examining the Gains from Operations for both companies and comparing the results with those in Table 5.3A for the coinsurance transaction, there is no visible difference in earnings. The difference is in the statutory Balance Sheets. The Balance Sheet shows that XYZ Re has an accounts receivable item of $900 while ABC Life has an accounts payable liability of $900. The combined gains, invested assets, policy reserves, and surplus for the two companies remain unchanged from any of the previous examples. In this case however, a "paper asset" and a "paper liability" in the amount of the initial funds withheld have been created.

The reinsurance report for funds withheld coinsurance shows a total due XYZ Re of $900, just as in the coinsurance example. In this case however, ABC Life does not remit the $900. This is the amount of its initial accounts payable and the amount of XYZ Re's initial accounts receivable.

ABC LIFE
REINSURANCE REPORT - YEAR 1

Funds Withheld Beginning Balance:			$ –0–
Ceded Premium:		$1,000	
Less: Allowances	$100		
Benefits	–0–		
Mod-co Adjustment	–0–		
Experience Refund	–0–	(100)	
Total Due XYZ Re:		$ 900	
Less: Risk Charge Paid		(–0–)	900
Funds Withheld Ending Balance:			$ 900

TABLE 5A

STATUTORY FINANCIAL STATEMENTS
FUNDS WITHHELD COINSURANCE – YEAR 1

GAIN FROM OPERATIONS

	ABC LIFE	XYZ RE
Revenue:		
Premiums:		
Gross	$ 1,000	$ 1,000
Ceded	1,000	0
Net	$ 0	$ 1,000
Investment Income:		
Surplus	0	0
Reserves	0	0
Total	$ 0	$ 0
Reinsurance Allowances	$ 100	$ 0
Mod-co Adjustment	0	0
Misc. (Experience Refund)	0	0
TOTAL REVENUE	$ 100	$ 1,000
Benefits:		
Claims and Surrenders		
Gross	$ 0	$ 0
Ceded	0	0
Net	$ 0	$ 0
Reserve Increase:		
Gross	$ 1,000	$ 1,000
Ceded	1,000	0
Net	$ 0	$ 1,000
Experience Refund	0	0
Mod-co Adjustment	0	0
TOTAL BENEFITS	$ 0	$ 1,000
Expenses:		
Expenses and Commissions	$ 0	$ 0
TOTAL EXPENSES	$ 100	$ 100
GAIN FROM OPERATIONS	$ 0	$ (100)

TABLE 5.7B

STATUTORY FINANCIAL STATEMENTS
FUNDS WITHHELD COINSURANCE – YEAR 1

BALANCE SHEET

	ABC LIFE	XYZ RE
Assets		
Invested Assets	$ 900	$ 100
Accounts Receivable	0	900
TOTAL ASSETS	$ 900	$ 1,000
Liabilities and Capital		
Policy Reserves:		
Gross	$ 1,000	$ 1,000
Ceded	1,000	0
Net	$ 0	$ 1,000
Accounts Payable	900	0
TOTAL LIABILITIES	$ 900	$ 1,000
Surplus	$ 900	$ 1,000
TOTAL CAPITAL	$ 0	$ 0
TOTAL LIABILITIES AND CAPITAL	$ 900	$ 1,000

XYZ Re, again, establishes an outstanding surplus account in its ABC Life file. In the initial transaction it shows that it has advanced ABC Life $100 which will be repaid out of future gains.

ABC LIFE
OUTSTANDING SURPLUS ACCOUNT
END OF YEAR 1

Beginning Balance:		$ –0–
Plus: Statutory Gain		(100)
Less: Investment Income on Surplus	$ –0–	
Risk Charge	–0–	(–0–)
Ending Balance:		$ (100)

Second Year Results. Tables 5.8A and 5.8B show the statutory Gains from Operations and Balance Sheets in the second year for the funds withheld coinsurance transaction. The transaction no longer looks like pure coinsurance.

A strange thing has occurred in the second year of this transaction – ABC Life now shows ceded premium of $90 and XYZ Re has gross premiums of $90. This $90 represents the investment income on the $900 which ABC Life retained rather than paying to XYZ Re. Statutory accounting rules regarding the treatment of this particular item are not specific and some companies treat this item as some form of miscellaneous revenue.

The investment income is now divided between the two companies in the same manner as was the case with no reinsurance since each maintained its original amount of invested assets. XYZ Re still pays ABC Life the $1 experience refund and reimburses it $5 for benefits. XYZ Re is holding all the reserves on its books. Again, this results in a $1 gain for ABC Life and a $24 net income for XYZ Re.

The statutory Balance Sheet shows that the accounts receivable item has grown to $981. ABC Life's invested assets have grown to $982 which is exactly $3 less than its invested assets in the no reinsurance example shown in Table 5.2B. The difference is attributable to the risk charge which it paid XYZ Re. Conversely, XYZ Re's invested assets are $3 higher than in the no reinsurance example because of the receipt of this $3 of risk charge. Again the combined gains, invested assets, policy reserves, and surplus remain unchanged for both companies as in the previous examples.

TABLE 5.8A

STATUTORY FINANCIAL STATEMENTS
FUNDS WITHHELD COINSURANCE – YEAR 2

GAIN FROM OPERATIONS

	ABC LIFE	XYZ RE
Revenue:		
Premiums:		
Gross	$ 0	$ 90
Ceded	90	0
Net	$ (90)	$ 90
Investment Income:		
Surplus	$ 0	$ 0
Reserves	90	10
Total	$ 90	$ 0
Reinsurance Allowances	$ 0	$ 0
Mod-co Adjustment	0	0
Misc. (Experience Refund)	1	0
TOTAL REVENUE	$ 1	$ 100
Benefits:		
Claims and Surrenders		
Gross	$ 5	$ 5
Ceded	5	0
Net	$ 0	$ 5
Reserve Increase:		
Gross	$ 70	$ 70
Ceded	70	0
Net	$ 0	$ 70
Experience Refund	0	1
Mod-co Adjustment	0	0
TOTAL BENEFITS	$ 0	$ 76
Expenses:		
Expenses and Commissions	$ 0	$ 0
TOTAL EXPENSES	$ 0	$ 0
GAIN FROM OPERATIONS	$ 1	$ 24

TABLE 5.3B

STATUTORY FINANCIAL STATEMENTS
FUNDS WITHHELD COINSURANCE – YEAR 2

BALANCE SHEET

	ABC LIFE	XYZ RE
Assets		
Invested Assets	$ 982	$ 113
Accounts Receivable	0	981
TOTAL ASSETS	$ 982	$ 1,094
Liabilities and Capital		
Policy Reserves:		
Gross	$ 1,070	$ 1,070
Ceded	1,070	0
Net	$ 0	$ 1,070
Accounts Payable	981	0
TOTAL LIABILITIES	$ 981	$ 1,070
Surplus	1	24
TOTAL CAPITAL	1	24
TOTAL LIABILITIES AND CAPITAL	$ 982	$ 1,094

In order to see the growth of the funds withheld balance, the reinsurance report must be examined. It shows an initial funds withheld balance of $900. ABC Life now has ceded premium of $90, the amount of the foregone investment income on the withheld funds. It nets the benefits and experience refund against this amount for a total due XYZ Re of $84. However, ABC Life pays XYZ Re only $3, the amount of the risk charge. The remaining $81 increases the funds withheld balance.

ABC LIFE
REINSURANCE REPORT - YEAR 2

Funds Withheld Beginning Balance:			$ 900
Ceded Premium:		$ 90	
Less: Allowances	$ -0-		
Benefits	5		
Mod-co Adjustment	-0-		
Experience Refund	1	(6)	
Total Due XYZ Re:		$ 84	
Less: Risk Charge Paid		(3)	81
Funds Withheld Ending Balance:			$ 981

At the end of the accounting period, XYZ Re updates its outstanding surplus account for the ABC Life treaty. As in the previous examples, the ending balance is $89.

ABC LIFE
OUTSTANDING SURPLUS ACCOUNT
END OF YEAR 2

Beginning Balance:		$ (100)
Plus: Statutory Gain		24
Less: Investment Income on Surplus	$ 10	
Risk Charge	3	(13)
Ending Balance:		$ (89)

Alternatively, this may be looked at as follows ignoring XYZ Re's investment income on its original assets:

ABC LIFE
OUTSTANDING SURPLUS ACCOUNT
(ALTERNATIVE CALCULATION)
END OF YEAR 2

Beginning Balance:		$ (100)
Plus: Reinsurer Premium		90
Less: Benefits	$ 5	
Reserve Increase	70	
Experience Refund	1	
Risk Charge	3	(79)
Ending Balance:		$ (89)

This result is the same as in the original calculation. The alternative calculation is more likely to be used in practice.

Funds Withheld Modified Coinsurance

Funds withheld modified coinsurance looks like regular mod-co in the initial transaction. The initial premium, allowance, and mod-co adjustments will be the same. The difference between the two is that under funds withheld mod-co, the reinsurer retains the initial allowance, setting up an accounts payable item for that amount. The ceding company then sets up a corresponding receivable item for the same amount.

Advantages. The principle advantage of funds withheld mod-co is that the reinsurer retains the initial allowance. It is freed from having to liquidate any assets to pay the allowance and minimizes future capital loss exposure. The reinsurer also has a lessened risk in the event of the ceding company's insolvency compared to regular mod-co as it is holding the assets underlying the initial allowance.

Disadvantages. A major problem of funds withheld mod-co is that it adds just one more layer of complexity to the administration of the treaty. The mod-co adjustment is complicated because the ceding company did not receive the allowance in cash. A special adjustment must be made to the interest element to reflect the fact that the ceding company has not earned interest on the allowance.

Funds Withheld Mod-co Illustrations. Assume that ABC Life has entered into a funds withheld mod-co transaction with XYZ Re on the same basic terms as the mod-co transaction.

First Year Results. Tables 5.9A and 5.9B show financial effect in the first year of the funds withheld mod-co initial transaction. When looking at the statutory Gains from Operations for both companies, the transaction looks exactly like mod-co transaction shown in Tables 5.5A and 5.5B. The difference appears in the statutory Balance Sheets. In this example, ABC Life has an accounts receivable asset of $100 while XYZ Re has an accounts payable liability of $100. Combined gains, invested assets, policy reserves, and surplus for both companies remains unchanged from the other examples.

The reinsurance report shows how the initial funds withheld amount is calculated. As in regular mod-co, the report shows that XYZ Re owes ABC Life a balance of $100 after the initial transaction. XYZ Re does not pay this amount, and instead sets up an accounts payable item.

ABC LIFE
REINSURANCE REPORT - YEAR 1

Funds Withheld Beginning Balance:			$ –0–
Ceded Premium:		$1,000	
Less: Allowances	$ 100		
Benefits	–0–		
Mod-co Adjustment	1,000		
Experience Refund	–0–	(1,100)	
Total Due XYZ Re:		$ (100)	
Less: Risk Charge Paid		(–0–)	(100)
Funds Withheld Ending Balance:			$ (100)

The outstanding surplus account for the ABC Life treaty again shows an initial balance of $100.

TABLE 5.9A

STATUTORY FINANCIAL STATEMENTS
FUNDS WITHHELD MODIFIED COINSURANCE – YEAR 1

GAIN FROM OPERATIONS

	ABC LIFE	XYZ RE
Revenue:		
Premiums:		
Gross	$ 1,000	$ 1,000
Ceded	1,000	0
Net	$ 0	$ 1,000
Investment Income:		
Surplus	$ 0	$ 0
Reserves	0	0
Total	$ 0	$ 0
Reinsurance Allowances	$ 100	$ 0
Mod-co Adjustment	1,000	0
Misc. (Experience Refund)	0	0
TOTAL REVENUE	$ 1,100	$ 1,000
Benefits:		
Claims and Surrenders		
Gross	$ 0	$ 0
Ceded	0	0
Net	$ 0	$ 0
Reserve Increase:		
Gross	$ 1,000	$ 0
Ceded	0	0
Net	$ 1,000	$ 0
Experience Refund	0	0
Mod-co Adjustment	0	1,000
TOTAL BENEFITS	$ 1,000	$ 1,000
Expenses:		
Expenses and Commissions	$ 100	$ 100
TOTAL EXPENSES	$ 100	$ 100
GAIN FROM OPERATIONS	$ 0	$ (100)

TABLE 5.9B

STATUTORY FINANCIAL STATEMENTS
FUNDS WITHHELD MODIFIED COINSURANCE – YEAR 1

BALANCE SHEET

	ABC LIFE	XYZ RE
Assets		
Invested Assets	$ 900	$ 100
Accounts Receivable	100	0
TOTAL ASSETS	$ 1,000	$ 100
Liabilities and Capital		
Policy Reserves:		
Gross	$ 1,000	$ 0
Ceded	0	0
Net	$ 1,000	$ 0
Accounts Payable	0	100
TOTAL LIABILITIES	$ 1,000	$ 100
Surplus	$ 0	$ 0
TOTAL CAPITAL	$ 0	$ 0
TOTAL LIABILITIES AND CAPITAL	$ 1,000	$ 100

ABC LIFE
OUTSTANDING SURPLUS ACCOUNT
END OF YEAR 1

Beginning Balance:			$ –0–
Plus:	Statutory Gain		(100)
Less:	Investment Income on Surplus	$ –0–	
	Risk Charge	–0–	(–0–)
Ending Balance:			$ (100)

Second Year Results. In the second year of the funds withheld mod-co transaction, the companies must first calculate the mod-co adjustment:

ABC LIFE
MOD-CO RESERVE ADJUSTMENT - YEAR 2

Ending Policy Reserves:		$1,070
Less: Beginning Policy Reserves	$1,000	
Interest on Beginning Policy Reserves	90	(1,090)
Mod-co Adjustment:		$ (20)

In the regular mod-co example, the mod-co reserve adjustment resulted in a $30 payment to XYZ Re. In the funds withheld mod-co example, this amount is reduced $20 because ABC Life did not have all the necessary assets to support the reserves. It offsets its reserve increase by the amount of investment income on the funds retained by XYZ Re. This is reflected in the statutory Gains from Operation shown in Table 5.10A.

The only difference in the statutory Gains from Operations in the funds withheld mod-co arrangement as compared to that for the regular mod-co arrangement is in the case of funds withheld. XYZ Re now has earned investment income on the amount of the retained allowance and has received a correspondingly smaller mod-co adjustment. ABC Life has earned less investment income and paid a smaller mod-co adjustment. The gain to ABC Life remains $1, while the gain to XYZ Re remains $24 as in the previous examples.

TABLE 5.10A

STATUTORY FINANCIAL STATEMENTS
FUNDS WITHHELD MODIFIED COINSURANCE – YEAR 2

GAIN FROM OPERATIONS

	ABC LIFE	XYZ RE
Revenue:		
Premiums:		
Gross	$ 0	$ 0
Ceded	0	0
Net	$ 0	$ 0
Investment Income:		
Surplus	$ 0	$ 0
Reserves	90	10
Total	$ 90	$ 10
Reinsurance Allowances	$ 0	$ 0
Mod-co Adjustment	0	20
Misc. (Experience Refund)	1	0
TOTAL REVENUE	$ 91	$ 30
Benefits:		
Claims and Surrenders		
Gross	$ 5	$ 5
Ceded	5	0
Net	$ 0	$ 5
Reserve Increase:		
Gross	$ 70	$ 0
Ceded	0	0
Net	$ 70	$ 0
Experience Refund	0	1
Mod-co Adjustment	20	0
TOTAL BENEFITS	$ 90	$ 6
Expenses:		
Expenses and Commissions	$ 0	$ 0
TOTAL EXPENSES	$ 0	$ 0
GAIN FROM OPERATIONS	$ 1	$ 24

TABLE 5.10B

STATUTORY FINANCIAL STATEMENTS
FUNDS WITHHELD MODIFIED COINSURANCE– YEAR 2

BALANCE SHEET

	ABC LIFE	XYZ RE
Assets		
Invested Assets	$ 982	$ 113
Accounts Receivable	89	0
TOTAL ASSETS	$ 1,071	$ 113
Liabilities and Capital		
Policy Reserves:		
Gross	$ 1,070	$ 0
Ceded	0	0
Net	$ 1,070	$ 0
Accounts Payable	0	89
TOTAL LIABILITIES	$ 1,070	$ 89
Surplus	1	24
TOTAL CAPITAL	$ 1	$ 24
TOTAL LIABILITIES AND CAPITAL	$ 1,071	$ 113

The statutory Balance Sheet in Table 5.10B shows that ABC Life's invested assets have grown to $982, the same as in the funds withheld coinsurance illustration, which is $3 less than the invested assets in the no reinsurance illustration. Again, this $3 is the risk charge which ABC Life paid XYZ Re. XYZ Re's invested assets are now $113, which is the same as in the funds withheld coinsurance situation and exactly $3 more than in the no reinsurance example.

The reinsurance report for the second year shows a decrease in the funds withheld balance of $11. The total amount due is $14, but only the $3 risk charge is paid.

ABC LIFE
REINSURANCE REPORT - YEAR 2

Funds Withheld Beginning Balance:			$ (100)
Ceded Premium:		$ –0–	
Less: Allowances	$ –0–		
Benefits	5		
Mod-co Adjustment	(20)		
Experience Refund	1	14	
Total Due XYZ Re:		$ 14	
Less: Risk Charge Paid		(3)	11
Funds Withheld Ending Balance:			$ (89)

XYZ Re, at the close of the accounting period recalculates the outstanding surplus account for the ABC Life treaty. The result is, of course, the same as in the other examples. In this situation, it is equal to the funds withheld balance.

ABC LIFE
OUTSTANDING SURPLUS ACCOUNT
END OF YEAR 2

Beginning Balance:		$ (100)
Plus: Statutory Gain		24
Less: Investment Income on Surplus	$ 10	
Risk Charge	3	(13)
Ending Balance:		$ (89)

The alternative calculation is as follows:

ABC LIFE
OUTSTANDING SURPLUS ACCOUNT
(ALTERNATIVE CALCULATION)
END OF YEAR 2

Beginning Balance:			$(100)
Plus:	Reinsurance Premium	$ –0–	
	Mod-co Adjustment	20	20
Less:	Benefits	$ 5	
	Experience Refund	1	
	Risk Charge	3	(9)
Ending Balance:			$ (89)

Partially Modified Coinsurance

Partially modified coinsurance,[5] or part-co, is a combination of coinsurance and modified coinsurance. In a part-co treaty, the initial coinsurance reserves are set equal to the initial reinsurance allowance. The remaining reserve liabilities are reinsured on a modified coinsurance basis. This results in no cash transfer at the inception of the treaty. In renewal years, the proportions of the coinsurance and modified coinsurance are adjusted. The adjustment may be scheduled in the treaty or it may be allowed to float with the increase in coinsurance reserves and the surplus relief repayment. Some states disapprove of the coinsurance percentage increasing from its initial point because this typically indicates increased surplus relief without the reinsurer paying its share of cash losses. This is not necessarily improper, but it does call for explanation.

Advantages. The chief advantage of part-co is that there is no cash transaction initially. It also eliminates the need to create the paper assets and liabilities required under a funds withheld situation. In this sense, there is less regulatory question about the transaction.

---

[5]This combined form of reinsurance is also referred to as "co/mod-co" or "split co/mod-co."

Disadvantages. The chief disadvantage of part-co is that it is very complicated to comprehend and to administer. If the coinsurance reserves are going to follow the amount of the outstanding surplus, two statutory gains from operations calculations must be made. The preliminary statutory gain from operations calculations is necessary to determine the amount of the surplus repayment. The finalized statutory gain from operations will than be created to show the change in reserves from coinsurance to modified coinsurance.

Part-co Illustrations. Assume that ABC Life has entered into a part-co transaction with XYZ Re. Since the initial allowance was $100, the initial amount of the coinsurance reserves is equal to $100. This is equal to 10% of the total reserves. The initial mod-co reserve is set at $900. Other assumptions are unchanged.

First Year Results. Tables 5.11A and 5.11B illustrate the financial effect in the first year of the initial part-co transaction. The statutory Gain from Operations shows that ABC Life receives a mod-co adjustment of $900 and is holding $900 in mod-co reserves. XYZ Re's statutory Gain from Operations shows that it is holding $100 of coinsurance reserves and has paid out a $900 mod-co adjustment.

    The statutory Balance Sheet for ABC Life shows that it has retained its $900 of invested assets and has decreased its reserve liabilities to a matching $900. XYZ Re has kept its $100 of invested assets and has increased its reserve liabilities to $100.

    The reinsurance report for the initial transaction shows ceded premium of $1,000 less allowances of $100 and a mod-co adjustment of $900 for a total amount due of $0. No cash has been transferred.

ABC LIFE
REINSURANCE REPORT – YEAR 1

Ceded Premium:			$1,000
Less:	Allowances	$100	
	Benefits	–0–	
	Mod-co Adjustment	900	
	Experience Refund	–0–	(1,000)
Total Due XYZ Re:			$ –0–

TABLE 5.11A

STATUTORY FINANCIAL STATEMENTS
PARTIALLY MODIFIED COINSURANCE – YEAR 1

GAIN FROM OPERATIONS

	ABC LIFE	XYZ RE
Revenue:		
Premiums:		
Gross	$ 1,000	$ 1,000
Ceded	1,000	0
Net	$ 0	$ 1,000
Investment Income:		
Surplus	$ 0	$ 0
Reserves	0	0
Total	$ 0	$ 0
Reinsurance Allowances	$ 100	$ 0
Mod-co Adjustment	900	0
Misc. (Experience Refund)	0	0
TOTAL REVENUE	$ 1,000	$ 1,000
Benefits:		
Claims and Surrenders		
Gross	$ 0	$ 0
Ceded	0	0
Net	$ 0	$ 0
Reserve Increase:		
Gross	$ 1,000	$ 100
Ceded	100	0
Net	$ 900	$ 100
Experience Refund	0	0
Mod-co Adjustment	0	900
TOTAL BENEFITS	$ 900	$ 1,000
Expenses:		
Expenses and Commissions	$ 100	$ 100
TOTAL EXPENSES	$ 100	$ 100
GAIN FROM OPERATIONS	$ 0	$ (100)

TABLE 5.11B

STATUTORY FINANCIAL STATEMENTS
PARTIALLY MODIFIED COINSURANCE – YEAR 1

BALANCE SHEET

	ABC LIFE	XYZ RE
Assets		
Invested Assets	$ 900	$ 100 *
Accounts Receivable	0	0
TOTAL ASSETS	$ 900	$ 100
Liabilities and Capital		
Policy Reserves:		
Gross	$ 1,000	$ 100
Ceded	100	0
Net	$ 900	$ 100
Accounts Payable	0	0
TOTAL LIABILITIES	$ 900	$ 100
Surplus	0	0
TOTAL CAPITAL	$ 0	$ 0
TOTAL LIABILITIES AND CAPITAL	$ 900	$ 100

* Note: Assume XYZ Re held $100 of assets prior to R/I transaction. Example is difficult to follow as loss in yr 1 is (100) offsetting an initial surplus position of $100. No cash transfers are assumed - see pgs 142/143

The outstanding surplus account established for the ABC Life treaty again shows that XYZ Re has provided it with $100 of surplus.

ABC LIFE
OUTSTANDING SURPLUS ACCOUNT
END OF YEAR 1

Beginning Balance:		$ –0–
Plus: Statutory Gain		(100)
Less: Investment Income on Surplus	$ –0–	
Risk Charge	–0–	(–0–)
Ending Balance:		$ (100)

Second Year Results. At the end of the second year of the part-co treaty, both companies calculate the preliminary gain from operations. The first calculation is the preliminary mod-co adjustment. Ninety percent (90%) of the reserves were ceded on a mod-co basis, therefore, $90 of the reserve increase is on a mod-co basis. The mod-co reserve adjustment is as follows.

ABC LIFE
PRELIMINARY MOD-CO
RESERVE ADJUSTMENT - YEAR 2

Ending Policy Reserves:		$ 963
Less: Beginning Policy Reserves	$ 900	
Investment Income on Surplus	–0–	
Interest on Beginning Policy Reserves	90	(990)
Preliminary Mod-co Adjustment:		$ (27)

This $(27) mod-co adjustment compares to the $(30) mod-co adjustment made in the pure mod-co illustration and to the $(20) mod-co adjustment in the funds withheld mod-co illustration. Coinsurance reserves have increased from $7 to $107.

Tables 5.12A and 5.12B present the Preliminary Statutory Financial Statements for the second year for ABC Life and XYZ Re. The preliminary statutory Gains from Operations reflect the division of 10% coinsurance and 90% modified coinsurance.

TABLE 5.12A

PRELIMINARY STATUTORY FINANCIAL STATEMENTS
PARTIALLY MODIFIED COINSURANCE – YEAR 2

GAIN FROM OPERATIONS

	ABC LIFE		XYZ RE	
Revenue:				
Premiums:				
Gross	$	0	$	0
Ceded		0		0
Net	$	0	$	0
Investment Income:				
Surplus		0		0
Reserves		90		10
Total	$	90	$	10
Reinsurance Allowances	$	0	$	0
Mod-co Adjustment		0		27
Misc. (Experience Refund)		1		0
TOTAL REVENUE	$	91	$	37
Benefits:				
Claims and Surrenders				
Gross	$	5	$	5
Ceded		5		0
Net	$	0	$	5
Reserve Increase:				
Gross	$	70	$	7
Ceded		7		0
Net	$	63	$	7
Experience Refund		0		1
Mod-co Adjustment		27		0
TOTAL BENEFITS	$	90	$	13
Expenses:				
Expenses and Commissions	$	0	$	0
TOTAL EXPENSES	$	0	$	0
GAIN FROM OPERATIONS	$	1	$	24

TABLE 5.12B

PRELIMINARY STATUTORY FINANCIAL STATEMENTS
PARTIALLY MODIFIED COINSURANCE – YEAR 2

BALANCE SHEET

	ABC LIFE	XYZ RE
Assets		
Invested Assets	$ 964	$ 131
Accounts Receivable	0	0
TOTAL ASSETS	$ 964	$ 131
Liabilities and Capital		
Policy Reserves:		
Gross	$ 1,070	$ 107
Ceded	107	0
Net	$ 963	$ 107
Accounts Payable	0	0
TOTAL LIABILITIES	$ 963	$ 107
Surplus	1	24
TOTAL CAPITAL	$ 1	$ 24
TOTAL LIABILITIES AND CAPITAL	$ 964	$ 131

The Preliminary Statutory Balance Sheet shows that ABC Life has invested assets of $964 and XYZ Re has invested assets of $131. ABC Life has mod-co reserves of $963, while XYZ Re has mod-co reserves of $107. As in the other examples, the gain and statutory surplus for ABC Life is $1 and for XYZ Re, $24.

Now that the preliminary gains from operations have been calculated, XYZ Re can calculate the outstanding surplus account.

ABC LIFE
OUTSTANDING SURPLUS ACCOUNT
END OF YEAR 2

Beginning Balance:			$ (100)
Plus:	Statutory Gain		24
Less:	Investment Income on Surplus	$ 10	
	Risk Charge	3	(13)
Ending Balance:			$ (89)

As in the other cases, the outstanding surplus account shows that $11 has been repaid out of XYZ Re's gain on the business. This surplus repayment is used to calculate the final mod-co adjustment. This is shown below:

ABC LIFE
FINAL MOD-CO RESERVE ADJUSTMENT - YEAR 2

Preliminary Mod-Co Adjustment:		$ (27)
Plus: Coinsurance Reserve Increase	$ 7	
Surplus Repayment	11	18
Final Mod-co Adjustment:		$ (9)

In other words, the original mod-co adjustment is changed to reflect the $7 increase in coinsurance reserves which are to be reinsured on a mod-co basis as well as the transfer of coinsurance reserves to mod-co reserves in the amount of the surplus repayment of $11. This $18 transfer of coinsurance reserves to mod-co keeps the coinsurance reserves equal to the amount of outstanding surplus. For the next year, coinsurance reserves will be $89 (107−18), or 8.32% of the total of $1,070. The mod-co reserve will be $981 (900+ 63+18).

When this transaction has been calculated, the Final Statutory Financial Statements are calculated for both companies. These are shown in Tables 5.13A and 5.13B.

The mod-co adjustment is now $9. The distribution of coinsurance and mod-co reserves has been adjusted to reflect the transfer of the increase in coinsurance reserves and the surplus repayment of $11. Notice that the $11 surplus repayment equals XYZ Re's release of reserve. Also, the $9 mod-co adjustment equals the sum of XYZ's share of benefits ($5), the experience refund ($1), and the risk charge ($3). All other things being equal, the $3 is the only cash transfer necessary. However, in the event of negative experience, XYZ could be required to pay ABC Life.

The gains for both companies remain the same. XYZ Re's invested assets are now $982 on its statutory Balance Sheet. This is the same as in the funds withheld transactions. XYZ Re's invested assets are now $113, again, the same amount as in the funds withheld examples. ABC Life's mod-co reserves are now $981, while XYZ Re's coinsurance reserves are $89, the amount of the outstanding surplus.

ABC LIFE
REINSURANCE REPORT – YEAR 2

Ceded Premium:			$ –0–
Less:	Allowances	$ –0–	
	Benefits	5	
	Mod-co Adjustment	(9)	
	Experience Refund	1	3
Total Due XYZ Re:			$ 3

The reinsurance report in Year 2 shows that total due from ABC Life to XYZ Re of $3.

TABLE 5.13A

FINAL STATUTORY FINANCIAL STATEMENTS
PARTIALLY MODIFIED COINSURANCE – YEAR 2

GAIN FROM OPERATIONS

	ABC LIFE	XYZ RE
Revenue:		
Premiums:		
Gross	$ 0	$ 0
Ceded	0	0
Net	$ 0	$ 0
Investment Income:		
Surplus	$ 0	$ 0
Reserves	90	10
Total	$ 90	$ 10
Reinsurance Allowances	$ 0	$ 0
Mod-co Adjustment	0	9
Misc. (Experience Refund)	1	0
TOTAL REVENUE	$ 91	$ 19
Benefits:		
Claims and Surrenders		
Gross	$ 5	$ 5
Ceded	5	0
Net	$ 0	$ 5
Reserve Increase:		
Gross	$ 70	$ (11)
Ceded	(11)	0
Net	$ 81	$ (11)
Experience Refund	0	1
Mod-co Adjustment	9	0
TOTAL BENEFITS	$ 90	$ (5)
Expenses:		
Expenses and Commissions	$ 0	$ 0
TOTAL EXPENSES	$ 0	$ 0
GAIN FROM OPERATIONS	$ 1	$ 24

TABLE 5.13B

FINAL STATUTORY FINANCIAL STATEMENTS
PARTIALLY MODIFIED COINSURANCE – YEAR 2

BALANCE SHEET

	ABC LIFE	XYZ RE
Assets		
Invested Assets	$ 982	$ 113
Accounts Receivable	0	0
TOTAL ASSETS	$ 982	$ 113
Liabilities and Capital		
Policy Reserves:		
Gross	$ 1,070	$ 89
Ceded	89	0
Net	$ 981	$ 89
Accounts Payable	0	0
TOTAL LIABILITIES	$ 981	$ 89
Surplus	1	24
TOTAL CAPITAL	$ 1	$ 24
TOTAL LIABILITIES AND CAPITAL	$ 982	$ 113

ABC LIFE
ALTERNATIVE OUTSTANDING SURPLUS ACCOUNT
END OF YEAR 2

Beginning Balance:			$ (100)
Plus:	Mod-co Adjustment		9
Less:	Reserve Increase	$ (11)	
	Benefits	5	
	Experience Refund	1	
	Risk Charge	3	2
Ending Balance:			$ (89)

REGULATION AND TAXATION

Prior to about 1984, financial reinsurance was in an "anything goes" situation, that is, there was very little effective regulation. The early 1980's saw an enormous amount of activity in the financial reinsurance marketplace. A large number of these reinsurance transactions were designed to reclassify components of taxable income which dramatically reduced federal income tax revenues from the life insurance industry. Reinsurance also figured prominently in a number of insurance company insolvencies, primarily in the property and casualty area. The excessive use in reinsurance in these two situations, and a resultant cavalier treatment of reserve credits and treaty provisions, brought about many changes in the way such reinsurance is regulated.

One of the major changes concerns the tax treatment given to reinsurance transactions. Section 845 of the Tax Reform Act of 1984 grants the IRS broad authority to change individual company tax returns if significant tax avoidance is found to be present. While substantial tax avoidance is not defined, a disproportionate sharing of risks and tax benefits is an indication of such avoidance. Since inforce blocks are typically very stable, it is possible that the use of such blocks to secure surplus relief, at least in the ways most prevalent in the market, might be judged to be disproportionate.

In many cases, reinsurance transactions have been used to mask the true financial condition of a life insurance company. Often very little, if any, risk was actually transferred to the reinsurer. There have been sufficient insolvencies where reinsur-

ance transactions have only postponed the inevitable liquidation
without providing any significant benefit, risk transfer, or economic
security to the insolvent company. This has caused state insurance
departments to review reinsurance agreements closely for risk
transfer.

The Internal Revenue Service (IRS) and state insurance
departments are both concerned that a reinsurance treaty provide
legitimate risk transfer. Several state insurance departments have
recently begun to challenge certain reinsurance treaties, disallowing
reserve credits and receivable assets, based on an apparent lack of
risk transfer. It would appear that the departments have valid
concerns. Specific reinsurance treaty terms which have caused
concern include the following:

(1) Scheduled gains to the reinsurer, regardless of the under-
     lying experience of the block of reinsurance.
(2) Reinsurer never having to pay out benefits, just building
     up a payment due liability.
(3) Reinsurer having the right to terminate the agreement or
     automatic termination of the agreement if either
     (a) the reinsured becomes insolvent,
     (b) the reinsured has a change in management, or
     (c) the business reinsured proves to be unprofitable.

The appearance of these and similar terms cause negative
reactions by the regulators. As a result, several states have come
to challenge all "cashless" reinsurance. However, it appears that
the states will accept reinsurance agreements of a cashless nature if
there is some reasonable risk transfer. Conditions which should be
included in treaties in order to gain acceptance include the
following:

(1) The reinsurer must have an actual obligation to pay
     benefits should experience reach a certain level.
(2) Gains to the reinsurer must be based on the actual
     experience of the reinsurance.
(3) No event, such as insolvency or management change,
     should automatically terminate the reinsurance in force.
     However, reinsurance may be terminated due to a certain
     level of earnings being attained.
(4) Inforce reinsurance cannot be terminated unilaterally by
     the reinsurer, except for nonpayment of premiums.

(5) Interest paid or credited via the reinsurance should be reasonable in relation to the investment markets or the assets involved.

(6) The ceding company should not be forced to pay back losses except for voluntary termination.

The state regulators object to allowing reserve or receivable credits when the risk transferred is disproportionate to reserve credit. Adherence to the guidelines above should assist in qualifying agreements.

SECURITY CONSIDERATIONS

In recent years, the use of funds withheld and similar cashless reinsurance programs has come under criticism from both state regulators and the IRS. This criticism results from the apparent lack of risk transfer often associated with these types of agreements. In response to this criticism, and for other reasons relating to protection of assets, preserving reserve credits, minimizing currency fluctuations, and protection in the event of insolvency of either party, the use of trusts, escrow accounts, and letters of credit has increased in recent years.

Trusts and Escrow Accounts

With these concepts, a trust or escrow account is established to hold, identify, or further segment the relevant assets of one or both parties to a reinsurance transaction. A trust is used to secure amounts that are owed or might become owed from the company that establishes the trust to the company that is the beneficiary of the trust. Legal title to the assets is in the trustee.

A common use of a trust is to transfer assets relating to reserves of an inforce block. The trust enables the investment performances to be tied to the assets owned and for the same assets or replacements to be transferred back upon recapture. In the examples above, consider the coinsurance model. In this model, the transactions would be the same except the asset held by the reinsurer would be placed in the trust. Trusts can be used in any reinsurance agreement, but they are most common as alternatives to funds withheld transactions.

Escrow accounts are frequently confused with trusts, but the differences are probably greater than their similarities. Escrow accounts are used to earmark assets, usually for potential transfer under specified conditions, rather than actually transferring the ownership of the assets as is the case with a trust.   In a typical transaction, an escrow account might be used to support a funds withheld agreement.   In a funds withheld coinsurance case, the assets left with the ceding company would be placed in an escrow account.   The escrow agreement would outline the various rights of companies.   If certain conditions were to occur, the assets in escrow would be transferred to the reinsurer.   Events which could trigger such a transfer might include the following:

(1)   Surplus dropping below an agreed upon level.
(2)   Change in management.
(3)   Financial performance of the reinsurance below expected levels.

     Trusts and escrow agreements are valuable tools to add protection to one or both parties in a reinsurance agreement while maintaining flexibility.   The treatment of trusts and escrow agreements is not standardized in all states and is currently under review.   Any agreement contemplating use of either of a trust or escrow account should be reviewed in the light of the latest developments for the state insurance department involved.

Advantages.   The use of the trusts and escrow accounts has the following potential advantages:

(1)   Assets are separate and identifiable.
(2)   Investment income can be limited to the performance of specific assets.
(3)   If the reinsurer is not licensed or admitted in the ceding company's state of domicile, a properly structured trust or escrow will permit the ceding company to take appropriate reserve credit.
(4)   In the event of recapture, the assets of the trust or escrow account can be used to effect payment, thereby reducing or eliminating dispute over market values.
(5)   A trust is a true transfer of ownership and should be less suspect to both state regulators and the IRS.
(6)   Upon default, the beneficiary has the right to withdraw assets as a secured creditor.   Additionally, the trust or escrow account may be constructed to give certain privi-

leges and rights to each party. In such instances, these are valuable tools providing assurance that the secured party receives its contractual benefits to the extent of the trust assets, not at a reduced value determined by a liquidator.

Disadvantages. Potential disadvantages in the use of a trust include the following:

(1) Use of a trust or escrow account creates additional expense which may or may not be of significance in a given agreement.
(2) A trust or escrow account can result in restrictions on investment management. The degree of control of either party or the investment policy may be negotiable, but unless some real element of management transfer is effected, it may be held that investment risk transfer did not occur.
(3) Transfer of assets into a trust is a transfer of ownership and may necessitate recognition of capital gains and losses for tax purposes, or the recognition of current market values for statutory statement purposes. The agreement should specify which party takes the capital gains or losses.
(4) If a trust is used to transfer ownership of assets, the company giving up the assets will suffer a reduction in the magnitude of assets it reports.
(5) Should the need to reverse the asset transfer occur, returning ownership to the original party, a depreciation in market values could create a surplus strain. This is occasioned because some assets may be carried for statutory purposes at book values in excess of market values. On transfer, new book values are established based on current market values. In some cases, it may be possible to avoid this by having assets returned at book value.

Letters of Credit

When a reinsurer is not licensed or admitted in the ceding company's state of domicile, state insurance departments are reluctant to give annual statement credit for the reserve liability ceded to the reinsurer as that state insurance department does not have the authority to enforce the terms of the contract or supervise the financial operations of the reinsurer. This problem can be avoided through the use of mod-co or a trust. However, as noted earlier, the use of mod-co places the assets outside of the control of the reinsurer. The use of a trust or escrow account may give the reinsurer more control over the assets but administration of a trust or escrow account is more expensive. A letter of credit is another solution.

Most states allow a ceding company to take annual statement credit for the reserve liability ceded to a nonadmitted reinsurer if the reinsurer provides the ceding company with a letter of credit for the amount of the reserves. A letter of credit is obtained from a financial institution and provides that the beneficiary, in this case the ceding company, may draw the funds on demand.

The chief advantage of a letter of credit is that it may be obtained for a nominal fee, often as low as .2% to .3% per year, although in certain situations the fee can exceed 1%. Letters of credit also require very little administration.

The major disadvantage of a letter of credit from a reinsurer's viewpoint is that the ceding company may actually draw down on the letter without warning. In this situation the reinsurer would be required to reimburse the financial institution.

From the ceding company's viewpoint, the major concern regarding letters of credit is its ability to withdraw the funds when actually needed. Most rules covering letters of credit address the specific concerns. These rules are discussed in Chapter 10, Reinsurance Regulations.

The Securities Valuation Office (SVO) of the National Association of Insurance Commissioners (NAIC) is authorized to develop a list of acceptable providers of letters of credit.

Administrative and Functional Considerations | Part Two

6 | The Reinsurance Treaty

Reinsurance agreements are legal contracts between two insurance companies.[1] In the past it was common practice to refer to a "gentlemen's agreement" between the two parties; this circumstance too frequently may have served as an excuse for the principals to ignore the need for proper documentation, relying on mutual integrity and good will to resolve any difficulties or uncertainties. Increasingly, events have proved such reliance to be costly or unwise. Large sums may be involved and questions regarding the original intent of the agreement may arise after one or both of the primary participants have passed from the scene. Today, it is considered good business practice to define the agreement as clearly as possible in the reinsurance treaty and not to rely on the good faith or memories of the individuals involved.

The reinsurance treaty, or contract, is the legal document which sets forth the agreement between the reinsurer and the ceding company. The reinsurance treaty is made up of a number of clauses or articles. These clauses deal with four major areas:

---

[1]See Schibley [13].

(1) Definition of Risks Reinsured
(2) Financial Terms
(3) Administration
(4) Special Provisions

In the case of indemnity reinsurance, the reinsurance treaty is solely between the ceding company and the reinsurer. The treaty does not create any legal relationship between the reinsurer and any of the ceding company's policyholders. In the event of the insolvency of the ceding company, the policyholders are not allowed to bypass the ceding company and deal directly with the reinsurer. The reinsurer is also not a party to any disputes between the ceding company and the policyholders.

An assumption reinsurance treaty transfers the contractual obligations of the ceding company to its policyholders to the assumption reinsurer. The precise nature of the reinsurance arrangement will dictate the provisions of the treaty. In this chapter, most of the provisions described pertain primarily to indemnity reinsurance arrangements.[2]

The common terms of most reinsurance arrangements are discussed in this chapter. For illustration purposes, a sample indemnity reinsurance treaty is provided as Appendix A. The actual language will vary to fit the needs of both parties.

DEFINITION OF RISKS REINSURED

One purpose of the reinsurance treaty is to define the conditions a policy must meet in order to qualify for reinsurance. These conditions vary between automatic and facultative reinsurance.

Automatic Reinsurance Treaty Provisions

An automatic reinsurance treaty sets forth very specific conditions which a policy must meet in order to qualify for reinsurance. Other provisions relate to the placing and timing of the reinsurance. The purposes of these are to facilitate the handling of policies requiring reinsurance and to assure that the reinsurer receives the type and quality of business it anticipated in pricing. These were discussed in some depth in Chapter 2 and are summarized here for reference:

---

[2]Provisions and characteristics appropriate to assumption reinsurance are described in Chapter 16.

Qualifications. The typical conditions which a policy must meet to qualify for automatic reinsurance include the following:

(1) The policy has been underwritten in accordance with agreed upon rules.
(2) The policy has been issued in accordance with normal guidelines.
(3) No facultative submission has been made to any reinsurer.
(4) The insured resides in a designated area.
(5) The ceding company maintains its full retention.
(6) The table rating and issue age fall within predetermined limits.
(7) The amount to be ceded is not less than the specified minimum cession size.
(8) The amount ceded to the reinsurer on all policies inforce in the ceding company does not exceed the binding limit.
(9) The total amount applied for and inforce in all companies does not exceed the jumbo limit.

Allocation among Reinsurers. If the application for insurance meets the conditions and limits for automatic insurance, and the policy is issued, the risk is ceded to the automatic reinsurer. If more than one reinsurer is participating in the automatic reinsurance, the treaty will define the method used to allocate the reinsurance. The common methods of allocation are:

(1) Assigning each reinsurer a portion of the alphabet and ceding by surname.
(2) Giving each reinsurer a stated percentage of each risk.
(3) Giving one reinsurer all cessions up to a certain amount, ceding any excess to a second reinsurer up to another amount, and so on.
(4) Assigning each reinsurer a group of issue ages or years of birth.
(5) Assigning each reinsurer a geographic location.
(6) Assigning the reinsurer by agent or source of business.

Commencement of Liabilities. The treaty defines when the reinsurer's liability begins on any policy reinsured. Under an automatic reinsurance treaty, the reinsurer's liabilities commence simultaneously with those of the ceding company as long as the automatic conditions have been met, even if the reinsurer has not been notified of the cession.

Conditional Receipt. If the application meets the conditions and limits for automatic reinsurance, and if the application included conditional receipt coverage, the automatic reinsurer would be on the risk during the period covered by the conditional receipt, subject to any limitations the reinsurer may place on the coverage in the treaty.

Facultative Reinsurance Treaty Provisions

Most automatic treaties provide for facultative submissions. Some treaties provide only facultative coverage. The purpose of the conditions set forth for facultative reinsurance is to facilitate the handling of those policies which do not qualify for automatic reinsurance or which require special consideration. They also assure that the reinsurer has adequate opportunity to evaluate such risks. These conditions are discussed below.

Qualifications. Any application may be submitted for facultative review. After its underwriting risk analysis, the reinsurer may decline the risk or it may make an offer to the ceding company stating its conditions for accepting the risk. These conditions will usually include:

(1) The underwriting classification.
(2) The amount of the risk the ceding company must retain, if any.
(3) The amount of the risk the reinsurer will accept.

Sometimes, the reinsurer's offer will require the submission of additional information satisfactory to it before coverage can be effected.

Commencement of Liabilities. The treaty defines when the reinsurer's liability begins on any reinsured policy. This reinsurance liability normally begins when the ceding company has met the conditions and accepted the reinsurer's offer. Some treaties provide that the ceding company must accept the offer in writing. The reinsurer may also place a time limit for the ceding company's acceptance. Failure by the ceding company to make such a formal acceptance of the offer within the prescribed time period will relieve the reinsurer of any liability.

Conditional Receipt. Once an application has been submitted for facultative review, it no longer qualifies for automatic coverage. In this case, conditional receipt coverage is lost unless special provision has been made by the automatic or facultative reinsurer.

TERMS AND SPECIFICATIONS

The financial terms and specifications are part of the treaty. These terms include the policy forms, forms of reinsurance, premiums, and allowances.

Policy Forms

The treaty defines the policy forms covered. Some treaties may cover all of the ceding company's policy forms but it is not unusual for a treaty to cover only one policy form. On occasion, a treaty may be drafted to cover a single policy in a special circumstance.

Forms of Reinsurance

The reinsurance treaty specifies whether the policies reinsured under the treaty are reinsured on a coinsurance, mod-co, or YRT basis. If the reinsurance is to be on a YRT basis, the method for determining the net amount at risk will be defined in the treaty.

Any two or even all three plans of reinsurance may be integrated into a single treaty, and the treaty will define when and how each plan is to be applied. The reinsurance treaty may also require that facultative submissions be reinsured on a different basis than the one used for automatic reinsurance.

Coverage on supplemental benefits may be reinsured on a different basis from that used for the basic coverage. The reinsurance of substandard flat extra premiums may be administered in a different form from the basic coverage, usually using generalized allowances.[3]

---

[3]See Chapter 7, Reinsurance Administration.

Premiums and Allowances

If coinsurance or mod-co is involved, the treaty defines the reinsurance premiums and allowances. If YRT reinsurance is involved, the YRT premium rate scale will also be included in the treaty. The terms for reinsuring ancillary benefits, substandard ratings, and riders will be defined in the treaty.

Coinsurance Limit

In a coinsurance or mod-co treaty, the reinsurer may set a coinsurance limit. The amounts reinsured on a single life in excess of this limit are reinsured on a YRT basis. A coinsurance limit is placed because of the reinsurer's own retrocession costs.

ADMINISTRATION

Much of the reinsurance treaty deals with administrative procedures. The type of data needed, the type of administration, and the timing of reports should be specified in the treaty. The standard treaty clauses dealing with administrative matters are discussed below.

Notification

The reinsurer must be notified when a a risk is ceded. The form and timing of the notification depends on the type of administration used: individual cession or self-administration.

Individual Cession. Under an individual cession arrangement, the contract specifies that the ceding company is to deliver a reinsurance cession card[4] to the reinsurer. This card contains the basic information which the reinsurer requires to set up its accounting and valuation records, and provides the reinsurer with the necessary information to search its own records to determine if any portion of its retention on the insured has previously been filled.

Self-Administration. When the ceding company is performing the basic administration of either traditional or financial reinsurance, the ceding company provides the reinsurer with a listing of all

---

[4]*Ibid.*

automatic cessions at predetermined intervals. This listing contains the basic information of the reinsurance cession card, or at least enough data to provide an audit trail and to avoid uncertainty regarding liability. This information may be sent as hard copy or in computer-readable form. The reinsurer reviews information and searches its records to determine if any of the lives on the list have previously been reinsured with it.

Premium Accounting

The reinsurance treaty describes the billing procedures to be used. The procedures will vary between individual cession and self-administration. In either case, the reinsurer retains the right to terminate reinsurance for cessions where the premiums are in default. The reinsurer normally gives the ceding company a 30-day grace period and a 30-day notice of termination. During this 30-day grace period the reinsurer will continue to be liable for claims. The reinsurer will allow the ceding company to reinstate terminated reinsurance within the 60-day period after the effective date of termination if all unpaid reinsurance premiums are paid in full. No evidence of insurability is required. However, the reinsurer is not liable for claims occurring after the termination of the reinsurance policy and prior to reinstatement.

Individual Cession. Most reinsurance treaties specify that the reinsurance premiums are payable on an annual basis regardless of how the insurance premiums are payable to the ceding company. Under an individual cession treaty, the reinsurer sends the ceding company a monthly billing statement listing first year and renewal premiums which are due during that month, less refunds and allowances. If the statement shows that a net reinsurance premium is due the reinsurer, the ceding company must pay this balance within a specified period of time. If the statement shows a balance due the ceding company, the reinsurer must pay the ceding company within a certain period of time.

Self-Administration. Under a self-administered treaty, the ceding company periodically prepares a statement with the same type of information as is normally contained on the individual cession premium billing report. The reinsurance premiums on a self-administered treaty may be payable at specified intervals regardless of the basis of payment of the basic coverage or the premiums may be payable on the same mode as the basic coverage.

In a financial reinsurance arrangement, the reinsurance premiums are normally calculated on the same mode as the ceding company receives them as this greatly reduces the administrative effort required of the ceding company. Reinsurance premium payment is normally on a net basis and enacted on a quarterly or annual basis.

Reductions, Terminations and Changes

This section of the reinsurance treaty outlines administrative procedures in the reapportionment of liabilities should one of the policies reinsured under the agreement be changed from its original terms. In most circumstances, if the amount of insurance is reduced, the amount of the reinsurance is reduced proportionately. If the policy had been reinsured with more than one reinsurer, the amount ceded to each company is reduced in proportion to the original amount ceded. The ceding company is not required to hold more than its original retention on the policy even though it has subsequently raised its retention limit. If the reduction affects more than one cession on the insured, this provision explains how the reduction should be applied to the reinsurance. If the policy reinsured is terminated, the reinsurer's liability is terminated. If another policy on an insured life that is not reinsured or that is reinsured with another company is terminated or reduced, it may result in a reduction in reinsurance on other policies inforce on the same life. Certain treaties require that the ceding company maintain its full retention by recapturing a portion of the reinsurance in the event of the termination or reduction of any policy reducing the amount retained on the life of an insured.

Should the policy be changed, the treaty explains how the changed policy is to be reinsured.[5] The treaty generally specifies that if the policy is continued under another policy form with no new business underwriting, the policy is a continuation and is covered under the treaty under the appropriate point-in-scale rates. If the amount of insurance of the policy is increased or if the original mortality rating is changed, the treaty specifies that normal procedures for new issues be followed.

The treaty also explains how the reinsurer is to be notified of a change. In the case of an individual cession contract, the reinsurer must receive a formal reinsurance cession card with the change. If the treaty is handled on a self administered basis the ceding company must supply the reinsurer periodically with a

---

[5]See Chapter 22, Selected Additional Reinsurance Topics.

listing of all changes containing the appropriate information. This listing must be provided at the intervals agreed upon in the treaty.

Increase in Retention and Recapture

Neither party may unilaterally terminate existing reinsurance under a treaty, but a treaty may be terminated with respect to new business upon proper notification. Many reinsurance treaties provide that if the ceding company increases its retention on risks reinsured under the treaty, the ceding company may, at its option, recapture amounts reinsured under the agreement subject to written notification of the reinsurer and subject to the terms of the recapture clause. Most reinsurance treaties require that a policy must be reinsured for a specified period of time[6] before recapture is allowed. This is designed to allow the reinsurer to recover its acquisition expenses.

The general conditions for recapture permit the ceding company to recapture reinsurance on each life for which it retained its maximum retention limit in effect at the time of the cession. If the policy is reinsured by more than one reinsurer, the reduction in reinsurance may be in proportion to the amount of reinsurance on the life carried by all reinsurers or applied to the top automatic layer first. The ceding company must recapture reinsurance on all like policies; that is, it cannot pick and choose which specific policies it wishes to recapture and which it does not. Policies may be recaptured on the anniversary following the increase in retention provided that the recaptured duration has been attained. Reinsurance cannot be recaptured and then ceded to another company.

Provisions requiring recapture under certain circumstances such as a change in ownership, financial conditions, or upon insolvency were included in some financial reinsurance agreements prior to 1984. However, the Tax Reform Act of 1984 gave the Internal Revenue Service broad powers to reallocate income and liability items under such contracts and very few, if any, contracts written today provide for forced recapture. New York Regulation 102 also limits these provisions.[7]

Reinstatement

If the policy reinsured under the treaty has lapsed for nonpayment of premiums to the ceding company and has subsequently been

---

[6]See Chapter 8, Managing Ceded Reinsurance.

[7]See Chapter 10, Reinsurance Regulations.

reinstated according to the reinstatement rules of the ceding company, the reinsurer generally provides that reinsurance can be reinstated on the policy by payment of all premiums in arrears by the ceding company. This provision reduces administrative work for both parties. However, under certain circumstances involving facultative cessions, the reinsurer may require some evidence of insurability.

Expenses

The reinsurance treaty generally provides that the ceding company is responsible for all expenses in connection with issuing and maintaining the policy. This includes the cost of medical reports and tests which the reinsurer may require on facultative submissions.

Claims

The claim section of the reinsurance treaty outlines the terms and conditions under which the reinsurer is liable for claims incurred under the reinsurance agreement. When a claim is incurred, the ceding company is required to inform the reinsurer within a defined period of time. Normally, if the contestable period of the reinsured policy has expired, and if the ceding company has retained more than 50% of the risk, the reinsurer will abide by the claim as it is settled by the ceding company. When the ceding company requests reimbursements for the claim, it must deliver all papers concerning the claim to the reinsurer.

If the ceding company retained less than 50% of the insurance, some treaties require the ceding company to submit all claim papers to the reinsurer first and await the reinsurer's recommendation on the claim before it settles the claim. To avoid unnecessary delay in payment to the claimant, the treaty may provide that the reinsurer must respond within a limited period of time and, if no response is given, the ceding company may assume that the reinsurer has no objection in settling the claim. Even if the ceding company has full claim settlement authority, it is expected to act in good faith.

If a claim is incurred during the contestable period of the policy, regardless of the amount retained, some reinsurers require the ceding company submit claim papers prior to settling the claim. The ceding company must wait for the reinsurer's response before settling the claim. Again, a time limit is generally placed on the reinsurer's review, but this limit is usually longer than the limit placed on incontestable claims as the questions involved in contestable claims may be more involved.

If the ceding company contests a reinsured claim, and if such contest results in a reduction of its liability, the reinsurer would also share in this reduction in proportion to the amount of reinsurance ceded on the life. If more than one reinsurer is involved, all would share proportionately in relation to the amount of coverage reinsured with each company. However, if a reinsurer declined to participate in the contest of the claim, it would discharge all of its liability by paying the full amount of the reinsurance to the ceding company. Under this circumstance, the reinsurer would not share in any subsequent reduction in the liability. Such an action by a reinsurer is infrequent.

The ceding company is expected to pay all routine expenses in connection with settling claims, including the cost of routine investigation reports, although some reinsurers may pay part of this expense. The reinsurer may share expenses in connection with the settlement of the claim which are not routine. These non-routine expenses would normally be incurred in connection with the contest of a claim, or by a decision on an individual claim. The expenses would be shared in proportion to the reinsurance ceded under the contract. However, in the rare event where the reinsurer has declined to participate in the contest of the claim and has paid the full amount of the reinsurance to the ceding company, the reinsurer would not share in any expenses of the contest.

The treaty typically requires that the ceding company provide timely notice of a claim. This is particularly important in the case of a litigated claim when extra-contractual or punitive damages may be involved. If the notice is late, the reinsurer may deny coverage. Case law has supported this position.

The payment of reinsurance proceeds under a life policy is generally made in a lump sum. The reinsurer normally does not participate in settlement options. However, the reinsurance proceeds for an in-benefit annuity contract or the benefits under a health policy are generally paid as incurred.

In a financial reinsurance agreement, the ceding company generally has much more latitude in settling claims. In most cases claims can be settled without reinsurer review.

SPECIAL PROVISIONS

The remainder of the treaty focuses on problem prevention and solving. These special provisions have evolved over the years in response to the change in the basic nature of reinsurance relationship from that of a longstanding partnership to more of a business relationship.

Oversights, Errors, and Omissions

The oversights, errors, and omissions clause covers unintentional clerical errors and oversights. This clause is unique to reinsurance treaties and minimizes disputes and the need for arbitration or litigation. These oversights and errors most frequently involve the failure of the ceding company to notify the reinsurer of a cession or incorrect entries made in the completion of the cession form.

The clause provides that both companies will be restored to the position they would have occupied if the oversight had not occurred. Some reinsurers require that the oversight be corrected within a reasonable period of time after its discovery.

In the case of the failure of a company to provide the reinsurer with information concerning a cession, the ceding company would be required to pay all reinsurance premiums from the date of the cession. If a claim is incurred, the reinsurer would be expected to reimburse the ceding company for its share of the claim upon the receipt of the back premiums. However, should the oversight involve the reinsurance of a facultative submission which the reinsurer had previously notified the ceding company it would not accept, the reinsurer would deny liability in the event of any claim.

Extra-Contractual Damages

The original concept of the gentlemen's agreement did not anticipate the large awards for extra-contractual or punitive damages which have been incurred in recent years. In some instances, the ceding company perceived that the reinsurer had "deeper pockets" and contended that the reinsurer should cover all costs of extra-contractual damages in excess of the ceding company's retention. Reinsurers have responded by adding provisions to the treaty regarding extra-contractual damages.

The extra-contractual damage clause holds that the reinsurer has no liability for any extra-contractual damages awarded against the ceding company as a result of the acts, omissions, or course of conduct committed by the ceding company in connection with any insurance ceded under the treaty. The reinsurance treaty normally provides that if the reinsurer was in some way a party to the act, omission, or course of conduct which resulted in the award of such damages, it will share a portion of the damages with the ceding company. It is important that the reinsurer not make the ceding company be perceived as its agent in settlement claims; otherwise it may become directly liable to the policyholders.

The amount of payment for extracontractual damages is usually in proportion to the amount of the risk reinsured. However, the amount may not be fixed in advance as the circumstances are difficult to predict and define. As such, the concept of the gentlemen's agreement still comes into play in this situation.

Extra-contractual damages are generally the result of specific actions by one of the parties. Therefore, it may be reasonable for the reinsurer to share in the cost to the extent it participated in the action or the decisions leading to it. On the other hand, if the reinsurer had no participation in the decisions or action, it may be equally reasonable for the reinsurer not to share in the extra expense. It may be difficult to determine the degree to which the reinsurer may have been a party to the act which resulted in the damages. Different reinsurers have different opinions as to the requirements of equity on the decision whether to participate in extracontracual or punitive damages.

Inspection of Records

The reinsurer reserves the right to inspect any of the records of the ceding company which pertain to the reinsurance ceded under the terms of the agreement. As a matter of good business practice, the reinsurer should audit both individual cession and self-administered accounts on a regular basis. Depending on the size of the account and its history, the audit may be conducted annually or less frequently. This audit ensures that cessions have been properly underwritten, recorded, accounted for, and meet the conditions of the treaty. This audit is particularly vital for self-administered accounts as the reinsurer maintains very few records on the policies reinsured.

Arbitration

The arbitration clause exemplifies the gentlemen's agreement concept. In the event that any disagreement or claim arises out of the contract, both parties to the contract agree that such disagreement is to be settled amicably and with good faith. If the parties cannot agree among themselves, these disputes are settled through arbitration rather than litigation in the courts.

The clause generally explains the arbitration procedures. Typically, the treaty will specify many details of the arbitration procedure. Alternatively, some treaties may specify that arbitration will be conducted in accordance with the Commercial Arbitration Rules of the American Arbitration Association which are in effect at the date of the disagreement.

The typical clause calls for three arbitrators who are current or past officers of life insurance companies other than the two parties to the contract. Each party to the contract appoints one arbitrator and the two arbitrators select a third. If one company fails to appoint an arbitrator or if the two arbitrators are unable to agree to a third arbitrator, the treaty will specify a method for selecting the third arbitrator.[8] The arbitrators determines how the expenses are apportioned.

The terms of arbitration clauses vary relative to the guidelines provided for the arbitrators in considering the dispute. Treaties frequently require that the intent of the parties, equity, and normal business practices be considered rather than a strict application of the law. Newer treaties direct that the arbitrators first look to the terms of the treaty and, only if they are unclear, should equity be considered.

The decision of the arbitrators is final and may not be appealed. The appropriate court may be approached to enforce a decision.

Parties to the Agreement

The reinsurance treaty creates a contractual relationship between the reinsurer and the ceding company. The indemnity reinsurance agreement specifies that it does not create any relationship between the reinsurer and the ceding company's policyholders or beneficiaries. This prevents the policyholders from taking action against the reinsurer. The reinsurer normally finds that desirable.

In some states, it has been possible to provide for a direct liability to this policyholder through a "cut-through" clause which

------

[8]In the past, many treaties have specified that in the event the first two arbitrators cannot agree on a third, the President of the American Council of Life Insurance (ACLI) will choose the third one. The ACLI, however, has requested that it not be so named.

provides for direct claim payment in the event of the insolvency of the ceding company. Since this clause may result in some beneficiaries receiving a larger portion of their claims than beneficiaries not covered by the agreement, many states prohibit or limit the use of such a clause.

Insolvency

In order for the ceding company to take financial statement credit for reserves on reinsurance ceded in most states, the reinsurance treaty must contain an insolvency clause which guarantees that reinsurance is payable to the liquidator without decrease or diminution in the event of the insolvency of the ceding company.[9] It normally does not prohibit the reinsurer's right to offset payments by monies owed it.

This clause is necessary because the basic reinsurance agreement provides that the reinsurer is required to pay only those claims which represent actual losses incurred by the ceding company. When an insolvency occurs, the liquidator may be able to pay only a portion of each claim, but the reinsurer should not benefit from a windfall. If the reinsurer has received full payment of premiums, it should pay full benefits.

Offset

The offset clause in most reinsurance treaties provides that mutual debits and credits may be offset against each other, even in the event of the insolvency of one of the parties to the treaty. For example, any reinsurance premiums or other amounts due the reinsurer may be deducted from any amounts owed the ceding company or its successor by the reinsurer. The offset clause is more fully discussed in Chapter 11 dealing with insolvency.

Duration of the Agreement

The duration of agreement clause affirms that the treaty cannot be terminated with respect to the inforce business except by mutual consent. It provides that the reinsurance take effect as of the effective date of the treaty. Following this clause, the treaty is executed by the signatures of officers of both companies.

---

[9]See Chapter 11, Insolvency and Reinsurance, and Chapter 10, Reinsurance Regulations.

PREPARING THE TREATY

The reinsurance treaty is the basic tool available to both parties to the reinsurance agreement for accounting and administrative purposes. As such, the wording should be clear and unambiguous. Those persons drafting the treaty should be familiar with the purpose of the treaty. If a professional reinsurer is involved in the arrangement, the reinsurer generally provides the treaty. In some instances, when a nonprofessional reinsurer is involved, the ceding company may prepare the treaty.

Review

Both parties should carefully review any reinsurance treaty before placing it in effect. The reviewers would normally come from the accounting, actuarial, administrative, and legal areas of the company. The goal of any review is to assure that the treaty accomplishes its purpose, clearly defines the intent of the parties, and does not violate any regulations.

Pre-Approval and Filing

In most states, reinsurance treaties do not need to be approved by the state insurance department. Some states require that treaties be filed and approved prior to execution. Other states require only that a copy of the executed treaty be filed with the department. The insurance department reviews all treaties at the time of the triennial examination.

In some circumstances, a ceding company may seek pre-approval of the treaty before signing it. This is generally done for financial reinsurance agreements or when the company has questions about the treaty's acceptability. The pre-approval process is frequently used for treaties that are attempting to do something new for which there are few precedents to follow.

Standardization of Provisions

Professional reinsurers have constructed treaties with standardized provisions for the ease of their administration. However, provisions of treaties will vary among reinsurers. It is to the ceding company's advantage to standardize provisions among the reinsurers that might be sharing the reinsurance on any given product. For example, it would be useful to have the same claim procedures for all reinsurers. It would also be useful to have the same binding limits, coinsurance limits, jumbo limits, and minimum cessions.

Use of Side Letters

Until recently, side letters were frequently used in conjunction with reinsurance treaties. These side letters spelled out the intent of the treaty. Sometimes, the side letters were the precursor of the treaty. The side letter states the intent to put the treaty into effect as of a certain date. This is done in situations where the companies are not able to draft the treaty before the effective date. In other cases side letters were used to clarify the intent of a reinsurance treaty when the intent was not obvious in the treaty itself. In other cases, side letters were used to circumvent the terms of the main treaty, or to provide additional security to the reinsurer.

The use of side letters is discouraged today. Regulators are interested in clear and unambiguous treaties without a hidden purpose. Many treaties contain a clause which states that the treaty constitutes the entire agreement between the parties. If side letters do exist, the regulators typically require that they be fully disclosed and included in the overall analysis of the treaty.

Industry Practices

While the reinsurance treaty is very important, the common practices of ceding companies and reinsurers are also relevant in administering and interpreting a reinsurance agreement. The typical treaty is more abbreviated than most legal contracts and good faith is assumed of both parties. Common industry practices are assumed or implied; terms and phrases of art are widely used without definition. Any reinsurance agreement should be reviewed with such practices and understandings in mind and any significant deviation from them should be specifically referenced.

Pitfalls

There are many pitfalls in the drafting of a reinsurance treaty. Even the work of professional reinsurers should be reviewed since they may make mistakes. Particular care should be taken when reviewing a treaty prepared by a nonprofessional reinsurer.

The most common mistake made in drafting a treaty is to copy another company's reinsurance treaty. This presupposes that the other company drafted its treaty correctly. This is not always

the case.   Also, if the purposes of the two treaties are not exactly
the same, the new treaty may not accomplish the desired results.
Any company copying another company's reinsurance treaty
should be certain it understands the purpose of both treaties and
carefully review the treaty before finalizing it.

It is also important that the person drafting the reinsurance
treaty understand the rules and regulations governing the conduct
of reinsurance.   If the contract violates these regulations, the
ceding company may not receive reserve credit on its statutory
statement for the reinsurance ceded, or may even increase its total
liability.

7 | Reinsurance Administration

To some degree, reinsurance transactions affect almost every area of the typical life insurance company. Reinsurance influences such diverse functional areas as accounting, actuarial, agency, claims, data processing, investment, legal, policyholder service, underwriting, and executive. Reinsurance administration activities include: drafting treaties, ceding individual policies, making premium payments (net of reinsurance allowances), paying claims and surrender benefits, making policy changes, valuing and opining on policy reserves, and recapturing as the result of an increase in retention.

This chapter explores the basic principles of reinsurance administration, especially as they pertain to proportional reinsurance. Just as treaties vary according to the particular provisions and companies involved, so does the administration. However, the basic functions of treaty negotiation, premium calculation, and claims determination remain for all treaties, even those for nonproportional coverages.

BASIC ADMINISTRATIVE PROCEDURES

The goal of effective reinsurance administration is to see that all policies requiring reinsurance are ceded properly, and that information regarding the policy status and policy values flow on a timely basis between the ceding company and reinsurer.[1] In order to have effective reinsurance administration, one must first understand the basic transactions and the methods available for administering reinsurance.

Reinsurance Transactions

The administrative processing of a typical insurance policy begins with the reception of the application, followed by the underwriting and issue of an individual policy. Throughout the lifetime of most policies, premium and commission accounting and reserve valuations occur on a regular basis. While an insurance policy is inforce, there may be scheduled changes in premiums and benefits or nonscheduled changes in these amounts at the policyholder's request. Depending on the nature of the contract, the policyholder may take out a loan; receive annuity, dividend, or disability benefits; surrender all or a portion of the policy; apply for accelerated benefits; or elect a nonforfeiture status. Eventually, all policies terminate through either death, conversion, maturity, expiration, lapse, or surrender.

Reinsurance transactions tend to mirror the basic transactions affecting the original policy. For example, in a traditional reinsurance arrangement, the reinsurance is ceded at the time of policy issue. Nonscheduled changes in the reinsured policy, such as a change in benefits, change of plan, or the removal of a substandard or smoker rating, normally affects the reinsurance and must be reported to the reinsurer promptly. In some instances, the ceding company can make such noncontractual changes unilaterally without the reinsurer's agreement. In other situations, the reinsurer must give its approval or else it is not bound by the insurer's action. The reinsurer can seldom prohibit a noncontractual policy change, as it is not a party to the contract between the ceding company and the policyholder. However, it can insist that it be kept in the same position as though no change had occurred.

Changes in premium rates affect coinsurance and mod-co. Policy loans or changes in the dividend scale may or may not affect the reinsurance depending on the terms of the reinsurance treaty. Benefit payments will normally result in some sort of reinsurance

---

[1] In this chapter, examples pertain to proportional reinsurance, including financial reinsurance. For a discussion of administration of nonproportional reinsurance, see Chapter 15.

transaction, unless the benefit involved is a disability or annuity benefit reinsured on the basis of a cumulative amount of claims payments. Termination of a policy results in termination of reinsurance ceded on that policy and may affect reinsurance ceded on other policies inforce on the same life. A change to nonforfeiture status also may affect the reinsurance.

Administrative Methods

There are two major methods used to administer reinsurance. The traditional method is known as individual cession administration. Under this form of administration, the ceding company and reinsurer both maintain individual records for each policy ceded and the reinsurer provides the ceding company with the premium, allowance, and reserve reports. Today, the reinsurer's records are usually kept on a computer; the ceding company's records may be on a computer data base or on an index card system.

The second type of administration is called self-administration. This may also be called "bulk" or "bordereaux." Under this type of administrative arrangement, the ceding company maintains individual records of each policy, but the reinsurer does not. The reinsurer relies on the ceding company to provide it with all information necessary for processing the reinsurance.

CEDING COMPANY ADMINISTRATION

Efficient ceding company administration requires that employees in all areas understand their responsibilities in the administrative process and the requirements of the each reinsurer. These requirements vary between individual cession administration and self-administration.

Functional Responsibilities

In general, the insurance company functional unit involved in a particular transaction with the individual policy is also responsible for reporting the companion reinsurance transaction to the reinsurer.[2] The exception to this is the company that has such a

---

[2]Actually, in many companies the administration of reinsurance falls in the actuarial department. In some, especially those companies too small to have an actuarial department, reinsurance is administered by the underwriting department.

large volume of insurance ceded that it can justify having a special reinsurance department to handle the administration. Some of the reinsurance duties of the various functional areas are discussed below.

The underwriting department has primary responsibility for seeking facultative reinsurance. The underwriter decides when an application should be submitted for facultative review and chooses the reinsurer with which the cession is to be placed. This includes both facultative policies which do not qualify for automatic reinsurance and those which otherwise would be automatic. The underwriting department may have input in choosing automatic reinsurers as the choice may affect its facultative arrangements.

The issue department is involved in the actual cession of reinsurance on individual policies. Employees in this area must be familiar with the terms and conditions of each treaty and with the reinsurance arrangement for each policy form. Under a traditional individual cession treaty, the issue department fills out the cession card and forwards it to the reinsurer. In a self-administered situation, it does not fill out the individual cession card but, depending on the system design, it may be involved in some manner in the processing of the cession. With either type of administration, it is important for the ceding company to forward cession information on a timely basis so that the reinsurer can process retrocessions, where necessary.

The accounting department typically handles direct premium and commission payments as well as the accounting for reinsurance premiums and allowances and for any reinsured benefit payments. The accounting department also prepares financial statements integrating the reinsurance transactions. It is involved in both individual cession and self-administered reinsurance.

The actuarial department normally handles the solicitation of reinsurance proposals, evaluates reinsurance costs, and may choose the reinsurers. The actuarial department is also responsible for reserve valuation. It performs this function for both individual cession and self-administered contracts.

The claim department is responsible for investigating claims and notifying the reinsurer of any reinsured claims. Depending on the terms of the particular agreement, the claim department may be able to settle claims without the reinsurer's recommendation or approval, or it may be required to submit claim papers to the reinsurer for review prior to payment of the claim.

The data processing department is involved in the creation of the reinsurance database either for internal use for individual cession reinsurance or for the administration of a self-administered contract. It works with the other areas to produce the reports necessary to track the experience of the reinsured business and is involved when a new product, having special reinsurance processing needs, is developed.

The agency department may become involved in choosing the reinsurer, particularly if it believes that the company should have a reinsurance relationship with a particular company for agent morale. The agency department generally is concerned with the reinsurer's product or underwriting reputation.

The executive area may become involved in making the decision to seek a special reinsurance arrangement or in selecting reinsurers. Generally, the executive area is concerned with the reinsurer's reputation and any longstanding relationship with a reinsurer.

The primary reinsurance function of the investment department involves identifying and transferring assets, if necessary, or coordinating investment policy with the reinsurer in financial reinsurance transactions. In a traditional reinsurance arrangement, the investment department may be involved with products such as annuities which feature a large investment element. These products require a higher-than-average rate of return for competitive purposes and the investment policy must be coordinated with the reinsurer. Reinsurance payments may have a significant effect on cash flow.

The legal department is concerned with the treaty terms. It may review the treaty prior to finalization and advise in the case of ambiguities in the treaty language or in disputes and assist in drafting specific language for unique provisions. The legal department should also be aware of any unusual treaty provisions which may be required or prohibited by certain state insurance departments.

The policyholder service department notifies the reinsurer of any policy changes which affect reinsurance. Under individual cession reinsurance administration, the policyholder service area fills out a form similar to the cession card notifying the reinsurer of the change in reinsured policy. Its responsibility in the self-administration situation will vary with the type of administrative system.

Individual Cession Administration

Individual cession administration has been in use since the beginning of reinsurance. Procedures for ceding, reporting, and record keeping are well-defined with only slight variations among reinsurers.

Individual Cession Card. When reinsurance is ceded on an individual cession basis, the ceding company notifies the reinsurer by filling out an individual cession card. This card contains the policyholder's name, date of birth, sex, plan of insurance, amount of insurance, amount reinsured, policy or cession number, premium rating class, premium, smoker status, riders, and other information necessary for the reinsurer to set up its computer records.

Records and Reports. The ceding company's reinsurance records may consist of only a copy of the cession card or it may have its reinsurance records on a computer system. Under an individual cession arrangement, the reinsurer sends the ceding company a monthly billing report listing all policies with anniversaries falling within the month. This report provides sufficient information to enable the ceding company to trace the policy on its records. The report also lists all changes, such as deaths, surrenders, increases or decreases in amount of premium, reported since the last monthly report. The report shows the reinsurance premium due less any allowances.

The ceding company checks the reinsurer's report against its records to determine if the records are in agreement. Once the monthly premium report has been checked, it is normally sent to the accounting department for processing of the payment.

At least annually, the reinsurer provides the ceding company with the listing of all inforce policies detailing the reserve information necessary for the company to complete its statutory financial statements. The ceding company verifies these listings to determine that all cessions have been properly recorded. The actuarial department reviews the reserves for reasonableness. For interim financial statements, the ceding company generally uses other methods of producing statutory reserves.

Because there may be items in transit or because the reinsurer may use a different valuation basis for its own purposes, it may be appropriate for the ceding company to make its own reinsurance reserve calculations for statutory purposes.[3] This calculation is difficult if the necessary reinsurance information is not contained in the basic policy records on a computer file. Companies which prepare GAAP financial statements must make provision to adjust the GAAP values to reflect reinsurance ceded.[4] This function usually falls to the actuarial department.

For a ceding company with a moderate amount of reinsurance business, individual cession administration may be the most economical as it is usually less expensive to verify reports than to produce reports to the reinsurer's specifications. Now that it is possible to transfer reinsurance data electronically via disk, tape, or direct computer interface, individual cession reinsurance may become even more economical.

Self-administration

Individual cession administration was created before modern data processing equipment and removed the burden of detailed reinsurance administration from the ceding company. As modern data processing systems were developed for insurance administration, reinsurance was frequently neglected. Self-administration shifts the burden back to the ceding company and requires a complex data processing system.

Considerations. The ceding company will typically use the individual cession method for traditional reinsurance and do its own administration for financial reinsurance. However, in certain circumstances, the ceding company may choose to self-administer traditional reinsurance. Reasons why the ceding company may chose to self-administer the business include:

(1) The volume involved may be so great as to make it more economical for the ceding company to administer the business using a computer system rather than to prepare individual cession forms.

(2) The ceding company may be involved in a joint venture with the reinsurer using a quota share arrangement which

---

[3]For a more thorough discussion of valuation considerations, see Chapter 12, Statutory Accounting for Reinsurance.

[4]For a discussion of GAAP treatment for reinsurance ceded, see Chapter 13, GAAP Accounting for Reinsurance.

is most easily administered by the ceding company. Frequently, in this situation, the amounts of risk per life are small, so the reinsurer will not need to retrocede any risks, thus eliminating one reason for individual insured information.

(3)   The product reinsured may necessitate special calculations that the reinsurer normally is not prepared to make. This would include interest sensitive products where the ceding company desires that the net amount at risk be calculated monthly for reinsurance premium and death benefit purposes.

(4)   The ceding company may believe that it can administer the reinsurance more economically than the reinsurer and that the reinsurer will pass the cost savings on to the ceding company in the form of lower reinsurance costs.

Reporting. In a self-administered system, the ceding company is responsible for providing the reinsurer with all of the information regarding the ceded policies. This reinsurance information usually is communicated on paper, but it can be communicated with the use of disks, tapes, or direct interfacing between computers. The ceding company must provide the reinsurer with premium reports, policy change reports, and claim information, as well as the information necessary to complete its annual statement.

There are no standardized procedures for transferring this information between the ceding company and the reinsurer. The details of this information transfer are usually subject to negotiation. Some of the considerations include the frequency and timing of the reports, the physical form of the report, and the format of the reports. Of course, computer-to-computer methods require careful coordination.[5]

The reinsurer may require that the reports be received monthly, although in some instances, quarterly reporting is permitted. In most cases, the reinsurer requires that the reports be received in time for its normal financial reporting cycles, although on occasion, a reinsurer may be willing to accept reports in arrears.

---

[5]Such methods are fairly new and standards are emerging. Basically, these techniques involve the ceding company producing an "electronic individual cession card" for both new business and changes which the reinsurer can use with manual intervention.

The amount of detail required in the reports is subject to negotiation. Typically, detailed information on an individual policy level is required for new business, changes, and claims. The reinsurer may require that detailed reserve reports be provided at least on an annual basis. In any event, the ceding company must maintain sufficient policy detail information in its office for audit purposes. When detail is required, the reports normally contain the policy number or cession number, insured's name, sex, date of birth, issue age, policy duration, policy date, plan name or plan code, underwriting or premium class, amount issued, amount reinsured, and premium.

The type of transaction must be identified. The most common transactions include the payment of first year and renewal premiums, including reinsurance premiums and allowances due, reported separately for life, ADB and waiver of premium. There would also be an indicator for policy changes. Transactions which must be documented include not taken, lapse, surrender, reinstatement, conversion, increase or decrease in face amount, recapture, death, expiration, and other policy changes. The transaction date must be included. If facultative reinsurance is being ceded on a self-administered basis, a facultative indicator is necessary.

Systems Design. Entering into a self-administered reinsurance arrangement, other than on a pure quota share basis, is not a step to be taken lightly by the ceding company. Any sort of reinsurance system requires a significant amount of systems development. If the ceding company cannot devote the time and the money to building this system, it should not enter into such an arrangement.

In designing the system, it should be made as flexible as possible in order to adapt to new products. The systems design should allow for coinsurance, mod-co and YRT rates; variations in the treatment of smokers and nonsmokers as well as males, females, and unisex; and different retention limits by plan or policy. Special consideration should be given to the treatment of accidental death benefit and waiver of premium riders, other riders, automatic and facultative cessions, replacements and continuations, recapture, multiple policies on the same life, and multiple reinsurers on the same policy.

When reinsurance is ceded under a quota share arrangement, for either traditional or financial reinsurance, the reporting is not normally as complex.[6]   Quota share arrangements are used to keep things simple.   Percentages are applied to the pertinent amounts such as premiums, claims, reserves, and other benefits.   In the case of financial reinsurance, a special adjustment for reinsurance already in force may be required.   The ceding company is still required to provide all of the necessary information for the reinsurer to complete its financial statements and usually produces a special report of all ceded policies annually.

Facultative Cessions.   Facultative cessions often create special problems in a self-administered reinsurance arrangement.   The ceding company may keep a reduced or no retention on facultative submissions.   This may require special handling in the administrative system.   If the reinsurance is to be handled through the self-administered system, the company may have to require that facultative business be placed only with those reinsurers that are in the automatic arrangement to minimize administrative problems. This may limit the ceding company's ability to place certain substandard policies at a competitive rate.

The reinsurer requires special notification of facultative cessions.   This would normally be handled outside of the automated system.   If the automatic reinsurance is ceded on a pool basis with each reinsurer receiving a percentage of each policy ceded, facultative policies must be handled separately since these are not normally shared.   The reinsurer also may charge different premiums or grant different allowances for policies reinsured on a facultative basis, again complicating systems development.   For these reasons, it is not uncommon for facultative policies to be handled on an individual cession basis.

Appendix B contains the Guidelines for Reporting Self-administered Reinsurance developed by the Reinsurance Administration Committee of the Reinsurance Section of the Society of Actuaries.   These guidelines provide more detail on the considerations in self-administered reporting and illustrate sample report formats.

---

[6]For certain situations even the reporting for quota sharing arrangements can become somewhat complex.   For example, if the ceding company's share exceeds its retention, individual excess reinsurance will be needed.   Facultative coverage always requires special notices.

Choice of Method

Before deciding to enter into a self-administration arrangement with a reinsurer, the ceding company must look at the system, the costs, the anticipated volume, and its reasons for pursuing self-administration. It must make an honest estimate of the costs and of the anticipated reinsured volume to see if the volume will justify the costs of the administrative system.

If, for example, the ceding company's only purpose for entering the self-administered reinsurance arrangement on a universal life product is to calculate the reinsurance premiums on a monthly basis to match the monthly changes in the net amount of risk, it may find that a mutually agreed upon approximation procedure will produce satisfactory results on an individual cession method for far less cost.

The ceding company must also make a realistic estimate of the time required to complete the system. More than one insurance company has committed to producing monthly reports on a self-administered basis and found itself manually processing these reports each month for a year or more after the first cession was made.

REINSURER ADMINISTRATION

The reinsurer has many of the same basic functions as the ceding company. The major difference between the two is in the market: the ceding company markets to individuals and corporations while the reinsurer markets to insurance companies.

Functional Responsibilities

Almost every unit in a professional reinsurance company has a dual function. The first function is its primary purpose, such as accounting, pricing, and underwriting. The second function is marketing assistance.

Basic Functions. A professional reinsurer's functional organization is much like that of a direct writing insurance company. Its various functional personnel perform much the same duties as their ceding company counterparts.

One major difference in the work performed by a reinsurer occurs because of the volume and complexity of the transactions involved. For example, the reinsurance underwriter will review far more complex cases than his ceding company counterpart and tends to become more expert.

The reinsurance pricing actuary prices hundreds of products in a given year, far more than his direct counterpart. He is able to do so because he works within the confines of the final product design and does not have the complex implementation or policy form problems faced by a ceding company actuary.

The reinsurance valuation actuary will normally have far more plans to value than the typical ceding company valuation actuary. This results in an enormous valuation file.

Much time is spent creating and maintaining valuation records. The reinsurance valuation actuary faces particularly complex problems in preparing GAAP reserves for reinsurance assumed. The major problem occurs with the self-administered business where the valuation actuary has very little data on which to base his calculations.[7]

The reinsurance claims department is not responsible for the administrative aspects of a claim such as checking wills and beneficiaries or building the claim file. However, reinsured claims tend to be large and are often very complex.

Reinsured claims often require extensive review and discussion with the ceding company claims personnel. Sometimes, legal counsel is required. Even if the direct company is able to settle its claims without reference to the reinsurer, the reinsurer is often consulted on large and complicated claims as it may have more experience in these unusual circumstances.

Since a reinsurer does not deal directly with policyholders as a ceding insurance company does, the reinsurer does not have a policyholder service department as such. It does, however, have an administrative department dedicated to creating new cessions and making policy changes. This department interfaces with the ceding company's policyholder service department. Service to the reinsurer's policyholders, the ceding companies, is not centralized in any one department but is shared among all the departments.

The reinsurer may have a service department which responds to special requests from its clients or prospects. Such a department may coordinate visits to the reinsurer by reinsurance client or prospective client staff or prepare information for distribution.

---

[7]Some of these problems are discussed in Chapter 13, GAAP Accounting for Reinsurance.

A reinsurance company is responsible not only for preparing its own financial reports, but it must also provide premium and allowance reports for its client companies and check client reports. It prepares special financial reports for treaties which include experience refund provisions. Premium tax reimbursement calculations and claim accounting also need to be performed.

Marketing. The second major difference between the functions of a reinsurer's personnel and those of the ceding company occurs because of the differences in the clients and the products. The ceding company has two clients: the agent and the policyholder. The reinsurer has only one client: the ceding company. The ceding company must service both the agent and the policyholder.

Servicing agents includes paying commissions, issuing policies promptly, and developing new products for the agents to sell. Servicing the policyholder involves issuing the policies, providing information on policy values, making policy changes, and paying policy benefits.

The reinsurer performs the same functions, but services only the ceding company. This involves developing reinsurance products, billing premiums, paying allowances, and paying reinsurance benefits. It also includes answering accounting questions, providing assistance in systems development, providing underwriting services, and providing assistance in product development.

A ceding insurance company may have an extensive portfolio of products to sell with several whole life, interest sensitive whole life, term, annuity, disability, and medical policies. The reinsurer has five generalized products: coinsurance, mortality risk reinsurance, health reinsurance, financial reinsurance, and underwriting expertise. It uses these products to cover the range of the ceding company's portfolio and its needs.

A consequence of this difference is that the reinsurer has a different marketing organization than a direct writing company. A reinsurer does not employ commissioned agents.[8] Instead, the reinsurer uses sales representatives who are compensated through a

---

[8]Most life reinsurance, and much of health reinsurance, is conducted through sales representatives who work for one reinsurer. Most property and casualty reinsurance, as well as many non-proportional life and health reinsurance agreements, are negotiated through reinsurance brokers who do not represent a single company but who purport to search the market for the best quotes.

salary and incentive bonus package.   Because the reinsurance
marketplace is relatively small in comparison to the direct
insurance marketplace, the reinsurer employs only a few sales
representatives. Typically, the number of sales representatives for
a single reinsurer would range from about four to twelve.

The reinsurance client is very sophisticated and the
reinsurance sales representative must deal with the key decision
makers, usually the actuary, the underwriters, and at times, the
accounting, legal, and agency department managers as well as the
chief executive officer.   Because of this, the reinsurance sales
representative should have a strong knowledge of insurance
products as well as general knowledge of insurance regulation,
taxation, administration, and underwriting. Frequently, the sales
representative will take a more technically qualified individual, such
as an underwriter or an actuary, on a call to discuss specific
matters.

Sales representatives are usually assigned to a specific
geographic area and call on clients and prospects in that area.
During the course of the reinsurance representative's call on a
client, he may have to discuss a variety of subjects.   When the
insurance company wants a reinsurance proposal, the sales
representative obtains the information necessary for the reinsurance pricing actuary to prepare the proposal.   The representative
also gathers other pertinent information, such as proposed administrative procedures or changes in marketing.

While a reinsurer may have only a handful of representatives calling on clients on a regular basis, the reinsurer's total sales
and service team is much larger.   This team may include
accountants, actuaries, administrators, and data processing and
underwriting personnel who may be called upon in specific sales
situations. In a direct sales situation, only the underwriter might
have contact with the agents or applicants on any regular basis. It
would be very rare for an accountant, actuary, or data processing
staff member to speak to an individual applicant or policyholder.
However, because of the nature of the reinsurance client and
product, it is not uncommon for any of these specialists to be
involved with the ceding company on a regular basis.

The reinsurance accountant is most likely to become
involved in the sale of financial reinsurance or a self-administered
program.   The accountant would work with the reinsurance
actuary to explain the reporting mechanisms involved in the
contract to the ceding company's accountant and actuary.   The

accountant might also be involved with the reinsurance administrator to explain the reinsurer's reporting requirements for self-administration to the ceding company. At any time during the life of a self-administered arrangement, the accountant may be in contact with his ceding company counterpart to answer questions or obtain information.

The reinsurance actuaries are involved in preparing proposals for any of the traditional reinsurance products and for financial reinsurance. In pricing a traditional reinsurance product, the actuary needs to understand the direct product and the assumptions used to develop it. In some instances the material given to the sales representative may be incomplete or unclear. In this situation the actuary may have to contact his ceding company counterpart. In some circumstances, the actuary may be involved by the sales representative early in the product development process to advise the ceding company actuary on product trends, experience, pricing assumptions, and the regulatory and tax aspects of the product involved.

In a financial reinsurance sales situation, the reinsurance actuary usually develops earnings projections. In order to prepare these projections, the reinsurance actuary needs the product features of the plans involved and the experience of the block. The actuary may be called upon to present the projections to the ceding company in order to explain how the proposed reinsurance operates.

Data processing personnel are sometimes involved in self-administered arrangements. If the ceding company is embarking on its first attempt at designing a reinsurance administration system, the reinsurer's data processing personnel may play an important advisory role during the design and implementation of the administrative system. In a traditional reinsurance sales situation, the data processing people may be called upon occasionally to discuss systems modifications necessary for unique product design features.

The reinsurance underwriter plays the major role in marketing the underwriting services of the reinsurer. The reinsurance underwriter may have almost daily contact with some of the clients, and a relationship built between the underwriters may be vital to the success of a reinsurance relationship. The success or failure of the underwriting service affects the success of the reinsurance program.

The successful reinsurer has to offer competitive products and service to its clients. Service crosses all areas of the company. To be effective, the reinsurer should have knowledgeable people in all positions that deal with the clients. Because there is relatively little product differentiation, the successful reinsurer must have a competitive price, provide good service, and be flexible and innovative in its approach.

Individual Cession Administration

Under an individual cession reinsurance arrangement, the reinsurer is notified of an automatic cession when it receives the individual cession card from the ceding company. This card is sent to the reinsurer's administrative department which is responsible for keying the data contained on the card into the reinsurance administration system. This system is similar to the administration systems of most direct writing companies. It will contain all of the pertinent information necessary to administer and value the policy such as plan of insurance, plan of reinsurance, and premium and allowance schedules.

When an individual cession card is received, the reinsurer searches or indexes its inforce file for other reinsurance on the policyholder. If any reinsurance inforce combined with the new cession causes the total amount to go over the reinsurer's retention, the reinsurer retrocedes the excess.

Retrocessions are usually handled under an automatic retrocession arrangement, but large amounts may require individual underwriting and acceptance by the retrocessionaire.

The reinsurance change department receives notification of all nonscheduled changes in reinsured policies. It updates the individual policy records to reflect the current status of the reinsured policy.

Each month, the reinsurer sends each ceding company a billing report listing all policies with anniversaries falling within that month. The report shows the reinsurance premium due as well as the allowance. This report also shows all the changes reported to the reinsurer. Sometimes, the changes result in a premium refund to the ceding company. The ceding company then remits the reinsurance premium due net of refund and allowances.

At least annually, the reinsurer provides the ceding company with a reserve report listing all inforce policies. This report provides the ceding company with all the pertinent information necessary for it to identify the policies on its records. This report also includes the statutory policy reserves for the ceding company's annual statement.

Annually, usually shortly after the close of the calendar year, the reinsurer prepares a premium tax reimbursement report for each treaty which provides for this allowance. A check is then sent to the ceding company along with the report.

Also, about this same time of year, the reinsurer prepares experience refund reports for all treaties which include that provision for distribution to clients. Checks are included for those clients qualifying for experience refunds.

Self-administration

When self-administration became popular in the 1980's, reinsurers and ceding companies entered into these arrangements somewhat blindly with the hope that the arrangement would be beneficial to both parties. This did not always prove to be the case. Many of the problems encountered could have been avoided by a more thorough appraisal of the factors involved.

Considerations. Before entering into a self-administered arrangement with any company, the reinsurer must consider the following:

(1) The ceding company's willingness and ability to produce the necessary reports on a timely and accurate basis.
(2) The ceding company's likelihood of producing a volume of business sufficient to justify the expenses involved in its administration.
(3) Its ability to verify and certify the policy reserves.
(4) Its GAAP reporting requirements.
(5) Its ability to produce the necessary experience studies.
(6) Its ability to audit these accounts on a timely basis.

The reinsurer must accurately judge the ceding company's ability to produce the necessary reports. If the ceding company must go for several months on a manual basis before the system is complete, both companies will suffer. If the information is not accurate or is not received on a timely basis, self-administration may be more expensive for the reinsurer than individual cession administration would have been.

When an insurance company prepares its statutory annual statement, the actuary must provide an actuarial opinion stating that, among other things, the reserves are computed in accordance with commonly accepted actuarial standards and make a good and sufficient provision for all unmatured obligations of the policies. It is, of course, impossible to opine on reserves that are supplied on a "blind" basis, that is, with no individual policy identification. Even if reserves are provided on a policy level basis, it will be difficult to form an opinion on reserves if sufficient policy detail is not provided.

One option available to the reinsurer is for the ceding company's actuary to provide an actuarial opinion similar to that provided for the statutory annual statement, limited to the reserves on the policies ceded to the reinsurer and for the reinsurer's actuary to place reliance upon this opinion when rendering his. While there are no guidelines as yet regarding actuarial opinions for reserve items prepared by the ceding company, as self-administered arrangements become more common and as regulators take more interest in reinsurance practices, such opinions should become more common.

For the reinsurers that prepare GAAP financials, self-administered reinsurance creates a whole new set of problems. It is almost impossible to transform a single statutory reserve amount total to the corresponding GAAP benefit reserve total, let alone develop the corresponding expense reserve or deferred acquisition cost asset. In order to calculate GAAP benefit and expense reserves, a breakdown of inforce by age and duration is needed. The reinsurer may ask the ceding company to provide this breakdown or it may prepare this from a computer file provided by the ceding company. In either case, a good deal of work may be involved, diminishing the cost benefits of self-administration.

From the reinsurer's point of view, a further drawback of self-administered treaties is that it looses valuable data for statistical studies. Experience studies enable the reinsurer to monitor its business and establish pricing assumptions. In the case of self-administered reinsurance, the reinsurer must either look to the ceding company to prepare the experience studies or obtain the data from the ceding company in a form compatible with its computer system. As a minimum, it must receive the data in a form which is understandable and useful for analysis. As an alternative, the reinsurer may opt to view experience on a treaty level basis only, foregoing lower level detail entirely.

The growing needs for audits and their associated costs, together with the increasing demand for valuation and experience data, has eliminated much of the anticipated cost advantages from self-administration. Many reinsurers now have full audit teams, and auditing has become an important part of the reinsurance process.

Reporting. It is not always easy for the ceding company to produce timely and accurate reinsurance reports providing the necessary information. In the negotiation process, the reinsurer, generally being the most knowledgeable about such matters and having an overriding interest in receiving this information, must take the initiative in the negotiations and very clearly state its needs. This should include the nature and the format of the reports as well as the timing. Samples of reports and written specifications should be presented early in the process. The reinsurer would, as much as possible, like to standardize reports from clients to alleviate problems for its personnel. This is not always possible, particularly if the reinsurer is involved in a pool with other reinsurers.

In a self-administered reinsurance situation, the reinsurer does not receive individual cession cards. In the place of these cards, it receives a listing of all policies issued within a given time period, commonly 30 to 45 days. This listing will provide all the information contained on the reinsurance cession card. The reinsurer usually checks all new issues against its current inforce file to ascertain that it has no other insurance inforce. If it has already filled all or part of its retention on a given insured, it must retrocede any portions of the policy in excess of its retention.

Since the purpose of self-administered reinsurance is to lower the reinsurer's administrative costs, the reinsurer will not, as a rule, create an individual policy record for each policy on the listing. Instead, these listings are maintained on file for future reference. In fact, if the amounts involved are low, the reinsurer may not even index the amounts, thus accepting that it will occasionally be over its retention on some lives.

The reinsurer also receives at the same interval a report listing of all changes since the prior report. This report contains the policy detail for each policy which has undergone a change. The reinsurer should be able to verify changes by tracing the policies back through the prior listings. This verification may be done on a random basis and is particularly important in case of any benefit payments. The report also contains a recap of all transactions, called a policy exhibit or reconciliation, showing the beginning balance, increases and decreases, and an ending insurance balance. The beginning balance must match the ending balance from the previous month. Any discrepancies are reported to the ceding company.

The ceding company also produces a billing report on the same frequency, incorporating the issues and changes.

Financial reinsurance agreements almost always are administered by the ceding company. Because these arrangements usually involve a quota-share method of ceding reinsurance, administration is greatly simplified since the ceding company need only to apply a common percentage to all policy values.

Self-administration became popular in the traditional reinsurance markets with the advent of interest sensitive whole life products. Many ceding companies were concerned that the net amount of risk could change dramatically from period to period and desired a monthly calculation of reinsurance premiums in order to reflect any changes in the net amount of risk. It was not feasible for reinsurers to perform a monthly calculation of the fund of the universal life product, so that task fell on the ceding company.

One premise behind the idea of self-administration is that the reinsurer's administrative costs will be decreased because it will not have to make entries into its administrative system and produce monthly reports or valuations. The reinsurer often priced these products with a lower expense assumption to reflect this cost savings, thereby returning the savings in the form of increased allowances or decreased reinsurance premiums. This made the reinsurer more competitive in the marketplace. In order to achieve the pricing results, it is important that the reinsurer realizes this cost savings. This is not always the case.

Systems Design. Because building a system to administer reinsurance is a large undertaking for any company, the reinsurer may be called upon to provide advice in the systems design. The reinsurer may help the ceding company evaluate its current capabilities, and it may help the ceding company with its cost estimates for systems development. The reinsurer should help the ceding company evaluate its needs and, if the anticipated volume of reinsurance does not justify the cost of a system, the reinsurer should suggest alternatives to self-administered reinsurance. For example, on an interest-sensitive life product, the companies may agree to the use of projected net amounts at risk for a period of three to five years under an individual cession arrangement unless actual values vary by more than 10% from those anticipated in a given year. If such a variation occurs, a new set of values will be developed for use for a new period.

Criteria for Self-administration. It is beneficial to both the reinsurer and the ceding company if the reinsurer develops criteria for self-administration. As part of any self-administration proposal, the reinsurer should clearly describe its reporting requirements. These reporting requirements cover premium and allowance accounting, the information necessary for the reinsurer to validate reserves for statutory statement purposes and to calculate satisfactory GAAP reserves, and to perform experience studies.

Auditing

Auditing is an important concern of reinsurers. This is a very time consuming process and is needed to ensure that all business is being properly ceded and administered. It is desirable to audit the ceding company's records every two to three years at the ceding company's home office.

The general purpose of any reinsurance audit is to satisfy the reinsurer that it is receiving all the business it is entitled to receive under the terms of the treaty, and that it is receiving only that business. Obviously, when pricing a reinsurance treaty the reinsurer anticipated a certain degree of profit, so it is important to the reinsurer that all eligible policies are being ceded to it. Policies which are being incorrectly ceded to it may represent lost profits to the proper reinsurer. If they result from errors in issue or underwriting procedures, they may not meet the requirements for reinsurance anywhere and are likely to have very poor experience. This part of the audit generally is done by randomly selecting policies and reviewing the individual policy files.

The reinsurer is also interested in confirming that all premiums, allowances, and reserves are being calculated correctly. This is verified by randomly selecting policies and checking the values produced by the ceding company's administrative system. The reinsurer also reviews all benefit payments, particularly claims, to make sure that proper procedures have been followed.

During the course of an audit, the reinsurer verifies that the ceding company has sufficient controls in its administrative processing to ensure that its procedures are being followed correctly. It assures itself of agreement with the ceding company regarding the terms and conditions of the treaty. To this end, it checks that the ceding company's treaty is up-to-date and consistent with its own files.

The reinsurer is interested in reviewing underwriting practices. It verifies that the proper new business underwriting rules are followed at all times and reviews rules concerning smoker status and conditional receipts. It also reviews rules used for continuations, changes, re-entries, reinstatements, and conversions.

The reinsurer's audit team may consist of some combination of an accountant, an actuary, an administrator, an underwriter, and a claims examiner. The exact composition of the team will vary from client to client because of different needs and problems. An audit requires a great deal of preparation. Before going to the client's office, the audit team should be thoroughly familiar with the relevant treaties and the existing reinsurance reports. It may wish to review the systems documentation before the actual audit begins. Based on this information, the audit team develops a plan for proceeding with the audit. When the audit is completed, a report is written for the reinsurer's management. Depending on the nature of the findings, all or portions of the report may be discussed with the ceding company's management.

8 | Managing Ceded Reinsurance

Ceded reinsurance can have a significant effect on the operations and financial results of a life insurance company. Most companies will have several reinsurance agreements in force at any time, using a number of different reinsurers to cover a wide variety of products. Since the early 1980's, each major new product usually has its own special reinsurance arrangements.

An insurance company must manage this array of ceded reinsurance just as it manages its direct insurance operations, with attention to both proper administration and monitoring of results. This chapter discusses the evaluation of new and existing reinsurance programs for automatic, facultative, and financial reinsurance.

RETENTION LIMITS

One of the key factors in any automatic reinsurance program is the retention limits. Each product line has its own retention limits: ordinary life, group life, group health, annuity, disability, and medical. Sometimes, a company has different retention limits for different products within a product line. Frequently a company will vary retention limits by issue age or underwriting classification.

Some companies allow each line to maintain independent retentions, but most establish a combined or company retention. In this instance, a separate limit is established for coverage in all lines where the combined retention is less than the sum of that of all the lines. For example, a company may have a $500,000 limit each for individual life insurance and group life insurance, but never to exceed $750,000 in total. If the company already had $350,000 of retention on an insured under a group policy, it would retain only $400,000 on an individual policy issued on the same life, not $500,000.

The key purpose of the retention limit is to allow the insurance company to manage fluctuations in earnings caused by fluctuations in claims. The retention limits of the company will normally increase as the size of a company increases, because the degree of fluctuation in the expected amount of claims reduces as the amount of inforce increases.

The retention limit also grows as the company's surplus grows, since the company is better able to withstand larger fluctuations in experience.

Most insurance companies wish to maintain a retention limit which balances the need for protection from adverse claim fluctuations against lower reinsurance costs and increased retained earnings. Periodically, a growing insurance company will review its retention limits in terms of reinsurance costs and claim fluctuation protection. There are four basic approaches which a company may use to evaluate its retention limit:

(1) Ratio method
(2) Model office projection
(3) Rosenthal's approximation
(4) Pentikäinen's approach

Ratio Method

The ratio method[1] is perhaps the most common and certainly the easiest and most practical method to use in evaluating a retention limit increase. In effect, this method assumes that, historically, the company has been satisfied with the results of its retention practices.

As a practical matter, the first step in evaluating a retention limit increase is to examine the changes in the ratios of

---

[1]This is also known as the "quick and dirty" method.

the retention limit to surplus, the retention limit to the amount of insurance inforce, the retention limit to premiums, the retention limit to assets, and the retention limit to expected claims since the last retention increase.

There are no published or accepted standards or guidelines concerning these ratios. A company would not normally make a radical change in the established ratio unless it had reason to believe that the ratio was unrealistic, either too aggressive or too liberal, when the last adjustment was made or that the risk or reinsurance cost factor had changed.

The second step of the ratio method is to review these ratios for peer companies with similar amounts of surplus and inforce and with similar growth patterns. A company would generally not want to be out of line with other companies in the peer group. While this approach certainly is not scientific, it is a good reference point. It can be easily communicated to nontechnical executives and demonstrates the range of comfort levels among the companies in the peer group.

As a final step, the company should also examine the distribution of the cessions by amount. While small retention increases may not be cost effective, it may be possible to reduce the number of cessions significantly with only a modest increase in retention and with a significant reduction in administrative costs. For example, a company with a $75,000 retention may eliminate almost half of its cessions by increasing its retention to $100,000. This will result in greatly reduced administrative costs to both reinsured and reinsurer. Also, it should increase the average size cession by decreasing the number of small cessions, perhaps allowing the reinsurer to offer more favorable terms and an additional savings. Most companies can tolerate a modest increase in retention with no significant change in their exposure to fluctuation.

This approach is used by companies that do not have the resources to do more technical work. It also is used by large companies in conjunction with another method. The advantage of the ratio method is that it does not take much time and the results are easily communicated. To the extent that the prior ratios of the retention limit to the other values are reasonable and the company was able to find a good match with the other companies used in the ratio comparison, this method is probably adequate.

There are disadvantages of the ratio method. There are no set standards for the ratios, and the use of a small sample of peer companies may result in such a broad range of data that the results are difficult to interpret. There may be competitive pressures to set the retention at the higher end of the range which might not be appropriate. Because the costs of reinsurance are not directly reflected in this method, separate consideration of such costs is necessary since they constitute a major consideration in setting retention limits.

Model Office Projection

A more sophisticated approach to a retention limit increase would be to develop a model of all inforce reinsurance where the company has kept its stated retention, and explore the financial effect of any changes in the retention limits. Separate models by broad underwriting classifications may be informative. This approach may be used in conjunction with the ratio method or any of the other approaches.

The actual construction of the model may be very difficult. It would not be unusual for a company to have coinsurance, mod-co, and YRT reinsurance in its reinsurance portfolio. It may do business with several reinsurers, each on a different cost basis. In fact, some policy forms may be ceded to several reinsurers, with each reinsurer on a different cost basis.

Further, many direct administrative systems provide no reinsurance information other than the existence of reinsurance. Often, information regarding the company or companies to which the excess coverage is ceded, how much is ceded, the plan of reinsurance, the reinsurance premium, or the recapture provisions is not contained in the computer system. For many companies, this information is available only in a separate reinsurance cession file, which may simply be an index card system, or in the reinsurance treaty. This information would have to be transferred to a computer readable form, which could be a formidable task.

Some simplifying assumptions may be made. For example, it could be assumed that only amounts in excess of a company's retention on any one policy have been ceded. This assumption ignores the existence of multiple policies on one life, which would result in the amount of risk assumed to be retained on some lives being greater than the normal retention limit of the company. Of course, an estimated adjustment can be developed to account for this. It is also necessary to exclude all facultatively reinsured policies where a special or reduced retention was kept. These should be studied separately in any event. If several YRT reinsurance premium scales are in use, the model may use the two or three most prevalent scales. Treaties which produce a trivial amount of reinsurance may be modeled into similar treaties with more substantial amounts reinsured.

The ability to determine the effect of recapturing the reinsurance inforce which is eligible for recapture should be included in the model. This will allow the company both to include the savings due to recapture, if any, in the reinsurance costs and to determine if it wishes to recapture any business.

Once the model has been validated against current experience, a single test can be run with the proposed retention limit or a Monte Carlo approach may be used. In this latter approach, several scenarios can be constructed using different claim frequencies to test the retention limits. The retention limit chosen will be the one which best balances reinsurance costs, including both reinsurance premiums and the administrative costs of ceding reinsurance, against the retained mortality costs.

The advantage of the model office approach is that it places a value on the financial cost of the change in the retention limit. This value can be used by management in the decision making process. The disadvantages are that the value is only as good as the model; actual results may not equal those expected and models can be very time consuming to build and typically require extensive computer resources.

Rosenthal's Approach

For the purposes of this discussion, it is assumed that the reader is familiar with the concepts of individual and collective risk theory.[2]

The basic concept behind individual risk theory is that, in a group of insured lives, a claim probability can be associated with each life, and the amount of the claim is known in advance. The claim probabilities may change over time, but the probability of a claim for one member of the group is independent of the claim probability for another member.

The gain or loss on any given policy in any given period is the basic random variable. The total gain on the portfolio is equal to the sum of the gains of the individual policies. It is assumed that this distribution of gains follows the normal curve.

---

[2]If not, the reader is encouraged to review Chapters 2, 11, 12 and 13 of Bowers, et al. [1].

Assume that there are n_x^z policyholders in a group of N insured lives with an amount of insurance Z and a probability of dying during the year of q_x. It follows that $p_x = 1 - q_x$. Ignoring interest and lapses, the net premium for any policyholder equals the expected value of a claim, Zq_x. If the policyholder survives, the gain is Zq_x; if he dies, the loss is $Z - Zq_x = Zp_x$.

The expected value of the gain for one policyholder is

$$E(gain) \;=\; Zq_x p_x \;-\; Zp_x q_x \;=\; 0.$$

The variance of the gain for one policyholder is

$$
\begin{aligned}
V(gain) \;&=\; [Zq_x - E(gain)]^2 p_x + [-Zp_x - E(gain)]^2 q_x \\
&=\; (Zq_x)^2 p_x + (-Zp_x)^2 q_x \\
&=\; Z^2 p_x q_x \,(q_x + p_x) \\
&=\; Z^2 p_x q_x.
\end{aligned}
$$

The expected value of the gain for all n_x^z members of the cell with amount of insurance Z and probability of dying of q_x is equal to the summation of all the expected gains for each individual, or zero. The variance of the cell gain is equal to the sum of the variances

$$V(cell\ gain) \;=\; \sum_{n_x^z} V(gain)$$

$$=\; Z^2 n_x^z \, p_x q_x.$$

The variance of the class gain, where Z is fixed and X varies, is equal to the sum of the variances

$$V(class\ gain) \;=\; \sum_{X} V(cell\ gain)$$

$$=\; \sum_{X} Z^2 \, n_x^z \, p_x q_x.$$

The variance for the total portfolio of N lives is equal to the sum of the variations over all amount classes Z

$$V(total\ gain)\ =\ \sum_Z V(class\ gain)$$

$$=\ \sum_Z \sum_X Z^2\, n_x^z\, p_x q_x.$$

This, of course, involves a great many calculations, one for each policyholder. Rosenthal [11] developed an approximation for the variance. Let σ_R^2 represent Rosenthal's approximation, given by

$$\sigma_R^2\ =\ Npq \sum_Z \frac{Z^2\, N_z q_z}{Nq},$$

where

$$N\ =\ \sum_Z \sum_X n_x^z,$$

$$N_z\ =\ \sum_X n_x^z,$$

$$q\ =\ \text{average value of } q_x \text{ over the entire portfolio,}$$

and

$$q_z\ =\ \text{average value of } q_x \text{ over amount class } Z.$$

The Rosenthal approach involves estimating the variance in the amount of claims in a portfolio which would be in excess of the retention limit. The variance calculated can be used to determine the size of the risk reserve or claim fund necessary to absorb claims with a certain probability.

The Rosenthal approximation states that the approximation is conservative if, as is believed to be the case, there is a positive correlation between the series of Z's and the associated q's, that is, the approximation of the variance tends to be larger than the actual variance. As such, the probability that claims do not exceed a certain value based on the approximation tends to be less than the actual probability. However, there is no guarantee that this relationship will be true in every case and obviously the results may not be appropriate if a normal approximation is not appropriate. Furthermore, events may not be independent, which also affects the actual results as compared to those modeled.

For a given retention limit, the Rosenthal approximation can be used to calculate the probability that actual claims do not exceed those expected by a predetermined amount. This predetermined amount is the maximum claim loss the company is willing to absorb in any year.

The advantage of the Rosenthal approximation is that it assigns a value to the probability that losses in a year will exceed the fund provided for this loss. Management can use this information in its decision making process. The disadvantages are that it is a nontrivial calculation and results may be difficult to interpret. The question that needs to be addressed is "What is a suitable level of safety?" Is an 85% level sufficient? Is 99% sufficient or too conservative?

Pentikäinen's Approach

Pentikäinen [9] investigated the retention limits of Finnish insurance companies to study the probability of ruin within one year. This approach uses ruin theory[3] to evaluate a retention change. Ruin theory is used to estimate the probability that claims will exceed the claim fluctuation fund or risk reserve. The risk reserve at time t, denoted $U(t)$, is defined as

$$U(t) \;=\; u + K(t) + \lambda m - X(t),$$

where

$$
\begin{aligned}
u &= \text{ initial risk reserve at } t=0, \\
K(t) &= \text{ net risk premium} = \text{expected claim amount,} \\
\lambda m &= \text{ security loading where } m \text{ is the expected number of} \\
&\quad\ \text{ claims and } \lambda \text{ is the security loading factor (addition} \\
&\quad\ \text{ to net premiums), and} \\
X(t) &= \text{ aggregate amount of claims, a random variable.}
\end{aligned}
$$

Further, if p_1 is the first moment of the claim function or the average claim amount, mp_1 is then the expected amount of aggregate claims or $K(t)$.

For the purpose of this illustration, the following definitions will be used:

$$
\begin{aligned}
M &= \text{retention limit} \\
u' &= \text{initial risk reserve on January 1} \\
K'(1) &= \text{net risk premiums or expected claims} \\
U(u',1) &= \text{probability of ruin within a year}
\end{aligned}
$$

---

[3]For a discussion of ruin theory, see Bowers, et al. [1].

For various portfolios of insurance, Pentikäinen plotted the logarithm of the ratio of the retention limit to mean claim amount $\left(\frac{M}{P_1}\right)$ against the logarithm of j, where $j = \dfrac{u' + \lambda m}{\left(p_1 K'(1)\right)^{1/2}}$.

Pentikäinen discovered that for a given value of $U(u',1)$, the curves for the various portfolios were fairly close together for values of $\frac{M}{P_1}$, up to 50. Assuming a 1% chance of ruin within one year, he found that the straight line

$$\log j = \log \frac{M}{P_1} + \log 1.9$$

would give a conservative, or lower, value of M than the actual curves.

It then follows that

$$\frac{\log u' + \lambda m}{[p_1 K(1)]^{1/2}} = \log 1.9 \left(\frac{M}{P_1}\right)$$

$$\frac{u' + \lambda m}{[K'(1)]^{1/2}} = 1.9 \, M^{1/2}$$

and

$$M = \frac{(u' + \lambda m)^2}{3.61 \, K'(1)}$$

or

$$M = \frac{(u' + \lambda m)^2}{4 \, K'(1)}.$$

If M is at least fifty times the average claim amount, and there are at least 500 expected claims, Pentikäinen estimated the error in his formula to be 10-30% and seldom more than 50%.

For any given risk reserve or claim fluctuation fund U, values of M can be developed from the aggregate amount of expected claims and the security loading expressed in terms of the number of expected claims. These values of M can be used in management's discussions regarding a retention limit increase. The difficulties include quantifying the security loading and the amount of expected claims and in interpreting the results.

Practical Considerations

Despite the obviously technical questions involved, setting a retention limit is still generally the result of a team effort involving input from the actuary, underwriter, financial officer, and marketing officer, as any retention changes will impact these areas. A final check is the general attitude of the company toward risk and risk avoidance. It has been said that the retention limit should be the largest amount of a claim that the CEO would be willing to see on his desk on any given morning.

Many companies use reinsurance, in the form of coinsurance, to finance growth. A retention increase will reduce the volume of reinsurance, so the ceding company will need to be prepared to finance this additional business itself if it increases its retention.

Frequency of Review. Few companies review retention limits as often as annually; relatively small changes in the retention limit may be more of a nuisance than a real cost saving item. In general, a meaningful review should be made about every five years. It should also be noted that a company that generates a large volume of reinsurance as the result of a relatively low retention may receive more competitive reinsurance terms and better service than a company that produces very little reinsurance due to a higher retention.

Corridors. When setting the retention limit, the minimum cession size must be considered. This may be accomplished via a minimum cession definition, say $25,000, where the ceding company agrees to keep its normal retention, say $75,000, plus an amount up to, but not including, the minimum. If the issued amount were $100,000 or more, the $75,000 retention would apply; if an amount less then $100,000 were issued, the entire amount would be retained.

Alternatively, a corridor approach may be utilized. Under this method, the retention is the issued amount for all issues up to $99,999, and $75,000 for larger issues. The economic and mechanical effects are the same as for the minimum cession approach, but the treaty definition and wording are different.

Small cessions are typically very expensive to administer. By reducing the number of small cessions, a company not only saves the real mortality cost of reinsurance, it can save itself administrative expense and obtain a lower reinsurance cost due to the reinsurer's expense savings.

Variations. Many companies have reduced retentions for very high and low issue ages, say for 65 and above and 18 and below, and for certain substandard issues, say above Table 4. The theory behind this practice is that there is not enough experience at the extremes to smooth out fluctuations. This may be reasonable for some mutual companies where dividend classes are based on very fine distinctions.

From a practical viewpoint, if all issues ages and substandard classes are adequately priced and underwritten, there is little need to have significant variations in retention limits by issue age or by substandard classification, other than for increased dividend equity. A consistent retention limit will simplify administration and may create expense savings.

Ancillary Benefits. Companies may have separate retention schedules for the various ancillary benefits. Waiver of premium would normally follow the retention schedule of the base policy. Accidental death benefits usually have a separate retention schedule. Sometimes, accidental death benefits are 100% reinsured.

Recapture of Reinsurance Inforce. Once a decision has been made to increase the retention limits, the next decision facing the insurance company is whether to apply this retention increase to inforce business. While the increased retention schedule is obviously applicable to new business, the company is under no obligation to increase the retention on all inforce reinsurance. However, it is supposed to notify its reinsurer of any intention to recapture at the time of the retention increase. Failure to notify the reinsurer of plans to recapture is generally accepted as a forfeiture of the right to recapture. However, definitive correspondence is recommended in either event.

Retention increases via recapture can be applied on a treaty by treaty basis. If the ceding company decides to increase its retention under a certain treaty, it must recapture all business reinsured under that treaty. It cannot pick and choose.

Recapture is effected on all risks which are eligible for recapture at the time of the retention increase. Thereafter, recapture is effected on the policy anniversary on which the risks first become eligible. Thus, a recapture program may take years to be completed.

Considerations involved in the recapture decision include those involved in the retention increase analysis. One point to note is that the cost of reinsurance is usually high in the later years following the attainment of the recapture duration, especially if mortality or the other risk experience has improved. Typically, a reinsurer would want to price its business to have produced a reasonable return prior to the end of the recapture period.

All ceded businesses may not be eligible for recapture. First, the recapture duration must have been attained and the company must have maintained its normal retention, according to the terms of the treaty. Facultative, quota-share, and reduced retention cessions are usually not eligible for recapture.

Other Factors. A good deal of judgement is used is setting the retention limits. The company may choose to set a limit lower than the theoretical limit for several reasons.

(1) It simply may not feel comfortable with the maximum claim amount produced by the theoretical retention limit.
(2) It may wish to set a lower limit for a certain policy form which it feels has a higher degree of risk than the rest of its portfolio.
(3) The surplus strain on a given policy form may be so great that it must lower the retention in order to issue the policies.
(4) It may be able to get a better reinsurance cost if it maintains a lower retention on all or certain policy forms.

NEW BUSINESS

Reinsurance is frequently a vital concern in the development of a new product, especially for an innovative product design or marketing structure or a price competitive plan. It is desirable to have a reinsurance agreement in place, at least verbally, before a new policy form is introduced.

Assessing Needs

Before soliciting reinsurance proposals on a new product, the ceding company should review its needs and make some preliminary decisions about its wants and desires. The major points it must consider include the form of reinsurance, the form of administration, and any special terms needed.

The ceding company should decide if it wants coinsurance, mod-co, or YRT reinsurance on any new product. Coinsurance or mod-co would be the primary choice if surplus strain were anticipated to be a problem. Mod-co or YRT would be chosen if the ceding company wanted to maintain the assets in support of the reserves.

The ceding company may choose YRT because of its low annual cost. If the company wishes to use YRT reinsurance, it may decide to use its existing YRT reinsurance agreements or it may decide to solicit a special YRT scale designed to fit the new product. If the underwriting to be used is different from that normally used, a different YRT scale will be needed.

The ceding company should choose between self-administration and individual cession administration early in the product development process. Should it decide on self-administration, it should consider the demands of self-administration during the product development and implementation process.

Before soliciting any reinsurance proposal, the ceding company should determine any special needs it may have for the product. It may desire a special recapture period, or a special retention. It should consider how many reinsurers it would like to have participate on an automatic basis; the automatic capacity needed, any facultative needs, and how the reinsurance will be divided among the reinsurers.

Soliciting Proposals

When coinsurance or modified coinsurance is to be used, reinsurance proposals are requested late in the product development process after premiums, cash values, and reserves have been generated since this information is vital to the reinsurance pricing actuary. This information is also necessary if a customized YRT scale is desired. Occasionally, the insurance company works closely with one particular reinsurer throughout the product development process in order to benefit from the reinsurer's expertise in a new product area. The reinsurer may provide tentative reinsurance premiums early in the product development process to be used in pricing the product.

Usually, it is not difficult to find a reinsurer interested in submitting a proposal on a new product. Most large, professional reinsurers have sales representatives who call on clients or prospects on a regular basis. These sales representatives gather the information pertinent in developing a proposal. This information will include the premiums and other policy values, commissions, underwriting standards, and the general marketing plan. The sales representative may also ask questions regarding company mortality and persistency experience on similar products.

If the company is venturing into a new product line, market, or underwriting program, the sales representative may ask for information regarding the pricing assumptions and their source. All of this information is necessary for the reinsurance pricing actuary to develop a proposal with the appropriate assumptions. The ceding company actuary should also make known any special needs or preferences his company may have regarding the plan of reinsurance, administration, slope of the reinsurance premium scale, and recapture periods.

Evaluating Costs

When all the reinsurance proposals have been gathered, the task of financially evaluating the proposal generally falls on the pricing actuary. Because reinsurance costs may vary by duration, age and policy size, the most straightforward method of evaluating the proposals is to reprice the product at the various issue amounts with the normal company retention and original pricing assumptions. If the pricing system does not provide for the inclusion of reinsurance costs, special adjustments can be made with relatively little effort.

A typical alternative is to determine the expected profit from the various reinsurers' points of view, using a common set of assumptions. The proposal generating the lowest profit should be the lowest cost to the ceding company. Of course, sensitivity testing is advisable.

YRT. The YRT comparison is perhaps the most simple to perform. A simple spread sheet program can be written to calculate and compare the present value of YRT premiums using the anticipated net amounts at risk, discounted with interest and survivorship. The net amount at risk assumptions may make a critical difference in this comparison and should be chosen carefully when an interest sensitive product is involved.

Alternatively, the death benefit cost for the policy as a whole, including both the retained and ceded portions, can be determined by weighting the mortality rates and the reinsurance

YRT premiums in proportion to the retained and ceded coverage and using the weighted values as the mortality assumption.

Coinsurance. If the proposals are on a coinsurance basis, the profit tests can be run on the ceded portion only, treating it from the reinsurer's view. Profit tests are run treating allowances as commissions. Expenses, other than those directly related to ceding reinsurance, should be excluded as these must be born by the retained portion alone. The resulting reinsurance profit is the ceding company's cost on the amount ceded. The total profit on the combined ceded and retained portions can be found by deducting the reinsurer's profit from the profit for the entire amount issued assuming no reinsurance. However, this approach does not permit the calculation of the return on investment.

Care must be taken not to oversimplify the assumptions, especially regarding average size, premium bands, and expenses. Reinsurance will typically occur with much greater frequency for policies issued at higher amount bands which have lower per unit premiums, higher expenses for medical underwriting, and, perhaps, better mortality. Persistency may also be different on reinsured policies.[4] All factors must be taken into consideration when setting the assumptions for determining present values of reinsurance costs.

The most precise approach is to perform new profit tests using a program that allows direct input of the appropriate reinsurance parameters. Most currently available profit test programs have this feature. This approach permits the calculation of return on investment. In either approach, care must be taken with assumptions, as discussed above.

A simplistic approach is to compare the present value of reinsurance premiums net of allowances using anticipated mortality, persistency, and interest. This is similar to the YRT comparison. However, the values produced would be useful only to compare relative net reinsurance premiums among reinsurers, and not to evaluate the true reinsurance costs as they do not consider the effect of cash values, reserves, and interest.

Mod-Co. The evaluation of mod-co proposals is more difficult because of the effect of the mod-co interest rate. For the sake of

---

[4]Larger policies are often associated with more informed buyers, which can affect experience, with both positive and negative implications.

simplicity, mod-co could be treated as coinsurance, with the earned interest rate being the mod-co interest rate. This method fails to recognize any gains or losses resulting in the difference in the interest actually earned and that credited via the mod-co interest adjustment.

As an alternative, the original profit test can be modified to test both the ceded and retained portions together by adjusting the premiums and commissions to reflect the ceded premiums and allowances, adjusting the mortality to reflect the lower amount at risk, and adjusting the investment income to reflect the mod-co interest rate. Special adjustments can also be made to recognize the differences in earned interest and the mod-co interest rate.

Administrative Expense. When evaluating the reinsurance costs of any new product, the ceding company should have an understanding of the administrative expense involved in ceding reinsurance. However, evaluating these costs is not always easy. The major problem is identifying the actual expenses. A functional cost study is probably necessary, looking at both the fixed and marginal expenses associated with reinsurance.

Evaluating Nonfinancial Aspects

Price is not the only criterion in evaluating reinsurance proposals. The ceding company must be able to work with the reinsurer. There are many other factors which contribute to a satisfactory reinsurance arrangement. These will vary by company.

Service. The ceding company will want to be assured that it receives prompt and accurate service from its reinsurers. It will want cessions and claims processed promptly, and all reports produced on a timely basis. When dealing with a new reinsurer it may be difficult to evaluate the service issue. Often, service does not become an issue until it is found that the actual service does not meet expectations

Administrative Requirements. The ceding company should review administrative requirements. It will want little variation in requirements among reinsurers as this would complicate its own procedures. A ceding company would wish to avoid any burdensome or unusual requirements.

Underwriting Expertise. For many companies, underwriting service is very important. It may not be necessary that all automatic reinsurers provide the desired underwriting service. However, the company may maintain automatic reinsurance relationships with its desired facultative reinsurers. The degree of underwriting support to be provided by the reinsurer, and the level of competitiveness, should be discussed and agreed upon in advance. Sometimes a reinsurer will not offer facultative services on a selected automatic treaty, or it may do so only with higher costs or with a minimum placement ratio.[5]

Product Knowledge. Some companies depend on their reinsurer to provide them with the latest product information. They may seek information about product features, experience, regulation, and taxes.

Stability. For some companies, the stability of the reinsurer is important. Some companies view newcomers on the reinsurance market as less stable and prefer to deal with established reinsurers. Most companies want to work with a reinsurer that they expect to be in the reinsurance business for years to come. Individual perceptions of stability vary, but few companies wish to deal with a reinsurer that is in a precarious financial position or that is perceived as being less than fully committed to the business of reinsurance.

Capacity. The ceding company should be satisfied that the reinsurer will be able to accept all of its business. For most companies this is not a problem, because reinsurers are able to retrocede. Capacity may be a problem in facultative situations involving large amounts, if the reinsurer does not have adequate facultative retroceding facilities.

Capacity problems may be a function of the reinsurer's surplus rather than mortality risk protection. This problem can occur in either excess new business or financial reinsurance situations when the reinsurer does not have sufficient surplus to cover the surplus strain and does not have a ready source of surplus or retrocession capacity.

---

[5]See Chapter 3 for a discussion of facultative reinsurance and placement ratios.

Other.   Choosing a reinsurer can also be an emotional decision.
Some companies have built longstanding relationships with one or
two reinsurers.   There is a certain sense of security and trust
involved in knowing a group of people over a long period of time.
The administrative procedures are all in place, and everyone knows
how things work.   In addition, the individuals at one company
know who to contact at the other company with special requests or
problems.

INFORCE REINSURANCE

Periodically, every insurance company should review its ceded
reinsurance portfolio.   This review may be conducted in conjunction with the retention limit review.   The purpose of this review is
to examine individual reinsurance arrangements.

Reviewing Procedures

The major purpose of a reinsurance review is to assure that
procedures are being followed correctly.   It should ascertain that
policies requiring reinsurance are ceded properly, that policy
changes and lapses are reported promptly, and that claim procedures are followed correctly.

Improving Operations

The company should look for ways to streamline procedures
without sacrificing accuracy in order to lower its administrative
expense.
        The company may wish to standardize certain treaty
provisions relating to the administration of its contracts.   This
could greatly simplify new business and claim procedures.   It
should be kept in mind that changes in treaties typically affect only
new cessions.   Existing reinsurance will not be affected unless both
parties explicitly agree to such a change.

Recapturing Business

Typically, once automatically ceded business has been in force for a
given period of time, called the recapture period, the ceding
company may recapture or take back some of the reinsurance on a
policy.   This is allowed only if the company has increased its

retention since the policy was ceded and then only up to the new retention amount. For example, if a company had a retention of $75,000 and raises it to $100,000, it may, after the expiration of the recapture period, recapture the first $25,000 of reinsurance on each life. Any rules regarding minimum cessions must be maintained, and typically only automatic and not facultative cessions are available for recapture. The company must notify the reinsurer of its intention to recapture at the time of the retention increase, not at the end of recapture period.

If a company increases its retention, it may choose not to recapture reinsurance ceded prior to the retention increase. It cannot choose to recapture only some policies covered under a treaty, it must recapture on all or none. Recapture can be a significant cost savings tool in eliminating the administration of a number of small cessions. In evaluating a potential recapture, the ceding company should compare the present value of future reinsurance premiums and administrative expenses to the present value of reinsurance benefits less the expense of recapturing the business. A model office projection is useful in this comparison. For small changes in the retention limits, recapture may be too expensive to consider. However, if there is a sizeable retention increase, the ceding company may choose to recapture inforce business to provide additional stability for the retention increase.

Contracts involving only a handful of policies or involving the cession of amounts less than $10,000 should be reviewed. It may be more economical to both the ceding company and the reinsurer for these small cessions to be recaptured.

FACULTATIVE REINSURANCE

Periodically, the ceding company should review its facultative program to determine if its needs are being met and if its costs are reasonable. This review may be done annually.

Facultative Criteria

One part of the facultative review is to examine how policies are selected for the facultative program. In some companies, this may be a very informal procedure, the decision being left to the underwriter's discretion. However, an increasing number of companies have formal guidelines. For example, a company could decide to submit all applications rated above Table 4 for facultative review. In such a situation, the ceding company would want to determine if its needs have changed and it requires a different criterion. If the company finds it is making a large number of exceptions to the rules, it may wish to modify the rules to cover the exceptions.

Service

The ceding company should also examine its placement ratios with its various facultative reinsurers. It can be very expensive to deal with a large number of reinsurers. If it finds that a particular reinsurer is not providing the type of underwriting service needed, it may be beneficial to both parties to terminate the relationship.

Costs

The costs of facultative reinsurance should be an ongoing concern for all ceding companies. As mentioned in Chapter 3, reinsurance costs can vary a great deal by reinsurer. If an application is sent to more than one reinsurer for facultative reinsurance, it is wise to look at both the table rating and the reinsurance premiums before placing the case. Sometimes the reinsurance cost for a given rating is greater than that for a higher rating from another reinsurer.

The ceding company should periodically evaluate the internal costs and perceived benefits of its facultative reinsurance program. Facultative submissions can be expensive. The ceding company must consider if the costs of the facultative submission on the borderline applications is justified by its expenses in relation to the reinsurance premiums and claim recoveries on such business and any enhancement to agent relations.

FINANCIAL REINSURANCE

An insurance company enters into a financial reinsurance agreement for some specific purpose. These are usually one time agreements that do not involve new cessions, although this need not be the case. Termination may be accomplished at any point that the reinsurer's experience reaches a specified level. Because of the nature of these arrangements, the needs assessment and ongoing monitoring for the business are different from those of traditional reinsurance.

Assessing Needs

The needs assessment process in financial reinsurance will vary according to the motivation for the transaction. In a financial reinsurance transaction for surplus relief, the company generally realizes that it has a need for surplus but must ask itself "how much" and "for how long". The company should also consider the various alternatives to reinsurance.

The company must also consider which block it wishes to reinsure. Typically, an older block of business with stable experience and large reserves is chosen.

Monitoring Results

Most financial reinsurance transactions are of a short term nature. While the recapture period on traditional reinsurance is seldom less than ten years, most financial transactions can be terminated at any time subject to the provisions of the treaty. The usual provision is that the reinsurer is not to be left in a loss position. The treaty may provide that the ceding company pay any accumulated loss as a price for termination. Such termination should be voluntary, at the ceding company's option.

While the reinsurer will be monitoring all of its experience rated accounts, it is useful for the ceding company to also track the results periodically.

Changing Conditions and Needs

The ceding company must continually monitor internal and external conditions that may affect its financial reinsurance transactions. The two major external factors most frequently affecting financial reinsurance are regulation and taxation. Changes in these areas may occur at any time, and if any changes occur that would diminish the desired financial effect, termination should be considered.

Internal changes in the ceding company can also affect reinsurance. While most reinsurance treaties do not require termination upon a change of management or ownership of the ceding company,[6] the ceding company may wish to terminate the reinsurance if one of these events occur. It may do this because the new management or ownership has a different philosophy concerning financial reinsurance or because financial conditions have changed as a result of this change in ownership.

---

[6]See Chapter 5, Financial Reinsurance.

9 | Managing Assumed Reinsurance

Just as the ceding company manages its reinsurance portfolio, the reinsurer, whether it is a professional reinsurer or any other type, must manage its assumed reinsurance portfolio. The reinsurer will have both assumed and retroceded reinsurance in its portfolio. While this chapter primarily addresses professional reinsurers' activities, the considerations are important to other types of reinsurers. In addition, ceding companies that understand the concerns and operations of the reinsurer can avoid misunderstandings and improve relationships.

This chapter covers issues concerning the pricing of reinsurance, the setting of retention limits for assumed reinsurance, the managing of retrocession agreements, the monitoring of inforce assumed reinsurance, the designing and pricing of special features, and the special considerations of financial reinsurance.

PRICING

Reinsurance pricing[1] follows the same principles as traditional insurance pricing. The reinsurance pricing actuary reviewing an

---

[1]The material in this chapter applies primarily to traditional reinsurance. While the same principles apply to financial reinsurance, different techniques, such as model office projections, are more commonly used.

insurance plan of a particular ceding company must put itself in the shoes of his counterpart at that company and evaluate the plan in terms of the anticipated experience for the ceding company. The chief difference between direct pricing and reinsurance pricing is that the reinsurance actuary wears "several pairs of shoes" in one day and frequently produces a pricing quote in a week or less, a much shorter time frame than is given the direct pricing actuary. This is possible because the reinsurance actuary usually begins with a finished product.

Original Policy Values

The reinsurance pricing actuary must evaluate each plan of insurance from each company separately in order to develop appropriate pricing assumptions for the pricing of specific reinsurance plans. The pricing process begins with the original policy values supplied by the ceding company.

While the usefulness of the various values will vary depending upon the plan of reinsurance desired, the values are always of some significance. For example, in YRT the cash surrender values, or reserves, affect the net amount at risk and, therefore, the reinsurance premium to be received. The design of the product and its compensation influence overall persistency.

Premiums. The policy premiums are important when pricing coinsurance or mod-co because the allowances, and therefore the net reinsurance premiums, are based on the policy gross premiums. In the case of an interest sensitive product, the reinsurance may be YRT with premiums based on the cost of insurance rates, net of allowances.

While the gross premiums are used to develop the reinsurance allowances, the policy premium scales can also give an indication of the anticipated persistency. These considerations are discussed later in this chapter.

In today's market, most policy forms will have two or more premium bands. The reinsurance pricing actuary may perform profit tests on all premium bands if time permits. If time does not permit, the reinsurance actuary may only review bands for amounts over the ceding company's retention.

In some instances, the reinsurance pricing actuary may price only the highest band because the premiums are the smallest and the persistency probably the least favorable. Allowances based on the highest band may be applied to all bands. This will generally produce larger profits to the reinsurer because the lower band premiums are larger, resulting in a larger net reinsurance premium. Also, persistency is usually better for the lower bands. However, nonmedical underwriting may negate the additional profits.

Alternatively, the high band premiums and allowances may apply to all issues, regardless of the ceding company's actual gross premiums. In this case, the ceding company receives the benefit of the larger premium on the lower bands.

If a significant amount of reinsurance is anticipated at the lower bands where nonmedical underwriting is used, the reinsurance pricing actuary may want to price these bands separately. In any event, the actuary should review all bands to see if, in his judgment, testing of other bands is needed.

Most traditional reinsurance premiums are collected on an annual basis regardless of the premium mode although the unearned reinsurance premium is refunded in the event of an off-anniversary termination. The underlying distribution by premium mode of the product being reinsured is of interest to the pricing actuary to the extent that it affects persistency. For example, monthly premium business often has higher lapse rates than annual premium business, and certainly less premium is collected in any policy year due to off-anniversary terminations.

The primary exception to this annual premium mode rule is reinsurance involving interest sensitive products: excess interest whole life, universal life, variable life, and variable universal life where the reinsurance premium is calculated in the normal fund calculation cycle. Normally, this is a monthly calculation, and reinsurance premiums follow this pattern. However, reinsurance premiums may be remitted on a quarterly basis in arrears. Lost interest and the monthly lapse patterns should be reflected in the pricing.

Policy Fee. In most coinsurance and mod-co situations, the ceding company is allowed to retain the policy fee to cover its ongoing expenses, and it would be ignored in pricing. If the reinsurer is to participate in the policy fee, the fee should be considered in the pricing. The reinsurer should consider the effect on deficiency reserves of including or excluding the policy fee.

Cash Values. The original policy cash values are important in profit testing in order to determine surrender costs. Cash values are readily available on conventional products, but must be estimated in the case of interest sensitive products. For these products, the reinsurance pricing actuary should test several likely scenarios based on his judgement or the judgement of the ceding company's actuary.

Reserves. Policy reserves are also an important part of the expected profit analysis. In the case of conventional products, the reserves are generally provided by the ceding company, or may be calculated given the statutory reserve basis. In the case of interest sensitive products, the reinsurance pricing actuary must again use his best judgement. Both statutory and tax reserves are necessary for proper evaluation. For simplicity, cash values are sometimes used in lieu of the statutory and tax reserves, but this practice can distort expected profits.

Benefits. The reinsurance pricing actuary must carefully study the policy benefits and reflect these in profit testing. The pricing actuary must be aware of any automatic increases or decreases in the benefits and the point at which these changes may occur. If the policyholder has different options at any given point, the pricing actuary must examine each option.

Policy benefits affect mortality, morbidity, and persistency, and are discussed subsequently.

Net Amount at Risk. The net amount at risk is important in pricing because it determines the benefit costs. In a YRT case, it also determines the flow of premium income. If the net amount at risk is overstated in a YRT profit test, the profits may be overstated.

Because it is usually more readily available, the cash value may be used to determine the net amount at risk when pricing YRT reinsurance. For decreasing term coverage, the net amount at risk for reinsurance purposes depends on the death benefit schedule of the product and the retention method being used. If the ceding company retains a level retention, the amount reinsured may reduce quickly, causing the reinsurance to terminate prior to the contractual end of the term of the policy. In this case, it may be necessary to reduce first year allowances. A pro-rata retention will allow the reinsurer to continue to receive premiums and provide coverage throughout the term period, possibly permitting higher first year allowances. When providing reinsurance on mortgage protection products which do not follow a fixed amortization schedule but which vary with variable rate mortgages, the reinsurance actuary may wish to look at several scenarios to determine the average expected profitability of the product.

When pricing a YRT scale for an interest sensitive product, the choice of the net amount at risk may be quite difficult. Points to consider include the following:

(1) If large amounts of pour-in money are received, initial cash values may be quite large.

(2) In the case of flexible premium products, it may be difficult to predict premium levels. Premiums may not necessarily follow "target" premiums.

(3) Products sold on "vanishing" or a limited premium basis may result in reduced cash values in later years, compared to policies where premiums are expected every year. As a rule, "minimum" premium plans will produce minimal cash values.

The retention method used is also important. The same considerations apply as in the decreasing term situation.

Commissions. The reinsurance pricing actuary should examine the commissions paid by the ceding company on the policy. The ceding company usually desires that the reinsurance allowances cover its commission costs, and the reinsurance pricing actuary attempts to do this wherever possible.

Commission patterns affect persistency results, as will be discussed later in the this chapter.

Assumptions

In setting pricing assumptions, the reinsurance pricing actuary looks at the original policy values, the type of agent used in making the sale, the market for the policy, the ceding company's underwriting philosophy, the ceding company's recent experience, and the ceding company's pricing assumptions.

Mortality. One of the most critical assumptions in pricing any sort of life insurance product is the mortality assumption. The pricing actuary at a direct writing company is concerned with the expected nonmedical, paramedical, medical, simplified issue, or guaranteed issue mortality appropriate for his company. The reinsurance actuary must consider these assumptions for each company reinsured.

Intercompany mortality studies[2] have shown significant variation in mortality results by contributing company. A primary reason for this variation is the difference in underwriting standards among companies. While one company's underwriters may classify a specific life as a standard risk, a company using a more conservative underwriting approach may consider the life to be substandard by perhaps four tables or more.

Other factors which have a significant effect on mortality results include the type of agents, the market, and geographic concentration. For example, companies which specialize in the rural market often have very good mortality results at ages over 30, but may have very poor mortality results at younger ages due to a higher than average rate of accidental deaths. Companies which have a loyal career agency force tend to have better mortality than companies which have a substantial volume of brokerage business. The business insurance market tends to have worse mortality than the family market. Of course, no rule is ironclad, and individual analysis of each pricing request is advised.

Mortality will also vary by product type. Historically, term insurance mortality experience has been worse than that on permanent products due to antiselection at both issue and renewal.

Insurance plans with poor persistency experience tend to have poor mortality experience. Individuals who lapse are normally the healthy lives who could qualify for new insurance coverage, leaving the persisting group with poorer than average mortality.

Select and ultimate term has been a particular problem to the insurance industry. Pricing such a product is truly a challenge for both the direct writer and the reinsurer. In fact, the reinsurance experience on such products in the early 1980's was so poor that several reinsurers withdrew from this particular market, refusing to reinsure these plans.

In order to price a select and ultimate product, it is necessary to determine exactly how re-entries are to be handled.

---

[2]This information is collected by the Committees on Mortality and Morbidity Experience Studies among Lives Individually Insured and published annually in the *Transactions, Society of Actuaries, Reports.*

It is important to know how frequently re-entry will be allowed, the degree of underwriting which will be used on re-entries, as well as the amount of commission which will be paid upon re-entry. The mortality assumption for the re-entry group and the no-re-entry group are both affected by the level of re-entry underwriting and commission. In general, the more lives which would qualify for re-entry the worse the mortality is on the remaining group which cannot requalify for new select rates. One problem facing the reinsurance pricing actuary is that the re-entry rules often are not clearly defined or strictly followed. At this writing, there is little experience on which to base assumptions.

Select and ultimate products and other products with increasing premiums tend to have poorer persistency than level premium products. Products with re-entry provisions present a special problem concerning the re-entry assumptions. The inter-action between mortality and persistency is very clear in these products.

If large volumes of reinsurance are expected to be placed on a facultative basis, the reinsurance pricing actuary must consider the expected facultative mortality. Factors which influence auto-matic reinsurance mortality will also influence facultative coverage. Facultative mortality is further influenced by the number of reinsurers participating in the shopping program and the placement ratios.

Persistency. Another critical pricing assumption is persistency. There can be significant first year policy strain in a coinsurance or mod-co arrangement, exposing the reinsurer to the risk that poor persistency will prevent it from recovering its initial investment.

Persistency varies by type of agent involved in the sale. Business written by brokers tends to be replaced more frequently as the brokers look for new first year commissions. Business placed by true career agents, and sometimes business placed by salaried agents, may have very good persistency.

The market also affects persistency. For example, the employer sponsored plan market will tend to have persistency related to employee turnover rates. Companies which have upscale policyholders who are frequently exposed to other insurance agents may have poor persistency.

Policy size is an important factor in persistency. Larger policies tend to move more frequently than smaller policies because the commission dollars generated by a move are greater. Because reinsurers see large policies with great frequency, reinsurance persistency does not tend to be as good as the persistency of the ceding company.

The commission scale may affect persistency. High first year commissions attract business. Policies which feature high first year commissions generally have low renewal commissions. Agents have been known to move policies periodically in order to obtain new first year commissions. Persistency bonuses may improve short-term persistency on a product. Policies which have level commissions will tend to have better persistency than policies with heaped first year commissions.

The premiums and benefit patterns will also affect persistency. Policies with increasing premiums tend to have poorer persistency than level premium policies because the cost per thousand increases with increasing age. If a policy has select and ultimate premiums, any healthy person would be prudent to re-enter or replace his policy periodically to secure the lowest rate. Decreasing term policies often have poor persistency because the premium per unit of outstanding coverage increases each year. In later policy years, the amount of coverage may become trivial when compared to the premium, and the policyholder will lapse the policy.

Recapture. The reinsurance pricing actuary must reflect possible recapture of ceded business. Typically, this is done by increasing lapses once the recapture duration is attained. Several factors influence the assumption, including the length of time since the last retention increase, the current retention limit, and the growth pattern of the company. Because it is so difficult to predict recapture by company, a generalized approach may be used.

Expenses. Because of the very competitive nature of the reinsurance market, expenses are a critical item in pricing reinsurance. The successful reinsurer may only be able to provide for expenses of 5% to 8% of premium in order to remain competitive. This level is much lower than the expense level of most direct writing companies.

Issue expenses for an automatic reinsurer would be substantially less than issue costs connected with the direct product as the reinsurer will have no underwriting costs or agency expenses. It will usually have relatively fixed sales and administration expenses. Facultative underwriting costs should be less than the underwriting costs of the direct writing company as the direct writer will pay for the various medical reports. Facultative underwriting costs are related to the placement ratios experienced by the reinsurer. To keep the underwriting costs down, the reinsurer must maintain a reasonable placement ratio on its facultative submissions.

The quest for ever lower reinsurance costs as well as the introduction of universal life products has shifted some of the administrative burden of reinsurance from the reinsurer to the ceding company, with the reinsurer passing any administrative cost savings on to the ceding company. Self-administered reporting has resulted, however, in only marginal cost savings to the reinsurer. Reinsurers must spend a good deal of time reviewing the reports, auditing the accounts, and preparing financial statements. Overhead must also be considered. Given the low level of most reinsurance expenses, little real cost savings may be realized.

Expenses may be allocated on several bases: per policy or unit issued, per policy inforce, or percent of premium. If charged on a per policy basis, pricing results will be more favorable for larger policies. This is an advantage to the reinsurer if pricing the higher premium bands. If expenses are charged on a per unit basis, smaller policies will be favored. When expenses are charged on a percent of premium basis, low premium reinsurance, such as term coinsurance and YRT, will show more favorable pricing results. Normally, maintenance and routine issue expenses will be charged on a per policy basis which is related to the manner in which the expenses are incurred. Underwriting expenses may be charged on a per unit and/or percent of premium basis, which is related to the manner in which these expenses are incurred. Overhead expenses may be charged in any reasonable manner.

If maintenance and issue expenses other than underwriting are allocated on a per policy basis, the average size assumption is quite important. The average size is dependent on the company's retention and the type of product involved. For example, term products generate larger size policies than whole life products. The average size of a company's reinsurance cessions tends to increase as the retention limit of the ceding company increases.

Premium Tax. Some reinsurers routinely reimburse ceding companies for premium taxes on reinsurance premiums. In this case, an explicit premium tax assumption is necessary. This assumption may be client-specific or the reinsurance pricing actuary may employ a generalized assumption based on the overall premium tax rate. In most situations, there is little difference between the client's rate and the reinsurer's rate, particularly for clients doing business in a number of states. Small regional companies may have rates which vary significantly and special consideration may be given to these accounts.

Allowances. In some instances, specific reinsurance allowances are input in profit testing. The ceding company may provide the reinsurance pricing actuary with desired allowances which are used in the initial round of profit testing. In most cases, however, the pricing of coinsurance or mod-co is a matter of solving for allowances which provide the desired profit for the reinsurer.

Interest. The reinsurance pricing actuary must establish a reasonable interest assumption for investment income just as his direct counterpart does. This assumption is normally based on investment department and company objectives just as is the case for a direct company.

Reinsurance pricing involving term coinsurance or YRT scales gives little consideration to investment income. In pricing mod-co, the mod-co interest rate should be used, at least for interest on reserves. If pricing includes consideration of investment income on cash flows, the reinsurer's own earned rate should be used.

Special Facultative Considerations

Facultative reinsurance presents a particular set of problems for the reinsurance pricing actuary.

The major problem facing the reinsurance pricing actuary is relating underwriting action to pricing assumptions. It is very difficult to predict the effect of reinsurer underwriting actions on mortality experience. Aggressive underwriting is going to produce worse mortality experience than that produced by conservative underwriting. However, aggressive reinsurance underwriting will result in more business and, hence, more premium. There is no precise method to determine how mortality will change when underwriting standards change, but past facultative mortality experience should be helpful.

Even though facultative underwriting is a function of the reinsurer's underwriting standards, some variation in facultative mortality exists by ceding company. Different ceding companies produce different facultative mortality experience because of the type of business being facultatively ceded. Some ceding companies using conservative underwriting standards may reinsure a large number of marginally substandard policies in order to keep the standard risk classification clean for dividend purposes. The reinsurer might consider these cases standard by its underwriting criteria. Other companies may send out only highly rated cases.

Facultative mortality varies by the level of the placement ratio. As placement ratios increase, mortality will tend to decrease because the reinsurer is receiving a better spread of risks.

Techniques

The reinsurance pricing actuary employs many of the same techniques that the ceding company pricing actuary uses. However, because of differences in the nature of the business, there are some problems which are unique to reinsurance pricing.

Age/Sex/Underwriting Distributions. In the ideal situation, one set of coinsurance allowances or one YRT rate scale will produce uniform profits for all age/sex/smoker cells. This ideal situation rarely, if ever, occurs because of differences in the mortality and persistency assumptions used by the reinsurer and ceding company. However, a common set of allowances is desirable to ease administration. In order to produce a common set of allowances, the profit levels must vary by cell and must be weighted by cell in developing the overall profit level, a process sometimes employed by direct insurers. Distributions may vary by company and product. Monitoring actual-to-expected results is vital to achieve the desired profit goals.

Profit Objectives. The reinsurance pricing actuary employs the same sort of profit goals as his ceding company counterpart. The most common goals are expressed as a percent of premium, per unit issued, percent of mortality, and return on investment. A combination of goals may be used. The most common goal is the percent of premium goal where the present value of future profits is divided by the present value of future premiums. This goal may vary by product type, with higher premium products often using a lower goal. This goal is appropriate for both whole life and term pricing.

The profit per unit issued or profits expressed as a percentage of the death benefit is appropriate in pricing term coinsurance and YRT because it directly reflects the major risk involved.

The return on investment goal is usually confined to cash value products. When used with term insurance, exceedingly large values may be produced even if actual dollar profits are small or negative. Risk/reward ratios are not necessarily properly recognized, in that a very small shift in experience, especially mortality, may entirely eliminate these high expected profits. If losses occur in later years, multiple return on investment values may result. Reinsurers review profit margins in all years and try to avoid negative margins after the first policy year.

Profit Test Years. Most reinsurers base their profit objectives on the profits arising over a ten or twenty year period. The danger is that losses could develop after the period reviewed.

Sensitivity Testing. Because of the short time frame given the reinsurance pricing actuary, sensitivity testing is performed infrequently. The pricing actuary normally tests one scenario for three to six ages for each smoker status. If time permits, different sets of assumptions may be used for certain cells. Females are priced separately only if they are expected to constitute a significant portion of the reinsurance assumed. The value of sensitivity testing should not be overlooked because a seemingly small variation in assumptions can have a large impact on results in a competitive field like reinsurance where profit margins are slim.

RETENTION LIMITS

The reinsurer must examine its retention limits on assumed business periodically just a ceding company must. The reinsurer may use any one or a combination of the techniques discussed in the previous chapter for ceding companies. A reinsurer with both assumed and direct business should consider the retention limits independently because the expected mortality will be different or organizational considerations may require separation of the profits for the two blocks of business. The reinsurer may find that it should keep a different retention on its assumed portfolio than it does on its direct portfolio.

RETROCESSION AGREEMENTS

Professional reinsurers have retrocession agreements in order to retrocede amounts over their retention limits. In the past, reinsurers often had retrocession arrangements with some the their client ceding companies. This was called reciprocity,[3] an uncommon practice today. Today's reinsurers will retrocede to other professional reinsurers or to professional retrocessionaires.

A reinsurer may have more than one retrocession agreement for new business. Many have special retrocession agreements for selected business which allow the reinsurer to retrocede assumed policies on the original terms. This can result in cost savings and freedom in pricing for the reinsurer. Special facultative retrocession agreements may have YRT premium scales which vary by retrocessionaire.

A professional reinsurer might also have retrocession agreements for financial reinsurance contracts. This situation occurs when the reinsurer does not have sufficient surplus of its own and is acting on behalf of another insurance company. This other company has the surplus but does not have the expertise to design the arrangement and draft the treaty or does not have the proper resources or contacts to find companies needing surplus relief. Typically, each of these retrocession treaties is for a unique reinsurance treaty.

INFORCE

Periodically, the reinsurer must review its inforce assumed reinsurance portfolio. Unlike the ceding company which tends to look at its entire inforce block of ceded reinsurance, the reinsurer's review will often be at the treaty level. Some treaties call for an annual review of experience for experience refund, bonus, and chargeback calculations. The reinsurer will also want to review self-administered accounts and facultative programs periodically.

Experience Refunds

An experience refund is a mechanism to return some portion of the profits experienced on a block of ceded reinsurance to the ceding company. Experience refunds can be used for YRT, coinsurance, and mod-co.

---

[3]See Chapter 1, Introduction.

Generalized Formula. In reviewing experience refund treaties, it is typical to find the refund formula defined via algebraic symbols. A typical generalized formula would be as follows:

$$ER = f\{P + I - A - C - S - RC - PT - LCF(1+i) - F\}$$

ER — Experience refund
f — Percent of gains to be returned to ceding company
P — Premiums incurred
A — Allowances incurred
C — Claims incurred - mortality or morbidity
S — Surrender benefits incurred
PT — Premium taxes reimbursed
RC — Reserve charge (positive for increase and negative or decrease)
LCF — Loss or deficit carryforward
i — Interest rate to be used on LCF
I — Investment income from reserves and cash flow
F — Fee or risk and expense charge

Of course, some of these terms may not be necessary in a specific agreement, or other terms may be required to clarify or more easily accommodate a specific feature, such as a chargeback of allowances upon early lapse.

As can be seen, this is really a modified gain and loss statement. In theory, any item in the gain and loss can be included in the formula. Since reinsurance normally deals only with annual premiums, items such as due and deferred premiums are not needed. However, refund of premiums for off-anniversary terminations need to be recognized in calculating incurred premiums and allowances.

The experience refund formula can be made to accommodate any structure. For example, it is not uncommon to include only cash items. This is done largely to reduce administrative effort. In practice, certain modifications are common to certain types of treaties. Some typical simplifications are noted below.

The loss carryforward is a unique feature, representing the reinsurer's accumulated past losses under the treaty. Its inclusion in the experience refund calculation simply provides that the ceding company will participate in excess gains on the block only after any losses incurred by the reinsurer have been recovered.

The interest rate applied to the loss carryforward may vary with several factors. For example, it is not uncommon for two different rates to be used, especially in financial reinsurance treaties. One, relatively low rate, may apply to noncash lapses, but another, higher rate may apply to any actual cash outlaid by the reinsurer. This higher rate compensates the reinsurer for loss of investment income on the "missing" cash.

The fee, or risk and experience charge, is another valuable feature. It represents the profit and expense load which the reinsurer extracts before profits are shared with the ceding company. This fee may be stated as a percentage return on strain or losses, as a percentage of reinsured premiums, or as a flat amount per unit of inforce per year. In fact, any fee structure may be used, as long as both parties agree in advance. The fee may vary, depending upon the type of risk and the treaty structure.

Historically, the percentage of the profits which go to the ceding company was fairly uniformly set at 50%, but the percentage can be any mutually acceptable portion up to 100%.[4] Percentages less than 50% are rare.

YRT. Since little or no reserves are involved in YRT reinsurance and surrender benefits are not considered, the experience refund formula in a YRT treaty may be simplified.

A typical experience refund formula in a YRT reinsurance treaty may look like the following:

$$ER \ = \ f\{P - C - F - LCF(1+i)\}$$

Reserves are ignored as being insignificant and merely a timing matter. Allowances are not considered as the typical YRT treaty has no allowances.[5] In this example, premium taxes are also ignored, and presumably are covered by the expense and risk charge; they could be separately recognized.

Under a YRT treaty, the loss carryforward may be limited to a period of time. For example, a claim may be included in the

---

[4]The reinsurer which gives 100% of the profit back presumably has satisfied its objectives through the risk and expense fee.

[5]Actually, certain benefits and substandard extras are coinsured even under a YRT treaty and have allowances. If these benefits are included in the experience refund calculation, both the premiums and the allowances should be considered.

loss carryforward calculation for only a limited period of time, say five or seven years. If the reinsurer cannot recover its fee by that time, it will "forgive" the loss (loss forgiveness) and exclude it from future loss carryforwards. Obviously, in this case, the order of losses is important and any gains should be applied to the oldest eligible loss first.

Coinsurance. The generalized formula is applicable for the coinsurance situation. No special treatment is necessary, although investment income must be clearly defined. Frequently, an annual statement rate is used to determine the interest rate applied to reserves, or a fixed rate or outside index may be used. Usually investment income on cash flow is ignored, but some treaties make provision for it.

Mod-co. In theory, mod-co is no different than coinsurance in developing an experience refund. A key item is determining the interest rate to be used, which generally will be the mod-co adjustment interest rate. In some cases, the mod-co adjustment may be used directly in the formula. In this case, the formula would be

$$ER \ = \ f\{P - A - C - S - PT - LCF(1+i) - F - MCA\},$$

where MCA is the mod-co adjustment.

Bonuses

Some treaties call for the payment of production or persistency bonuses. Production bonuses vary by the level of production, which is generally measured in terms of new reinsurance ceded volume. The bonus would usually be stated in terms of cents per thousand of production. The reinsurer would generally review its new business reports for those accounts having production bonuses. The bonuses may be limited to a stated maximum volume per life.

Persistency bonuses may be paid for the achievement of a certain level of persistency. These bonuses are generally based on thirteen month persistency which is calculated by comparing first year volume of the previous year to the second year volume inforce at the end of the current year. Such bonuses are expressed as cents per thousand of inforce or percentages of premiums and may vary by level of persistency.

Production and persistency bonuses are infrequently used currently.

Chargebacks

When first year allowances exceed first year premiums, a charge-back feature often is included in the treaty. A chargeback provides for the reinsurer to receive its investment back on policies which lapse before premiums received exceed the allowances paid. In pricing, chargebacks may be handled as negative cash values.

Some sample chargeback calculations at various durations are illustrated below. For purposes of illustration, assume the following facts about a coinsurance treaty.

Premiums:	$1,200 annually
Allowances:	
First Year:	140%
Renewal:	20%
Premium Tax Reimbursement:	2%
Chargeback Provision:	Return of excess of allowance paid over premium received, if any, on a policy by policy basis.

Example 1 - Lapse at 12 months

Allowances:		
First Year:	$1,680	
Renewal:	–0–	$1,680
Premiums:		
First Year:	$1,200	
Renewal:	–0–	1,200
Chargeback:		$ 480

Note that premium tax is not included in this chargeback calculation. That, of course, depends upon the terms of the chargeback provision.

Example 2 - Lapse at 15 months

Allowances:
First Year:	$1,680	
Renewal:	60	$1,740

Premiums:
First Year:	$1,200	
Renewal:	300	1,500
Chargeback:		$ 240

Example 3 - Lapse at 24 months

Allowances:
First Year:	$1,680	
Renewal:	340	$1,920

Premiums:
First Year:	$1,200	
Renewal:	1,200	2,400
Chargeback:		$ (480)

In the last case, premiums exceed allowances, so no chargeback is incurred.

Chargebacks may be defined according to any mutually acceptable terms. For example, chargebacks may be unlimited in time, as above, or limited to terminations within a specific period, such as 12, 13 or 24 months from issue. Also, chargebacks may apply to the excess of something other than 100% of premiums, such as 90% or 110% of premiums.

Chargebacks do not afford complete protection against excess lapses for a reinsurer. Chargebacks are collectible only to the extent that future allowances payable to the ceding company can be reduced. The ceding company usually does not guarantee the chargebacks; to do so could create a statutory liability for the ceding company. If lapses are high enough, the future allowances may not cover the chargeback and the reinsurer could lose some of its lapse protection.

Self-Administered Accounts

Periodically, the reinsurer should review self-administered accounts. The reinsurer should look at the experience of the account to determine if it is getting the volume and profits expected in pricing. It would also look at the timing and the quality of the reports received. If it is not receiving reports on a timely basis, or if reports are incomplete, the reinsurer must address the problem. The reinsurer may want to audit the account.

Facultative Reinsurance

The reinsurer should review large facultative accounts periodically to make sure that anticipated placement ratios are being met and that it is receiving proper notification of cessions. Poor administration can lead to poorly defined liabilities, uncertainty, and potential losses.

The reinsurer should periodically review the experience of all facultative accounts. This review can help in establishing pricing assumptions for mortality, persistency, and expenses.

Monitoring of Results

It is important that the reinsurer monitor its results to make sure that business goals are being met. Monitoring should include mortality and persistency experience studies for both automatic and facultative reinsurance and profits by account vis-a-vis pricing expectations.

Effect of Marketing

The experience of inforce business, as well as the relationships built up during the time that the inforce business is on the books, can have a significant effect on a reinsurer's marketing efforts. Ceding companies and reinsurers tend to build up relationships with individuals and companies. From this point of view, reinsurers sometimes will price more competitively for a long-term existing account then they will for a new account. This tendency was very strong up until the mid-1980's when pricing competition became so great that old relationships seemed to take a back seat to sound pricing considerations.

One of the major influences of inforce upon marketing is the current experience that the reinsurer is having on a given client's business. If experience is very good and the reinsurer has continuing faith in the ceding company, it will tend to protect the account with more competitive pricing on new products and a higher level of service overall. If, on the other hand, the block is performing poorly, the reinsurer can logically be expected to take that into consideration when it sets its assumptions for pricing of new plans.

On occasion, reinsurers have even been known to give a discount on profitable inforce reinsurance in order to maintain their position with respect to new business.

FINANCIAL REINSURANCE

Financial reinsurance creates certain unique problems for a reinsurer; most of these have been discussed previously. However, certain aspects of managing an assumed portfolio of financial reinsurance deserve additional comment.

Ceding Company Stability

In evaluating a prospect for financial reinsurance, the long-term stability of that client company and the expectations of future stability have a major influence on the reinsurer's evaluation and willingness to establish a financial reinsurance relationship.

In most circumstances, a traditional reinsurance treaty carries a fairly well-defined risk and the economic loss is largely related to the mortality, persistency, and expense experience on that block of business. The reinsurer accepts a risk and establishes a profit objective which it considers appropriate for that risk.

In dealing with financial reinsurance, the reinsurer typically takes a lower level of profit and expects a lesser exposure to normal insurance risk. However, the reinsurer may take a significant risk with respect to surplus loss.

A financial reinsurance treaty may involve the ceding company holding and managing a large block of assets backing reserves for the reinsurer. If the ceding company mismanages the business it has reinsured or the corresponding assets, the reinsurer can have a significant loss. Therefore, the stability of the ceding company, while important in traditional reinsurance, becomes much more important in the financial reinsurance field.

External Changes

In financial reinsurance one needs to be very concerned about the occurrence of certain external changes. These can be environmental changes such as a drastic change in the economy. However, more frequently they center about the ownership and management of the company. In the past, some financial reinsurance treaties called for an immediate termination or recapture of the treaty, with any experience loss being repaid to the reinsurer, upon any significant change in management or ownership of the ceding company. In general, these types of clauses have been questioned because they leave the regulator with uncertainty as to the validity of reinsurance under all future circumstances. Since the reinsurer may not be able to rely on such clauses, the reinsurer needs to evaluate the management and ownership carefully.

Monitoring Results

Just as with traditional reinsurance, it is important for the financial reinsurer to monitor the experience. A typical way to do this would be to make a model office projection on a block of financial reinsurance at the time the treaty is written. Then, the reinsurer periodically compares the results of that projection with the actual results.

It is more common for subsequent changes to be made in a financial reinsurance treaty than in a traditional treaty. For example, if surplus relief is the initial objective of the treaty, the ceding company may desire to add additional business to the treaty in order to effect additional surplus relief. On the other hand, it may just wish to prolong the repayment of the surplus relief. Before any reinsurer would agree to this, it would want to review the existing reinsurance for trends and performance.

Any changes must be determined on a voluntary, negotiated basis. Any agreement outside the reinsurance treaty which is in place during the existence of the treaty should be considered a part of the treaty. An agreement, such as the ceding company agreeing to indemnify the reinsurer for any loss, might invalidate the reinsurance agreement for surplus relief purposes as far as the regulators are concerned. Therefore, it is important for the reinsurer to monitor the results of financial reinsurance treaties and try to negotiate improved terms, if necessary.

Regulatory, Accounting, and Tax Considerations

Part Three

Reinsurance
10 Regulations

Reinsurance is regulated like other forms of insurance by the laws and regulations of the various state insurance departments. There are far fewer regulations existing for reinsurance than there are for other forms of insurance because reinsurance is a transaction that takes place between two insurance companies rather than a transaction between an insurance company and an unsophisticated policyholder.

State insurance department regulation is concerned with many facets of insurance. A primary concern is the ability of the policyholder to rely upon the insurer's promise of payment of benefits. Statutory reserves and statutory accounting are designed to strengthen this promise of payment. Reinsurance, through the use of reserve credits, or sometimes asset receivables, allows the ceding company to "pass along" some of the responsibility and, in effect, hold lower reserves, and thereby strengthen its balance sheet. Therefore, regulators establish rules defining the acceptability of reinsurance treaties for statutory accounting purposes. These rules do not define the validity of a treaty in legal or economic terms, but only in statutory accounting terms. A treaty may very well be proper in its economic and legal terms and of benefit to the ceding company, but not meet the standards for statutory accounting purposes.[1]

With the occurrence of some prominent life and property and casualty insurance company insolvencies in the early 1980's, regulators became increasingly concerned that reinsurance transactions were being used or abused to mask a company's true economic position. To combat this, much of the recent regulatory activity has focused on reserve credits, mirror image reserving, nonadmitted reinsurers, and use of trusts and letters of credit. This chapter deals with some of the important issues in reinsurance regulations.[2]

RESERVE CREDIT

Insurance regulations in most states do not prohibit reinsurance transactions. The insurance commissioner would not normally disallow a reinsurance treaty but would, instead, disallow any reserve credit.[3] If the reserve credit is disallowed, the ceding company would have to increase its reserves to the pre-reinsurance level. Much of today's regulation concerns reserve credit issues, but review of additional liabilities, such as extraordinary premium payments or interest guarantees, are under consideration.

Regulatory Concerns

One major purpose of these regulations is distinguishing true reinsurance transactions where there is an appropriate transfer of risk from transactions that are in essence loans where the reinsurer seldom, if ever, is exposed to meaningful risk. The latter may be a

---

[1]For example, a coinsurance treaty with a nonadmitted reinsurer may produce perfect indemnity, but the treaty would still not qualify for reserve credit.

[2]Of necessity, this book discusses regulations as they are at the time of this writing, August 1990. Changes may have occurred since that time and the reader is advised to check current regulations before entering into any transactions.

[3]Actually, under statutory accounting, the appropriate treatment would be to take credit for the reinsurance as a reduction to the reserves, even though the reinsurer may not be admitted, and to establish a separate liability, as appropriate, for reinsurance in unauthorized companies. See Chapter 12, Statutory Accounting for Reinsurance.

legitimate business credit risk, but it is not a reinsurance risk and should not be accounted for as reinsurance on the ceding company's balance sheet.

The problem facing regulators is identifying what constitutes appropriate or sufficient risk transfer. Often, this definition is left to the discretion of the regulator. Recently, some states have implemented specific regulations or legislation to address the issue.

Regulatory Guidelines

Regulators are concerned that the reinsurer will not be able to pay its obligations to the ceding company when they are due. Most states require that the reinsurer must be licensed or accredited in the ceding company's state of domicile or that the reinsurer must provide some security either through funds withheld, a trust account, an escrow account, or a letter of credit.

The NAIC Model Law on Credit for Reinsurance establishes conditions that a reinsurer must meet in order for a domestic ceding company to take credit for reinsurance, either as an asset or as a reduction in liability for reinsurance ceded. Credit is allowed where reinsurance is ceded to a reinsurer under any of the following situations:

(1) The reinsurer is licensed to transact insurance or reinsurance in the state.

(2) The reinsurer is accredited as a reinsurer in the state. An accredited reinsurer is one which
   (a) files with the Commissioner evidence of its submission to the state's jurisdiction;
   (b) submits to the state's authority to examine its books and records;
   (c) is licensed to transact insurance or reinsurance in at least one state, or in the case of a U.S. branch of an alien insurer, is entered through and licensed to transact insurance or reinsurance in at least one state;
   (d) files annually with the Commissioner a copy of its annual statement filed with the insurance department of its state of domicile and a copy of its most recent audited financial statement, and either
      (i) maintains a policyholder surplus of at least $20,000,000 and has not been denied accreditation

by the Commissioner within 90 days of its submission, or

(ii) maintains a policyholder surplus of less than $20,000,000 and whose accreditation is approved by the Commissioner.

(3) The reinsurer is domiciled and licensed in, or in the case of a U.S. branch of an alien reinsurer, is entered through a state which employs standards regarding credit for reinsurance substantially similar to those applicable under the Model Law, and the reinsurer

(a) maintains policyholder surplus of not less than $20,000,000, and

(b) submits to the authority of the state to examine its books and records.

(4) The reinsurer maintains a trust in a qualified U.S. financial institution for payment of the valid claims of its U.S. policyholders and ceding insurers. Annually, the reinsurer must report to the Commissioner substantially the same information as that required on the NAIC Annual Statement to enable the Commissioner to determine the sufficiency of the trust fund. In the case of a single reinsurer, the trust shall consist of an amount representing the reinsurer's liabilities attributable to business written in the U.S. and the reinsurer maintains a trusteed surplus of not less than $20,000,000. In the case of a group of individual unincorporated underwriters, such as Lloyd's, the trust shall consist of a trusteed account representing the group's liabilities attributable to business written in the U.S. and a trusteed surplus of $100,000,000 held for the benefit of the U.S. ceding insurers of any member of the group, and make available to the Commissioner an annual certification of the solvency of each underwriter by the group's domiciliary regulator and its independent public accountants.

The model act also provides the following:

(1) Credit is allowed for a reinsurer not meeting the above requirements only with respect to the insurance risks located in jurisdictions where such reinsurance is required by law or regulation of the jurisdiction.

(2) If the reinsurer is not licensed or accredited to transact insurance or reinsurance in the state, the reinsurer must

also agree to perform its obligations under the terms of the agreement, and in the event that it fails to perform, it agrees to submit to the jurisdiction of any court of competant jurisdiction in any state of the U.S. and will abide by the final decision of such court or of any appellate court in the event of an appeal and will designate the Commissioner or an attorney as its true and lawful attorney for any action.

(3) A reduction from liability for reinsurance ceded to a reinsurer not meeting the above requirements is allowed in an amount not exceeding the liabilities carried by the ceding insurer will be in the amount of the funds held by or on behalf of the ceding insurer, including funds held in trust for the ceding insurer as security for payment of obligations under the reinsurance contract. The security may be in the form of

(a) cash;

(b) securities listed by the Securities Valuation Office of the NAIC and qualifying as admitted assets; or

(c) clean, irrevocable, unconditional letter of credit by a qualified U.S. institution.[4]

New York Regulations 114 and 133 and California Bulletin 87-10 further expand on the rules governing the banks permitted to be utilized for trusts and letters of credit.[5] The New York Regulations have specific rules concerning the actual form of the letter. The California regulation requires that all three parties must be unrelated and the agreement explicitly allows a conservator or liquidator to withdraw the funds from the trust or draw down the letters of credit. Unfortunately, the various state requirements are not only different, they are frequently in conflict.

Risk Transfer

The NAIC model regulation regarding life reinsurance addresses many of the risk transfer questions in financial reinsurance. This

---

[4]The Securities Valuation Office maintains a list of qualified institutions.

[5]At this time, the future of these regulations is uncertain. The industry is attempting to modify some terms, but the effect of the regulation is likely to follow that of the cited provisions.

model regulation on life reinsurance was designed to regulate surplus relief reinsurance. The objective of the regulation is to deny reinsurance credit for certain kinds of financial reinsurance transactions. This regulation was developed in response to a large number of reinsurance transactions which purported to provide a significant amount of surplus relief to the ceding company, but with little or no risk to the reinsurer. The regulation prohibits the ceding company from establishing any asset or offsetting any liability in its financial statements if any one of these eight conditions exist:

(1) If the primary affect of the agreement is to transfer only deficiency reserves or excess interest reserves to the reinsurer for a small charge and it does not provide for the reinsurer's significant participation in one or more of the mortality, morbidity, investment or surrender risks.

(2) If the reserve credit is not in compliance with the rules or regulations of the Insurance Department.

(3) If the reserve credit is greater than the underlying reserve for the policy obligations transferred to the reinsurer.

(4) If the ceding company is required to reimburse the reinsurer for negative experience. However, offsetting experience refunds against prior years losses or payment of an amount equal to prior year losses upon voluntary termination of the reinsurance are exempted.

(5) If the reinsurer can regain the surplus at its option or automatically upon the occurrence of some event except for nonpayment of reinsurance premiums.

(6) If the ceding company is required at some point scheduled in the agreement to recapture all or part of the reinsurance ceded.

(7) If the reinsurer is not required to make any cash payments prior to termination of the reinsurance agreement.

(8) If the agreement may require the ceding company to pay the reinsurer amounts other than the income reasonably expected from the reinsured policies.

The model regulation further requires that reinsurance agreements be in writing. The current model regulation has been adopted in only a few states.

Insolvency

In order to take a statutory financial statement credit for reinsurance ceded, all reinsurance agreements are required to contain an insolvency clause. The insolvency clause states that the reinsurance is payable to the liquidator without diminution because of insolvency. The insolvency clause is required because the basic understanding in a reinsurance contract is that the reinsurer is required to pay only those claims which represent actual losses incurred by the ceding company. U.S. courts have ruled that the liquidator may first collect reinsurance proceeds without paying any part of the loss. In fact, the liquidator may apply only a portion of reinsurance proceeds to pay the claim. The remainder of the reinsurance proceeds may be used to pay portions of other claims.

An important part of this clause and its interpretation is that the basic terms of the treaty are not changed by the event of insolvency. If the ceding company still makes premium payments, it is entitled to full claim payments. If, on the other hand, it fails to pay reinsurance premiums, the reinsurer is entitled to terminate the reinsurance. Consequently, the offset provision, allowing either party to offset amounts payable to it by amounts due to it, may provide an alternative to termination.[6]

The most important case in this area of insolvency is the Fidelity & Deposit Company vs. Pink.[7] In this case, the Southern Surety Company of New York was declared insolvent and the New York Superintendent of Insurance, Lewis H. Pink, took possession of the assets to begin liquidation proceedings. Pink approved a claim for payment but did not actually pay it. However, he demanded reimbursement from the reinsurer. The reinsurer refused to pay stating the language of the treaty was quite clear that it was only responsible for actual losses. It argued that, as no claim was paid, there was no actual loss. The United States Supreme Court agreed with the reinsurer. Superintendent Pink responded by introducing Section 77 of the New York Insurance Law which requires the inclusion of the insolvency clause in reinsurance contracts. Most other states have adopted similar requirements.

------

[6]See Chapter 11, Insolvency.

[7]Fidelity & Deposit Company v. Pink, 302 U.S. 224, 82 L.Ed. 213, 58 S. Ct. 162 (1937), *reh'g. denied*, 302 U.S. 780, 82 L.Ed. 603, 58S. Ct. 407 (1938).

MIRROR IMAGE RESERVES

The basic concept of mirror image reserves is that the ceding company is not allowed to take a reserve credit on its statutory annual statement for any reserves in excess of the amount of reserve the reinsurer is holding on the business. This is a very complicated subject and the NAIC has been studying the issues. However, only a few states currently have regulations in this area, and these differ significantly in their provisions.[8] Mirror image reserves is still the subject of much debate. Some of the arguments for and against mirror image reserving are presented.

Regulatory Concerns

Regulators are very concerned about liabilities that disappear or vanish in reinsurance transactions. This goes back to the solvency issue. The concern is that adequate provision has not been made for the liabilities if the statutory reserves vanish in the transaction and are not being held by the reinsurer.

Differences in Reserves

There are some legitimate reasons for the ceding company and the reinsurer to hold different reserves. These occur because of mechanical or logistical problems in communicating reinsurance information.

One of the most common reasons for reserves to differ between the ceding company and the reinsurer is because of the items in transit. There is always a lag between the reporting of new cessions, reinstatements, lapses, and other changes between the ceding company and the reinsurer. The reinsurer must close its books by a certain date in order to prepare its own financial statements and simply cannot wait an extra ten days to make sure that it has the majority of all transactions reported. The reserves on items in transit are usually insignificant in comparison to the total reserve, and some ceding companies may not make any adjustment because of time pressure in preparing their own financial statements.

---

[8]The fifth amendment to New York Regulation 20 requires "worldwide" mirror reserves. This obligates the ceding company to verify that its reinsurer and any of its retrocessionaires on a given block of reinsurance are holding mirror reserves.

Another reason why reserves may differ is that the reinsurer may be using a slightly different reserve valuation basis to simplify its procedures. The reinsurer is faced with valuing many different types of policies. It may have only a handful of policies on any one policy form. Where possible, the reinsurer may try to group policy forms which are similar but not quite identical into a common valuation reserve basis. For example, the ceding company may be reserving a policy form using the Illinois Method, and the reinsurer may value it on a CRVM basis rather than setting up a unique reserve file for that product. The differences are usually trivial, but they do exist.

A third reason for differences in reserves often occurs on self-administered reinsurance where the ceding company is supplying the reinsurer with the reserve information. Often, the ceding company is unable to produce the reserve reports before the reinsurer must close its books for the year. The reinsurer is forced to use the last reserve value it had from the ceding company. The reporting is typically only one month in arrears, but could be three months or more. Obviously, the longer the lag in reporting, the greater the difference in reserves will be.

Vanishing Reserves

Sometimes reserves vanish in a reinsurance transaction because the reserves are not required in the reinsurer's jurisdiction or the reserve requirements are less stringent and a lesser value is held. A prime example of this is deficiency reserves. Some states have a very stringent deficiency reserve requirements while a few other states have no requirements at all. A reinsurer in a state which did not require deficiency reserves could accept business with deficiency reserves and not set up any of these reserves on its statutory statement, while the ceding company might take full credit for the deficiency reserves on its statutory statement.

The problem is not limited to deficiency reserves. The situation is quite common in offshore sites which use a more flexible valuation system, such as the United Kingdom or Bermuda.[9]

---

[9]See Chapter 16, International Reinsurance.

NONADMITTED REINSURERS

Reinsurers which are neither licensed nor accredited to accept reinsurance on lives in a specified state are called nonadmitted reinsurers. While it is very rare for a professional reinsurer not to be admitted in all states, not all reinsurance transactions take place with the professional reinsurer. Many reinsurance transactions take place between specialty reinsurers, captive reinsurers, or affiliates which are nonadmitted in the ceding company's state of domicile.

Regulatory Concerns

Regulators are concerned about nonadmitted reinsurers because they have no jurisdiction over these reinsurers. This makes it very difficult for the regulator to enforce contractual reinsurance benefits due to the ceding company. Regulators also have no control over the financial condition of the reinsurer. Should the nonadmitted reinsurer become insolvent, the domestic ceding company's financial position could be severely impaired.

A special subset of the nonadmitted reinsurer problem concerns fronting. In this situation, the ceding company has issued policies on behalf of the reinsurer and may cede 100% of the risk to the reinsurer maintaining only a small fee for administration or use of its license. One concern of the regulator about fronting is that the reinsurer is circumventing the regulations of its jurisdiction by not complying with its regulations and becoming admitted in the jurisdiction. The company may not meet the standards set by that state and may even have been denied admission. Should the reinsurer become insolvent, the ceding company might be financially impaired as it would be responsible for the risks without having any premiums or reserves.

New York attempted to deal with this situation and proposed a regulation prohibiting certain transactions. While this regulation was never enacted, the prohibited transactions are included as an example of what future regulations may consider.

(1)   New York licensed life insurance companies are prohibited to cede directly or indirectly retrocede with an unlicensed insurer any policy covering residents of the state of New York if the reinsurance is a condition of the original placement of the policy with the licensed company and if the unlicensed insurer has the power to place such policies.

(2) No New York licensed insurer can cede 50% or more of its liability under any policy covering a resident of New York, either directly or indirectly, to an unlicensed insurer which controls or is controlled by or affiliated with the policyholder, producer, or any other entity which has the power to place these policies.

(3) No New York licensed insurance company is allowed to reinsure any part of its liability on a policy covering residents of the state to an unlicensed insurer if the reinsurer or any affiliate of the reinsurer performs any one or more of the following functions in connection with the policies reinsured: marketing, underwriting, policy owner service or claims.

The proposed regulation would have exempted group policies issued to multi-state employers if less than 10% of the covered employees resided in New York and if the unlicensed reinsurer did not control or was not controlled by or affiliated with the policyholder or producer. Reinsurance transactions involving affiliates of the ceding company were not prohibited if these transactions were performed under a nondisapproved service agreement. Further, facultative underwriting was not considered underwriting for the purpose of fronting.

Effect of Regulations

As stated in the section on Regulatory Guidelines, nonadmitted reinsurers are required to provide security through funds withheld, trust or escrow accounts, or letters of credit. Ceding companies will not receive reserve credit for reinsurance ceded to a nonadmitted reinsurer if the reinsurer does not meet these guidelines. In that event, there are special reporting guidelines in the statutory annual statement which flag these transactions.

TRUSTS, ESCROW ACCOUNTS, LETTERS OF CREDIT, FUNDS WITHHELD

Trusts, escrow accounts, and letters of credit are the principal instruments used as security for reinsurance transactions. Secruity may also be provided by structuring the reinsurance with funds withheld. Recent regulation has focused on defining specifications regarding these instruments to assure that they are indeed security for the transaction, not meaningless pieces of paper. Likewise, limitations have been placed on the admissability of assets under a funds withheld reinsurance treaty.

Regulatory Concerns

Regulators are concerned that funds set aside in a trust, escrow account, or letter of credit truly exist, are sufficient to cover the liabilities, and are actually available to the ceding company or its successor when necessary. Some recent insurance company insolvencies have demonstrated the difficulties experienced by the ceding company or the liquidator in actually obtaining funds seemingly committed by the reinsurance agreement. Regulators want to be certain funds are available. While regulators cannot dictate terms of a legal agreement, such as a reinsurance treaty, they can establish rules for statutory accounting of liabilities and acceptable assets. Regulations, therefore, set forth the conditions which must be met if favorable accounting treatment is to be allowed. Among other things, these regulations may define the type of assets acceptable in a trust and the types of financial institutions which are acceptable as participants, using these instruments.

Trusts and Escrow Accounts

New York Regulation 114 sets forth the requirements for provisions to be included in a trust agreement for reinsurers admitted in New York. The requirements include that the beneficiary of the trust, normally the ceding insurance company, has a right to withdraw assets from the trust account at any time without notifying the grantor, normally the reinsurance company. The trust agreement must provide that the trustee will receive and hold all assets and that these assets must be in such a form that the trustee may negotiate any of the assets in the trust without the consent or signature of the grantor. Assets deposited in the trust account must be valued according to their current fair market value. The assets must consist only of

(1) Cash,
(2) Certificates of Deposit, and
(3) Investments as specified by New York Insurance Law.

The assets may not be investments issued by a company which is in any way affiliated with the grantor or the beneficiary. The reinsurer must transfer to the trustee legal title of all the assets in the trust.

The reinsurance agreement must provide that the ceding company will be able to withdraw assets from the trust only for the following purposes:

(1) To reimburse the ceding company for the reinsurer's share of premiums returned to the owners of policies reinsured under the reinsurance agreement on account of cancellations of such policies.

(2) To reimburse the ceding company for the reinsurer's share of surrender benefits or losses paid by the ceding company pursuant to the provisions of the policies reinsured under the reinsurance agreement.

(3) To fund an account with the ceding company in an amount at least equal to the deduction for reinsurance ceded from the ceding company's liabilities for policies ceded under the agreement. Such accounts shall include, but not be limited to, amounts for policy reserves, claims and losses occurred and unearned premium reserves.

(4) To pay any other amounts the ceding company claims are due under the reinsurance agreement.

Letters of Credit

A letter of credit is a document issued by a bank on the orders of one party, in this case the reinsurer, which provides that the beneficiary, in this case the ceding company, will be able to withdraw funds up to a specified limit. It is a guarantee of payment which can be enforced, yet the use of a letter of credit requires no physical disbursement of assets by the reinsurer unless the ceding company actually requests disbursement of the funds. The letter of credit must be in writing. The actual contract between the bank and its customer does not affect the beneficiary.

Rules covering the use of letters of credit in reinsurance situations vary from state to state, therefore, it is important to review the position of the insurance department in the specific states affected by a given treaty. California and New York have specific rules regarding letters of credit. They require that the letter of credit must be "clean," "unconditional," "irrevocable," and "evergreen." A clean letter of credit requires that the beneficiary present only a demand for payment to the issuing bank and that no further documentation is necessary. "Irrevocable" means that the letter of credit can be modified only with the consent of the parties specified in the contract. The rules also require that the letter of credit be "evergreen", that is, that the letter of credit will be renewed automatically unless the issuing bank gives advance written notice of nonrenewal to both parties. This allows the parties to make other arrangements.

California requires the issuer be a member of the Federal Reserve System and be satisfactory to the Commissioner. The New York regulation requires that the reinsurance contract specifically call for the letter of credit. The NAIC Model Law on Credit for Reinsurance provides for the SVO to maintain a list of institutions qualified to provide acceptable letters of credit.

The financial institution issuing the letter of credit receives a fee commensurate with the degree of risk it is assuming by issuing the letter of credit. This fee is usually expressed as a percentage of the amount of the letter of credit and may be in the range of .2 to .3% per year, or up to 1%.

Funds Withheld

Another form of security is funds withheld by, or assets left on deposit with, the ceding company in support of the reinsurance. Either the ceding company withholds funds due the reinsurer or the reinsurer deposits funds with the ceding company in an amount at least equal to the reserve credit to be taken. The ceding company establishes a separate liability for the funds due the reinsurer and uses this as an offset in determining the liability for reinsurance in unauthorized companies.

This approach is generally viewed favorably by the regulators since the ceding company has in its possession assets sufficient to cover the reserve credit. The regulators do have a concern that the reinsurance agreement provide sufficient transfer of risk. In addition, they require that any interest paid or credited to the reinsurer on such funds be reasonable in relation to the ceding company's investment returns. If the regulators are not satisfied that these conditions have been met, they may disallow the offset in the determination of the liability for reinsurance in unauthorized companies.

OTHER AREAS OF REGULATION

Reinsurance Treaty Approval

Unlike an insurance policy form, a reinsurance treaty usually does not require approval of the state insurance department in order to be put into effect. As mentioned earlier, state insurance departments do not usually disapprove or disallow insurance treaties but rather disallow reserve credits or disapprove statutory accounting treatments. Obviously, it is highly undesirable to have a reserve credit disallowed. There are times when the parties to a financial reinsurance treaty may wish to consult with the state insurance department before effecting the treaty. It is impossible to define every occasion when this step should be taken, but it would usually involve issues which are known to be sensitive, when a new technique is used, or when the financial implications are significant.

Intercompany Reinsurance

Generally, the same rules apply to reinsurance between related companies as apply to independent entities. Some states do have special regulations regarding related party reinsurance, such as a requirement of prior approval of treaties. On the other hand, an unusual treaty between related parties may be viewed more favorably than one between unrelated parties, especially if both companies are domiciled in the same state and the stronger company is the reinsurer. Again, the primary concerns of the regulators are conformity with the applicable regulations and protection of policyholder interests.

IRIS

The NAIC Insurance Regulatory Information System (IRIS) was developed to assist state insurance departments in overseeing the financial conditions of insurance companies. All companies are required to file annual statements in all states in which they are licensed. Because no state insurance department is able to review all licensed companies' financial statements quickly and thoroughly, IRIS was developed to help the insurance department select those companies which may require more immediate attention. IRIS consists of a series of ratios which may be developed from the statutory annual statement. There are currently twelve IRIS ratios. Because reinsurance may affect the amount of assets, liabilities, surplus, investment income, premiums, benefits, or expenses reported in a company's annual statement, its use can affect, either favorably or unfavorably, a number of the ratios developed. A company should consider the effect on these ratios before entering into a significant reinsurance transaction. Alternative structuring of the treaty might produce significantly different effects on the ratios.

Certain of the ratios are intended to measure the effect of reinsurance. For example, Ratio #8 measures the amount of surplus relief. It is calculated by dividing commissions and expense allowances on reinsurance ceded by the capital and surplus of the company. A ratio of greater than 20% may trigger a further investigation into the nature of the reinsurance transactions. The greatest attention will be paid to those reinsurance agreements providing surplus relief.

Insolvency
11 and Reinsurance

Reinsurance treaties are unique legal contracts in that they affect not only the two parties to the transaction, but also the individuals insured by both parties, even those not covered by the reinsurance agreement. The ultimate worth of the treaty, and the ability to collect under its terms, must be clear, even in the event of an insolvency by one of the two parties. Therefore, special provisions are included in most reinsurance treaties clarifying the working of the treaty in such an event.

Few life insurance companies face insolvency. While some companies may approach the edge of solvency, most are able to avoid actual disaster by obtaining necessary funds from financial institutions, by slowing growth, by selling all or a portion of the business to another insurer, or by adding surplus through reinsurance transactions. If an insurer is declared insolvent, it is frequently due to some combination of fraud, mismanagement, under-reserving, inexperience, or an uncontrollable external event such as a war or plague.

MODEL ACT

Insurance companies are specifically excluded from the Federal Bankruptcy Act. The NAIC has recommended the Insurer's Supervision, Rehabilitation and Liquidation Model Act to guide the Commissioner in insolvency proceedings. The Model Act defines insolvency as either the inability to pay obligations when due or having admitted assets that do not exceed liabilities plus the greater of the legally required capital and surplus or the total par or stated value of authorized and issued capital stock.

Conditions

The Model Act allows the Commissioner to take charge of the troubled company in any of the following situations:

(1) The continued operation of the company might prove financially hazardous to its policyholders, competitors, or the public.
(2) There is fraud, embezzlement, or other dishonesty.
(3) The periodic financial reports are not filed and no adequate explanation is provided.
(4) The insurer attempts to sell or reinsure all or almost all of its business without the prior consent of the Commissioner.

The Commissioner may, at his option, attempt to rehabilitate the company. If the rehabilitation is successful, the management of the company is turned over to an approved management team. If the rehabilitation is not successful, the Commissioner can liquidate the company.

In the case of a liquidation, the Commissioner gathers the assets of the company. If a Guarantee Fund exists in the state, the fund will either assume the life, accident and health, and annuity business or reinsure it with a solvent company. The insolvent insurer's creditors are then paid on a class by class basis from the remaining assets. All creditors of a given class must be paid in total before any creditors in the next class may receive any payment.

Priority of Distribution

The model act defines eight classes of unsecured creditors for distribution purposes after the claims of secured creditors have been satisfied. These classes and their definitions are as follows:

Class 1.   The cost and expenses of administration.
Class 2.   Debts to employees for services performed.
Class 3.   Policy claims.
Class 4.   Claims for general creditors.
Class 5.   Claims of any federal, state, or local government.
Class 6.   Claims filed late.
Class 7.   Surplus, contribution notes, policyholder dividends, or similar obligations.
Class 8.   The claims of shareholders or other owners.

In an insolvency, the policyholders may receive only a portion of the benefits from their policies. The federal government, despite being classified as a Class 5 creditor, is usually paid before the policyholders.

The Ceding Company's Position

From time to time, a ceding company has tried to assert that it is a policyholder and therefore in Class 3. In one case, the Indiana Supreme Court found that the model act was designed for the protection of unsophisticated consumers and not reinsurers. In this case, one insurance company had fronted insurance for another company and had ceded 100% of the business to it for a small fee. When the reinsurer became insolvent, the fronting company was left with policy liabilities and no premiums. The court found that the fronting company was not a policyholder but rather a sophisticated insurance company which had entered into a reinsurance agreement. Accordingly, it was placed in Class 4.

The Reinsurer's Position

In the case of a ceding company insolvency, the reinsurer is considered to be in Class 4, a general creditor. General creditors rarely receive full payment for amounts owed them, so a reinsurer must either accept the fact that it will lose some or all amounts owed it in the event of a client's insolvency or make other provisions which will improve its position. The use of a trust may allow a reinsurer to become a secured creditor, moving ahead of all unsecured creditors.

THE INSOLVENCY CLAUSE

Most reinsurance agreements contain an insolvency clause stating that the reinsurance is payable to the liquidator without diminution because of insolvency. The insurance company is denied reserve credit for reinsurance ceded on its statutory financial statements unless this clause is included. The insolvency clause has been required by many states because the basic understanding in a reinsurance contract is that the reinsurer is required to pay only those claims representing actual losses incurred by the ceding company. U.S. courts have ruled that the liquidator may first collect reinsurance proceeds without paying any part of a loss. In fact, the liquidator may apply only a portion of the reinsurance proceeds to pay the claim. The remainder of the reinsurance proceeds may be used to pay portions of other claims.

Purpose

The effect of the insolvency clause is to override the normal treaty mechanics whereby the reinsurer pays only its proportionate share of any claims paid. It really provides that, in the event of an insolvency, the ceding company may not be able to pay all claims incurred. Instead it may pay a lesser amount. However, the reinsurer may not use this lowered payment as a reason to reduce its payment. In this event, the reinsurer must pay its share of the amount which would have been due the policyholder absent the insolvency.

The insolvency clause is required for a treaty to generate reserve credit, but is not a requirement for a valid treaty. For example, a coinsurance treaty which omitted this clause would have equal effect on cash flows, barring an insolvency, but would not provide reserve credits.

Nonproportional treaties may omit this clause altogether as reserve credits are not an issue. However, many treaties still include this clause as it provides clarification on a potential problem point. In any event, the clause should be useful in establishing the collectibility of claims due at year-end or at the point of insolvency.

Cut-Through

Until recently a "cut-through" or purchase of a claim has had unclear status in a liquidation. Reinsurers, from time to time, have attempted to pay a claim directly to the claimant, bypassing the liquidator without a specific authorization in the reinsurance contract. However, a liquidator is empowered to settle claims for less than their full value in a liquidation, and apply the remainder of the reinsurance proceeds to pay other claims.

In Ainsworth vs. General Reinsurance Corp.[1], the U.S. Court of Appeals for the Eighth Circuit upheld a decision that General Reinsurance was liable to the receiver of Medallion Insurance Company for policy proceeds that had previously been paid directly by General Reinsurance to the policyholder. In this case, the reinsurer paid a reduced amount directly to the policyholder in exchange for a release discharging the primary insurance company and its receiver from all liability in connection with the claim. The receiver, however, filed an action to recover the 100% of proceeds due from General Reinsurance. The court found that Missouri's Statutory Code for insolvencies mandated that the receiver collect all reinsurance proceeds and that the reinsurer was not free to pay the policyholder without the liquidator's consent. General Reinsurance had to pay the receiver as well as the policyholder.

Some states specifically allow cut-through provisions. In the event two parties to a reinsurance agreement wish to allow for a cut-through, the statutes and regulations of the states concerned should be carefully researched and the reinsurance treaties made very clear.

Set Off

In a reinsurance arrangement, large sums of money may pass back and forth between the reinsurer and the ceding company. These sums include premiums, expense allowances, and claim reimbursement. To simplify these transactions, frequently only the net balance is remitted. This is referred to as an offset or a set off.[2] A set off allows for the netting of amounts due arising out of different transactions.

In the event of the insolvency of one party to the contract, the right to set off becomes important. Courts have held that the

---

[1]Ainsworth v. General Reinsurance Corporation. 751 F.2d 962 (8th Cir. 1985).

[2]The term "set off" or "offset" comes from the fact that amounts due are netted, or set off against each other.

inclusion of the right to set off in a statute or a reinsurance agreement does not create this right, but merely affirms the already existing right of set off. In most states the right of set off is a part of the law. This right cannot be overridden by the courts, but it can be eliminated or abridged by statute. In states where this right is normally granted, the two parties can eliminate it through negotiation and mutual agreement. If the right of set off is prohibited by statute, the prohibition cannot be overriden by contract provisions.

In order to set off debts in a liquidation, the reinsurer must show that some equitable ground exists and that there is "mutuality." Mutuality of capacity is defined as debts that are "due to and from the same persons in the same capacity." In other words, there must be a relationship between the two parties, each acting as a principal and not as an agent or trustee. Mutuality of time provides that obligations incurred before liquidation be offset only against other obligations incurred prior to liquidation. Likewise, obligations incurred after liquidation may be set off only against other obligations incurred after liquidation. Under this concept, a party incurring obligations from one agreement can look to the obligations owed it from another agreement with the same party to offset payment of the debt.

The majority of states have enacted statutes concerning the right to set off in insurance company liquidations. However, only California, New York, Minnesota, New Jersey, Wisconsin, Missouri and Illinois have case law specifically interpreting the statutes. Other jurisdictions may look to these cases as precedent in interpreting their set off statutes.

Historically, the right to offset was well accepted within a single reinsurance treaty. There was even fairly widespread belief that obligations incurred could be set off against amounts due under a separate treaty between the same two parties. However, a case now in the California courts has challenged this position.

In this situation, a group of property and casualty insurers, known collectively as Mission Insurance, became insolvent and had many reinsurance agreements with many reinsurers, including several between some of its companies and some Prudential companies. Prudential argued, in essence, that all treaties between any Mission Insurance company and any Prudential company should be combined for purposes of determining the offset. The California Insurance Commissioner disagreed, and essentially asked the court to invalidate the offset provisions.

The trial court agreed with the Commissioner and denied the right of set off. Prudential appealed and the California Court of Appeals rejected the Commissioner's arguments, siding with Prudential and reversing the trial court.[3] The case is now on appeal to the California Supreme Court. The Court of Appeals' decision establishes the right to offset mutual debts and credits between ceding companies and reinsurers under California law. In any event, the final result of the litigation will provide an important precedent for states with similar laws.

An argument against offset is that it gives "reinsurers an unlawful preference against creditors in higher statutory priority groups." In addition, it has been argued that reinsurers should not be "entitled to share as claimants" in the insolvent company's assets. The recent litigation has pointed out the need to review this situation. Accordingly, the NAIC Rehabilitators and Liquidators Task Force was established to review the Insurer Supervision, Rehabilitation and Liquidation Model Act, especially Section 30 which provides specific authority for offset. Thus far, that group has supported the continuation of the intent of the Act, but is considering making changes in the wording.

The effect of this could include stronger underwriting of a ceding company's financial strength by the reinsurer, leaving less assets with the ceding company, and higher prices for financial reinsurance. Any company entering into a reinsurance treaty may be well advised to discuss the validity of this provision in advance with the various insurance departments.

CEDING COMPANY INSOLVENCY

When discussing insolvency, the focus is usually on a ceding company insolvency. There are many considerations, most of which should be addressed before entering into a reinsurance treaty.

In the event of the insolvency of an insurance company, the liquidator takes control of the company and begins to collect the assets. It also pays claims. The insolvency clause clearly states that the liquidator will receive the reinsurance proceeds on claims without reduction. The liquidator is under no obligation to pay

---

[3]Prudential Reinsurance Co. v. Superior Court. 265 California Reporter, 1986.

the claim with the reinsurance proceeds, the proceeds could be used for the payment of other claims. If the reinsurance is secured by a letter of credit or a trust or escrow account, the liquidator may actually draw out the funds.

The reinsurer is entitled to receive any monies owed it as a Class 4 general creditor. However, the reinsurer traditionally has had the right to offset any funds which it owes the liquidator of the ceding company by the amounts which the ceding company owes it. This is particularly important if there are a large amount of unpaid premiums, if the ceding company is maintaining the reserves under a mod-co arrangement, or if funds withheld coinsurance has been used and the ceding company is holding an accounts payable liability. In the absence of the right to set off, the reinsurer could be left in a critical situation. In the absence of the statutory right to do so, the reinsurer is not allowed to cut-through or pay claims directly to the policyholder, bypassing the liquidator.

REINSURER INSOLVENCY

The reinsurer can also become insolvent. This could have a dramatic effect on the ceding company's financial position. The recent insolvency of several property and casualty reinsurers has increased regulatory concern about reinsurance transactions.

The presence of an indemnity reinsurance agreement does not relieve the ceding company of its obligations to the policyholder. In the event of a reinsurer insolvency, the ceding company would be required to make full benefit payment to its policyholders even if the policies were 100% reinsured. This could be a problem in the case of any situation which is largely coinsured or in a funds withheld mod-co arrangement. This could conceivably impair the ceding company's financial situation. In these situations, some protection would be afforded the ceding company if there is a letter of credit or trust securing the reserves.

The ceding company would receive benefit payments from the reinsurer as a Class 4 general creditor, not as a Class 3 policyholder. It is quite likely in such a situation that the ceding company would not receive full reimbursement for the reinsured benefits. This situation is particularly critical where the ceding company reinsures 100% of the risk for a small administrative fee. This is one reason that fronting agreements should be considered only with caution.

The liquidator or reinsurer would expect to receive all monies which the ceding company owes to the reinsurer. The ceding company would be able to set off these monies by any amounts which the reinsurer owes it.

For those ceding companies utilizing reinsurance pools, the situation of the insolvency of a member of a reinsurance pool should also be considered. Unless otherwise specified in the treaty, each reinsurer is responsible only for its share of claims and liabilities. In the event of the insolvency of one member, the ceding company is in the same situation as it would be without the pooling arrangement; the pooling is merely an administrative tool. However, a pool could provide that the surviving members are responsible for the obligations of an insolvent member, but this would then be specified in the treaty. This latter approach is uncommon.

POLICYHOLDER RIGHTS

Policyholders are placed in Class 3 for benefit distribution in the case of ceding company insolvency. This places the policyholder ahead of the reinsurer and the other general creditors of the ceding company. While benefit payments may be delayed, state insurance departments work very diligently in the case of an insolvency to see that policyholders receive full benefit payment.

In the case of the Equity Funding and Baldwin United insolvencies, the policyholders eventually received full benefit payment. In the event of the reinsurer insolvency, the policyholders would expect full benefit payment within a reasonable period of time from the ceding company. Should the reinsurer's insolvency push the ceding company into insolvency, the policyholders would be treated as Class 3 creditors.

MANAGING THE INSOLVENCY RISK

The two major tools that the reinsurer has in managing the insolvency risk is carefully drafting the reinsurance treaty and underwriting proposed clients.

Contractual

From the contractual side, the most important provision for inclusion in the treaty is the set off clause. However, as pointed out earlier, this protection is not as invulnerable as it was once believed to be. The reinsurer might gain some additional protection by requiring that the ceding company maintain a trust to cover any unpaid premiums or fees. Inclusion of any requirements which would cause the reinsurance to be terminated in the case of a change of ownership or a change in management, or upon the insolvency of the insurer, would no doubt cause insurance regulators and the IRS to view this as other than a reinsurance contract.

The reinsurer may add a provision requiring quarterly or even monthly financial reports and conditions regarding asset and liability matching, investment restrictions, and rules covering the types of assets which the ceding company may purchase. These restrictions are not common in reinsurance treaties but are often required by institutional investors. If the reinsurer is making a major financial commitment to the ceding company, the reinsurer may consider imposing some sort of restriction on stockholder dividends paid. The reinsurer may place restrictions on the type, amount, or source of new business which the company can issue if it believes that such business would be detrimental to the long term health of the insurer. The reinsurer may also use an "indeterminate premium" form of reinsurance, allowing itself the right to charge a higher premium or lower allowance later should it view future expectations differently.

As noted earlier, the forced termination of reinsurance upon certain conditions, such as a change in management or insolvency of the insurer will cause the contract to be viewed as a nonreinsurance transaction. The ceding company would likely have to reserve for that eventuality. Also, requiring that the ceding company pay the reinsurer any amount of a negative experience refund will result in similar treatment. The exceptions to this rule are that the reinsurer need not pay an experience refund if there is a cumulative negative experience refund balance and the reinsurer can also require that unpaid losses be paid upon termination of the reinsurance.

Some treaties include a charge-back allowance which permits the reinsurer to recover allowances paid in excess of premiums received in the event of lapse or surrender of the underlying policies. Any amounts charged back are actually additional premiums or reduced allowances, and as such are subject to the same exposure as other funds owed.

In any event, any company advancing funds or establishing significant liabilities under a reinsurance treaty would be well advised to discuss that treaty with the insurance department of the states of domicile of each company to better understand those states' interpretation of the treaty's provisions.

Underwriting

Perhaps the best safeguard against insolvency is informed underwriting. While a few companies seek surplus relief for purely cosmetic purposes, most companies seeking financial reinsurance have true financial problems, such as limited capital available. The reinsurer must do its underwriting homework. As a minimum, the reinsurer should obtain and review the proposed client's statutory annual statements for the last three to five years and the last two triennial reports from the state insurance department. If the company produces GAAP financial statements, the reinsurer should review these also.

Other sources of information include the various publications of the A.M. Best Company and the National Underwriter. The Best's publications include a monthly magazine which contains news of new product trends and other happenings within the life insurance industry, a weekly newsletter, and an annual report which is available for microcomputers. The National Underwriter is a weekly industry newsletter which features some of the current events in the life insurance industry. Reports from other rating agencies, such as Standard & Poor and Moody, may also be useful.

Before providing any surplus relief, the reinsurer should examine the client's existing statutory and GAAP surplus. It should particularly review existing surplus relief contracts. The reinsurer should be careful with any company that has a large amount of surplus relief inforce with other reinsurers as this indicates that surplus has been a problem over the years. There may not be sufficient profitable, unreinsured business available for the transaction. A review of the non-financially oriented reinsurance is also important.

The reinsurer should look at the company structure. In some circumstances, it may be necessary to investigate some of the affiliates of the ceding company, especially subsidiaries, as their success or failure may affect the company's position.

The reinsurer should also appraise the client's managerial talent, and feel comfortable with the management team. The reinsurer must believe this management team can move the company in the necessary direction so that continued surplus relief will not be a permanent need.

In reviewing the company, it is important to look at the various products which the company has sold and is selling. Accident and health coverages can be very volatile. A company active in the term insurance market may also experience earnings fluctuations; companies with large amounts of annuity business may experience fluctuations with swings in experience due to changes in interest rates and economic conditions.

The reinsurer should also investigate any potential legal liabilities that could affect the company's financial position. The reinsurer must examine the asset side of the company. Items to consider include the amount of assets invested in real estate, the amount of assets invested in bonds and the quality of those bonds, and commercial paper carried by the insurance company. The reinsurer should pay particular attention to assets invested in affiliates as the market value of these assets could be quite small in reality, or may be overstated in the statutory books. Current reinsurance receivables should also be reviewed.

If the review of the prospect company generates concern, the reinsurer may wish to discuss the company with the company's domestic state insurance department, or its own insurance department. Most reinsurance transactions are negotiated in confidence, so a reinsurer normally would contact an insurance department only with the ceding company's prior knowledge and permission.

As well as underwriting the company, the reinsurer must also underwrite the business to be reinsured. It is important to review the product design and past experience to make an estimate of the future experience of the block. The pricing margins should be reviewed to determine if the margins are adequate to repay the existing relief and provide a healthy flow of profits in the future. The existing reinsurance contracts on the policies to be reinsured should also be reviewed.

The focus of the above comments has been on financial reinsurance, as those examples are clearest and the insolvency risks involved are often the largest. The same cautions and considerations should, however, apply to all reinsurance treaties.

12 | Statutory Accounting for Reinsurance

Until the middle of the 1970's statutory accounting requirements for reinsurance were fairly simple. For the most part, data was accumulated on worksheets and either entered directly in the annual statement[1] or embedded in the overall numbers. As reinsurance became increasingly important to the financial structure and solvency of many insurers, more data has been required to be detailed in the annual statement.

This concern became apparent after the problems surrounding the Equity Funding scandal and increased with the concerns following the Baldwin-United insolvency.[2] The insolvency

---

[1]In this chapter, the statutory report required to be filed annually with the various state insurance departments is referred to as the annual statement; the form developed by the NAIC Committee on Blanks used for the preparation and presentation of this annual statement is referred to as the convention blank.

[2]While reinsurance did not cause the insolvencies in either situation, it did play a prominent role as a vehicle for perpetrating one of the many frauds uncovered in the Equity Funding operations and in obscuring the true financial condition of the various insurance companies within the Baldwin United complex.

273

of several primary property and liability insurers due to the failure
of their reinsurers caused even more alarm among the regulators.

Throughout the 1980's, insurance regulators, actuaries, and
accountants attempted to create uniformity in statutory accounting and to highlight reinsurance transactions in the convention
blank.   One desired result was to provide enough scrutiny of
reinsurance transactions so that true reinsurance transactions be
treated as such, while any transactions that are in effect only loans
of surplus be treated as loans.   A further objective was that a
modest audit trail be established to allow examiners and other
interested parties to cross-check between the annual statements of
the ceding company and of the reinsurer.

This chapter will discuss the reinsurance related entries in
the annual statement.   The reader may find it helpful to have a
copy of a recent annual statement or convention blank at hand
when reading this chapter.   References to specific pages, exhibits,
schedules, or lines are based upon the convention blank used to
report for the year ended December 31, 1989.   Convention blank
format and specifications change annually and the reader is urged
to check the latest NAIC and specific state instructions and
requirements.

BALANCE SHEET

Pages 2 and 3 of the convention blank summarize the assets,
liabilities, and surplus and other funds for life insurance companies.   Special provision is made for reporting certain reinsurance
items.

Assets

Invested assets normally are not affected by the presence or
absence of reinsurance.   Assets held on behalf of a reinsurer are
usually reported as part of other assets of that generic type.

Policy loans are reported on line 5.   Coinsurance treaties
usually provide that the reinsurer will not participate in policy
loans. However, should the reinsurer share in policy loans, it would
include the appropriate amount on this line.   An interesting
question arises concerning the treatment of such policy loans on the
ceding company's statement.   There is no specific provision for
reduction of this asset even though coinsurance reserves are

specifically deducted from the gross reserves in Exhibit 8. The commonly accepted treatment for a ceding company in this situation is to show the net policy loan asset on line 5; this would be the gross policy loans less those funded by the coinsurer.

The subdivisions of line 11 summarize amounts due from reinsurers. Line 11.1 shows the total amounts recoverable from reinsurers. This item reflects the reinsured portion of benefits which have been paid by the ceding company but not yet paid by the reinsurer.

Line 11.2 is for commissions and expense allowances which are due and unpaid. Normally, amounts shown here are the result of a lag in processing, but they may also represent amounts withheld by the reinsurer under a financial reinsurance treaty.

Line 11.3 reflects experience rating and other refunds due on reinsurance ceded. This receivable is normally due to the fact that experience refunds are typically finalized and paid shortly after the end of the year.

Accounts receivable representing amounts for funds withheld by the reinsurer may be shown on line 21 for aggregate write-ins for other than invested assets.[3] If the amount represents allowances withheld, they would more likely appear on line 11.2; if they represent reserve adjustments or other amounts, line 21 may be more appropriate. The breakdown of the items aggregated on this line, as is the case with all aggregated write-in lines, is detailed at the bottom of the page.

Treatment of assumed reinsurance is usually straightforward. Any invested assets are reported with other such assets. Any amounts due the reinsurer are reported on the appropriate line. If premiums are due the reinsurer, they are included on line 14 for life insurance premiums and annuity considerations deferred and uncollected or on line 15 for accident and health premiums due and unpaid. Other amounts due for assumed reinsurance are more appropriately included on line 21.

Liabilities

In general, liability items are developed on a net basis with reference to reinsurance ceded. Liabilities arising from reinsurance assumed are treated just as though they arose from direct insurance policies, unless otherwise specified.

---

[3]Trust accounts or letters of credit provided for purposes of securing reserve deductiblity are not reflected in the balance sheet.

The aggregate reserve for life policies and contracts, net of reinsurance ceded, is shown on line 1 of page 3. A similar reserve for accident and health policies, net of reinsurance ceded, is shown on line 2. The derivation of these amounts is discussed in more detail subsequently in the discussions of Exhibits 8 and 9.

Likewise, the amounts shown for policy and contract claims on lines 4.1 and 4.2 are net of amounts recoverable from reinsurers and are developed in Exhibit 11, discussed subsequently.

As is the case with policy loans, reinsurers seldom participate in supplementary contracts or policyholder dividends. If they do, the amounts shown on lines 3, 5, 6, and 7 are reduced accordingly.

The various liabilities usually reflect any deductions or credits for reinsurance ceded, regardless of the admitted or nonadmitted status of the reinsurers. A separate liability for reinsurance in unauthorized companies is established on line 24.2. This liability reflects the excess, if any, of the total reserve and liability credits taken for each unauthorized reinsurer over the corresponding total of funds withheld, trusteed assets, letters of credit, and other funds held for the benefit of the ceding company. The details entering this determination for each unauthorized reinsurer are shown in Schedule S, Part 3B. Line 24.3 shows the amounts of the funds held under reinsurance treaties with unauthorized reinsurers used for the purpose of supporting the reserve and liability credits taken.

Any other amounts due reinsurers, such as those under a funds withheld arrangement with an admitted reinsurer, are usually shown as a write-in item on line 25.

Surplus and Other Funds

Reinsurance, even that done for surplus relief, will not change surplus directly. Instead, the effect of the reinsurance on the various liabilities and assets will in turn affect the level of surplus. Absent other changes, if reinsurance causes assets to increase or liabilities to decrease, surplus will increase.

SUMMARY OF OPERATIONS

The Summary of Operations is shown on page 4 of the convention blank and the Analysis of Operations by Line of Business is shown on page 5. The comments which apply to page 4 also apply to page 5.

Income Items

The premiums and annuity considerations shown on line 1 include premiums on reinsurance assumed and are net of premiums on reinsurance ceded. Line 5 shows commissions and expense allowances on reinsurance ceded. For a ceding company, any amounts reimbursed for premium taxes are included in allowances on line 5. Lines 1 and 5 must agree with Exhibit 1.

Line 5a is used to record reserve adjustments on reinsurance ceded. This line normally reflects the modified coinsurance adjustment due from the reinsurer. It should be remembered that this item includes the increase in reserve less the appropriate investment income. This may be viewed as balancing other income items; the investment income portion of the modified coinsurance adjustment is included in the ceding company's net investment income on line 4 and the reserve increase is included in the amount shown on line 17.

Line 6 for aggregate write-ins for miscellaneous income may be used for a variety of reinsurance related items. Some companies use this line to include allowances on annuity deposits reported on line 1A or for initial allowances when blocks of inforce business are ceded. Experience refunds earned are generally included here.

Benefit and Expense Items

All incurred benefit payments and increases in aggregate reserves on lines 8 through 18 are reported net of reinsurance ceded, including that ceded in unauthorized companies, and inclusive of reinsurance assumed. The change in the liability for reinsurance ceded in unauthorized companies is reflected on line 38 of the Capital and Surplus Account. Any change in liability for reinsurance ceded to unauthorized reinsurers is thus reflected directly in surplus and not in the Summary of Operations.

Commissions and expense allowances on reinsurance assumed are shown on line 21. Some reinsurers include experience refunds incurred on this line.

Any normal administrative expenses of reinsurance ceded or assumed are shown as general expenses on line 22. The premium tax on reinsurance assumed is included on line 23 for insurance taxes, licenses and fees.

The line for aggregate write-ins for deductions, line 25, may also be used for a variety of reinsurance related items. Experience refunds incurred by reinsurers may be included here, as might amounts incurred under modified coinsurance adjustments. Ceding amounts incurred under modified coinsurance adjustments. Ceding companies may use this line to reflect the amount of reserves transferred to reinsurers under an agreement covering an inforce block of insurance, rather than recording this amount on line 1 as premiums and considerations.

CAPITAL AND SURPLUS ACCOUNT

The Capital and Surplus Account is shown on page 4 following the Summary of Operations. A reconciliation of the change in capital and surplus funds for the year is provided. The effects of reinsurance, as reflected in the Summary of Operations, are included in the net income entered on line 35. Line 38 is used to record the change in liability for reinsurance ceded in unauthorized companies. This item includes the increase or decrease in the reserve credit taken for such reinsurance which is not admissible.

Reinsurance seldom has a direct influence on the other items of the capital and surplus account, but under special circumstances, it may. For example, some insurers reflect any change in deficiency reserves directly through surplus as a write-in on line 46 rather than through a change in reserves in the Summary of Operations. If this technique is followed, the change so reflected should be net of any credits for ceded deficiency reserves. Similarly, changes in reserves due to changes in valuation basis are reflected directly in surplus on line 39 and should also be net of reinsurance.

EXHIBITS

There are thirteen exhibits[4] in the convention blank which support the Balance Sheet and the Summary of Operations. Reinsurance transactions may have a direct effect on the first twelve exhibits.

Exhibit 1 - Part 1:
Premium and Annuity Considerations

Exhibit 1 shows first year, single, and renewal premiums by line of business for the insurance company. Separate classification is

---

[4]These exhibits are numbered 1 through 11, 13 and 14. Exhibit 12, Reconciliation of Ledger Assets, previously in the convention blank, has been deleted and the exhibits have not been renumbered.

provided for both reinsurance assumed and reinsurance ceded for deferred and uncollected premiums and for collected premiums. Total premiums are developed for first year, single, and renewal categories, and within these are shown for direct business, reinsurance ceded, and reinsurance assumed.

In most traditional reinsurance applications, reinsurance premiums are paid on an annual basis or on a true monthly premium basis, resulting in no deferred premiums. Therefore any items shown in the breakdown of deferred and uncollected premiums for lines 3 and 13 for reinsurance ceded or assumed are normally unpaid premium items under traditional reinsurance arrangements. If reinsurance premiums are paid on a modal basis other than annual, as in some traditional treaties or in many financial reinsurance arrangements, both deferred and uncollected premiums are reflected in the reinsurance lines.

Exhibit 1 - Part 2: Dividends and Coupons Applied, Reinsurance Commissions and Expense Allowances and Commissions Incurred

Reinsurance commissions and expense allowances incurred are summarized in Exhibit 1 - Part 2. Separate lines are provided for ceded and assumed for first year, single, and renewal commissions and expense allowances. Experience refunds on reinsurance may be treated as allowances in the annual statement. If so, the appropriate amounts would be included in this part of the exhibit. This treatment is consistent with United States federal income tax practice regarding experience refunds.

The total ceded commissions and expense allowances are recorded on line 5 of the Summary of Operations while the total commissions and expense allowances on reinsurance assumed are recorded on line 21 of the Summary of Operations.

Exhibits 2, 3, and 4: Investment Income and Capital Gains and Losses

There are no special entries in these exhibits for reinsurance ceded or assumed. The nature of the reinsurance agreement will have an effect on assets. Transactions which increase invested assets will normally increase investment income and transactions which decrease assets will tend to decrease investment income.

Investment income pertaining to modified coinsurance is a part of the overall net investment income for the ceding company, and is not separately identified in its annual statement. The reinsurer does not include any amounts in investment income for mod-co.

Exhibit 5: General Expenses

The general administrative expenses associated with reinsurance ceded and assumed are incorporated with direct expenses shown in this exhibit. Any unusual expenses incurred as a result of reinsurance operations could be included in the aggregate write-in on line 9.3.

Exhibit 6: Taxes, Licenses and Fees

Reimbursement of premium taxes for reinsurance assumed are included in the amount reported on line 3 for premium taxes on direct premiums. Any premium tax reimbursed on reinsurance ceded would be reported in Exhibit 1 as reinsurance allowances.

Exhibit 7: Dividends and Coupons to Policyholders

This exhibit would include any amounts for dividends or coupons incurred for reinsurance assumed less corresponding incurrals of reimbursements for reinsurance ceded.

Exhibit 8: Aggregate Reserve for Life Policies and Contracts

Exhibit 8 shows the aggregate reserve for life policies and contracts by valuation basis for each benefit type and line of business. The reserves on reinsurance assumed are combined with those for direct business under the appropriate valuation basis, benefit type, and line of business. The reserve credit for reinsurance ceded is shown in total by benefit type and line of business. The reserve credit for reinsurance ceded includes that for reinsurance ceded in unauthorized reinsurers, as noted previously.

Only coinsurance and YRT reserves are reflected in Exhibit 8. The total net reserve in Exhibit 8 goes to line 1 on page 3. The total credits for reserves on reinsurance ceded should balance to the totals documented in Schedule S.

Exhibit 9: Aggregate Reserve for Accident and Health Policies

Exhibit 9 shows the aggregate reserve for accident and health policies by type of reserve and by line of business or type of policy. As in Exhibit 8, reserves for reinsurance assumed are included in the totals for direct business and should balance to those listed in

Schedule S. The reserve credit for reinsurance ceded is shown in total and for each line of business or policy type, but is not segregated by type of reserve. The net reserve is carried to page 3, line 2.

Exhibit 10: Deposit Funds and Other Liabilities Without Life or Disability Contingencies

Exhibit 10 shows the deposit funds and other liabilities without life or disability contingencies by line of business. Part A shows details of liabilities net of reinsurance ceded and includes any liabilities for reinsurance assumed. Part B shows the total deductions taken for reinsurance ceded for the current and previous year.

Exhibit 11: Policy and Contracts Claims

This exhibit, which details claims by line of business, is divided into two parts. Part 1 shows the net claims liability at the end of the current year together with the components for direct business, reinsurance assumed, and reinsurance ceded. The net liability, separated as to life end accident and health coverages, is carried to lines 4.1 and 4.2 on page 3. The credits for reinsurance ceded are listed by company in Schedule S.

Part 2 develops the net claims incurred during the year together with the components for direct business, reinsurance assumed, and reinsurance ceded. The net incurred claims, separated as to benefit type, are carried to the appropriate lines of the Summary of Operations.

Exhibit 13: Assets

Exhibit 13 recaps the assets shown on the Balance Sheet, dividing them into ledger assets, non-ledger assets, assets not admitted, and the net admitted assets. The lines in this exhibit correspond to the lines on page 2 and the admitted assets from this exhibit should agree with the counterparts on page 2, by line and in total.

SCHEDULES

Reinsurance ceded and assumed amounts are directly recognized in Schedules H, S, and T of the convention blank.

Schedule H: Accident and Health Exhibit

Schedule H summarizes the experience and reserves for accident and health insurance by line of business and type of policy and is

divided into four parts. Part 1, an analysis of underwriting
operations, develops the underwriting gain. All values shown
include reinsurance assumed and are net of reinsurance ceded.

Part 2 shows the reserves and liabilities for accident and
health insurance. Premium reserves, policy reserves, and claim
reserves and liabilities are shown, inclusive of reinsurance assumed
and net of reinsurance ceded.

Part 3 is a test of the previous year's claim reserves and
liabilities. Again, all figures shown are net of ceded reinsurance
and include reinsurance assumed.

Part 4 is a summary of reinsurance. Premiums written,
premiums earned, incurred claims, and commissions are shown
separately by line of business and type of policy for reinsurance
assumed and for reinsurance ceded. No net numbers are developed.

Schedule S: Reinsurance

Schedule S itemizes information relative to all reinsurance, both
ceded and assumed, by specific treaty. It is divided into several
parts. Each part of Schedule S is divided so as to show the
information separately for affiliate reinsurers and non-affiliate
reinsurers. Each treaty with each company is identified in the
appropriate parts of the schedule by the company's federal I.D.
number, the effective date of the treaty, the company's name, and
the location (city and state or country) of the company. This
information is used by the insurance department staff to compare
corresponding items in the ceding company's and reinsurer's annual
statements.

*Part 1: Amounts Recoverable on Paid and Unpaid Losses for
All Reinsurance Ceded.* Part 1 is a schedule for reinsurance
ceded showing the amounts recoverable for paid and unpaid losses
by treaty as of the end of the year. Paid and unpaid amounts are
shown in separate columns. Separate lists and totals are shown
for life and for accident and health. While amounts are shown by
specific treaty, a treaty is not listed in this part unless there is a
claim amount due or pending at the end of the year.

The total of amounts recoverable on paid losses for
reinsurance ceded is shown on line 11.1 of page 2. This represents
amounts paid by the ceding company which have not yet been
reimbursed by the reinsurer and are normally a result of lags in
payment.

The amounts recoverable on unpaid losses should agree with the total shown in Exhibit 11 – Part 1 for reinsurance ceded. These amounts represent the reinsured portion of claims still pending or in the course of settlement and therefore not yet paid.

Part 2: All Accident and Health Ceded. Part 2 is another ceded schedule listing certain values for each ceded accident and health reinsurance treaty as of December 31. The code for the line of business and type of reinsurance, premiums, unearned premiums, and the reserve credit for other than unearned premiums is shown.

Again, these listings and totals are separated for affiliates and non-affiliates. Grand totals are developed and should agree with the appropriate parts of Exhibit 1 – Part 1 and Exhibit 9.

Part 3A: Reinsurance Ceded for All Life Insurance and Related Benefits. Part 3A lists certain information for reinsurance ceded on all life insurance and related benefits. This shows, by contract, the line of business and type of reinsurance code, the amount of reinsurance inforce, current and previous years' reserve credit, and ceded premiums. The total of the amount inforce at the end of the year corresponds to the reinsurance ceded at the end of the year shown on line 21 of the Exhibit of Life Insurance on page 15. The reserve credit taken should correspond to the reinsurance ceded totals of Exhibits 8, 9, and 10. The premiums should correspond to the appropriate lines in Exhibit 1 – Part 1.

Part 3B: Data on Life and Accident and Health Reinsurance in Unauthorized Companies. Part 3B shows certain balance sheet and other items for life and accident and health reinsurance in unauthorized companies. Information is shown separately for life and accident and health coverages, identifying the reinsurer and the treaty.

Items shown are the reserve credit taken, any amounts recoverable on paid and unpaid losses, other debits, deposits by and funds withheld from reinsurers, and other miscellaneous credit balances. Any deposits by and funds withheld from reinsurers are further identified as to whether they are a letter of credit, trust agreement, funds deposited by and withheld from reinsurer, or other arrangement.

The excess, if any, of the sum of the reserve credit taken, the amounts recoverable on paid and unpaid losses, and the other debits over the sum of the deposits by and funds withheld from the reinsurer and the other miscellaneous credit balances is developed separately for each treaty. The sum of the positive excesses only is entered on line 24.2 of page 3 and represents that portion of the total reserve credits taken which is not admissible.

It is important to note that any reserve or other credits for reinsurance in an unauthorized company is still taken in the same manner as credits for reinsurance in authorized companies. It is in Part 3B that the separate liability is developed for page 3. This additional liability is required because the reinsurer is not authorized and the insurance department cannot be as certain of collection as it would be with an admitted insurer. The net result is that reserve credit is allowed only to the extent of funds arising from the treaty which are readily available to the ceding company.

It should also be noted that an unauthorized company is one which is not admitted either as a direct writer or as a reinsurer in the state of domicile of the ceding company. If the reinsurer is admitted in every other jurisdiction but not in the ceding company's domicile, it is still unauthorized. The domicile of the reinsurer has no direct influence on authorized status; it may be domiciled in another of the United States or in another country.

Part 3C – Section 1: Data on Reinsurance Assumed for Life Insurance and Related Benefits. Part 3C – Section 1 shows information for reinsurance assumed on life insurance and other related benefits for each treaty. It shows the line of business and type of reinsurance code, amount of inforce at the end of the year, the reserve, premiums, and reinsurance payable on paid and unpaid losses. This is basically the comparable data to that which is developed in Part 3A for ceded life insurance and related benefits.

The total premiums should agree with Exhibit 1 – Part 1, line 20b, columns 2 through 7. The total reinsurance payable on paid and unpaid losses should agree with Exhibit 11 – Part 1.

Part 3C – Section 2: Data on Reinsurance Assumed for Accident and Health. Section 2 of Part 3C shows data for reinsurance assumed on accident and health insurance for each treaty. It shows the line of business and type of reinsurance code, premiums, unearned premiums, reserve liabilities other than unearned premiums, and reinsurance payable on paid and unpaid losses, paralleling the data developed in Part 2 for ceded business.

The total premiums should agree with Exhibit 1 – Part 1, line 20b, columns 8 through 10. The total reinsurance payable on paid and unpaid losses should agree with Exhibit 11 – Part 1.

General Interrogatories. This section consists of three interrogatories. The first interrogatory asks if any of the reinsurers listed as nonaffiliated are either owned or controlled, directly or indirectly, by the company, any representative, officer, trustee, or director of the company. If the answer is yes, details must be provided.

The second interrogatory asks if any policies issued by the company and reinsured by a company chartered in another country which is owned or controlled directly or indirectly by the policyholder, the beneficiary, creditor of the insured, or any other person not primarily engaged in the insurance business. Again, a positive response requires that details be furnished.

The third interrogatory consists of two parts. The answer to the first question determines whether it is necessary to complete Part 4. If required, the second part asks whether Part 4 has been completed and whether the instructions relating to credit for ceded reinsurance contained therein have been followed.

Part 3D: Five Year Exhibit of Reinsurance Ceded Business. Part 3D is a new schedule added beginning with the 1988 convention blank. It requires a listing of certain operations items, balance sheet items, and information on deposits by and funds withheld from unauthorized reinsurers for each of the last five years. This schedule permits the reader of the statement to determine quickly the effect of ceded reinsurance on the financial stability of company and to observe the trend of dependency on such reinsurance.

Part 4: Ceded Reinsurance Report. Part 4 is a ceded reinsurance report which must be completed only if certain adjustments in surplus would result in a reduction in surplus of 30 percent or more.

This report provides supplementary questions regarding terms of any reinsurance treaty which is considered unacceptable, such as one granting the reinsurer the unilateral right to cancel the treaty. Other questions deal with payments which would be owed reinsurers if they were to cancel the treaties and with reinsurance premiums and amounts paid in excess of premiums to be collected from policyholders.

Schedule T: Premium and Annuity Considerations

Schedule T allocates direct premiums and annuity considerations by state and territory; separate columns are used for life insurance premiums, annuity considerations, and accident and health insurance premiums.

Premiums for reinsurance assumed and reinsurance ceded are not allocated by state or territory but are added to and subtracted from the grand total at the end of the schedule. The total for direct premiums should agree with that in Exhibit 1 - Part 1; reinsurance ceded and assumed totals in Schedule T may not agree with those in Exhibit 1 since Schedule T may not reflect large reinsurance transactions on inforce blocks.

OTHER ANNUAL STATEMENT ITEMS

Reinsurance affects four other analyses in the convention blank.

Cash Flow

The cash flow analysis is shown on page 4A. With respect to reinsurance, all items should be reflected on the appropriate lines as cash is actually received or disbursed, for both ceded and assumed reinsurance transactions. Since incurred and non-cash items are not shown in this analysis, this may lead to significant differences in the amounts shown relative to the corresponding items in the Summary of Operations. For example, amounts withheld do not affect the cash flow reporting.

Only one item regarding reinsurance is specifically highlighted in the cash flow analysis. Line 4 shows allowances and reserve adjustments received on reinsurance ceded.

Analysis of Increase in Reserves and Deposit Funds During the Year

The analysis of the increase in reserves is shown on page 6. All items in this analysis are shown net of reinsurance. For example, reserves are shown net of ceded coinsurance amounts, but including the mod-co reserves held by the ceding company. The analysis includes any amounts for coinsurance and YRT assumed.

Exhibit 8A: Changes in Basis of Valuation During the Year

Any changes in the valuation basis of reinsurance assumed are shown in this exhibit. The changes shown are also net of any reinsurance ceded reserve credits.

Exhibit of Life Insurance

The Exhibit of Life Insurance on page 15 shows the increases and decreases in the life insurance inforce, number of policies, and current death benefits during the year separately for industrial, ordinary, credit, and group insurance. Reinsurance assumed during the year is shown on line 3. Deductions during the year for death, maturity, disability, expiry, surrender, lapse, conversion, and all other decreases include those for reinsurance assumed. Any assumed reinsurance which is recaptured during the year is shown on line 17. The amount of reinsurance ceded at the end of the year is shown on line 21, but the number of policies affected is not given.

OTHER CONSIDERATIONS

Self-Administration

Because of the limited amount of data which is received on self-administered treaties, the reinsurance valuation actuary may be faced with many special problems. The information provided may consists only of summaries with very little detail. The reinsurer will likely have to rely on the accuracy of the information provided by the ceding company.

In most instances the reinsurer will review the information provided for reasonableness and ask questions of the ceding company as needed. The information will then be included in the various exhibits and schedules. The audit trails provided are different than those normally used by insurance companies. New procedures and audit practices will be required to handle self-administered accounts. This should not cause a problem, but individuals who participate in assembling financial statements should be aware that information will be gathered and documented in a different manner.

The ceding company should be aware that it is responsible not only for the reinsurance data in its own statement, but for corresponding information in its reinsurer's statement. This is different than the situation with individual cession reinsurance where the reinsurer has enough data to prepare its own statements independently.

Financial Reinsurance

Financial reinsurance should be treated the same as any other type of reinsurance for statutory accounting purposes. All entries in the annual statement should be made with equal care and attention to detail. Most financial reinsurance is self-administered so the considerations discussed earlier for self-administration apply.

In many instances, financial reinsurance is expected to be short term in nature, so attempts are sometimes made to avoid distortions in the annual statement. For example, the ceding company might use an aggregate write-in line rather than the premium line to show the transfer of a large amount of initial reserves. A reinsurer might choose to net an initial premium under a mod-co treaty with the initial mod-co adjustment in order to minimize the distortions to the elements of its statutory earnings and cash flow.

Statement of Actuarial Opinion

Reinsurance is an important element to consider in forming the actuary's statement of opinion as to the adequacy of a company's reserves. The considerations of the actuaries of the ceding company and the reinsurer are different, but somewhat parallel. The mechanics of the process are described elsewhere in this book, but a brief discussion of some of the issues involved is appropriate.

Reliance. The ceding company's actuary can generally obtain all of the data necessary to form an opinion regarding reserve credits. The assuming company's actuary is not always in the same position. Frequently, especially when dealing with self-administered reinsurance, the reinsurer relies on the ceding company for all data, including the calculation of the statutory reserves and other actuarial items. In such cases it is common for the reinsurer's actuary to rely upon the ceding company's actuary as to the accuracy, appropriateness, and adequacy of the reserves and other items for the block of business reinsured.

The preferred practice is for the ceding company's actuary to provide the reinsurer with a statement that, in his opinion, the reserves and other actuarial items are calculated in accordance with generally accepted actuarial standards, meet the standards of the relevant jurisdictions, and make a good and sufficient provision for the policy obligations. The reinsurer's actuary then includes a statement of reliance on this statement of opinion in the appropriate section of his own opinion.

This practice does not allow the reinsurer's actuary to rely blindly on such an opinion. For example, if the reserves clearly do not meet minimum standards or are inadequate, the actuary may not opine that they do. The terms and benefits of a reinsurance treaty may be different than those of the direct policies underlying the reinsurance. The actuarial opinion of the reinsurer must address its own liabilities, not those of the ceding company.

Qualified or Limited Opinions. The actuary of either company may find himself in a position where he must give a qualified or limited opinion. For example, a ceding company's actuary may be uncertain about the recoverability of benefits from a reinsurer, or may believe that a given treaty does not transfer adequate risk. In this case, he may qualify his opinion appropriately, stating his reasons or concerns.

Likewise, a reinsurer's actuary may qualify his opinion if he is uncertain about the derivation, accuracy, or adequacy of reserve amounts given him by a ceding company. In some instances, the ceding company will not produce information in time for the reinsurer to use it in its statement. In such a situation, it would be appropriate for the reinsurer's actuary to qualify his opinion stating that the reserves for certain blocks of assumed reinsurance had not been reviewed due to lack of available information. Another approach would be to limit his opinion by stating that it excluded such blocks of business. In either event, the amount and classification of the reserves in question should be identified.

Valuation Actuary. For the most part, the valuation actuary for the reinsurer has the same considerations and concerns as any other valuation actuary. In the end, he must give his opinion as to whether or not the reserves established make good and sufficient provision for all obligations of the company. On the other hand, the ceding company's actuary must consider whether his company can rely upon its reinsurers to perform and whether or not any meaningful risk transfer results from each reinsurance agreement.

In July 1989, the Actuarial Standards Board adopted Actuarial Standard of Practice No. 11, entitled *The Treatment of Reinsurance Transactions in Life and Health Insurance Company Financial Statements.* This standard applies to any financial statements prepared for periods beginning after December 15, 1989. It applies not only to statutory, but also to GAAP and other financial statements. Any valuation actuary whose has responsibility for reinsurance, either ceded or assumed, should read and be familiar with this standard.

13 GAAP Accounting for Reinsurance

Generally Accepted Accounting Principles (GAAP) apply to reinsurance just as to any line of life insurance business, but certain idiosyncrasies of reinsurance call for special consideration. It is not the purpose of this text to define GAAP for reinsurance nor to delve into all of the intricacies involved. This chapter is intended to provide insight into the special problems which reinsurance and GAAP create for each other, as well as to develop a general approach to the solution of these problems.

BACKGROUND AND GENERAL CONSIDERATIONS

As for directly issued life insurance, GAAP is required for reinsurance only for certain stock life insurance companies. In dealing with any application of GAAP, it is important to review and be familiar with the applicable accounting pronouncements.[1]

---

[1] At the current date, these would include *Audits of Stock Life Insurance Companies*, American Institute of Certified Public Accountants, and "Statements of Financial Accounting Standards Nos. 60 and 97," Financial Accounting Standards Board (FASB).

There are also a number of available publications which deal specifically with the application of GAAP to reinsurance. (See, for example, Ernst and Ernst [4] and Robertson [10].) Recently, the accounting profession has issued an exposure draft of proposed guidelines[2] for financial reinsurance treaties. These references, which form the basis for most GAAP accounting for reinsurance as well as for much of the following discussion, address the basic concerns and techniques involved.

One of the central points of Robertson's papers is that the approach to GAAP accounting should vary by the type of the reinsurance involved (YRT, coinsurance, or mod-co) and by the position of the company (ceding company or reinsurer). The basic tenet of GAAP for reinsurance has been to recognize income in proportion to revenues. Reinsurance is subject to more variability than any other product line; some products, such as a traditional YRT plan, may produce no statutory surplus strain and perhaps even a profit at issue, while some produce significant strain. The degree of adjustment required for restatement from statutory to GAAP will vary accordingly. Therefore, generaliza-tion is difficult.

There is also the question of materiality. The vast majority of reinsurance accepted is in companies that make reinsurance a major line of business. In those cases, it would seem obvious that GAAP should be uniquely defined for the reinsurance line. However, many companies find that the ceded portion of their business is relatively small and immaterial in the overall financial reporting, and therefore not deserving of extensive effort.

Some state insurance regulators have endorsed the concept of mirror image reserves for statutory purposes, suggesting a system whereby reserve factors are identical for the ceding and accepting companies. This is clearly not a valid approach for GAAP.

The assumptions a ceding company uses across an entire block of business may be inappropriate for the reinsurer on the reinsured portion of that same business. This is fairly obvious when one considers items such as expense factors, commission and allowance patterns, and other acquisition costs. Different mortality or persistency assumptions also may be appropriate on the reinsured and retained portions of the business. If it represents

---

[2] "Transfer of Risk in Reinsurance Contracts and Accounting for Reinsurance Contracts," Proposed Statement of Position, AICPA, April 1, 1988.

the reinsured and retained portions of the business. If it represents a relatively small portion of the business, there is no need for the ceding company to develop unique assumptions for its ceded business. The reinsurer will most likely have different assumptions. Because of this, it is unlikely that the GAAP reserves, for either benefits or expenses, would be the same for the ceding company and the reinsurer on any block of business.

GAAP FOR CEDED REINSURANCE

Under statutory accounting principles, premiums paid for reinsurance ceded are deducted from premiums received and the net amount is reported as premium income. Claim reimbursements from the reinsurer are offset against total claim payments and, similarly, any cash value or other surrender benefits received from the reinsurer are offset against the appropriate transaction account. If an experience refund is payable, the refund is generally recorded as miscellaneous income, although refunds can be considered negative reinsurance ceded premiums.

For purposes of GAAP, all of these elements must be matched against the appropriate revenue or benefit base in a manner consistent with that required of the GAAP treatment for directly issued business. Although different techniques may be used, Robertson's paper calls for the calculation of an annual "expected cost" of reinsurance according to GAAP valuation assumptions. For reinsurance ceded purposes, the assumptions used in developing the valuation premium should be consistent with the original assumptions used in developing the direct GAAP reserves.

As with statutory accounting, GAAP accounting usually involves calculating direct and ceded factors for benefit reserves and deferred acquisition costs and using these to develop gross numbers. The ceded values are then subtracted from their gross direct counterparts to develop net retained assets and liabilities.

The final net benefit reserve and net deferred acquisition cost asset are the important items. While the direct and ceded pieces may be calculated separately, it is the net value that matters. If the company expects experience to be significantly different on its reinsurance ceded portion than on the entire block of business, it should consider different assumptions for the reinsurance ceded calculations. Affiliated companies filing reinsurance ceded from one entity to the other. Otherwise, the ceded and accepting companies need not use the same assumptions.

The type and extent of GAAP reporting necessary for a ceding company will vary with the type of reinsurance and according to how material reinsurance is to the bottom line. For many companies, ceded reinsurance never has been considered to be material and no GAAP adjustments have ever been made. Even some large companies with significant volumes of reinsurance business use the statutory reserve adjustment for GAAP reporting for reinsurance ceded. This practice has become less common in recent years as the use of reinsurance has increased and as more of it is of a coinsurance type. The question of materiality should be kept in mind in reviewing GAAP procedures for reinsurance ceded.

Yearly Renewable Term

Yearly renewable term reinsurance requires the simplest accounting (GAAP, statutory, or tax) of any form of reinsurance. The simplest way to handle ceded YRT is merely to recognize the premiums, the claims and any experience refunds as incurred. Implicit in this treatment is an assumption that the YRT cash premium is relatively proportional to the mortality rates assumed throughout the life of the business; this may or may not be so.

For example, YRT may be purchased on a zero first year premium basis. In this case, the theoretically correct way to handle it would be to develop benefit reserves based upon the mortality assumption of the ceded business. An implicit first year premium equal to expected mortality, and an equal allowance, may be used to develop a deferred acquisition cost asset which, in effect, spreads the expected actual first year cost over the life of the business. Otherwise, the ceding company takes into earnings any first year claim recovery which would theoretically be repaid in future years through higher reinsurance premiums than would be the case if a first year premium were paid. A simpler method is to develop a negative deferred acquisition asset to account for the zero premium.

Coinsurance

Coinsurance is more complicated than YRT. Benefit reserve factors might reasonably be assumed to be the same for reinsurance ceded as for the original policy. The investment rate assumed should be that of the ceding company and not the assumed should be that of the ceding company and not the reinsurer. Alternatively, it is possible to develop a net benefit reserve for the ceding company based strictly upon the retained portion of the policy, but most administrative systems do not allow this approach.

The amount and incidence of reinsurance expense allowances seldom match those of the actual acquisition expenses and commissions of the ceding company. If these are reasonably similar, it may be possible to use the same deferred acquisition cost factors to net ceded coinsurance out of the deferred acquisition cost asset developed for the corresponding directly written business. However, if they are not similar and the ceded business is material, then separate deferred acquisition cost factors should be developed for the ceded portion of the business.

For a quota share coinsurance treaty, it is possible to develop factors based upon the net retained portion taking into account the percentage of the business retained versus the percentage ceded and the differing patterns of expense and allowances. In effect, a net factor can be developed for the entire block, based on net retained revenues and benefits.

Modified Coinsurance

In calculating GAAP factors for mod-co, the ceding company can take the same approach on deferred acquisition asset factors as it would for coinsurance. However, calculation of benefit reserve factors should be adjusted for the fact that the statutory reserve is held by the ceding company. This can be a complicated adjustment depending on the basis for selecting the interest rate used to calculate the mod-co adjustment.

For example, some treaties call for a permanent guarantee of a specific interest percentage. In this case, benefit reserve factors can be calculated based upon that interest rate. In other cases the ceding company's net earned rate is used in the interest adjustment. In this case, the same interest rate should be used for the reinsurance as is used for the originally written business. In statutory accounting, the ceding company holds the reserve under mod-co. However, under GAAP accounting, the ceding company's benefit reserves are decreased by the amount of the benefit reserve which it holds for the reinsurer.

While not technically correct, mod-co may be viewed as involving a loan from the reinsurer to the ceding company, creating an asset in the amount of the statutory reserve and an interest obligation, as defined in the mod-co adjustment provisions of the treaty. This results in a total benefit reserve for the ceding company equal to the "benefit reserve calculated without considering reinsurance, reduced by the portion reinsured, plus the statutory reserve held by the reinsured company."[3]

It is important to use the actual interest rates expected in calculating the benefit reserves. In essence, the way to do this is to assume that the portion of the GAAP reserve which corresponds to the statutory reserve is earning interest at the rate established for the mod-co interest adjustment. Any remainder of the reserve should be assumed to earn interest at a rate consistent with the original interest assumptions.

A satisfactory approximation in most cases would be to use the same approach as for coinsurance, substituting for the interest rate assumed in the original policy pricing the one used in determining the mod-co adjustment. This introduces an error which is related to the product of (1) the difference between the mod-co interest rate and the direct interest rate and (2) the difference between the GAAP benefit reserve and the statutory reserve. For most companies this would be relatively small and immaterial.

Special Provisions

Certain reinsurance transactions require special consideration for GAAP.

Chargebacks. Some reinsurance treaties call for allowances at acquisition which exceed 100% of the first year premium. These treaties frequently call for a chargeback of excess allowances if a certain persistency level is not maintained. A common feature calls for a refund of all allowances in excess of 100% of premium for any policy which does not pay the 13th month premium. Such provisions call for special GAAP accounting treatment if the reinsured inforce is significant.

For statutory purposes, there is no general requirement to make provision for this chargeback in most situations. For GAAP purposes this provision, like any other affecting cash flow, should be recognized. Those policies which lapse with a chargeback create negative statutory revenues; this is charged against the revenue over the life of the policies for GAAP.

---

[3]See Robertson [10].

This chargeback is, in effect, an offset of overstated first year revenue. Just as the deferred acquisition cost asset spreads the excess first year acquisition expense and commission over the life of the policy, so should it spread chargeback expenses. In effect, while first year allowances in excess of 100% create statutory and, generally, tax gains for the ceding company, they do not necessarily create GAAP gains. Proper GAAP accounting, in fact, calls for both excess first year allowances and chargebacks to be spread over the life of the policies in proportion to expected premium revenues. This prevents inappropriate front-ending of GAAP earnings and reduces the GAAP cost to the ceding company of a surrender.

Recapture. As discussed earlier, most reinsurance agreements carry some form of recapture provision. This leads to the possibility of additional termination of reinsurance even though the base policy has not terminated. Theoretically, it is appropriate to take expected recaptures into account in determining both benefit reserve factors and deferred acquisition cost factors. However, as a practical matter, this is seldom done. Recapture generally is allowed only after a specific period of time has elapsed following the original policy cession, and then only if a retention increase has taken place. While it is appropriate for a reinsurer to take into account recapture, it is not necessarily required that a ceding company consider recapture in calculating reserves. If it does not, it will likely have GAAP gains or losses upon recapture.

If recapture is to be taken into account, it should be treated as an additional provision for termination in both the benefit reserve and the deferred acquisition cost calculations. Obviously the earliest point of this additional termination provision is at the earliest point of recapture allowed in the contract. Companies which do take this into account may introduce a significant increase to the termination rate at that point and a smaller increase thereafter. As a practical matter, most ceding companies ignore recapture in GAAP calculations.

Experience Refunds. Experience refunds, being subject to wide fluctuations, are difficult to handle in GAAP accounting. Good experience in one contract year can create a refund, while poor experience in another year can generate a smaller refund or no refund, perhaps even eliminating future refunds. Most companies choose to ignore experience refunds in calculating GAAP factors, allowing any refunds to flow through earnings as they are incurred on the statutory basis.

Theoretically, a test using GAAP valuation assumptions should be made to determine if an experience refund is expected. This test should be made in aggregate over the life of the block of business. If a refund is expected, then that refund should be taken into consideration along with other revenues. This will generally result in reducing the expected annual cost of reinsurance. Relatively few traditional reinsurance agreements of recent years include an experience refund provision.

Self-Administration

The recent emphasis on self-administration has created exceptional problems for reinsurers in the accounting arena, but it has not created particular problems for ceding companies. Since the principles of GAAP accounting do not vary with the manner in which reinsurance is administered, ceding companies should be able to handle GAAP in a straightforward manner, regardless of the type of administration.

Special treaties, such as those used for surplus relief or other forms of financial reinsurance, do require special treatment for GAAP, as discussed subsequently.

Retrocessions

In determining GAAP benefit reserves and deferred acquisition cost for retroceded business, the principles of ceded reinsurance generally apply. To the extent the retroceded premiums or allowances are equal to the accepted premiums and allowances, then the assumed GAAP factors can be used for the retroceded factors. To the extent that different premiums or terms are included in the retrocession agreement, then different factors should be developed. Again, the degree of materiality should be considered. If retroceded business is a very small portion of a company's reinsurance assumed operations, it may choose to do nothing special regarding retroceded GAAP factors.

Facultative Cessions

Facultative cessions will generally exhibit different mortality and termination results. Also, reinsurance expenses may be different from those for automatic business. Depending upon the volume and the differences involved, the insurer may develop different GAAP factors for facultative cessions, but usually will not.

GAAP FOR ASSUMED REINSURANCE

Reinsurers have unique problems in determining GAAP factors. Few treaties have enough experience to be independently credible, and few are large enough to necessitate or deserve separate treatment for calculating GAAP factors. Trying to generalize factors for use with several treaties from different companies is difficult as premiums and allowances are generally distinct for each individual agreement. The reinsurer seldom has the option to avoid developing GAAP factors.

Another problem faced by reinsurers is dealing with the type, or lack, of detail available. For individual cession business, the reinsurer has extensive detail on each life. However, many individual cession reinsurance treaties may have less than 100 policies inforce; the expense and effort needed to develop special factors for such small numbers may be prohibitive. For large accounts, it is possible and practical to develop separate GAAP factors. The reinsurer should develop GAAP factors based upon its expected experience and the plan of reinsurance, but it may group several ceded treaties together for administrative simplicity. The reinsurer must constantly decide whether a given contract is different enough from other contracts to justify separate assumptions, or should it be combined with similar contracts.

Yearly Renewable Term

In developing GAAP factors for a YRT scale, the reinsurer should consider the expense, persistency, and mortality assumptions used in developing that scale. This is a straightforward procedure; the factors so developed can be applied to business produced using the rate scale until a new GAAP era is started.

Just as with the ceding company, the zero first year premium YRT contract requires additional consideration. No special rules are required for this form of YRT reinsurance, as regular GAAP guidelines apply, as is illustrated in the following discussion.

A zero first year premium YRT treaty in essence provides for the recovery of the first year reinsurance claims and expenses out of future premiums. While this is economically no different than coinsurance on an annually renewable term plan with a 100% first year allowance, it creates problems as there are no first year revenues. A benefit reserve should be calculated based upon actual premiums to be received, adjusted for an implied first year premium. The implied first year premium and 100% allowance generates a deferred acquisition cost asset.

An alternative procedure which should produce algebraically the same result calls for no deferred acquisition asset and for benefit reserves to be based upon the zero actual premium received. This leads to a negative first year benefit reserve which is amortized over the life of the policy. Both procedures have been used. If persistency experience diverges from assumptions, more consistency between factors may be maintained with the latter approach.

Coinsurance

Coinsurance is more difficult than YRT to handle for reinsurance assumed. In theory, every plan from every insurer should have a separate set of factors based upon the expected premiums, interest, mortality, persistency, and allowances. Some reinsurers have tried to adhere to this approach, but others have found it administratively more convenient to combine several plans. This may produce some variations among plans, but these will typically offset each other. In fact, reinsurers can develop a model plan or a series of model plans for each of type of policy reinsured and, at the time of pricing, assign the product to a model plan. For large accounts or plans, separate factors should be developed.

In developing the factors, the reinsurer should take the same approach as does a direct writer, matching revenues and expenses over the life of the policy, using realistic assumptions for mortality, persistency, and expense with reasonable provision for adverse deviation. Development of deferred acquisition cost factors is the same for coinsurance as for a direct issue, with allowances being used for commissions. The calculation of factors for coinsurance is not difficult, but the application and administration can be very tedious and complicated.

Modified Coinsurance

Mod-co may be treated exactly the same as coinsurance, except that the interest rate assumed for the benefit reserve has to be consistent with that used for the mod-co adjustment. This can introduce a slight error since the statutory reserve will likely be different than the GAAP benefit reserve and the mod-co adjustment interest rate may be different from the rate which is assumed to be earned by the reinsurer. However, the reinsurer's assumed earned rate may be used as a matter of simplification unless there is a significant difference in rates. If the difference between the reinsurer's assumed rate and the mod-co adjustment rate is significant, then the reinsurer's assumed rate should be used. Many reinsurers use their assumed rate in the mod-co reserve factors for simplicity.

Deferred acquisition cost factors should be identical for mod-co and coinsurance if the allowances, premiums and mortality and persistency assumptions are the same.

Special Provisions
As was the case with ceded reinsurance, the following transactions require special consideration for GAAP.

Chargebacks. As noted in the section on ceded reinsurance, chargebacks need to be considered in developing GAAP factors. The benefit reserve factors do not change with the presence of a chargeback. However, the presence of a chargeback will have an effect on deferred acquisition cost factors. The additional first year allowance should be treated as an additional first year expense. A chargeback should be treated as income in the year in which it is expected to be received, based upon the lapse assumptions. This can lead to distortion of revenues. An alternative method is to treat the additional first year allowance as an expense in the year it occurrs and chargebacks as negative surrender values.

In any event, chargebacks should be recognized in determining the reinsured deferred acquisition cost and the revenue to which it should be related is the base premium, not an inflated premium including the chargeback. The total expense, including both the additional allowance and the chargeback, is spread in proportion to revenues over the life of the policy.

Recapture. Recapture is an interesting problem for reinsurers. While it is generally reasonable and appropriate for a ceding company to ignore recapture, it is probably not prudent for a reinsurer to do so since it is likely that some ceding companies will exercise this option.

A typical pricing decision might be to assume that 50% of the business will be recaptured at the earliest opportunity, with an additional 5%-10% recaptured annually thereafter. For GAAP purposes, such an approach is reasonable. This leads to faster amortization of the acquisition costs, but the effect on benefit reserves is unpredictable.

It is reasonable to assume that if a block of business is producing negative results for the reinsurer and is expected to continue to produce negative results, then recapture will not occur. On the other hand, if the ceding company can prudently reduce reinsurance costs by recapture, it is reasonable to assume it will exercise its recapture options subsequent to any retention increase. In short, recapture is more likely on profitable business than on unprofitable business.

It would be appropriate for a reinsurer not only to assume additional lapses for potential recaptures, but also to assume a deterioration in mortality on the remaining business following recapture, reflecting the fact that the accounts which do not recapture may choose not to do so because of negative expectations. Depending upon the premium pattern of the policy and the underlying benefit structure, this could lead to either higher or lower benefit reserves.

Experience Refunds. In the past, a substantial part of the coinsurance and mod-co written on a traditional basis contained experience refund provisions. While less frequent today, refund business still occurs and significant blocks of inforce business are subject to experience refund rating. In addition, many YRT treaties were written with experience refund provisions. The presence of experience loss carryforwards introduces a complication in integrating experience refunds into the GAAP factors, as timing differences must be considered as well as expected values.

In theory, when a contract is written with an experience refund provision, the expected refunds should be taken into account in determining the benefit reserves and deferred acquisition cost assets. In practice, this is often not done. Instead, refunds are recognized as incurred. If a loss occurs, the experience refund account is cast in a loss carryforward position and it is appropriate to review that individual account to determine if some or all of the loss is expected to be recovered in the future. To the extent that the loss is expected to be recovered in the future, that amount, discounted for interest, may be set up as a GAAP asset. Paid refunds may be directly reported for GAAP without adjustment.

Self-Administration

In principle, the application of GAAP to the self-administered reinsurance[4] is the same as for individual cession business. The choices of an appropriate model and appropriate assumptions are identical in concept. One significant difficulty is that the reinsurer seldom has sufficient detail to apply the factors accurately. The reinsurer is supposed to receive some sort of detail by plan, issue, age, and year of issue, but often does not. A significant challenge is faced by the reinsurer attempting to account for a self-administered assumed reinsurance treaty on a GAAP basis. A dynamic worksheet approach to deferred acquisition costs and a concurrent review of statutory results may achieve the stated goals of GAAP, but the theoretical basis for the resulting financial entries may be weak.

The purpose of self-administration is to simplify administration for both the reinsurer and the reinsured while minimizing the volume of data transferred from one party to another. The systems used to produce reports are often those used for other purposes and the reinsurance data is only a by-product. There may be significant realistic limitations to the amount of detail available. In addition, self administration generally assumes a very low level of expense.

Models. To add additional administration for GAAP is self-defeating to the purpose of self-administration, so a model approach is both desirable and necessary. The construction of a model and the development of factors for benefit reserves and deferred acquisition costs are essentially the same as those for individual cession business, but there are some differences. The same basic steps need to be undertaken for both individual cession and self-administered contracts. These are as follows:

(1) Selection of Various Model Segments: Some self administered agreements include only one plan and others include many. In addition, it may not be practical to develop GAAP factors for every contract. Some grouping is an administrative necessity. The grouping should be based upon plans of similar characteristics and expected profit levels. Smoker/nonsmoker and other such special underwriting categories and premium classifications should

---

[4]For a more detailed discussion of the intricacies of self-administered reinsurance and GAAP accounting, see Tiller [16].

be recognized whenever possible. GAAP accounting will nearly always require more segments than will statutory accounting since GAAP issue era groupings are used.

(2) Assumption Selection: Most companies have found that a few, say three, issue age groups per plan are adequate. This should be consistent with the standard of the company on other products and lines. Other assumptions should also be selected consistent with this standard.

(3) Projection of New Issues: A key part of modeling bulk accounts is a projection for new issues. This earnings projection should be made on both GAAP and statutory bases and should produce by-products such as inforce volume, inforce premium, and inforce statutory reserves. This projection will be used not only in determining deferrable expenses and initial reserves, but in the development of factors for the inforce.

(4) Factor Application: Once the factors have been developed for the model in the prior step, they can be applied to summaries of the inforce business which are provided by the ceding companies. In this case, factor application is identical to that for individual cession business.

(5) Model Validation: Checking assumptions, especially persistency assumptions, is extremely difficult for self administered contracts. For example, if a distribution of the inforce business by issue age within issue year is available, then a model can very easily be tested for credibility. Self-administered contracts generally do not provide that data and other tests have to be devised. In any event, comparisons should always be made of the aggregate statutory reserves, the volume inforce, and the premium produced by the model to that actually reported by the reinsured. These are general checks and can help identify problem areas.

With any model, it is reasonable to expect that over time actual results will differ from those projected. The purpose of the model validation is to determine the accuracy of results and to assist in determining when corrections or modifications to the model are necessary. Even if only one assumption, such as persistency, is out of line, the model can produce extremely inaccurate results. Since profit results vary by issue age, if the assumed issue age distribution is not representative, the model can produce distorted earnings. While validation can never be perfect, it can provide a level of comfort for relying on the results. What this modeling technique accomplishes, in effect, is a substitution of a "per account" factor in the place of a "per thousand dollar unit" factor.

The most important consideration in developing GAAP factors for self-administered treaties is dealing with the data available or, more typically, not available. The reinsurer must adapt itself to the data available on the submitted reports. It is important that the reinsurer take GAAP as well as statutory and cash reporting requirements into account when entering into bulk accounting agreements and in designing bulk accounting report forms.

It may be difficult to identify substandard issues on self-administered business. The validation process should obviously take substandard business into account and assumptions should reflect the percentage of substandard policies. This is an extra layer of administration complexity, but not conceptually difficult.

Once a model has been validated, it needs to be checked at least annually. As long as the validation continues to show the model to be reasonable, it can continue to be used. If a check shows that actual results are deviating significantly from the model, then a new model may be appropriate, based upon more current assumptions. This need may conflict with GAAP rules regarding assumption lock-in except in cases of loss recognition. It should, however, not be considered in the same light as a loss recognition or a recoverability issue, but rather as the correction of an accounting error.

Unless it is necessary, due to loss recognition or recoverability problems, the underlying GAAP factors should not be changed. But the model should be adjusted to reflect the appropriate age or smoker/nonsmoker distribution, for example. There is generally little reason to change the mortality or persistency in a model unless loss recognition or recoverability is involved. Even if persistency is significantly different, it is not appropriate to change the future expected persistency in the model. The inforce should be adjusted, effectively writing off the deferred acquisition asset in proportion to excess terminations.

Adjusting for Time Lag. The time lags in reporting are also a difficulty in self administered agreements. While individual cession business is generally reported on a fairly current basis and has relatively few items in transit, a self administered contract may have a whole quarter or perhaps an entire year of activity unreported.

Some reinsurers accept this and allow the books to be one reporting period behind for such clients. Others attempt to project both statutory and GAAP results through the end of the current accounting period, then adjust the estimates to actual results when results are received. The latter approach is preferred as being technically correct, but extreme care must be taken that earnings are not distorted. Techniques which produce conservative statutory results may lead to excessive GAAP gains, creating a misleading impression of the performance of the reinsurer and management problems, since any excess earnings must be "made up" later.

Recoverability and Loss Recognition

Recoverability and loss recognition criteria are similar for self-administration and individual cession reinsurance and are basically the same as for directly written business. These types of tests should be performed on reinsurance accepted just as they are for direct written business. In performing loss recognition or recoverability tests for a direct writer, reinsurance ceded should obviously be taken into account. If a problem appears to be developing with either recoverability or loss recognition, additional refinement of models and investigation of experiences should be completed before a loss or reduction in deferral is accepted.

Facultative Business

Facultative business provides a challenge for reinsurers, since experience will differ from that of automatic business. For individual cession business, facultative factors can be developed using different mortality assumptions. For some reinsurers facultative business is not material and it is not necessary to develop separate GAAP factors.

GAAP factors can take into account the weighted average of mortality and of persistency for facultative and automatic business and develop one set of factors to apply overall. If a company wishes to do the detailed administration, it can also develop separate factors for facultative business.

Facultative reinsurance can be a problem for self-administered treaties. It may be difficult to identify the proportion of facultative cessions reinsured.

FINANCIAL REINSURANCE

In theory, financial reinsurance treaties may be treated the same as any other reinsurance agreement. The economic effect on both the ceding and reinsuring companies is usually quite different from that of the gross numbers which flow through the reinsurance treaties. It is generally accepted that the economic effect of the treaties must be considered with the GAAP accounting reflecting primarily the net cash transactions and risk transfer involved in the treaty. For a typical surplus relief treaty, the gross numbers may be shown from a statutory or tax basis, but it is common to "collapse" the transaction to show merely the risk fee or cash transfer for the GAAP accounting. On this basis, the risk fee would be the only item to show up on either the ceded or accepted statements for GAAP purposes. For the ceding company, the risk fee would be reinsurance ceded premium, resulting in a reduction in the premium and, eventually, a bottom line reduction in earnings. For the reinsurer, this same fee would produce premium income that would drop to the bottom line as earnings.

In GAAP accounting, both parties in the transaction need to take account of the statutory and tax considerations. In determining whether or not a full GAAP or a collapsed GAAP treatment is appropriate, the parties should take into account items such as expected recapture and experience refunds relataive to the permanency of transfer. It is quite possible to have a long term risk transfer which is not expected to be permanent.

For example, a surplus relief treaty may transfer fully the risks for persistency and mortality. However, if properly priced, it may be that in five to ten years the block of business would "repay" the initial surplus relief and fees and begin to produce a profit. At this point the ceding company may wish to terminate. If the expectation is that the block of business will be profitable enough to premit termination or to produce significant experience refunds, then those expectations should be reflected.

This would be an argument for collapsing the treaty down to the expected cash transaction of a risk fee. If, however, this is less certain or if termination is not specifically included as an option in the treaty, then more permanent and larger scale GAAP accounting may be necessary. The accounting profession believes it is important not to distort the income of the two parties by moving income from one carrier to another and then, upon recapture, moving it back.

OTHER CONSIDERATIONS

It is beyond the scope of this text to discuss the GAAP implications of accident and health reinsurance. The principles discussed in the examples regarding life insurance should be of instructional value in applying GAAP accounting for accident and health reinsurance.

Special treaties, such as stop-loss and catastrophe covers, have a variety of options under GAAP accounting. Under traditional statutory accounting, these policies merely take the premium into income, treat the current year's claims, if any, as benefits, and the net result is the statutory earnings. Many companies follow the same approach for GAAP. However, some companies build up a catastrophe or contingency reserve under GAAP, statutory, or both bases.

Under this approach, some portion of the premium, perhaps the net premium, is accumulated in a reserve fund. Under this approach, in any year that claims are less than some portion of the premium, say the net premium, a specified percentage of the excess is added to and accumulated in the contingency reserve. In any year that claims exceed the net premium, the excess, or some portion of the excess, is charged to the contingency reserve. This has the effect of smoothing the earnings, and, as a result, the reserve is sometimes referred to as a fluctuation reserve. This reserving approach has gained acceptance for both statutory and GAAP reporting for highly volatile benefits such as these. Other companies will allow surplus to perform this function of a catastrophe reinsurance reserve.

GAAP requires that future income taxes on GAAP income which has not yet been taxed be shown as a "provision for deferred taxes." This is designed to prevent the over-reporting of income. Any current cost tax savings which will be reversed later in the life of the agreement should be included in the deferred tax provision.

14 | Tax Effects of Reinsurance

Taxation of reinsurance has many implications and degrees of complexity, ranging from the mundane routine of premium taxes to exotic international tax issues. Taxes can be a major expense of an insurance company; a competent management group will explore reasonable, legal options to reduce expenses, including taxes. Many reinsurance transactions have been either largely motivated by tax benefits or have had a number of their terms dictated or at least influenced by tax considerations.

The intent of this chapter is to introduce the subject of reinsurance taxation and to describe some of the tax considerations which must go into the analysis of a reinsurance arrangement. The focus of this chapter is on taxation within the United States. Some considerations of taxation of treaties which cross international borders are also included.[1]

Taxation is an extremely important subject which should be approached with caution. This book is not intended to be a handbook on taxation; specific court cases and precedents are not always cited. The actual circumstances surrounding an agreement can change the tax treatment. Qualified tax practitioners or

---

[1]Additional international tax considerations are discussed in Chapter 18, International Reinsurance.

counsel should always be involved in the analysis whenever a reinsurance treaty has significant tax implications.

PREMIUM TAXES

In most jurisdictions of the United States, reinsurance is excused from a premium tax based upon the fact that the premium taxes for any business reinsured have already been paid by the direct company. Many reinsurance agreements call for the reinsurer to reimburse the ceding company for premium taxes on the reinsurance premiums to the extent that the reinsurer is not otherwise taxed on those premiums. Other agreements call for no explicit reimbursement for premium tax, but implicitly the reinsurer may have increased allowances or otherwise reflected the fact that it is not paying premium tax on this business.

The payment may be either an exact reimbursement based on the actual premium taxes paid or a specified percentage of reinsurance premiums. Economically, the latter is just an additional allowance. The specified percentage may be stated in the treaty or agreed upon for administrative convenience.

If the treaty calls for premium tax reimbursement, the reinsurer participates in any change in the premium tax rate. If the treaty specifies a percentage allowance, only the ceding company is affected by any change in premium tax rates.

Other state and local taxes, licenses, and fees are sometimes charged on insurance. These are not covered nor reimbursed under any form of reinsurance. The reinsurer is responsible for any such taxes, licenses, or fees it incurs as a business entity.

UNITED STATES FEDERAL INCOME TAX

Tax law and the basis on which life insurance companies in the United States are taxed is fluid.[2] However, since 1958, taxes have been based upon total income or the principal components of

---

[2]There are several references on the taxation of insurance companies in general and life insurance companies in particular, including VanMieghem and Brown [18]. The Internal Revenue Code itself, the discussions in the various "Blue Books," and *The Congressional Record* are the ultimate sources.

earnings of the company, with some limitations on the deductibility
of policyholder dividends.   Companies will frequently use
reinsurance to lower their taxable income and, under certain
circumstances, to increase current taxable income.

Background

Taxation of life insurance companies has always been a complicated
matter, due to the long-term nature of their liabilities.   Over the
last 80 years, the United States has used many bases for taxation
of life insurance companies.   Originally, total income was taxed.
Later, only investment income was taxed.   From 1958 through
1981, the Life Insurance Company Tax Act of 1959, commonly
referred to as the 1959 Act[3], applied.   Many of the current
reinsurance practices with regard to financial reinsurance treaties
and the effect of taxation upon reinsurance agreements evolved
under the 1959 Act.   Therefore, some basic understanding of the
provisions of the 1959 Act is important in understanding both the
history of reinsurance taxation and the current law.

Tax Phases.   Under the 1959 Act there were three situations, or
phases, of taxation.   In the first of these, commonly known as
"Phase I," taxes were based on investment income.   Companies in
this   situation   most   frequently   were   large   mutual   insurers.
Dividends could not be used to reduce taxable income.

       "Phase II Negative" companies were taxed on the operating
income of the company, including investment income.   These
companies   were   often   smaller   stock   companies   or   companies
showing significant growth and strain.

       "Phase II Positive" companies, those where operating
income exceeded investment income, were taxed on the average of
those two amounts, with the untaxed operating income being
placed   into   a   notional   deferred   tax   account,   known   as   the
Policyholders' Surplus Account.   This account, which included
certain other untaxed items and deductions, is governed by "Phase
III" tax rules.   The Phase III tax is assessed in the event of certain
disbursements,   loss   of   life   company   status,   accumulation   of
amounts in excess of specified limits, or liquidation of the company.

---

[3]Public Law 86-89; June 25, 1959; Sections 801-820 of the Internal
Revenue Code.

Section 820 and its Effect. In the late 1970's, it became obvious that the 1959 Act was not functioning properly, particularly for companies in a Phase I situation. At a time of high interest rates, the tax on marginal investment income often exceeded 100%. In addition, the investment income on tax qualified pension contracts of some life insurance companies was being heavily taxed despite the obvious intent of the law that such income would not be taxed. Companies in this situation were forced either to subsidize tax qualified business or to be noncompetitive.

As a result, in the late 1970's companies in a Phase I position began to make increasing use of an hitherto little used provision of the 1959 Act, Section 820. Under Section 820, modified coinsurance could be treated as though it were coinsurance for tax purposes. The effect was to make it possible to move investment income from the ceding company to the reinsurer, using the mod-co interest adjustment combined with a Section 820 election, and return it to the ceding company as operating income via an experience refund or a return of reinsurance premium.

The use of Section 820 resulted in the recharacterization of investment income as operating income for tax purposes, with a significant tax reduction. This allowed more dividends to be deducted from taxable income by the ceding company, lowering its taxes. Typically the reinsurer was taxed only on the profit it retained from this business, and often the transfer of tax exempt investment income benefits sheltered this and other income from taxation.

In effect, significant amounts of investment income could escape taxation through this treatment. The total tax bill of the life insurance industry was drastically reduced. As the federal government became aware of this and other problems involved in taxing life insurance companies, it moved to change the law. Section 820 is no longer a part of the Tax Code although many treaties which included Section 820 elections are still in existence.

Section 818(c)(2) and its Effect. Another provision unique to the 1959 Act was the more broadly used Section 818(c)(2). Introduced as an equalizer between large and small companies, this provision allowed for modified statutory reserves to be treated as net level premium reserves for tax purposes without an exact recalculation but using an approximation formula adjustment.

The importance of this feature was that it allowed for a deduction in excess of the actual statutory reserve established at issue of a new policy. This resulted in a significant tax loss at issue while reducing tax deductions in renewal years for persisting policies and creating additional taxable gains at termination of a policy. After considering the time value of money, the effects on taxable income generally resulted in an overall gain to the company.

Of significance to the reinsurance industry was that policies issued on a modified reserve basis and reinsured on either a coinsurance basis or on a mod-co basis with the Section 820 election passed the 818(c)(2) benefits to the reinsurer. Often, the ceding company could not utilize all of these special deductions while the reinsurer could, so the total taxes paid by the insurance industry were reduced.

Phase III Concerns. The 1959 Act placed limitations on the maximum amount which could be accumulated in the Policyholders' Surplus Account. These limits were expressed as functions of premium income or reserves. If the premium income and reserves both became too low, a Phase III tax would be incurred on the amount in excess of the limit.

A number of companies facing a potential Phase III tax turned to reinsurance as a solution. Assumed reinsurance was used to increase the level of premium or reserves, thereby avoiding the imposition of a Phase III tax. At first, the IRS challenged the use of reinsurance in this manner, but the courts upheld this activity and the practice become relatively common. The later enactment of Section 845, as discussed subsequently, could cause new concerns for companies using this approach.

Effects on the Industry and Congress. The use of reinsurance significantly reduced life insurance industry taxes and played a major role in both the development of life insurance taxation as it exists today and the overall structure of the life insurance industry. Section 820 treaties made an increasing number of people aware of the potential for financial reinsurance and educated a whole generation in the use of reinsurance for financial planning. Section 818(c)(2) encouraged and subsidized the growth of cheaper term and term-like products.

The rapid growth of many life insurance companies was fueled by reinsurance financing in terms of both allowances and risk bearing, and much of this financing was motivated, or at least assisted, by tax benefits to the reinsurer. Many companies were writing large term and term-like policies with average sizes well in excess of their retention limits, requiring significant reinsurance. Many reinsurers took advantage of the Section 818(c)(2) election to generate tax losses. In some instances, plans with no pre-tax profit for either the direct writer or the reinsurer produced significant after-tax profits for both. This led to very high coinsurance allowances on some plans and helped to justify the rapid reduction in term insurance rates in the early 1980's, probably to the detriment of the life insurance industry.

Probably the most significant result of the tax-related reinsurance activity of the 1970's and 1980's was the change in the tax code. Congress changed the tax laws for life insurance effective in 1982 and again in 1983. Several of the changes were aimed directly at reinsurance. Both Congress and the IRS are very aware of the past use of reinsurance for tax reductions and view any use of reinsurance with considerable skepticism.

Reinsurance under DEFRA

The tax laws passed in 1982 and 1984 eliminated the provisions of Sections 818 (c)(2) and 820 from the Internal Revenue Code. There are no similar provisions in today's tax law. However, many companies became aware of the advantages of shifting losses and gains from one company to another via reinsurance; that process continues today, both in the financial or surplus relief reinsurance transactions and in the more traditional lines. Just as reinsurance can be used to accomplish many financial purposes for a company, reinsurance can also be used to provide other, more sophisticated tax-related benefits.

A responsible practitioner should be aware that tax law for life insurers is under constant scrutiny, subject to seemingly continual change. There are numerous cases in litigation, as well as constant legislation and IRS activity regarding reinsurance. The law as of this writing is basically that as passed by Congress in 1984, with some modifications.

The 1984 law was part of a major overhaul of the federal income tax system of the United States, the Deficit Reduction Act of 1984, commonly referred to as DEFRA. The portions unique to insurance companies include Sections 801 through 847. Sections 801 through 818 specifically address life insurance companies and Section 845 addresses reinsurance.

---

[4]IRS Rev. Rul. 82-69, 1982-1 C. B. 102.

Taxation of Gains and Losses. If a reinsurer provides statutory surplus for a company's growth, the reinsurer typically would have a statutory loss and could expect some degree of tax loss also. That loss creates a tax deferral on a current cash basis, allowing the reinsurer to shelter some of its income from taxes or at least defer the taxation. To the extent tax rates vary from one year to another or from one company to another, additional opportunities utilizing reinsurance may be created.

Historically, income from reinsurance has been taxable in the year it occurs, whether the company is a ceding company or a reinsurer. This continues to be the case. Losses due to reinsurance have been subject to various treatments, depending upon the facts of a particular situation.

Losses incurred by a ceding company are generally deductible in the year they occur. Typically, this would arise because reinsurance premiums exceed the sum of allowances, benefits, and reserve credits. However, in some circumstances it may be appropriate to spread a reinsurance cost over more than one tax year. This might occur in the event of a single premium intended to prepay mortality reinsurance on a YRT basis, where no reserve credit is taken. Such circumstances have been very rare.

Usually, a reinsurer will show a statutory loss, or surplus strain, when it puts new reinsurance on its books, especially in the case of a surplus relief agreement. This will typically translate into a tax loss, but the timing of that loss depends upon the terms and form of the reinsurance. In any event normal tax reserves must be used and the other peculiarities of tax accounting must be observed.

Under an assumption reinsurance treaty, any tax deductible strain incurred by the assumption reinsurer may not be deducted immediately, but must be amortized in the future, roughly in proportion to expected income over the "useful life" of the business. The rules for determining the useful life of the business assumed are not precise, but generally it can be determined as either the expected life of the reinsurance agreement, if it can be determined, or the average life of the business assumed. Under this treatment, the assumption reinsurer will incur statutory strain without an accompanying tax deduction. However, the determination of useful life is such that the deductions typically can be "front-ended."

Until recently, the situation was less clear under an indemnity agreement. Historically, the strain calculated on a tax basis was considered deductible by the reinsurer in the year the strain was incurred. In 1982, the IRS issued Revenue Ruling 82-69[4] which extended the previously described treatment for assumption reinsurance to indemnity reinsurance of blocks of inforce business. The IRS position was challenged in the courts with mixed results; in some cases the court involved upheld the taxpayer's position while other courts agreed with the IRS. This created uncertainty as to the appropriate position to be taken by the reinsuring company.

In June, 1989, the Colonial American case[5] reached the United States Supreme Court. This case concerned the deductibility of the strain, or "ceding commission," in an indemnity reinsurance agreement. Under the agreement, a block of inforce business was ceded to Colonial American Life Insurance Company. Colonial American deducted the strain in the year it occurred. The IRS contended that this was really the acquisition of an asset and should be treated as would the acquisition of any asset under general tax accounting; specifically, the ceding commission should be capitalized initially and amortized over the useful life of the business.

The Supreme Court agreed with the IRS, clarifying the conflict which had existed between the different lower court opinions. As a consequence, the ceding commission or strain arising from indemnity reinsurance on inforce business should be amortized and not deducted immediately, a treatment identical to that accorded assumption reinsurance.

However, uncertainty remained regarding the proper treatment of strain or ceding commission on indemnity reinsurance of new issues as well as the proper methods for applying the decision in practice. The situation was largely clarified with the June 1990 release of Revenue Proclamation 90-36.[6] This document describes an administrative procedure under which reinsurers can apply the Colonial American decision. A brief discussion of the pertinent points follows.

The Colonial American decision and Revenue Proclamation 90-36 address the reinsurance of inforce blocks of business. Reinsurance allowances which parallel the expenses incurred by the

---

[4]IRS Rev. Rul. 82-69, 1982-1 C. B. 102.

[5]Colonial American Life Insurance Company v. Commissioner of Internal Revenue, No. 88-396.

[6]Internal Revenue Bulletin 1990-27, July 2, 1990.

ceding company for acquisition, administration, and service of new issues should be deductible by the reinsurer as incurred, in accordance with Letter Ruling 8752003 of the IRS.

Revenue Ruling 82-96 was largely restated as applying to indemnity reinsurance of blocks of inforce business. Ceding commissions spent for purposes of acquiring the block are to be treated as capital expenditures to acquire an asset and amortized over the anticipated life of the asset.

An "annual ceding commission" which is paid by the reinsurer to reimburse the ceding company for the reinsured portion of current expenses of servicing and administration may be deducted in the year in which they are incurred.

The amortization applies only to the portion of the business retained by the reinsurer. Any portion of the ceding commission which is attributable to business which is retroceded may be deducted in the year of the retrocession. This balances the fact that any ceding commission received by the reinsurer from the retrocessionaire will be included in that year's taxable income.

The "up-front ceding commission" to be amortized is defined as "the excess of the increase in the reinsurer's tax reserve liabilities resulting from the transaction... over the value of the net assets received."

The ceding commission is to be amortized over the life of the reinsurance agreement. If possible, the expected life of the reinsurance agreement is to be used. This may be determined from the terms of the agreement, such as any rights of termination or recapture after a specified period of time. If the life of the reinsurance agreement is indeterminate, the "reasonably estimated life of the underlying policies" may be used. The amortization may be on a straight-line basis or done in a manner consistent with the anticipated income, including both premiums and investment income.

The revenue proclamation also laid out rules for changing the accounting methods with respect to inforce agreements in order to comply with the proclamation and further provided that it applied only to life insurance companies, not to property and liability insurers.

Life Company Status. An insurance company is taxed as either a "life company" or a "non-life company." While there are many nuances to consider, essentially a company is considered to be a life company for tax purposes if it meets three criteria:

(1) It is primarily engaged in the business of insurance.
(2) It is engaged in the issuance or reinsurance of life insurance policies or annuity contracts.
(3) Over 50% of its reserves are held for "life insurance" plans[7], including annuities.

Life insurance companies are taxed differently than other companies. There may be advantages to a specific company to be taxed either as a life company or a non-life company. Reinsurance is one means of managing to achieve the preferred status. One way to increase life reserves and thereby establish or maintain life company status is by assuming reinsurance. Ceding non-life reserves may accomplish the same objective. Ceding life reserves or assuming non-life reserves are ways to establish or maintain non-life status. Reinsurance has been used in both situations and its treatment has been upheld by the courts. However, the IRS may still challenge agreements if significant tax avoidance results or if there is inadequate transfer of risk under the agreement.

Phase III Status. A potential Phase III tax liability arising from the 1959 Act still exists for many companies. If a company with a positive Policyholders' Surplus Account balance loses its life company status or if its premium income or life reserves drop below a certain level, a Phase III tax is incurred. Reinsurance has been used to maintain appropriate levels of reserves or premiums.

Small Company Status. Under DEFRA, a "small company" is allowed a special deduction which effectively reduces its taxable income by as much as 60 percent. This deduction is available only to life companies that have less than $15 million of taxable income and also less than $500 million of assets in its corporate group. The deduction grades from 60 percent for taxable income of $3 million or less to zero for taxable income of $15 million or more.

It is conceivable that reinsurance could be used to reduce either assets or income below the applicable limits.

Section 845. Congress, the Treasury Department, and the IRS apparently realized that they could never anticipate and legislate

---

[7]For tax purposes, noncancellable accident and health insurance policies are considered to be life insurance. A life insurance policy must meet the rules of Section 7702 or it is not considered to be life insurance for tax purposes.

all situations in which reinsurance could be used. However, they were apprehensive about the possible usage of reinsurance to reduce insurance industry taxes significantly. To that end, DEFRA included the creation of Section 845. Although significant reduction of taxes through reinsurance was primarily a phenomenon of life insurance companies, this provision applies to all insurance companies, including property and casualty companies.

There are two parts to Section 845. Under the first part, Section 845(a), the IRS is given very broad latitude to reallocate tax items between two companies which are related. To many practitioners, this is merely a reaffirmation specific to reinsurance of a broader rule concerning related party transactions stated elsewhere in the Internal Revenue Code. Even prior to the enactment Section 845, companies usually established "arm's length" standards for reinsurance when related parties were involved. It is unknown what reinsurance terms will be considered unacceptable, given the IRS' broad powers to reallocate items in the tax returns.

Section 845(b) deals with reinsurance transactions between unrelated parties. Again, the IRS has broad latitude to reallocate income and deduction items between the two parties, but not as broad as provided under Section 845(a).

The IRS has the option to reallocate various income and deduction items within a single company's return if there is a "significant tax avoidance effect." Significant tax avoidance is not defined, but is left to the discretion of the Treasury Secretary, or in effect, to the IRS. Evidence of fraud or intent to avoid taxation is not required, merely the presence of tax avoidance. The IRS has the authority to reallocate items where only one party is a domestic insurer, subject to United States federal income taxes.

The law does not require that adjustment be made to the tax returns of both parties to the reinsurance agreement; the IRS can reallocate items in one party's tax return and not change the other's. For example, the IRS could reclassify a reinsurer's commissions and allowances, eliminating its deduction, but leave the income the allowances generated for the ceding company with the ceding company. In effect, the application of Section 845 could result in double taxation.

The background documentation of the development of Section 845 shows that Congress and the IRS intended for this provision to be used to prevent reinsurance abuses which distort taxable income. Certain exclusions and safe harbors were contemplated. As an example, taking over the business of a company near insolvency would normally not be subject to reallocation. Proportionality is considered a safe harbor. Proportionality exists when allowances are constructed such that the strain is divided between the ceding company and the reinsurer roughly in proportion to the division of the business between the parties. Because this is a relatively new provision, care should be taken in interpreting these exclusions and safe harbors.

The IRS is concerned about legitimate risk transfer as opposed to agreements where only paper liabilities are involved and no cash loss can ever be incurred by the reinsurer. Therefore, a major consideration in constructing an agreement which needs favorable tax treatment is that some meaningful element of risk be transferred from the ceding company to the reinsurer, i.e., that it not be a sham transaction. The more risks that are transferred, and the greater the degree of those risks, the more likely it is that the desired tax treatment will result. This is an important reason to utilize experienced reinsurance and tax advisors when considering such a treaty.

Loss Carryovers. The tax code for corporations provides that if taxable income is negative for a given year, the loss can be applied to income in other years. This is accomplished by the use of "loss carryovers."

If a company has gains in prior years, it may use the current loss as a "loss carryback" to offset those gains and recover taxes previously paid. Any tax recovery is limited to prior taxes actually paid. The period of time for which losses can be carried back is subject to change by Congress, but is currently three years. Losses must be carried back to the earliest possible year and applied to that year first; any remaining losses are then applied to the next qualifying year.

If a company does not use the loss as a carryback, it may use it as a "loss carryforward." In this case, the loss is carried into future tax years and used to reduce future taxable income. A loss carryforward may be less valuable than a carryback because a carryback will result in current cash income, where a carryforward has no current cash benefit. The actual benefits will vary according to the facts in the case. Currently, the limitation on tax loss carryforwards is fifteen years.

Reinsurance can be used to take advantage of loss carryover situations. If a company has a loss carryforward, it might choose to use reinsurance to accelerate future income which would be sheltered from current taxes. In this manner, it could realize a current cash benefit from a loss carryforward. On the other hand, a reinsurer may create a current tax loss and use it as a carryback to recover taxes already paid.

Special Mutual Company Taxes. Under DEFRA, mutual life insurance companies have a special tax[8] assessed on their surplus. The rules for this are very complex, but the important fact is that for most mutual life insurers, additional surplus creates additional tax. For this reason, some mutual companies have found that they can use surplus to finance reinsurance. This has a twofold benefit: earnings are increased by the profits on the reinsurance and the special tax on surplus is reduced to the extent that the additional business generated from reinsurance requires surplus.

Alternative Minimum Tax. DEFRA also introduced the concept of the alternative minimum tax, or AMT. AMT applies to all businesses, not just insurance companies. It is a tax on certain tax-preferred income items as well as the excess of "book" income over normal taxable income.

For stock life insurance companies, book income is based on GAAP income; for mutual life insurance companies, statutory income is the base. Specific adjustments must be made to base income to determine AMT income; the guidelines and procedures are not yet known.

In computing the AMT, gains and losses from reinsurance are treated the same as those from direct insurance. A company should be aware of its position with respect to the AMT when estimating the effect of reinsurance on its taxes.

If a company finds itself in a position where it will pay tax on an AMT basis because book income exceeds its normal taxable income, it may be able to cede a block of business and recognize the future value of the earnings on the block at a low marginal tax rate. This can occur because the income from the reinsurance would effectively be taxed only on the excess of the normal tax rate over the AMT rate. Alternatively, a company in the AMT

---

[8]This tax is technically a reduction in the deductibility of policyholder dividends for mutual companies and is known as the tax on differential earnings. The provision for this tax is contained in Section 809. As of the current date, Congress is considering changing this provision.

position may find that losses due to reinsurance have less tax benefit than expected.

In reinsurance planning it should be kept in mind that effective tax rates can change, either because of legislative action or because a company's circumstances change. An example of this would include a company moving from a small company position to a normal tax position or moving into or out of the AMT situation.

If possible, a company would prefer to incur tax losses at high tax rates and gains at low rates. This is not always under the company's control, but to some extent reinsurance may assist in planning to maximize such opportunities.

Offshore and Foreign Treaties. Many foreign countries have tax bases which are significantly different from that of the United States. In the past, it was not uncommon for a United States insurer to reinsure business with a foreign based company to improve the total tax position of both companies by capitalizing on the differences of the two systems of taxation. That practice is much less common today. The presence of Section 845 allows for the reallocation of income and deduction items and therefore makes the use of an international reinsurance treaty less certain.

However, saving taxes is not the only, nor even the primary, motivation for reinsurance treaties, either domestic or international. As a result, many international reinsurance treaties exist today. Certain provisions of the tax code and regulations apply to these treaties.

Reinsurance ceded outside of the country to a non-United States taxpayer calls for an excise tax. This tax is in lieu of an income tax on the reinsurer and is the responsibility of the ceding company. The current excise tax for life and health insurance products, both direct and reinsurance ceded, is 1% of premiums. The rate on property and casualty products currently is 4% of direct premiums and 1% of reinsurance ceded premiums.

The excise tax is waived for reinsurance to companies domiciled in certain countries. Any such waiver is granted as part of a tax treaty between the United States and the other country. Historically, the most important countries with such treaties have been the United Kingdom and France. The cost of the excise tax should be considered like any other expense.

The list of countries which have such treaties changes frequently; anyone involved with international reinsurance should check the current status of such treaties. The status could change after the initiation of a treaty, thus affecting the expenses involved in maintaining the agreement.

International reinsurance may be subject to other taxes, such as those pertaining to controlled foreign corporations, to passive income, or to foreign tax credits. While these topics are well beyond the scope of this book, it is important to identify all possible tax implications and include them in any analysis relating to reinsurance.

TAX PLANNING

Reinsurance should be consummated for reasons other than tax savings. Overall financial stability and pre-tax income are typically the primary motivations. But tax considerations can be very important. Taxes are an expense, and it is a legitimate goal of management to reduce expenses. It is reasonable to consider the tax implications in designing and analyzing reinsurance agreements; one design might lead to increased taxes while another might be tax neutral or might reduce taxes. In addition, reinsurance is a source of capital and should be analyzed as such, including the tax effects. Therefore, tax planning and reinsurance planning often go hand-in-hand.

Tax planning involving reinsurance has become much more difficult since 1984. Prior to 1984, there were straightforward methodologies and specific provisions within the law favoring tax planning using reinsurance; the situation is almost completely reversed today. There are no specific provisions, such as the since-repealed Sections 818(c)(2) and 820, allowing for any tax-favored reinsurance transaction. And, to the contrary, Section 845 now grants the IRS broad reallocation authority.

Nonetheless, many companies continue to enter into reinsurance transactions which result in significant tax benefits. This should be done with care and with the use of tax and reinsurance experts. One thing which is certain is that uncertainty will continue for some time in this arena. It should not be concluded from this discussion that tax planning using reinsurance is impossible, only that it is complicated.

Special Topics and Applications | Part Four

15 | Nonproportional Reinsurance

One way of classifying reinsurance is as being either proportional or nonproportional. Proportional reinsurance is that type where the sharing of the risk between the ceding company and the reinsurer is determined at issue. The majority of this book is devoted to a discussion of proportional reinsurance. Nonproportional reinsurance is that type where the reinsurer's participation in the risk depends upon the actual number of amount or claims, or some combination thereof.

Proportional reinsurance is used to limit the exposure of the ceding company on a given risk, such as a single life. Nonproportional reinsurance is a means of limiting the overall risk on a block of business or reducing the exposure to a particular type of hazard. In particular, nonproportional reinsurance is useful in reducing fluctuations in the total claims on a block of business; proportional reinsurance is useful to prevent any one claim from having too large a negative impact on a company's surplus.

Nonproportional forms of coverage are frequently used for accident and health as well as property and liability coverages. It is not the intent of this book to discuss all of the ramifications of nonproportional reinsurance and it's applications. This chapter provides a brief introduction to the more common forms of nonproportional reinsurance: stop loss, catastrophe, and spread loss coverages.

STOP LOSS

Stop loss coverage provides protection against an excessive number or amount of claims in any given contract period. While stop loss coverage may be used alone, more frequently it is used in conjunction with proportional forms of reinsurance. The use of stop loss coverage may allow the ceding company to increase its retention limit.

For life insurance, stop loss applies to a block of policies, not just to one life. For accident and health and other open-ended benefit coverages, stop loss may apply either in "aggregate" to collective risks or in "specific" form to a single risk. In a stop loss arrangement, the reinsurer pays only claims in excess of an "attachment point." This point is usually expressed in terms of a percentage of expected claims. A typical attachment point might be 110% of expected claims after deduction for reimbursements from any proportional reinsurance. When the attachment point has been exceeded, the stop loss reinsurer will pay a percentage of all net claims up to a predetermined maximum. Terms of a typical stop loss agreement for life insurance might be:

Maximum Retention:	$100,000 per life.
Expected Claims:	$500,000 (defined by formula as, say, 105% of a specified experience table).
Attachment Point:	110% of expected claims, subject to a minimum of $610,000
Limits:	90% of all claims in excess of the attachment point up to a total maximum of $1,000,000, with a maximum on any single life of $100,000.

The attachment point is typically set as an amount equal to at least one maximum claim above the expected amount of claims.

The premium charged for stop loss coverage is often expressed as a percentage of expected claims plus a fixed fee. In theory, stop loss net premiums are easy to calculate using risk theory methods. However, parameters such as catastrophes, epidemics, and other nonindependent events, as well as the high probability of fluctuation, must be considered and create significant complications. In reality, the gross premium charged may be several times the net premium.

The method used to determine expected claims is obviously critical and must be carefully defined in the reinsurance treaty. Coverage is usually restricted to net retained claims in order to avoid duplication of reinsurance. Both expected and actual claims are determined on the net amount at risk, not the gross death benefit.

The actual calculation of claims and premiums may be difficult because of the problem of assembling the appropriate data. Because of this and the reliance on typical excess per life reinsurance, few insurance companies seek to buy the coverage despite its obvious usefulness in protecting surplus. Proper use of stop loss coverage could lead to lower long term reinsurance costs.

Relatively few North American reinsurers offer stop loss coverage on life insurance because it is a very low premium coverage with a risk of significant deviation. While the probability of a claim is low, the cost, when one occurs, is high. It is difficult to write enough stop loss coverage in any year to provide an adequate spread of risk and balance premiums and claims. Those reinsurers that write the coverage sometimes do so only as an accommodation to existing clients and with some reliance on the trend of improving mortality experience. The reinsurer has a very low probability of recouping any losses incurred on a case because the ceding company would normally terminate a contract rather than pay the increased premium which would likely result from a year of bad claims.

CATASTROPHE COVERAGE

Catastrophe coverage is more commonly used than stop loss for life insurance. Catastrophe coverage protects the ceding company against multiple single claims from a single event such as a plane crash, a fire, an earthquake, or some other accident or natural disaster. The covered events must be carefully defined and may exclude specific events, epidemics, wars, riots, or nuclear hazards. Certain types of risks may also be excluded such as sports teams, airline personnel, credit card and travel accident coverage, long term disability, and assumed reinsurance.

Each "cat cover" is individually negotiated and is unique. The premium for the coverage is usually expressed in terms of a rate per million of mean inforce business. The contract will specify a minimum required number of claims per event as well as the maximum amount of claims covered.

A per life limit is used to limit claims. Only the net amounts at risk will be used in determining premiums and claims. This is a very useful coverage and is quite common as both large and small companies are exposed to multiple deaths from a single event. In fact, larger companies may have a higher probability of loss from any one accident because of a larger exposure. Usually, the coverage kicks in only after the occurrence of three, four, five, or more deaths from a single event. Large deductibles are common. The availability of catastrophe coverage is unlikely to replace a company's traditional proportional reinsurance portfolio or allow the company to increase its retention limit.

Some companies desiring a large amount of catastrophe coverage purchase two or more contracts in layers. Each layer would have a deductible which would include all layers below it.

SPREAD LOSS

Basically, a spread loss agreement provides coverage if a company's losses in a given year exceeded a specified attachment point. The attachment point and reinsurer's participation can be defined in a manner similar to that used for stop loss. If a claim occurs, the reinsurer would pay the ceding company. The ceding company would then repay the amount of the claim with interest over a period of years, thus spreading the loss. The repayment is frequently accomplished by an increase in the premium following incurral of a claim. In its traditional form, spread loss reinsurance is not really a form of reinsurance, but is more a means of changing the timing of cash flows. Premiums are somewhat arbitrary and are subject to negotiation.

This type of coverage most likely would not qualify for any type of reserve credit. Any cash benefit received by the company would almost certainly require a liability be established for repayment. Obviously this type of coverage is useful for protecting the cash flow of a company but it does not ultimately protect surplus.

The risks to the reinsurer are not among the normal ones of mortality, morbidity, persistency, interest, or default, but rather those of cash flow timing, credit, or insolvency. In essence, spread loss reinsurance is a type of loan.

If the ceding company becomes insolvent during the period of time it owes the reinsurer a spread loss payment, the receiver would likely terminate the reinsurance agreement and the reinsurer would not be repaid. In short, any claim that the reinsurer paid would be repaid only subject to the continued solvency of the ceding company.

RESERVE CONSIDERATIONS

There are no firmly established standards for reserves for nonproportional reinsurance. Judgement, as well as familiarity with Actuarial Standard of Practice No. 11 on reinsurance, is important.

Ceding Company

One point common to most nonproportional reinsurance is that it seldom qualifies for any reserve credit in the convention blank. Since nonproportional reinsurance generally covers only risks beyond those covered by normal reserves, no reserve credit is taken. However, it is possible to construct a stop loss agreement in such a manner that it transfers a risk which is covered by the basic reserves. For example, it is possible to construct a stop loss coverage with the attachment point set at 80% of the valuation mortality table rates. In this case, it may be possible for some reserve credit to be justified.

Historically, reserve credits for nonproportional coverages have not generally been acceptable to the regulators. Given the recent introduction of Actuarial Standard of Practice No. 11 on reinsurance by the Actuarial Standards Board, forms of nonproportional reinsurance which permit reserve credit may be developed. The issue is not really the form of the reinsurance as much as it is the transfer of risk. Many regulators have historically insisted on proportionality before they would permit any reserve credits.

If in the course of producing the statutory annual statement, it is determined that monies are owed to a ceding company as the result of a nonproportional reinsurance agreement, that company may include those amounts as a credit just as it would for a proportional reinsurance ceded due and unpaid claim. The amount of credit would be subject to the normal rules regarding authorized and unauthorized reinsurers.

In reviewing reserve credits for nonproportional reinsurance, it is necessary to consider the terms of the agreement. In a normal stop loss or catastrophe coverage situation, any claims recoverable would be treated as any other reinsurance claims recoverable. However, in a spread loss situation, any claim due most likely would be offset by future premiums which would be an offsetting liability for the ceding company.

On a GAAP basis, a benefit reserve credit might be appropriate if a model based on GAAP assumptions demonstrates that a recovery is expected. Premiums typically would flow through as incurred.

Reinsurer

For statutory purposes, some companies take the gross premiums into earnings; others reserve all or part of the net premium. If a reserve is established, a claim payment usually reduces the reserve before it affects surplus. Regardless of its practice regarding reserves, the reinsurer should maintain adequate surplus in relation to its risk for nonproportional reinsurance.

If a claim is incurred, the reinsurer should establish a reserve for the discounted value of the amount it expects to pay.

In its GAAP financial statement, the reinsurer would, in theory, reserve all or some portion of the net premiums. The loading would flow through earnings.

Assumption
16 Reinsurance

The majority of this book has dealt with indemnity reinsurance, which is by far a more common occurrence than is assumption reinsurance. Assumption reinsurance differs from indemnity reinsurance in one very major regard: under assumption reinsurance the obligations and the relationship to the policyholder shifts from the original direct writing company to the assumption reinsurer. The assumption reinsurer issues the policyholder a certificate of assumption which is to be placed with the policy. All contacts with the policyholder and the agent, including premium collection, commission payment, and benefit notification, are handled by the assumption reinsurer.

This treatment obviously differs from that of indemnity reinsurance where the policyholder is generally not aware of its existence. Basically, indemnity reinsurance allows the direct writer increased capacity and ability to underwrite more risks than it otherwise could. Assumption reinsurance, on the other hand, is the sale of the original insurer's interest in the block of business, a permanent transfer of all interest and obligations similar to the sale of any asset from one business to another.

THE ASSUMPTION PROCESS

The two companies, the ceding company and the assumption reinsurer, must negotiate an assumption reinsurance agreement covering the sale or transfer of the block of business. Generally, there is no provision for recapture as the transfer is intended to be permanent in nature and the direct insurer will have no further interest in the policies. Subsequent to the assumption, it is as though the policies had always been issued by the assumption reinsurer. Typically, the ceding company would be responsible for any claims incurred up to the point of the assumption and the assumption reinsurer responsible for any thereafter. If both parties' objectives are to be met and disputes avoided, it is important that they agree upon the liabilities and any assets that are to be transferred.

In some states, the insurance department has either regulatory or defacto power to approve or prevent an assumption transaction. In other states, the regulators believe that they have no control over this process. Most states require that an assumption reinsurer be directly licensed in the ceding company's state of domicile. Some regulators believe that as long as the assuming company is reasonably sound financially and is admitted as a reinsurer in that state, there should be no objection. The regulators are concerned about the benefits promised to the policyholders and generally review any assumption agreement to see if the policyholders would be adversely affected by the proposed transaction.

Effect on the Policyholder

Under the indemnity reinsurance process, the direct writing insurer has made promises to the policyholder based upon the terms of the policy. The policyholder can look to that company to perform, but he cannot look to the reinsurer. In fact, most indemnity reinsurance treaties carry a clear statement that no third party, including any policyholder, has any rights established under the reinsurance treaty. The indemnity reinsurance treaty is strictly a bilateral agreement between the ceding company and the reinsurer.

Under assumption reinsurance, the opposite occurs. The assumption reinsurer assumes the direct obligation to the policyholder and the original writing company expects to be removed from any further obligations regarding the policyholder. In normal operation, the policyholder has all of his future dealings with the new carrier and no further contact with the original carrier.

The policyholder is not absolutely helpless. In legal theory, the policy is a two-party contract between the insurer and the policyholder and cannot be unilaterally transferred by either one of the parties without the consent of the other. In a situation of assumption reinsurance, if that consent is given, a novation, or new contract, is created between the policyholder and the assumption reinsurer. This consent can be either specific or implied. Some state regulators require the specific consent of the policyholder while others deem that the policyholder has consented if he pays premiums or submits claims to the assumption reinsurer.

Courts have been divided on this issue. Most recently, however, a California appeals court held that an original insurer was liable to the policyholder for benefits following the insolvency and default of the assumption reinsurer.[1] In this case, the court held that the submission of claims to the new insurer did not imply consent by the policyholder as he had no other course of action. Both legal and regulatory decisions have been divided regarding the need for consent of the policyholder and what constitutes consent. Any parties considering entering into an assumption reinsurance transaction are well advised to obtain competent legal counsel.

Sometimes policyholders are concerned about an assumption, believing that the rules have been changed and promises modified, and that they have no say in the matter. This concern is greatest if the new carrier is less well known or is viewed as being less sound than the original insurer.

For this reason, there is frequently an increased lapse rate shortly after the assumption transaction, as policyholders surrender the existing policies and replace them with those of companies of their own choosing, usually subject to new underwriting by the new carrier. This in turn may cause the mortality or morbidity of the remaining block to deteriorate. Consequently, the value of a block of business may change as the result of the assumption.

Of course, many assumption reinsurance transactions result from a company selling business in order to generate immediate value. In this case, the policyholder may actually end up with a more secure position if a stronger company or one which specializes in that particular type of business assumes the obligations of the original company.

---

[1] Baer v. Associated Life Insurance Company. 248 California Reporter 1989.

Certificates of Assumption

Once the assumption agreement is finalized, the assumption reinsurer has a limited period of time, such as 60 days, during which to notify the policyholders of the change in insurers. This is usually done through a certification of assumption which the assumption reinsurer issues to each policyholder, identifying the new carrier and describing how to contact that carrier. From that point forward, the assumption reinsurer typically takes over the responsibilities for policy administration.

Typically, the insurance departments of the states of domicile of the ceding company and the assumption reinsurer must both approve the certificate of assumption. The departments differ in their requirements. Some are fairly flexible and others are quite rigid. For example, New York usually requires that the certificate include a place for the policyholder to sign, indicating his acceptance of the assumption. If he does not accept, his policy is not part of the assumption.

The certificate of assumption becomes a part of the policy and the policyholder is advised to keep it with his policy just as he would any other endorsement or rider.

Original Insurer Responsibilities

Under assumption reinsurance, the original carrier expects to have no further responsibilities to the policyholder. The two companies agree as to the consideration to be paid for the business. They also negotiate the type and amount of assets which should be transferred to meet the obligations and satisfy the reserve requirements of the reinsured policies. They should document specific agreement regarding responsibility for claims incurred prior to the assumption date and for claims in course of settlement and claims incurred but not reported as of the assumption date.

There are both ethical and business responsibilities on the part of the ceding company to ensure that the assumption reinsurer has the ability to pay future benefits. While there may not be a specific regulation or law requiring this, it would be prudent for the ceding company to exercise some reasonable judgment. For example, if the assumption reinsurer were to become unable to pay reasonable future benefits, and it was obvious that the reinsurer was financially unsound at the time of the transfer, there might be some contingent liability left with the ceding company.

It is probable that if bad faith or fraud could be demonstrated, the original insurer would have liability for the failure of the reinsurer to perform. It is also logical that this liability would lessen over time. For example, if the assuming company was rated highly by the various rating agencies and was apparently sound at the time of the transaction, but became insolvent 25 years later, it is unlikely that such action would prevail.

The legal profession has been reluctant to issue any clean opinions that a ceding company would be absolutely free of future liability following an assumption agreement. Until recently, there were few trial cases where the original company was found liable for the assumption reinsurer's failure to perform. The Baer case[2] has caused many insurers to reassess their position regarding selling a block of business through assumption reinsurance since they could become liable if the new carrier fails to perform.

The intricacies of an assumption reinsurance agreement will vary depending upon the parties involved, the type of business involved, the state that is involved in the transaction, and the economic conditions surrounding it. It is always important that both parties receive proper legal, tax, accounting, and actuarial advice as the agreement is being negotiated.

Once the assumption has taken place and the certificates issued, the original reinsurer has no further responsibilities beyond those outlined in the reinsurance treaty, barring some legal action.

The block of business which is being sold or transferred using assumption reinsurance may be subject to coverage under one or more indemnity reinsurance treaties. In the absence of any specific treaty provisions addressing termination or recapture in the event of subsequent assumption reinsurance, the indemnity reinsurance coverages would normally remain in effect.

The existing indemnity reinsurer, the ceding company, and/or the assumption reinsurer may wish to negotiate a termination or recapture of this coverage. In any event, the assumption reinsurer should take into account the terms and financial effects of all existing indemnity reinsurance agreements.

---

[2] *Ibid.*

FINANCIAL EFFECTS

Assumption reinsurance has permanent effects on the statutory and GAAP financial statements of both the ceding company and the assumption reinsurer, as well as their tax returns. Some of these effects are discussed in this section.

Ceding Company

The financial effects of assumption reinsurance on a ceding company are fairly straight forward. For most purposes, it treats the transaction as a surrender. On a statutory basis, it would release its reserves, other than reserves for claims in course of settlement and incurred but unreported claims, in compliance with the terms of the reinsurance treaty. It would cease to receive premiums and pay commissions.

On the asset side, it typically would transfer any policy loans to the assumption reinsurer, eliminating its own account. It would also transfer any assets to the assumption reinsurer as provided in the agreement. In some cases, there might be future contingent payments by the assumption reinsurer to the ceding company based upon experience which would be booked when incurred. Any allowance would be reported as earned.

On a GAAP basis, the ceding company would normally write off its deferred acquisition asset and eliminate its benefit reserves, adjusting invested assets and cash according to the terms of the treaty. Again, reserves for any unsettled claims would be handled in accordance with the terms of the treaty.

Treatment of any trailing commission or future commission would be dependent upon the terms of the treaty. In most cases, the amounts would probably fall directly through to earnings as they are incurred.

Tax treatment for the ceding company is relatively straight forward. In a typical assumption reinsurance treaty, assets would be adjusted according to any net transfer involved and tax reserves would be set to zero. Any income flowing out of that transaction, including any ceding consideration, would flow through taxable income accordingly.

Assumption Reinsurer

Financial reporting of assumption reinsurance for the assumption reinsurer is more complicated than it is for the ceding company. The treatment is similar to that used when a new policy is issued, but certain elements of accounting relating to the purchase of an asset apply to assumption reinsurance.

Statutory Reporting. The assumption reinsurer will report assumption reinsurance in the same manner as for indemnity reinsurance for statutory purposes. It will immediately establish the appropriate reserves for the risks assumed. For example, if an assumed policy is in its tenth policy year, the reinsurer should establish liabilities based on tenth year mortality, not that of a newly issued policy.

The assumption reinsurer will generally treat as an immediate expense the full amount of any initial consideration or allowance. Any initial allowance may be shown in the Summary of Operations of its annual statement on either line 21, as commissions and expense allowances on reinsurance assumed, or on line 25, as a write-in item.

After the assumption, the treatment of premiums and commissions is just as though the assumption reinsurer had insured the business from issue. Any premiums received are shown on the direct premiums and considerations lines, not on the reinsurance premiums line; any commissions paid would be treated as direct commissions, not as reinsurance allowances. Assumption reinsurance is not reported in Schedule S.

GAAP Reporting. Typically, the assumption reinsurer under assumption reinsurance will treat the block of business under a method similar to GAAP accounting for a purchase transaction. This would require that it match future earnings to future revenues on the block in a manner designed to produce no immediate GAAP gain or loss as a result of the original transaction. The initial consideration and allowance are usually capitalized and amortized over future revenues.

Unless the assumption reinsurer is a professional reinsurer, this may involve a more detailed approach than it would apply to other blocks of reinsurance. It would definitely be more detailed than the GAAP reporting normally accorded financial reinsurance treaties.

GAAP deferred taxes for both parties would have to be adjusted according to their situations.

Tax Reporting. Tax reporting for the assumption reinsurer is clearly defined and has been for some time. Basically, the block of business is treated as the purchase of an asset and any ceding commission or strain resulting from the transaction must be amortized over the useful life of the block of business. The useful life may be determined to be the average life of the business, or it may have another definition. Competent tax counsel should be consulted in making this determination.

A major point to remember is that assumption reinsurance definitely does not create a major tax deferral. Although it may be possible to somewhat front-end the tax deduction, the operating mechanism still involves amortizing any ceding commission. Prior to the Colonial American case[3], it was believed that the deduction for assumption reinsurance would be amortized, but indemnity reinsurance would create an immediate deduction. As discussed in Chapter 14, that is no longer the case, at least for the indemnity reinsurance of inforce blocks of business. For the reinsurer, the tax treatment of indemnity reinsurance and assumption reinsurance is the same for inforce blocks of business.

STRATEGIC CONSIDERATIONS

Assumption reinsurance is most frequently the result of strategic decisions and considerations about allocation of resources. An understanding of some of these considerations and their implications is important to the understanding of the applications of assumption reinsurance.

Ceding Company

Ceding companies may use assumption reinsurance as a vehicle to implement a strategy to exit a given product line or to sell a block of business. It will thereby recognize immediately a gain representing a measure of the value of future gains on this business. Typically, the ceding company will receive a higher value from assumption reinsurance than it would from indemnity reinsurance. Indemnity reinsurance may be subject to future recapture, which may reduce its value to the reinsurer. Assumption reinsurance may give the reinsurer more control over the future of the business, its administration, and therefore may offer more opportunity for profits.

Also, assumption reinsurance involves a transfer of invested assets. Just as the assumption reinsurer may believe that it can

---

[3]Colonial American Life Insurance Company v. Commissioner of Internal Revenue, No. 88-396.

make more money from the assumed business than it can by investing its capital elsewhere, the ceding company may choose to recognize future gains now and free up both cash and its surplus for reinvestment elsewhere to its advantage. As previously mentioned, this strategy may allow some companies to focus on more preferred opportunities.

One important point which must be recognized by both parties, especially the ceding company, is that assumption reinsurance is intended to be an irrevocable step. It may be possible for the ceding company to repurchase a block of business, but assumption treaties typically do not include provisions for either recapture or repurchase. Any such provisions would have to be separately and carefully negotiated.

Just as assumption reinsurance is less common than indemnity reinsurance, it is also more permanent. If a company wishes to stay in a line of business and to maintain its field force, it would likely use indemnity, not assumption, reinsurance to raise cash or surplus or to limit its risks.

A ceding company may use assumption reinsurance if it decides it no longer wants to be at risk or deal with the policyholders and agents on a particular block or line of business. It has been used by companies recently to exit from group life and health business and, on some occasions, to exit from other lines of business such as credit or industrial insurance. Basically, assumption reinsurance allows the sale of a line or division of business without selling the entire company and without any transfer of ownership or control.

While this transfer is similar to the sale of stock, it does not require the involvement of investment bankers or SEC approval. It is also less likely to require stockholder approval or discussion, although approval of the board of directors is usually required to assure the other party of the legitimacy of the transaction.

As discussed earlier, the ceding company should be careful in its selection of an assumption reinsurer. If the assumption reinsurer becomes insolvent or otherwise fails to honor the original commitments to the policyholders, the original company may have a contingent liability. Therefore, it is logical that the ceding company perform reasonable due diligence on any perspective assumption reinsurer, including both its ability and its intentions to meet fully the guarantees and obligations towards the policyholders.

The risk of future insolvency is difficult to analyze for the indefinite future. Therefore, some companies have required a trust for the assets committed to the obligations of its former policyholders. Such a trust can be referenced in the assumption reinsurance agreement, allowing the original company to take over both the assets and the policies should the assumption reinsurer become insolvent, or more prudently, should its capital and surplus fall below a reasonable, specified minimum.

This approach may not be fully acceptable to an insurance department trying to liquidate an insolvent company, but at least it will provide some protection for the ceding company and the policyholders. The insurance department may believe that this will lead to favored treatment for one group of policyholders at the expense of others. This can be partially mitigated by having future earnings from such a block be paid to the assumption reinsurer or its successor, except for reasonable administration fees.

Assumption Reinsurer

Assumption reinsurers typically enter into assumption reinsurance agreements for strategic reasons which are perhaps the reverse of those of the ceding companies. While the ceding company may find that a block of business is too small for it to administer effectively, an assumption reinsurer may want to assume several blocks of similar business in order to benefit from its administrative capacity. Recently, several insurers have searched for blocks of a specific type of business, such as industrial insurance, traditional ordinary insurance, or universal life policies, because they have excess administrative capacity. As a result, they expect to administer many additional policies at a very low marginal cost. This, in turn, will drive down their effective expenses per unit. The cost per unit for one company may be increasing due to a shrinking line of business, but adding that business to another company's inforce might reduce its per unit costs. This differential in expense factors can make an assumption transaction attractive to both parties. In short, the business may be worth more to the assumption reinsurer than to the ceding company.

The assumption reinsurer must be careful, however, to review the business to ensure that it can effectively administer it on a low cost basis. The cost of adding the new policies to the existing inforce system may be prohibitive, especially when including the cost of conversion to the new system.

An assumption reinsurer should also consider the "shock lapse" factor, where lapse rates almost always increase temporarily immediately following notification to the policyholders of an assumption agreement. This can affect the value both by reducing the future premiums and by leaving higher than average risks on the books.

There is not one specific reason why shock lapses occur. One theory is that any unusual activity causes insureds to reexamine their needs and their coverages. Frequently, assumption reinsurance occurs after the original company has had publicized financial difficulties or changes in ownership. Such events may either disturb some policyholders or offer opportunities for agents, either the original ones or others, to leverage policyholder uncertainty or concern into replacement sales. Terminations continue after assumption largely because of the momentum developed prior to the assumption.

Frequently, shock lapses are the result of the former agents contacting the policyholders to offer new options, especially if the agents are now allied with another insurer, not the assumption reinsurer. Accordingly, it is important for the reinsurer to consider the agency relationships before determining the price it can offer for a block of business.

On the other hand, persistency may improve following an assumption agreement. This can result if the new insurer is perceived by the agents and the policyholders as being more stable and desirable than the original company. This is most likely if the assumption occurs before the policyholders or agents have had time to develop significant concerns.

Companies sometimes use assumption reinsurance to buy a field force and to give it a larger line of business. This occurred in the group insurance business in the late 1980's. Several carriers decided to exit or limit their group business while others decided to increase their group business, in essence buying the customer lists and distribution capabilities of the ceding companies.

Companies may have excess surplus which they believe can be invested in an additional block of business for an acceptable return. Sometimes, the blocks of business transferred are closed blocks and involve no field force or ongoing sales capabilities. These transactions should be viewed merely as investments. Of course, the considerations of persistency, mortality or morbidity, expense, and investment income should be reviewed carefully.

Insurance departments frequently utilize the assumption reinsurance process as a method to provide for the security of policyholders of insolvent or financially impaired companies under their jurisdiction. This is frequently accomplished by letting bids. Since the insurance departments' primary concern is the security of the policyholders, this process can result in favorable terms to the successful bidder.

On occasion, the ceding company will continue to perform some or all of the administrative functions for the assumption reinsurer, at least for a period of time. This service usually is compensated for with a service or administration fee.

In some situations, a reinsurer may choose to defer any decision relative to assumption reinsurance. An indemnity reinsurance agreement may be established which gives the reinsurer the right to assume the business directly at some point in time or upon the occurrence some event. For example, the reinsurer may not be licensed in the appropriate states, so indemnity reinsurance might be used until it is licensed. Even if the reinsurer is licensed, indemnity reinsurance may be used until the appropriate regulatory approval for the assumption transaction is secured.

In other instances the reinsurer may prefer indemnity reinsurance, but want the right to convert to assumption reinsurance if the ceding company's capital and surplus become too low. This may offer the reinsurer some protection and clarity in the event the ceding company were to become insolvent or otherwise impaired.

Other reasons may lead the two parties to prefer the "right of assumption" feature over immediate assumption. In any event, the tax implications need to be carefully considered; the existence of the right of assumption followed by actual assumption within a few years may lead the IRS to contend that the treaty was assumption reinsurance all along and was never indemnity reinsurance.

The reinsurer must also consider its state licenses. For indemnity reinsurance, it is generally sufficient for the reinsurer to be licensed in the ceding company's state of domicile. Even if it is not licensed in that state, most regulatory concerns can be satisfied by placing assets backing the reserves in trust or escrow. This is not the situation for assumption reinsurance. The assumption reinsurer has a direct relationship with the policyholders and the regulators may want more protection or authority.

Some experts contend that the assumption reinsurer must be licensed, or at least an authorized reinsurer, in all states where the affected policyholders reside. Others contend that it is sufficient to be licensed only in the ceding company's state of domicile, especially if the insurance departments of both that state and the reinsurer's state of domicile approve the transaction. Certainly assumption transactions have occurred where the reinsurer was not licensed in all the involved states.

17 | Captive Reinsurance

For the most part, the transactions described in this book have been between a life insurance company and one of the reinsurers actively accepting reinsurance business in North America. These reinsurers are typically in the business of reinsuring for economic gain and are relatively indifferent as to the source of business, as long as that source is acceptable to the reinsurer. Reinsurance is not limited to transactions involving such reinsurers. Countless reinsurance transactions take place between insurance companies and special purpose reinsurers, often referred to as captive reinsurance companies.

The primary purpose of this captive reinsurance is to increase sales in the direct insurer by sharing some of the underwriting and investment gains with the producer of the business. This sharing is accomplished through reinsurance.

CAPTIVE REINSURERS

The term captive reinsurance company refers to an insurance company formed with the purpose of reinsuring insurance policies from a particular, captive source. Captive reinsurers have many common problems and considerations.

Purposes

The producer of the business that is reinsured is normally the owner of the reinsurance company. The owner may be called the "sponsor" and the reinsurance company is usually referred to as the "captive." Historically, most well-known captives have been formed to reinsure property and casualty risks, primarily workers' compensation and liability coverages. These captives have been formed to provide the sponsor with more control over the price of the coverage, especially the fluctuations in price, and with tax advantages in some instances.

This chapter is primarily concerned with captives formed to reinsure policies sold by certain key agents of insurance companies and to reinsure risks related to credit insurance. Captives may also have other special applications, such as to facilitate risk and profit sharing in a joint venture or risk management in a self-insurance program.

Typically, the sponsor of the captive wants additional compensation for selling its business through a particular insurer. The insurer may not wish to pay such additional amounts directly and immediately, either because of statutory limitations or because the risk of loss would then be too great. The sponsor may also believe that it will receive tax advantages by participating in a captive rather than collecting direct commissions. Such additional compensation is usually subject to the actual experience of the block of business reinsured.

Location Considerations

Because of the limited purpose of captives, such companies are generally licensed in only one jurisdiction. In order to realize a reasonable return on investment, startup costs and ongoing administrative expenses need to be kept as low as possible. Most participants choose jurisdictions that have very low capitalization requirements, regulatory fees, and taxes. The amount of time required to establish a new company, the filing requirements, and the approval process are also considerations.

For these reasons, Arizona, Louisiana, and Texas are homes of many captive reinsurers.[1] Because of the large number of companies domiciled in these states, some sponsors prefer to license

---

[1]This is not intended to imply that any state or jurisdiction is lax in its regulation of insurers. However, the capitalization requirements and the receptiveness to new companies do vary among jurisdictions.

the insurance company in another state. Delaware is currently a popular choice, as it is perceived to have a more prestigious license.

Offshore sites such as Bermuda, the Bahamas, Barbados, the Cayman Islands, and the Virgin Islands are also popular jurisdictions for the formation of captives. These islands often offer very attractive tax treatment as well as less stringent or more flexible reserving and capitalization requirements, lower fees, and quicker implementation. Drawbacks to an offshore site include the perception that such sites are less prestigious or reputable than one in the United States, the federal excise tax on premiums ceded outside of the United States, and the difficulty of the ceding company to take statutory reserve credit for reinsurance ceded.

State Insurance Regulation

Any insurance company chartered in one of the United States will have to comply with the insurance laws and regulations of that state. The insurance company must maintain the standards for capital, surplus, and reserves. Most captives are licensed in only one state. Unless the ceding company is domiciled in the same state or the reinsurer provides appropriate security, the ceding company will not be allowed to take reserve credit on business ceded.

Sponsors often choose the domicile of the captive based on the requirements for capital of that domicile. However, that question must be carefully studied. In at least one instance, a captive has been forced to meet the higher capital standards of another state because the vast majority of its risks were on lives residing in the second state.

SEC Regulations

Normal rules and regulations of the Securities and Exchange Commission (SEC) apply to the formation of a captive reinsurer if the formation of the captive or the distribution of its shares takes place in the United States. Broad interpretation of these guidelines is usually applied. Even if there is a single owner, such as a corporation, the formation will probably have to be disclosed in certain financial or regulatory reports.

The SEC requires that companies with more than a minimum number of shareholders (currently 24) must be registered with the SEC. To avoid this registration, most captives have a limited number of participants. Even so, the SEC requires a private placement memorandum which contains some of the same information that would be required in a prospectus, including information as to the limited marketability of the shares and the risk of loss from the operation.

Ceding Company Motivation

Ceding companies work with captive reinsurers in order to increase their own profits. The increased profits are expected to result from an enhanced ability to attract, motivate, and retain producers resulting in an increased production of quality business.

Attracting New Producers. The willingness to cede business to a captive reinsurer can be a useful marketing tool for a ceding company to attract top quality producers. Many large producers expect to share in the profitability of their business. In fact, use of a captive is often a prerequisite for any insurer wishing to write business with that production source; otherwise, the producer will go elsewhere.

Retention of Key Producers. Just as many companies have employee stock ownership plans as an incentive to retain key employees, insurance companies may cede insurance to a producer-owned captive in order to retain the key producers. Retaining high quality producers would boost the ceding company's retained profits.

More Production. If the producers realize a profit on the assumed reinsurance, it is anticipated that they will write more business in order to receive more profits. The ceding company benefits from the increase in volume of business, both in terms of the direct profits realized on the additional business and the ability to spread its costs.

Better Experience. Because the producers are sharing in the profits of the business ceded, it is anticipated that they will write higher quality business in order to increase their share of the profits. High quality business also increases the ceding company's profits.

Reinsurer Motivation

In a captive reinsurance situation, the reinsurer is the producer of the business. The primary reinsurer motivations include more income, tax benefits, and increased influence and status.

More Income. Producers enter the reinsurance arrangements in order to receive income from the profits of the business. These profits are in addition to the normal commission income. If the producer is confident that he is writing high quality business, he would anticipate a steady flow of income from the reinsurance.

The individuals owning the stock of the captive anticipate that it will increase in value over the years, presumably by retaining earnings and in recognition of future earnings from the business reinsured.

Tax Benefits. The producer frequently expects to defer income and reduce taxes by creating and using a captive. In the past, the producer hoped to avoid current ordinary income taxes and instead receive capital gains treatment when he sold the shares of stock at an increased value. This strategy is desirable when capital gains are taxed at a lower rate than ordinary income. However, as recent experience has shown, the existence of a preferential rate for capital gains may or may not be available when the shares are sold.

Another common objective is to shelter income from current taxation, deferring the recognition of income and the payment of the tax into the future. A major reason for doing this is to permit reinvestment of income without first paying tax on it in anticipation of a lower tax rate in the future or upon retirement.

Increased Influence and Status. Normally, only the top producers of an insurance company are invited to participate in the reinsurance of their business. As partners in the future profitability of the business, they often exert a great influence on the sponsoring insurance company. These producers may receive special products, commissions, and service from the sponsoring companies.

Owning an insurance company may give some producers a feeling of increased status.

Tax Considerations

The tax considerations for reinsurance discussed earlier apply to captive reinsurance as well. In addition, a number of other factors require consideration in the captive situation because the benefits of the captive are frequently tied to stock ownership which, in turn, raises a number of income issues. Before entering into any sort of captive reinsurance arrangement, both parties should retain competent tax counsel to assist in the design and structure of the arrangement in order to increase the likelihood of obtaining the desired tax treatment.

If the captive is domiciled in the United States, it will be taxed on its earnings as determined in accordance with its tax status as a life or non-life insurance company. One benefit of a captive is that it may qualify for the small company deduction,[2] resulting in a lower effective tax rate. In order to qualify for the special small company deduction, the captive usually must not be deemed to be a part of the sponsoring life company. Accordingly, the sponsoring company should own less than 80% of the voting stock or total value of the captive. If the sponsoring company has entered into an agreement to repurchase the stock in the future, the IRS may deem this to be constructive ownership of the shares.

If the captive is domiciled outside of the United States, it may escape current United States taxation entirely but it is still subject to the taxes of its domicile. Whenever the income is repatriated, it will be subject to United States taxation. The applicable regulations are very complex.

AGENT-OWNED REINSURANCE COMPANIES

An agent-owned reinsurance company (AORC) is formed for the purpose of allowing key agents to participate in the profitability of their own business or as a means to defer compensation, either for tax or financial planning reasons. Typically, a select group of agents, chosen according to standards of quality and production, is invited to participate in the ownership of the captive company. The agents purchase shares in the captive and the ceding company places a portion of all business written by these agents into the AORC.

The agents most likely to become involved in an agent-owned company are those who are engaged in sophisticated upscale markets and those who use group marketing techniques such as salary savings. Competition to attract these agents is quite strong and is expected to grow. Companies which have established

---

[2]The small company deduction is available only to life companies in which the "controlled group" has less than $500,000,000 of assets.

AORC's may be in a good position to retain these agents in the future.

Form of Reinsurance

The reinsurance arrangement generally involves coinsurance or mod-co. These arrangements are usually designed to minimize first-year surplus strain and to produce a positive cash flow in the first year of operation. The sponsoring company will seldom cede more than 50% of the business placed by the participating agents in the agent-owned company. To control fluctuations in experience, the AORC will often limit its mortality exposure with relatively low retention limits, retroceding the balance of the risk on a YRT basis. In some cases, the retrocession may be to the ceding company. The level of actual risk sharing desired in the captive will dictate the financial terms of the arrangements.

Some AORC agreements involve only YRT reinsurance. Under these, the agent can participate in mortality experience, but has little or no exposure to investment, persistency, or expense risks and the profits that can arise from them. Some of these agreements are designed largely to increase commissions without doing so directly.

Ownership and Participation

In forming the company, it must be determined whether each agent will share in the overall profits and losses of the business or if each agent will be assigned a special series of stock or an account which would reflect only the profits and losses from that agent's business.

The advantage of separating each individual agent's business is that the agent's financial incentives are then tied directly to the actual profitability of the business he sells. If profits are distributed in proportion to stock ownership rather than in relation to the business submitted and profits produced, some agents will gain a windfall from the efforts of others and the others will not receive the rewards anticipated. Agents with good experience may become dissatisfied if their profits are diminished due to the poor experience of business submitted by other agents.

Agent Considerations

There are several reasons for a life insurance agent to join an AORC. The principal ones include increasing his earnings through

the profits of the reinsurance company and deferring or reclassi-
fying earnings for tax purposes.

Increased Earnings. An agent would not enter into a reinsurance
agreement unless he anticipated that he would share in future
profits as the result of the business which he produced in addition
to his normal commission income.

There are drawbacks from the agent's view. The primary
motivation of many agents is the level of first year compensation
received on business written. In order to reduce surplus strain and
the investment required in the AORC, the level of first year, and
perhaps even renewal, commissions is sometimes reduced.
Participation in an insurance company is not a risk free endeavor;
both the initial investment in the purchase of shares and any
foregone commissions are exposed to loss as the result of the future
experience and operations of the AORC. It is possible for losses on
the business reinsured to reduce, not enhance, the agent's total
compensation.

Further, most agents have very little knowledge of or
control over the pricing of insurance products. These factors tend
to limit an agent's willingness to defer immediate compensation in
order to participate in an uncertain endeavor.

Taxation. One of the major considerations in forming an AORC
will be the effect on the individual producer's personal federal
income tax. Some of the factors which may influence income tax
treatment are discussed below.

Buy-back Agreement. If the arrangements with the agents include
some predetermined buy-back formula for repurchasing their stock,
the IRS may consider any change in value as current income.
Despite this fear, many companies use such agreements with their
AORC's because some agents prefer the added security.

Risk Participation. Most tax practitioners believe that the greater
the degree of risk participation by the agent stockholders, the lower
the likelihood that gains in the captive will be treated as current
income to the shareholders. The argument is that when there is a
true risk sharing, any income deferred is exposed to the risk of loss
and is, therefore, not current ordinary income.

Constructive Receipt. If the agent can, at his option, receive lower
commissions on the policies which are placed in the captive

reinsurance company in order to increase future profits, the IRS may argue that this optional reduction in commissions amounted to constructive receipt of the profits, at least to the extent of the commission reduction. This argument might be countered by allowing only one set of commission scales for use in the agent-owned company.

Market Value. The IRS may argue that the price paid by the agent for stock in the company, usually the book value, is less than the true market value of the stock. This could result in the excess of the imputed true market value over the price paid for the stock paid being treated as ordinary income.

Pooling of Risk. If several agents share in the experience of a common book of business, then the ownership of shares is more likely to be viewed as an investment. If a given agent's participation is tied directly to his business alone, there is more exposure to IRS challenge. Therefore, the pooling of risks and experience is an important consideration.

Percentage Ownership. In order to receive the desired tax treatment, no producer should own ten per cent or more of an AORC. Ownership of ten per cent or more will cause the proportionate share of the captive's income to be included in the agent's taxable income for the year. Therefore, AORC's usually have at least eleven agent shareholders.

Ceding Company Considerations

The ceding company, or direct insurer, typically sponsors an AORC in order to protect or build its distribution system and to increase its total earnings or premium income.

Distribution Systems. Good agents are valuable and there is always competition for their services. Many insurance companies consider the establishment of an AORC as a excellent recruiting and retention tool. In addition, some companies believe that good agents attract other good agents; having an AORC with some good agents shows the company's concern for its agents, and that will attract others.

If the captive achieves adequate profits, the agents will be satisfied; otherwise they may become very unhappy. It is anticipated that the formation of an AORC that allows the agents to share in the profits of the business will create a team or partnership arrangement where the agents and the insurance company are working towards the same goal. However, formation of an AORC may also create an agent power structure which could make future negotiations difficult.

Earnings. Companies forming AORC's believe that total profits will grow as a result. Their philosophy is that keeping, say, 50% of the profits on an agent's sales, while passing some of the strain and experience risk back to the agent, is better than receiving none of that agent's business.

The ceding company anticipates improving its profits by writing higher quality business and by writing more business. However, sponsoring an AORC will create an additional level of expense. The ceding company may have to supply the capital and surplus for the newly formed company.

The sponsoring company may have to commit home office staff to the formation and ongoing operations of the captive company. It may have to divert human and computer resources from other projects for some period of time. There is no guarantee that this additional effort will result in more or better quality production. In one way or another, the sponsoring company may pass on to the AORC the cost of capital to start the AORC and its marginal expenses, but it can rarely recover any overhead involved.

Control. The ceding company will want to maintain some degree of control over the AORC to ensure that funds are available to pay benefits and that any seed capital is protected. It is in the sponsoring company's interest to prohibit the reinsuring of business written by the agents with other carriers in its AORC.

Typically, the ceding company will provide the day-to-day management of the AORC. It will also retain management or voting control, frequently through the use of preferred stock. Under this approach, the ceding company's preferred stock would have voting control and the agents' common stock would provide for profit participation and ownership. The common stock would reflect the value of the reinsured business. The preferred stock would allow the ceding company to maintain control and to receive dividends for the use of capital. At some point, the management rights of the preferred stock might be transferred to the common stock.

The main disadvantages of separating each individual agent's business are that the agent's share of AORC income is more likely to be considered as current taxable income and the administration is more complicated. Also, the company may need to purchase stop-loss insurance for each agent's account so that a few early claims do not bankrupt an account.

In most successful AORC programs, the insurer has set high standards for continued agent participation in the AORC. If the standards are not met, the agent is disqualified and either bought out or not allowed to have any further business reinsured in the company.

There is always the possibility that an agent could launch a minority shareholders lawsuit against the agent-owned company. Such a lawsuit might be filed because the agent wishes to remove his accumulated share of the profits before the scheduled time or because another agent has placed unprofitable business with the company, lowering the profits for the entire group. The risk of such lawsuits can be minimized if flexible rules for withdrawals are established at the beginning and if consistent underwriting standards and qualification standards are established and maintained. The sponsoring insurance company's exposure relative to such lawsuits might be reduced by not being a majority shareholder in the AORC or through the use of segregated classes of stock.

CREDIT CAPTIVE REINSURERS

The credit insurance industry, unlike most branches of the insurance industry, is characterized by "reverse competition." Credit insurance is normally sold in conjunction with retail or consumer credit, including credit cards. The insurance company's primary consumer is the producer, such as the financial institution or retailer involved in the loans being covered by the credit insurance.

Lenders, and therefore producers of credit insurance, include banks, savings and loan associations, finance companies, automobile dealers, furniture dealers, and other retailers. Any of these may offer credit insurance as a service to their customers and as a source of profit to itself. These institutions may become sponsors of captive reinsurers.

In order to attract these institutions, insurance companies frequently compete by paying as high a commission and charging as high a premium as possible. Insurance departments have sought to control this situation by regulating the level of premiums and commissions used in conjunction with credit life and credit disability coverages. In order to allow the sponsoring institution to share in the profits of the credit insurance business and thus retain its high volume outlets, insurance companies will sometimes reinsure a portion of the business written through that sponsor into a reinsurance company formed and owned by the sponsor.

Form of Reinsurance

Reinsurance to a credit captive is normally ceded on a coinsurance basis.

Ongoing premium credit insurance, such as monthly outstanding balance coverage sold in conjunction with revolving credit accounts, is usually coinsured using monthly premiums. The captive does not have to set up reserves and does not experience a surplus drain.

In the case of single premium credit coverages, cessions on a typical "written" basis[3] can result in a significant surplus drain to the captive, especially in the case of credit disability coverage where the initial reserve is equal to the gross single premium. To alleviate this strain, the disability coverage, and sometimes the life coverage, may be ceded on an "earned" basis.[4]

Sponsor Considerations

Banks and savings and loan institutions have complicated regulations regarding the ownership of an insurer, or even an agency. Rules vary between federally chartered and state chartered institutions. Automobile dealerships, other retailers, and finance companies typically do not face such restrictions on their activities.

Profits and Leverage.   One reason for forming a captive reinsurance company would be the anticipation of making additional profits. The sponsor may also believe that it will gain more influence over the ceding company, resulting in better service and more control over the products.

---

[3]See Chapter 21, Reinsurance of Other Lines and Products.

[4]*Ibid.*

Ceding Company Considerations

The ceding company's reasons for working with a credit captive are similar to those for establishing an AORC. In particular, it would expect higher sales and increased earnings from its credit business.

Sales Results. The ceding company would anticipate increased sales by attracting and retaining large distributors as the result of allowing the distributor to share in the profits of the business. The insurer may also attract new distributors by setting them up in the reinsurance business.

Profit. As in any endeavor, the ceding company hopes to make a profit on the business which it retains. The profits are anticipated to come from the volume and the quality of the business produced by the large distributors.

Any increase in profits may be partially offset by increased expenses. Depending on the terms of the reinsurance agreement, the ceding company may prepare all the necessary financial reports and perform many of the routine administrative functions for the reinsurer. The ceding company normally makes a charge for this service. This charge is often stated in terms of the percentage of premiums and referred to as the reinsurers "retention." This charge is designed to cover the ceding company's expenses and to provide a margin for profit and contingencies. Sometimes, the distributor will perform all the administrative functions itself, including managing the assets and valuing the reserve liabilities.

OTHER USES OF CAPTIVES

The use and structure of captives appears to be limited only by the creativity of insurers and producers, subject to tax and regulatory considerations.

Many insurance companies are interested in using a joint venture with another entity to combine administrative capacity, distribution potential, and financial strength. Reinsurance is one means of allowing both parties to share in the risks and profits. This may be accomplished either by reinsuring business from one company to another or by using a jointly owned subsidiary to assume the risks underwritten by the venture.

Some noninsurance companies use captive reinsurers to participate in the risk and gain from the insurance benefits resulting from certain of their employee benefit plans. The terms of such participation are limited by the provisions of the Employee Retirement Income Security Act of 1974, commonly referred to as ERISA, and other statutes.

18 International Reinsurance

As used in this book, international reinsurance refers to the ceding or assuming of reinsurance involving a company domiciled outside of the United States. This chapter addresses only reinsurance involving Canada, the United Kingdom, Australia, Continental Europe, and offshore sites such as Bermuda and the Virgin Islands. The intention of this chapter is to introduce the basic concepts and considerations of international reinsurance and should not be considered to be a full discussion of the topic.

The general principles of reinsurance discussed throughout this book are applicable to international reinsurance transactions. The three basic plans of reinsurance, coinsurance, mod-co, and YRT, are used throughout the world and the basic contract terms are universal. This should not be surprising since reinsurance was not invented in the United States.

Edward Lloyd is credited with starting the first reinsurance underwriting system in his London coffee house in the late 17th century. However, widespread abuses ultimately led to strict government regulations which curtailed most English reinsurance activity. The Germans brought reinsurance to the United States, and the Germans and Russians dominated the United States market until World War I. Since reinsurance was transacted on a coinsurance basis at that time, United States insurers were faced with major problems relating to the transfer of funds and recovery of benefits during the war. This encouraged the development of the domestic reinsurance industry.

While property and liability reinsurance is distributed worldwide, over fifty percent of the life reinsurance in the world originates in the United States. Most of this is written with domestic United States insurers; a number of these are foreign owned, but they operate as United States carriers and hold most of the assets relating to United States risks in the United States.

MOTIVATIONS FOR INTERNATIONAL REINSURANCE

Despite the excess capacity for reinsurance which currently exists in the United States market, a large number of international reinsurance transactions take place annually. There are several factors which might motivate a company to enter into an international reinsurance agreement.

Availability of Specialty Coverages

An insurance company may seek reinsurance outside of the United States either because it is unable to obtain the coverage domestically or because it can obtain the coverage at a better cost. The types of reinsurance most commonly purchased abroad are catastrophe and stop loss protection and certain forms of health reinsurance. Traditional life insurance risks are less likely to be reinsured internationally for a lower cost because of the current oversupply of such reinsurance capacity in the United States.

Business Purposes

In some instances, a United States company doing business in a foreign country will be required to cede a portion of the business to a company in that country. In other instances, a United States carrier may cede domestic risks to a foreign insurer as part of an international sharing or cooperation in business. Group coverages on employees of international firms is sometimes shared among companies domiciled in several of the countries served by that firm.

Some United States insurers are part of a international family of insurers. Reinsurance between these companies may occur for many reasons. It may be an efficient way of sharing capital and surplus among the various companies, allowing the stronger to help finance the weaker. It may also prove to be more profitable than having to buy coverage in the reinsurance marketplace as any profits on this reinsurance would stay within the group.

Surplus Relief or Financing Growth

United States life insurance companies have fairly inflexible, perhaps stringent, statutory reserve requirements when compared to those of the rest of the world. In many instances, a United States company is required to set up a significantly greater reserve than would a foreign company for the same policy. This is particularly true for situations requiring the recognition of premium deficiencies and interest guarantees.

Since the use of surplus creates a cost, the reinsurer that incurs the least surplus investment can usually offer a better price. Much reinsurance has been placed outside of the United States, particularly in offshore sites such as the Bermuda, because of the different reserve requirements. Letters of credit and similar instruments are frequently used instead of "hard assets." Should regulators establish mirror image reserving requirements, this practice would be curtailed.

Insurers that need surplus or cash to finance growth may look to international insurers at times, especially if the need is long term in nature. Such reinsurance differs from traditional surplus relief in that it typically involves a longer payback period and probably entails greater risks. Cash transfer is also more likely to be required.

Differences in Taxation

A domestic insurance company may place reinsurance outside the United States to take advantage of differences in tax laws. If an insurance company can reinsure business to a company in another country that has a lower effective tax rate or a more favorable tax standard, the benefits of lower taxes might be shared with the ceding company in the form of lower reinsurance costs.

Historically, tax related reinsurance has been common in offshore sites, but changes in the Internal Revenue Code have made it increasingly more difficult to create any advantages from international reinsurance. However, it is probably safe to assume that few, if any, international reinsurance agreements result in more combined taxes being paid than if both parties were in the same country.

CONSIDERATIONS

Before entering into a reinsurance arrangement with a foreign company, the ceding company must complete an in-depth analysis of the regulatory, tax, and political situations involved. Such an analysis is beyond the scope of this book. There are, however, certain key issues which are of a general interest.

Regulation

Regulation of insurance companies is significantly different in other countries. In some countries regulation is more liberal, granting the insurers a great degree of freedom. Elsewhere, the government may control nearly all aspects of the business. Quite frequently, reinsurers have more freedom of action than do direct writers.

Reserving. When a domestic insurance company cedes business to a nonadmitted reinsurer, whether it is domiciled in a neighboring state or halfway around the world, the ceding company is usually unable to take credit in its annual statement for the reserves on the business ceded. Many international reinsurance contracts are structured so that no asset transfer occurs to avoid this reserve credit problem. This may involve the use of mod-co or funds withheld coinsurance. Other treaties may be structured as stop loss in order to avoid the reserve credit issue.

Alternative solutions usually involve the use of a letter of credit, a surety bond, or a trust or escrow account.

Solvency Requirements. Most countries have specific solvency or surplus requirements. In the case of the European Economic Community (EEC), a solvency margin has been prescribed that is the minimum amount of surplus which insurance companies domiciled in the EEC may maintain. There is a basic agreement as to the level of solvency margins, but each country has historical definitions and these sometimes override the EEC's general rules.

In the United Kingdom, the required solvency margin is the greater of the aggregate required solvency margin for all classes of long term business and the Minimum Guarantee Fund, described subsequently. This level of surplus is, in effect, an investment on which some return is expected, and thereby affects the cost of reinsurance. The concept of solvency margins is similar to that of target surplus in the United States, except the solvency margins are specified by law.

The classes of long-term business defined for solvency margin purposes are as follows:

Class	Business
I	Life and Annuity
II	Marriage and Birth
III	Linked Long Term
IV	Permanent Health
V	Tontines
VI	Capital Redemption
VII	Pension Fund Management

The solvency margin for a given company is based on a percentage of its amount at risk and a percentage of its reserves. For example, the formula for Class I, life insurance and annuity business, may be expressed as (a)(b)+(c)(d),

where:

(a) is 4% of the policy reserves;
(b) is the greater of (1) and (2),

　　where:

　　(1) is the factor 50% for pure reinsurers (85% for all other companies), and
　　(2) is the ratio of the policy reserves after reinsurance ceded to the policy reserves before reinsurance ceded;

(c) is a percentage of the sum at risk (defined below) for a given type of business; and
(d) is the greater of (3) and (4),

　　where:

　　(3) is the factor 50%, and
　　(4) is the ratio of the sums at risk after reinsurance ceded to the sums at risk before reinsurance ceded.

The percentages which apply in item (c) for life and annuity business are:

(1)   10% for contracts of durations three years or less,
(2)   15% for contracts with original durations of more than three years but not more than five years,

(3)   30% for contracts with original durations of five years or more, and
(4)   10% for risk premium business of a pure reinsurer.

These percentages vary by class of business and may be changed from time-to-time.

The guarantee fund is calculated as the greater of one-third of the margin of solvency or the Minimum Guarantee Fund, which is approximately 500,000 pounds.

Companies are allowed to reduce this required solvency margin or surplus by an amount based on profits in the last five years. This obviously penalizes newer or faster growing companies that do not have sizable profits because of surplus strain.

In the United Kingdom, the somewhat reduced margins apply to both reinsurance and direct business. Some other EEC member countries have interpreted the directive as being totally inapplicable to assumed reinsurance. In general, direct companies are allowed to reduce their solvency margins at least partially for reinsurance ceded.

The assets which can be used to satisfy the solvency margins vary by country. Some countries are very liberal; others, such as the United Kingdom, are more conservative.

Taxation

Tax treatment of insurance companies and products varies significantly from country to country. It is important that the parties to any international reinsurance agreement understand the ramifications to their company before entering into such an agreement. It is also helpful to understand the tax implications to the other party if the treaty benefits are to be optimized.

It is beyond the scope of this book to explore fully or document the tax ramifications in every country with respect to reinsurance. The subject is too broad and too fluid; tax codes and bases are political in nature and are subject to sudden and major changes. Instead, this section is intended to provide an insight as to areas which should be considered in developing an international reinsurance treaty.

Income Taxes. As discussed previously, Section 845 of the United States Internal Revenue Code gives the IRS broad powers to reallocate items in an insurance company's tax return if it believes that a reinsurance arrangement entered into by the company results in significant tax avoidance or is without a reasonable risk transfer. Specifically, this allows the IRS the authority to reclassify elements of the tax return of the domestic carrier without requiring an offsetting treatment to a foreign carrier.

The tax bases of foreign domiciled reinsurers may vary significantly from those of domestic companies or from each other. The United States tax basis is essentially one of all gains from all sources. In the United Kingdom, the tax base is largely total investment income less insurance related expenses, with underwriting gains largely untaxed. Other countries have different bases or may allow great flexibility in establishing reserves or in determining taxable income. It is important that both parties to an international reinsurance transaction understand the tax ramifications of the treaty in both countries.

Excise Tax. The United States imposes a federal excise tax on premiums involving domestic risks reinsured outside the country. This tax is set currently at 1% of all premiums reinsured for life insurance, annuities, and health insurance. This tax is in lieu of United States federal income tax on the foreign reinsurer, but its payment is the responsibility of the United States ceding company.

Reinsurance ceded to companies domiciled in the United Kingdom, France, and a few other countries is exempt from this tax. This exemption is due to tax treaties which exist between the United States and these countries. As of this writing, reinsurance ceded to companies in Canada is not exempted, but discussions to alter this situation have been held.

Obviously this tax can add to the cost of reinsurance, so the benefits of the treaty must be carefully studied before it is consummated. It is important to verify the existence of the tax or any exemption before entering into an agreement. As with any tax, the situation is subject to change.

Stamp Duties. Some countries, most significantly the United Kingdom, impose a "stamp duty"; all insurance policies issued or reinsured must be "stamped" and a fee paid to the government. The duty is based on the amount of death benefit and is payable one time only.   The amount of the duty varies with the initial duration of the contract.   For durations greater than two years, the current duty in the United Kingdom is fifty pence per thousand pounds, or a rate of .05 percent.   For contracts with an initial duration of two years or less, the stamp duty is presently five pence per thousand pounds, a rate of .005 percent.

If the reinsurance arrangement involves a significant amount of insurance being ceded to a company in the United Kingdom, the stamp duty can be quite costly.   On the other hand, annuities do not create a stamp duty.

The United Kingdom is scheduled to remove the stamp duty in 1990 but, of course, this may not occur or the duty may be reinstated later.

Withholding Tax.   At one time, the United States imposed a withholding tax on all investments by foreign companies in the United States.   This withholding tax, in the amount of 30% of investment income, was removed by the Tax Reform Act of 1984. When it was in effect, companies domiciled in the United Kingdom and certain other countries were exempt from this tax.   It is mentioned here because such a tax could be reenacted in the future;   any revival of the withholding tax could affect not only new treaties, but any inforce agreements as well.

Foreign Tax Planning.   Before entering into any agreement involving a foreign country, it is important to become familiar with the taxation system of that country.   Many European countries and Japan have very conservative definitions of statutory earnings and, therefore, insurers operating there pay relatively little in income taxes.   In addition, the government functions differently in these countries with respect to taxation;   the typical situation is for the government to raise a certain amount of tax, and the government can change the tax base and rules rather quickly.   As a result, companies in these countries historically have had little motivation to enter into tax related reinsurance agreements.

Economic and Political Factors

In considering an international reinsurance arrangement, certain factors not usually relevant to domestic reinsurance, may be of overriding importance.

Currency Exchange Risk. In the event that the assets backing the policy reserves are transferred outside of the United States, the company is subject to the risk of fluctuations in the currency exchange rate. These fluctuations could cause wide swings in earnings or in asset values, potentially affecting the reserve credits. This risk can be eliminated for the ceding company if all amounts are based on its currency; the risk is then transferred to the reinsurer.

Inflation. Even a low rate of inflation can be a problem to a life insurer because of the long term nature of most risks coupled with guaranteed or fixed premiums. Severe inflation can quickly eat into profit margins. Before entering into any agreement in a foreign country, the insurance company should consider the economic situation in that country and the potential effect of inflation on the agreement.

Political Instability. Because of the risks involved in asset transfer, any insurance company contemplating reinsurance with a company in a foreign country should be aware of the political situation in that country. Not all countries have orderly changes in government, nor do all countries consistently respect private property rights, especially those of foreign individuals or companies.

While it may quite difficult to predict political turmoil or coups, when these do occur, social and economic upheaval follows. Assets could easily be devalued or confiscated, investment income could be disrupted, or reinsurance premiums or benefits withheld.

SELECTED INTERNATIONAL REINSURANCE MARKETS

Most developed countries in the world, with the possible exception of China and certain of the Soviet block countries, currently afford some degree of life and health reinsurance market potential. The following is a brief description of the principal international reinsurance markets dealt with by United States life insurance companies.

Canada

Canadian insurance companies may be federally or provincially incorporated or registered. Most are federally registered and are under the jurisdiction of the federal Superintendent of Insurance. There are over 150 federally registered insurance companies, about sixty of which are incorporated. The remainder are branches of foreign companies.

The larger Canadian insurers are sophisticated and knowledgeable in the United States insurance market. Some are active in the United States reinsurance market. Most professional reinsurers in Canada have "domestic" United States branches which are licensed to do business in most, if not all, of the states.

By ceding reinsurance to a United States branch, all monies involved remain expressed in terms of U.S. currency, eliminating the currency exchange risk and the federal excise tax. The branch of the Canadian company can retrocede the business to its parent without triggering the excise tax or can otherwise combine its financial results at the corporate level. Because of this use of branches, a United States ceding company is typically indifferent to the choice between a domestic reinsurer or a United States branch of a Canadian reinsurer.

Canadian valuation and nonforfeiture laws are less rigid than those of the United States. A Canadian valuation actuary has more freedom in setting reserves, but must file a lengthy report detailing and justifying his choice of assumptions. Canadian valuation actuaries seldom establish premium deficiency reserves as such, whereas they are required by law in many states. The United States branch of a Canadian company is subject to the reserve requirements of its state of entry, but any deficiency reserves would normally be "lost" in the consolidated overall statement of the Canadian company.

Prior to the introduction of indeterminate premium products, Canadian reinsurers may have had a slight edge in pricing premium deficient products for the United States market as the Canadian companies did not have the same degree of surplus strain in total as many domestic reinsurers. This was not a significant advantage, and the use of indeterminate premium products as well as the possibility of mirror image reserve requirements have further reduced its significance.

Canadian life insurance companies are taxed like other Canadian corporations; there is little opportunity for tax-driven reinsurance. Because of the valuation and nonforfeiture laws, surplus strain is minimal in Canada. It is difficult to provide surplus relief in Canada because of the valuation laws.

Most surplus relief contracts are designed to be repaid through future profits returned by the experience refund mechanism. To the extent that many of these surplus relief agreements have little or no risk, the Canadian valuation practices would require that a reserve be established for the repayments or, if no risk was really transferred, that no reserve credit be available. This is a by-product of having reserves determined by actuaries rather than legislative fiat.

In 1956, Canadian life insurance companies formed the Canadian Reinsurance Conference. This group meets annually and its purpose is to establish guidelines for the conduct of reinsurance. This is not a regulatory body and does not have any authority to police the business. However, its 1984 Reinsurance Guidelines established standardized reinsurance procedures and is valuable in the administration of reinsurance. It is used as a reference for generally accepted industry practices. No such guidelines exist in the United States but, because of the similarities between the countries, the Canadian guidelines are recommended reading.

It is fairly common for a United States life insurance company to cede traditional reinsurance to a Canadian company, but it is less common for a Canadian insurer to cede any business to a United States carrier. There are basic differences between the direct insurance markets of these countries. Differences in valuation and nonforfeiture laws have resulted in different products and practices.

United Kingdom

There are two distinct reinsurance markets in the United Kingdom, the conventional market and the specialty market of Lloyds.

Conventional Market. Insurance companies in the United Kingdom are regulated by the Department of Trade and Industry (DTI). The insurance market has historically been more savings oriented than that of the United States, with a large portion of sales coming from variable life type products. Valuation actuaries in the United Kingdom have far more discretionary powers in setting reserve liabilities than their United States counterparts, but they are also accountable for reserve adequacy. As a consequence, reserves may not necessarily be lower than those required in the United States.

In the past, some reinsurance between companies in the United States and the United Kingdom occurred because of the different tax structures of the two countries. United Kingdom life insurers are taxed on the excess of "I," investment income, over "E," expenses. This difference, known as "I minus E" determines taxable income.

It may be instructive to review an example of how this difference in tax systems could motivate international reinsurance which was to the benefit of both parties.

United States business involving relatively large amounts of commission and relatively little investment income were ceded to a United Kingdom company. Term coverages were good candidates, but short term credit insurance was better because the stamp duty was lower and the solvency margins required were less.

The result was that the United Kingdom insurer would have higher "E" with no increase in "I," thus reducing the amount of "I minus E." The tax saving could be shared with the ceding company in the form of higher allowances. In effect, the reinsurer could lose money on the underwriting and make it up, and then some, from tax savings.

This technique was seldom used, largely because the United Kingdom tax authority, the Inland Revenue Service, disapproved of the transactions. In the United Kingdom, the definition of taxable income is more dependent upon practices and history and less on formal legislation than in the United States. The Inland Revenue Service has broad authority to disallow the effects of any reinsurance treaty which it believes blatantly takes advantage of the laws. In general, tax savings from reinsurance are less common and less pursued in the United Kingdom.

Lloyds Market. Lloyds of London is composed of a group of syndicates. Each syndicate is made up of a group of individuals known as "Names." Each Name has an unlimited liability and must show sufficient financial strength to qualify. Initially, each Name must show readily available assets of 100,000 pounds. Neither Lloyds nor the syndicates are insurance companies in the traditional sense. Lloyds acts only in the capacity of a clearing house and establishes requirements.

Lloyds cannot offer regular life insurance coverages. It primarily handles property and liability risks, but it also offers a wide range of health and medical coverages, including accidental death benefits. Since it cannot reinsure regular life insurance risks, life insurers have little contact with Lloyds on a regular basis. It can and does offer stop loss and catastrophe covers for life and health insurance.

Australia

Life insurance in Australia is regulated under the Life Insurance Act of 1945 by the Life Insurance Commissioner. There are forty-nine registered life companies, six of which are professional reinsurers.

The Australian life market is very competitive and more savings oriented than the United States market. Australia is far more advanced in the integration of financial services.

The larger life companies have very large surpluses and many are having difficulties sustaining growth in the Australian market. Little need for surplus relief or financial reinsurance exists. In fact, some of these companies may find overseas investment or reinsurance attractive.

The tax situation is Australia is similar to that which existed in the United States under the 1959 Act. It might be possible to use mod-co to reclassify investment income as underwriting income to result in a more favorable tax for the Australian company, but a true transfer of risk would be necessary. To date, this has not been done to any significant extent.

Continental Europe

In general, the practices of Continental Europe are similar to those of the United Kingdom. Solvency margins are similar, as previously described. Taxes vary by country, as do reserve requirements. With the planned integration of the EEC in 1992, even more similarity of practices are expected to emerge. However, doubt has been expressed that practices and regulations will ever be identical in all countries.

Reinsurance tends to be organized in many pools, with risks shared in small pieces among many carriers. Reinsurance from companies in Europe tends to go to the larger reinsurers. It is very uncommon to find a reinsurer that is also a direct insurer. Europeans view this largely as a conflict of interest. Of course, many reinsurers and direct insurers have common or cross ownership. Most life reinsurers are part of organizations or companies which offer both life and property and liability reinsurance. In general, the European reinsurers are more conservative in analyzing risk than are the United States and Canadian reinsurers.

Several large reinsurers based in Europe are active in the United States. They generally function through United States subsidiaries, although branch offices are occasionally used. Dutch, English, German, Swedish, and Swiss reinsurers have significant subsidiaries in the United States. Until recently, there was also a significant French reinsurance subsidiary.

The principal Continental European reinsurance markets are described briefly.

The Netherlands. The Dutch insurance market is well developed and one of the most sophisticated in all of Continental Europe. It is dominated by three large companies and is not regarded as being competitive. All three companies enjoy comfortable market shares and profit margins.

The market is limited, and these three companies have looked for investment opportunities outside the Netherlands. These companies are familiar with United States reinsurance practices through their subsidiaries. Capital gains and all other taxable income are taxed at a rate of 45%. However, capital gains may be sheltered somewhat by rolling them into replacement assets.

Switzerland. Switzerland's life insurance market operates on a tariff system like that of many other countries in Continental Europe. Under a tariff system, life insurance premiums are defined by law on a basis comparable to that for statutory net premiums in the United States. A set percentage of the profits must be returned to the policyholders in the form of dividends. Because of the tariff system, there is very little price competition, and therefore it is difficult for new companies to increase their market share. The Swiss regulatory system is geared to producing conservative earnings. Swiss insurers would be likely to engage only in extremely profitable foreign ventures.

France. The French life insurance market is relatively unsophisticated but growing. The market operates on a tariff premium basis such as that used in Switzerland but which is not as rigid.

Germany. The German insurance market operates on the tariff system. It is important to remember that the German life insurance market has been wiped out twice in this century because of wars and hyperinflation. Regulation of the German market is therefore geared toward solvency. Because of the strength of the Deutchmark, German insurers have not been particularly interested in assuming currency exchange risks. While the current efforts to reunify East and West Germany may have a significant effect on the future domestic German insurance market, it is not likely to have any effect on its foreign reinsurance operations.

Japan

The Japanese life insurance market is approximately two-thirds the size of the United States market and growing rapidly. There are only twenty domestic life insurance companies operating in Japan, so they are incredibly large in relation to the average United States insurer. In the past, the Japanese have tended to be very conservative and rather unsophisticated in insurance and reinsurance. However, most life insurers have very large surpluses and may be interested in United States insurance company investments.

Offshore Sites

Offshore sites, such as Bermuda, Barbados, the Bahamas, the Cayman Islands, and the Virgin Islands, are popular jurisdictions for the formation of reinsurance companies. It is much easier to start an insurance company in the islands than in the United States, Canada, or the United Kingdom because of the lower capitalization requirements and lower fees. Also, a company can usually be formed more quickly in the Islands than in the United States.

The Islands also have a very attractive tax treatment and less stringent reserve requirements which add to their popularity. More investment flexibility is allowed, with higher yielding investments available. Premiums ceded to the islands are subject to the United States federal excise tax; that tax was suspended recently for some islands, but it is expected to be reinstated. Recent tax rulings have curtailed certain other benefits.

These islands are the home to many captive reinsurance companies for the reinsurance of the credit insurance, workers' compensation, and agent owned companies. While there is a certain exotic appeal to doing business in the islands, there is also a certain stigma because of the image of lower surplus and reserve requirements.   This need not be the case, and many island based reinsurers are financially solid and very well run.

19 Health Reinsurance

Many of the principles and practices described earlier relative to life reinsurance also apply to the reinsurance of accident and health risks. For example, the concepts of risk sharing, reserve credits, and accounting are the same for both life and health risks. Reinsurance of accident and health risks is nearly always the result of traditional risk transfer needs. Financial reinsurance of accident and health plans, especially medical insurance, was once not uncommon, but is rare today.

Accident and health reinsurance does, however, involve some unique features and practices. In this chapter, some of these features and considerations of accident and health reinsurance are discussed, with reference to disability income and medical indemnity coverages as the primary plans of insurance.

Health insurance is written on both individual and group bases. The benefit structures and the reinsurance considerations are similar for both types of insurance. The discussion in this chapter applies to the reinsurance of both group and individual health insurance.

373

DISABILITY INCOME

Perhaps the largest volume of accident and health reinsurance is on disability income or loss of time coverages.[1] These products cover permanent disability, and, in some instances, partial disability. Waiting periods and benefit periods can vary by cause, and policies may include features for cost of living increases, return of premiums, or return of cash value. Some policies provide benefits only if the disability is caused by an accident.

Insurance companies reinsure disability income for largely the same reasons that they reinsure life products. One reason is the surplus strain associated with the disability income claims. Even if the monthly cash benefit outlay is a reasonable amount, the necessary claim reserve can be significant, especially for a small or moderate sized insurance company.

A second major use of reinsurance for disability income plans is product expertise. A company whose primary business is individual life may wish to offer a health insurance line as an accommodation to its agents and want to access the reinsurer's expertise in areas such as product design, pricing, rate structure, policy forms and rate filings, underwriting, valuation, policy administration, and claims administration. The reinsurer's involvement can vary from providing excess risk coverage to providing virtually all administrative services related to a disability income line of business in addition to the risk coverage.

Retention Limits

There are three common approaches to setting retention limits for disability income coverages, one of which is unique to disability or periodic income coverages. To some extent, the retention limits and the type of reinsurance are interrelated.

In determining its retention, it is common for a company to consider the present value of benefits. The maximum present value of benefits would serve as a guideline in determining the maximum monthly benefit to be retained. For example, if the disability income line were roughly the same size as the life insurance line, it might set limits for disability income which would produce present values of benefits which were roughly the same as the maximum retention for life insurance. If the disability income line were smaller than the life insurance line, it might use a lesser retention.

---

[1]For purposes of this book, hospital indemnity and other forms of periodic cash benefit coverages are considered to be disability income plans.

This method is logical if the claim reserve is viewed as a lump sum benefit at the time of claim incurral; the intent is to keep the maximum incurred benefit at a reasonable level. Of course, the potential effect of fluctuation and the carrier's attitudes on risk avoidance by product line are major considerations.

Fixed or Excess Share. A fixed, or excess share, reinsurance of disability income is a proportional reinsurance coverage which closely resembles the typical retention situation for life insurance, except the retention and the reinsurance coverage amounts are stated in terms of dollars per month of benefit, instead of a gross dollar amount. Under an excess share arrangement, the ceding company retains a fixed, level amount of disability income coverage for the entire benefit period. For example, a company may elect to retain $200 per month per life for a certain coverage type.

Retention limits may vary by policy form or benefit period. The company may decide to retain less for longer benefit periods or shorter elimination periods. It may decide to retain 100% of any hospital indemnity coverages if the benefit amounts involved are relatively small. This type of variation in retention makes sense when the maximum possible present values of the various benefits are taken into consideration.

Quota Share. Quota share reinsurance is another form of proportional coverage where the ceding company retains a fixed percentage of each risk. This corresponds to the quota share method used in life reinsurance. The only difference between excess share and quota share reinsurance is in the determination of each party's share of the risk. The quota share method simplifies reinsurance administration and is often used when disability income is not a major product line of the ceding company, but rather an accommodation to its agents. Quota share coverages usually result in more reinsurance and less earnings effect on the ceding company.

Extended Wait. Extended wait, or extended elimination period, reinsurance is a nonproportional coverage. Under this method, reinsurance benefits begin only after the claim has reached a specified duration. This period of delay in reinsurance participation is known as the extended wait or the extended elimination period. Since the ceding company's share of the benefit payments is larger before the expiration of the extended wait period than afterwards, this larger share can be viewed as a large deductible which must be met before reinsurance coverage begins.

For example, the ceding company may retain all amounts for the first two years of benefits and then reinsure 75% of amounts payable after that point. Alternatively, a flat amount, such as $200 per month, may be retained after the extended wait period. While the carrier could seek to cede 100% of the benefits after the extended wait period, reinsurers generally prefer to keep the direct insurer involved in the ongoing claim review and its economic implications.

Extended wait coverage is also used in combination with excess share or quota share reinsurance. This is especially true of lifetime accident and sickness benefits, where extended wait coverage eliminates the reinsurance administration of a number of short duration claims. The ceding company retains a portion of each claim for a given period and a lesser amount thereafter. This makes the reinsurance package as a whole into a nonproportional plan. The extended wait coverage and the basic coverages (excess share or quota share) may be with the same reinsurer or with different reinsurers, even for the same insured life.

Plans of Reinsurance

Just as with life insurance, there are three major plans of reinsurance for disability income: YRT, coinsurance, and mod-co. Unlike life insurance, these are seldom used in combination.

Yearly Renewable Term. The simplest and perhaps most common method of reinsuring disability income coverages is the use of YRT reinsurance. This method is quite similar to the use of YRT reinsurance in the life insurance situation. Under this plan, a schedule of YRT premiums for $100 of monthly benefit is developed for each issue age, benefit period, and waiting period.

YRT works particularly well in the case of the excess retention method and can also be used with the quota share method. For individual cessions, YRT is relatively easy to administer, especially for the reinsurer. In addition to less complicated administration and increased clarity, YRT offers relative ease in the event of recapture.

There are two major differences between YRT reinsurance for life insurance and disability income coverages. For life insurance, the amount of coverage reinsured is the net amount at risk, or the face amount of the policy less the policy reserve. For disability income coverage, the policy reserve does not enter into the determination of the amount reinsured.

The second difference concerns the amount of surplus relief available as the result of reserve credits. For life insurance, YRT does not develop significant reserves, and, therefore, does not provide meaningful reserve credits. However, in the case of disability income coverage, the per unit active life reserve under YRT may be close to that of the original policy.

Yearly renewable term reinsurance is often designed and priced to cover only total disability benefits. Such a product may be inappropriate for partial benefits.

Coinsurance. The use of coinsurance for disability income reinsurance closely parallels the use of coinsurance for life insurance. The reinsurer accepts the ceding company's premium on the business reinsured and pays an allowance to cover the ceding company's commissions and expenses. This allowance is normally larger in the first year to cover acquisition costs. The reinsurer then holds its share of all policy reserves and pays its share of policy benefits.

Coinsurance is most frequently used in the quota share retention method because it greatly simplifies administration. The ceding company need only apply the quota share percentage to its premiums, reserves, and benefits to determine the reinsurer's share. Allowances are easily determined from the reinsurance premiums. The pricing of allowances is unique to each ceding company's premium and benefit structure.

As in the case of life insurance, when coinsurance is used, the policy cash values or reserves are usually paid to the ceding company at recapture. Most basic disability income coverages do not have cash values, although many have return of premium or cash value riders. Therefore, if coinsurance is used, a basis for recapture should be negotiated either at the time recapture is requested or at the time the treaty is written.

If the treaty provides for recapture, it must be clear regarding what amount, if any, is to be paid by the reinsurer to the ceding company on recapture, if disputes are to be avoided. This is more difficult than it is for life insurance because disability income reserves are less rigidly specified or defined than are life insurance reserves where cash values may represent a reasonable substitute.

Modified Coinsurance. Mod-co is rarely used for disability income reinsurance, although it could be. More common would be the use of funds withheld coinsurance if the reinsurer is not authorized in the appropriate domicile.

Pricing

The reinsurance pricing actuary has to consider many factors in developing rates for disability income. While the process is generally the same as that for life reinsurance, there are some special characteristics which merit further review.

Benefits. The reinsurance pricing actuary must carefully study the policy form and rate charts. Different definitions of disability will influence experience of the product, as will variations in occupational classifications and in the length of benefit and elimination periods.

Market. The market environment of a product also affects its ultimate experience. The actuary must consider whether the product is sold as a major marketing effort or only as an accommodation to agents. The actuary must also consider if the product is going to be marketed only to certain income levels or occupational groups, or in certain geographic regions. Any of these factors can affect experience and rates. Also, it is important to determine whether the plan will be sold only as a stand alone policy, a rider, or both.

Underwriting. Insurance claim management begins with good underwriting. This is particularly true for any accident or health product. The reinsurance pricing actuary or underwriter needs to evaluate the ceding company's underwriting rules, as well as its underwriters and their experience.

Claim Procedures. A company's claim procedures can have a significant effect on the profitability of any health product. Claims should be handled promptly and professionally in order to avoid adverse legal action, and not be allowed to continue beyond the point defined by the terms of the policy.

Retention. The ceding company's retention is also important to reinsurance experience. If an excess share retention is being used instead of quota share, the reinsurer will have a relatively narrow base of risks over which to spread its claim costs. Larger amounts of risk exhibit different experience than do smaller ones. The ceding company should have sufficient exposure to risk on the reinsured policies to ensure proper claims review and management. Otherwise, the company could pay claims with relative impunity to avoid hassles with policyholders and agents.

Experience. It is important to examine the ceding company's previous experience in the market. If the company has had little or no experience, the pricing actuary should be more cautious than he would with a company which has substantial positive experience.

Special Considerations

Administration of a disability income reinsurance agreement is similar to that of life reinsurance. Two points, recapture and valuation, warrant special discussion.

Recapture. As mentioned previously, recapture of disability income reinsurance may be complicated because of a lack of defined reserves and an absence of cash values. Any expectations or rules regarding recapture should be defined in the treaty. Otherwise, recapture should be considered to be prohibited, unless, of course, the parties can agree on terms later. Policies with open disability claims are not normally recaptured until the cessation of the claim.

Valuation. The reinsurer needs a flexible valuation system to develop the reserves for disability income products, as each ceding company's benefit and premium structure is likely to be different. All reinsured benefits should be considered in determining the reinsurer's reserves and the ceding company's reserve credits. Claim reserves must also be computed. Extended wait coverages will generate claim reserves when the claim is first identified as being expected to go beyond the wait period, not when the wait period is finally breached.

MAJOR MEDICAL AND COMPREHENSIVE

Low limit hospital and medical expense insurance create little need for reinsurance. However, major medical and comprehensive health insurance may expose a company to very large claims, necessitating reinsurance.

Insurance companies reinsure medical coverages for the most basic of reasons: protection against adverse fluctuations in experience. Medical coverages usually provide benefits on an indemnity basis; the amount of a claim depends upon many factors, not just a defined lump sum as for life insurance. Because of this, the majority of reinsurance on medical plans is nonproportional.

A carrier may wish to accommodate its field force by issuing medical coverages and reinsuring them, as described in the section on disability income, but this is rare. The reinsurer would almost certainly require the company to retain part of the medical coverage risks, a step many carriers will refuse.

Retention

There are two methods used to determine retention for medical coverages: quota share and extended deductible. These correspond roughly to the quota share and extended wait methods used for disability income reinsurance.

Quota Share. The quota share method of reinsuring medical benefits is identical in practice to the quota share method used in life and disability income reinsurance. A fixed percentage of all policies is reinsured. Under this method, the reinsurer has an equal stake in every claim. Coinsurance of major medical and comprehensive plans must be quota share, although that share may vary with the deductible of the policy form.

Extended Deductible. The extended deductible is a nonproportional method of reinsurance developed for major medical which is applicable to individual policies. It corresponds to the extended waiting period used for disability income reinsurance. The reinsurer does not pay a claim until a certain level of payments to one individual or to all persons insured under a policy has been reached by the ceding company. For example, the reinsurer may agree to pay 75% of claims for any individual in excess of $25,000. The reinsurer's participation in claims may increase as the total amount of the claims increases to higher levels.

Types of Reinsurance

There are two types of reinsurance for major medical and comprehensive insurance: coinsurance and stop loss. Mod-co can be specified, but funds withheld coinsurance is more likely if the reinsurer is not authorized in the appropriate jurisdictions. The concept of YRT does not apply to these coverages.

Coinsurance. Coinsurance of medical coverages is rare, but if used, it is typically on a quota share basis. The reinsurer shares in premiums, claims, and reserves in proportion to its share of the business. Expense allowances are negotiated and priced in a manner similar to those for other coverages. Coinsurance usually is intended to last for the life of the policy.

Medical coverages vary by renewability guarantees, such as guaranteed renewable, noncancelable, collectively renewable, and nonrenewable. The terms of the coinsurance agreement should reflect the original policy's terms. It may also define the reinsurer's participation in the renewal premium setting process, if any.

Stop Loss. Today most reinsurance of medical coverages is done on a stop loss basis. Two kinds of stop loss are used and both can be applied to the same group of policies. Specific stop loss provides excess loss coverage on each policy or individual. Aggregate stop loss provides protection on an entire block of policies.

For example, specific stop loss may be set to provide payment of 90% of claims on a specific policy, or group certificate, when total claims exceed $25,000, up to a maximum of $50,000 per policy. Aggregate coverage may kick in if total retained claims exceed $500,000. Aggregate coverage likely would have maximum limits and coinsurance participation also.

In order to ease the claims administration effort, stop loss coverage is typically based on the date of services rendered within a defined coverage period, such as a calendar year. It is possible to relate stop loss coverage to all services rendered as the result of a given occurrence or event, but this is very difficult to administer.

Specific and aggregate coverages are usually provided by the same reinsurer, but they need not be. Each stop loss coverage has a deductible and a maximum limit. Some insurers purchase additional protection by adding one or more excess layers of stop loss over the lower coverages, with the deductible of each higher layer equal to the sum of the deductible and maximum coverage of the next lower limit. This procedure, called layering, is not common.

Stop loss reinsurance is usually guaranteed for periods of only one to three years. Rates may change with each period, or the reinsurer may decide to not renew the coverage. The ceding company can move the coverage to another reinsurer if more favorable terms are available. However, there is no guarantee that the desired coverage will be available in the future.

Special Considerations

There are more differences between medical coverages reinsurance and life reinsurance than there are between disability income reinsurance and life reinsurance. This is to be expected since the original benefits and forms are so different. Some of these differences necessitate different practices and procedures.

Covered Benefits. In developing the treaty for any medical reinsurance arrangement, the reinsurer and the ceding company must agree as to which benefits are covered and which are excluded. Among other things, this includes definitions of when coverage for individuals will begin, when coverage will end, and what claims are covered.

The ceding company and the reinsurer should discuss experimental procedures and whether such procedures are to be covered by the reinsurance agreement. Given the constant introduction of new medical techniques, medicines, and technology, there is little prospect of including an exhaustive list in the treaty. Therefore, it would be prudent to define a procedure for deciding on the role of the reinsurer regarding new procedures.

Recapture. Recapture of reinsurance on medical coverages is rare. Coinsurance is not really designed for recapture, and special terms would be needed. Stop loss is renewable for only short periods, so recapture is not a factor.

Administration. Administration of premiums and allowances, if any, is a fairly simple accounting procedure. Claims administration may be more difficult. If coinsurance is used, the reinsurer is responsible for a fixed percentage of claims and therefore reserves, so claims sharing is fairly simple. For stop loss however, running tallies of losses per individual policy or group are needed for coverage.

OTHER BENEFITS

Many varieties of medical, accident, and health coverages exist, and more are being created. Reinsurance for each may be designed in a unique manner, but the principles described in this chapter and elsewhere in this book would be expected to apply. These coverages include hospital surgical, dread disease, and travel accident benefits, among others. Stop loss, coinsurance, extended wait or extended deductible, and combinations of these may be applied as appropriate. A detailed discussion of all the possible products and reinsurance designs is beyond the scope of this discussion.

20 | Annuity Reinsurance

Until the mid-1980's, the reinsurance of annuities was relatively rare, largely because annuities were not a major product line with most insurers. However, as the "unbundling" of the protection and savings elements of insurance products spread, consumer interest in annuities grew and sales increased rapidly. This growth was spurred by certain tax deferral opportunities offered by annuities.

Along with this growth in sales of annuities came a demand for reinsurance of annuities. This demand flowed from the sometimes high surplus strain created by the sale of annuities, not from a need for mortality or morbidity risk protection. This need has led to the creation of different reinsurance techniques designed to share investment and asset risks and to provide surplus relief, while meeting regulatory requirements.

The principles of both traditional and financial reinsurance discussed elsewhere in this book also apply to annuities. This chapter addresses certain of the various products sold as annuities and some of the specific points to be analyzed or documented in developing a reinsurance agreement covering annuities.

ANNUITY PRODUCTS

For purposes of this chapter, annuity products are classified in two major groups based upon the guarantees provided. The first of these groups includes annuities with benefits that are sensitive to interest rates declared periodically by the insurer, based on its investment results. While some guarantees are present, the ultimate benefits are highly dependent upon the future interest credited to the contract. The other group includes those with guaranteed benefits only and which are, therefore, independent of the insurer's investment results.

Interest Sensitive Benefits

Interest sensitive annuities function largely as savings accounts, with interest being credited to the contract holders' funds on deposit. Generally there are long term guarantees at or below the maximum permitted statutory valuation interest rate and shorter term guarantees based upon a current interest rate declared by the insurer. Annuity purchase rates are guaranteed, creating some long term risks regarding interest rates and mortality. In a number of contracts, these guarantees are relatively modest and provision is made for allowing more favorable rates based on the insurance company's current practice at the time of annuitization.

Interest sensitive annuities are used largely as asset accumulation vehicles and can be classified according to the premium payment expectations. Generally, they are known as deferred annuities because the annuitization is to occur in the future, not immediately. The two principal types of interest sensitive products are single premium deferred annuities and flexible premium deferred annuities.

Single Premium Deferred Annuities. Single premium deferred annuities (SPDA's), as the name implies, are annuities purchased with a single premium and containing some long term guarantee as to annuity purchase rates. Generally, the contract holder can withdraw his money in a lump sum rather than accept an annuity, but there may be a penalty imposed for this option.

The primary risks of SPDA's are those relating to the reinvestment of assets and asset default. Favorable annuity purchase rate guarantees can create substantial risks if mortality improves rapidly or interest rates decline significantly. Surplus strain is created by acquisition expenses and by initial interest guarantees which exceed the corresponding statutory valuation interest rates.

Frequently, the strain of acquisition expenses is partially offset during the first seven to ten contract years through the use of surrender charges which reduce both surrender values and reserves. As the surrender charges reduce, reserves increase accordingly. As a result, insurers may wait for many years before realizing statutory profits on their SPDA sales.

Reinsurance opportunities arise from the strain created at issue. While the strain per unit may be low when compared to that for life insurance, the large volumes of SPDA premium can create enormous strains for some carriers. In addition, rating agencies and regulators want annuity issuers to maintain additional surplus, often referred to as required surplus. Reinsurance can be arranged which both offsets the initial statutory strain and transfers or reduces the required surplus target.

Initially companies ceding annuity reinsurance tended to use financial reinsurance to create surplus relief. However, as regulators increased the requirements for reserve credits or balance sheet improvement, companies turned increasingly to more permanent forms of risk transfer reinsurance. Some ceding companies now use reinsurance to realize immediately a significant portion of future earnings on the SPDA's, creating statutory earnings and surplus which can be used to support other new issues or pay dividends.

Perhaps the largest problem in reinsuring SPDA's is negotiating and documenting mutually acceptable investment and interest crediting strategies. This will be discussed in more depth later in this chapter.

Flexible Premium Deferred Annuities. Flexible premium deferred annuities (FPDA's) are similar to SPDA's in that they are primarily accumulation products with permanent annuity purchase rate guarantees. Like SPDA's, strain is caused by acquisition expenses and interest rate guarantees. Unlike SPDA's, FPDA's are designed to permit the payment of renewal premiums, usually on a flexible basis, although scheduled payments may be planned at issue.

Commissions on first year premiums for FPDA's are higher than those on SPDA's, but renewal commissions tend to be somewhat lower. Interest guarantees are similar to those of SPDA's, so the higher commissions can lead to greater strain as a per cent of premium. Surrender charges are employed similar to those on SPDA's.

The basic reinsurance considerations are the same for FPDA's as those for SPDA's, with two exceptions. SPDA's have only one premium, so there is no commitment regarding new money. FPDA's are designed to permit the payment of renewal premiums, so interest commitments on new money are important. This point must be considered in drafting the reinsurance agreement.

A more significant difference may be that a certain level of renewal premiums may be necessary to recover the initial strain created by the commission on the first year premiums. This situation is similar to that which occurs with most life insurance products with high first year commissions. The first year commission on an FPDA, however, is almost certain to be lower than that of a corresponding life insurance product.

Reinsurance pricing must take into account both the initial strain as well as the need for renewal premiums and the commitments regarding interest on those renewal premiums.

Guaranteed Benefits

Annuities which are designed to guarantee payments to a beneficiary provide a greater challenge to both the insurer and the reinsurer than do accumulation annuity products. At one time, all deferred annuities were of the guaranteed type. Today, this type of annuity is rare and virtually all guaranteed benefit annuties are variations of single premium immediate annuities (SPIA's). These products usually do not have any renewal premiums.

Rather than focus on crediting current interest on an accumulation account, these annuities guarantee the payment of certain amounts at certain points in time. Sales competition is based largely on purchase price, along with stability and reputation of the issuing company. Since payments may be guaranteed for many years in the future, the reinvestment risk is more significant on these products than on interest sensitive annuities.

Just as the credited rate is important to the profitability of interest sensitive annuities, the interest rate assumed in pricing the guaranteed benefits, referred to as the pricing rate, is key to profitability of guaranteed benefit annuities.

Structured Settlement Annuities. Structured settlement annuities are SPIA's sold in response to a need to structure a series of payments, instead of a lump sum, typically as an award or in settlement of a claim or lawsuit. For example, settlement of a workers' compensation claim for a job related disability may consist of a lifetime income, with lump sums at specified intervals for college expenses of dependents. Payments may increase annually as a provision for inflation.

Some of the benefits may not become due for fifty or more years. This presents a significant risk regarding reinvestments as few investments are available for such long periods.

Commissions are fairly uniform and the structured settlement market is controlled by a relatively small group of brokers. Competition is based almost entirely on price, once the stability and integrity of the insurer are established. When market interest rates are high in comparison to statutory valuation interest rates, gross premiums, net of commissions, are much lower than initial reserves. This, of course, can create a significant surplus strain.

Reinsurance of structured settlement annuities has been rare, probably because most major writers of this business are large, well capitalized insurers. However, the high strain has led some insurers to seek reinsurance for surplus relief purposes. Like SPDA reinsurance, structured settlement reinsurance started as financial reinsurance to provide short term surplus relief, but traditional coinsurance and modified coinsurance are growing in usage.

The use of coinsurance implies that the reinsurer assumes most or all of the risks of asset default, lower interest rates, and reinvestment. The reinsurer will know the stream of benefit payments promised and may invest the funds it receives as it wishes.

The use of mod-co is more complicated as the assets and their management are left with the ceding company. Depending on the terms of a specific agreement, the reinsurer will assume the interest rate and reinvestment risks. The asset default risk, together with the opportunity for capital gains and losses and the recognition of unrealized capital gains and losses, may be left with the ceding company or passed to the reinsurer. In either event, the reinsurer will wish to be comfortable with the ceding company's investment philosophy and practices, both initially and for the long term.

Structured settlements may involve substandard lives where injury or medical impairment is anticipated to reduce normal life expectancy. If these settlements involve any payments contingent on survival, competition for the business will be affected by the insurer's underwriting practices as a higher substandard rating will result in a more competitive premium. Both insurers and their reinsurers are advised to examine carefully the underwriting to ensure acceptance of desirable risks while minimizing exposure to unprofitable segments of the market.

It is generally believed that any type of insurance or annuity can be reinsured on an assumption basis if agreement can be reached between the ceding company and a reinsurer. Structured settlement annuities may be an exception to this generalization. Many structured settlement annuities are issued at the direction of a court, specifying a particular insurer or rating for the insurer. Questions have been raised as to whether or not the original company can transfer structured settlement obligations through assumption reinsurance. This point should be addressed before any assumption reinsurance of structured settlement annuities is finalized.

Guaranteed Investment Contracts.   Guaranteed investment contracts (GIC's), guarantee a lump sum payment at some specified point in the future. The periods of time involved are usually relatively short, such as three to seven years. Mortality risk and annuity purchase rate guarantees are usually limited, if they exist at all. The risks are basically those of asset default and interest guarantees.

Reinsurance on GIC's can arise from an insurer's desire to reduce its exposure to these investment risks. It is more likely, however, that reinsurance will result from the need for surplus relief. If interest guarantees exceed the statutory valuation interest rates, significant surplus strain can result; financial reinsurance is a common response[1]. In any event, the reinsurer must assume some of the guarantees in order for reserve credit to be granted.

Traditional mod-co may be used to reinsure GIC's if the reinsurer is comfortable with the ceding company's investment practices. The treaty must be clear as to the reinsurer's participation in realized or unrealized capital gains and losses or in asset defaults.

Terminal Funding Annuities.   Terminal funding annuities are a combination of deferred and immediate annuities sold in a specific application to fund pension obligations. The phrase "terminal funding" arose from the purchasing of annuities to fulfill obligations under pension plans which were being terminated. The most publicized usage has been in leveraged buy-outs or corporate

---

[1]See Chapter 5, Financial Reinsurance.

takeovers where the pension plans were over funded. Purchase of annuities to meet all earned commitments freed the excess funds for other uses, such as payment of corporate debt.

Terminal funding annuities, like structured settlements, are price-competitive. When market interest rates are higher than valuation interest rates, strain can result. Reinsurance considerations are similar to those of structured settlement annuities.

Variable Annuities

Reinsurance of variable annuities is rare. The investment risks are borne by the contract holder, so the need for risk transfer is small. However, strain can result from acquisition expenses and there are mortality guarantees. Reinsurers can participate in these elements, especially those relating to benefit purchase rates.

Once annuitized, variable annuities may have either fixed or variable benefits. Fixed benefits are determined in the same manner as for SPDA's and FPDA's, based on annuity purchase rates. These rates have mortality and interest guarantees which can be reinsured in the same manner as any SPIA or deferred annuity. Even those benefits which are variable may have mortality and minimum interest guarantees which can be reinsured in a similar manner.

SPECIAL CONSIDERATIONS

The basic principles of reinsurance discussed previously in this book apply to the reinsurance of annuities, as well. This section addresses some of the unique aspects of such reinsurance.

Plans of Reinsurance

Although some attempts have been made to create a form of YRT reinsurance for annuities, most, if not all, annuity reinsurance is on a coinsurance or mod-co basis. The funds withheld versions and combinations of the two are frequently used to minimize cash flows, especially if surplus relief is the objective and recapture is expected.

Reserve Requirements

As with any reinsurance, the combined reserves of the ceding company and the reinsurer must at least meet the minimum reserve requirements. If coinsurance is used, the reinsurer is responsible for the reserves on the reinsured portion of the business.

Control of Assets

In any annuity reinsurance agreement it is necessary to determine which party will own the assets, manage the assets, develop the investment strategy, and establish the crediting or pricing interest rate. These functions do not necessarily always lie with the same party. A defined process for setting credited rates or pricing rates is necessary if the reinsurer is to make a profit on the business and the ceding company is to maintain good faith with its contract holders.

In a coinsurance agreement, the reinsurer has the responsibility for the assets backing the reserves and their investment, but the ceding company has the responsibility for setting the credited rates for any interest sensitive product. The reinsurer obviously needs the credited rate to be one that it can reasonably support with its investment income.

In a mod-co agreement, the ceding company both manages the assets and sets the credited rate. The reinsurer is not directly concerned with the earned rate on the assets , but rather with the mod-co adjustment interest rate. The reinsurer will want the mod-co adjustment interest rate to show a spread above the credited or pricing rate which is sufficient to meet its profit objectives. The ceding company will want the mod-co adjustment interest rate to bear a reasonable relationship to the earned rate so the ceding company is not otherwise subsidizing the reinsurer.

The ceding company retains the responsibility for and obligation of dealing with the contract holder, including establishing credited interest rates. The reinsurer either benefits from a large spread or suffers from one which is too small. Therefore, it is suggested that the two parties negotiate and document a planned investment strategy prior to signing a treaty. This should include a discussion of both the methodology for establishing credited or pricing rates and the management of assets. These may not be absolutely binding, but they will serve as a guide and document the original intention of the parties.

Some companies have turned to the use of trusts to ease the questions of asset control, ownership, and management. For example, the reinsurer in a coinsurance agreement can place the assets invested in support of the reinsured business into a trust for the benefit of the ceding company. These assets can be restricted to certain classes of investments based on maturity, quality, duration, and other significant features. The two parties to the reinsurance agreement should then agree on an investment strategy and a crediting strategy. While each party maintains its individual rights and obligations, this process can make it easier to agree on investment issues.

In addition, if the reinsurer fails to perform or develops solvency or solidity problems, the ceding company may be able to take control of the trusteed assets directly to protect both itself and its contract holders.

Transfer of Risk

If reserve credits or surplus relief are expected to result from an annuity reinsurance agreement, legitimate risk transfer is a requirement. While mortality risks are inherent in some annuities, significant risk transfer involving other elements of annuities is possible. The reinsurer need not be involved in all risks on a contract for legitimate risk transfer to occur. Reserve credit or surplus relief will likely be allowed to the extent that any risk or risks have actually been transferred.

In particular, reserve credits should be allowed only for risk elements which are considered in the original insurer's reserves. For example, if the reinsurance agreement provides for payment by the reinsurer only in the event of annuitants living beyond the end of the mortality table, there should be no reserve credit granted. This may be a valid reinsurance need, but it is unlikely that any insurer would use that assumption in establishing its reserves.

There are several types of risk which can be transferred in a reinsurance agreement. The primary exposures are discussed in the following paragraphs.

Interest. The immediate element of risk in most annuities is the interest guarantee. Every annuity carries either an interest guarantee or a pricing interest assumption on the funds involved. The risk involved is whether or not the insurer will earn the interest assumed. If the reinsurer accepts that risk, then some risk transfer has occurred.

For example, if an SPDA guarantees to credit ten per cent for the next twelve months and the reinsurance contract passes that guarantee to the reinsurer along with the assets, then the reinsurer has accepted the interest rate risk. On the other hand, if a mod-co treaty contains a formula for the mod-co adjustment interest rate to be the contract credited rate plus a guaranteed spread, then the transfer of the interest rate risk is questionable.

In any event, the transfer of the interest rate risk is dependent upon the terms of the entire reinsurance agreement. Careful examination is advised to determine if any portion of the treaty might negate the risk transfer.

Asset Default. Another major risk element in annuities is asset default. Except for some market value adjusted and variable annuities, any asset loss is absorbed by the insurer, not by the contract holder. This is especially true for immediate annuities. If the reinsurer participates in asset default risks, then it has achieved transfer of risk. This is most obviously the case with coinsurance in its simplest form, without funds withheld, additional guarantees, or other modifications. The reinsurer assumes the guarantees and manages the assets; if any of the assets fail, the reinsurer must make good.

Participation in the asset default risk does not necessarily mean that reserve credits will result. Asset default is not a specific element of normal reserves. A reinsurance agreement which only protects the ceding company from capital losses may not reduce the ceding company's reserve liability even though the reinsurer is definitely at risk.

Voluntary Termination. A reinsurer can be on the persistency risk for annuities just as it can for life insurance. This risk arise in at least three ways: contract surrender, partial withdrawal, or premium reduction or cessation.

For either SPDA's or FPDA's, there can be a risk that the contract will surrender before the acquisition expenses are fully recovered. Partial withdrawals which are higher than expected have much the same effect as increased surrenders. Higher than expected outward cash flows can also lead to disintermediation, where assets might have to be sold below their book value in order to fund the cash payments, compounding the risks associated with voluntary terminations.

With flexible premium contracts, there is the added hazard that renewal premiums will not be as large as assumed, leading to lower profits or nonrecovery of all of the acquisition expenses.

Single premium immediate annuity contracts of the type discussed in this chapter generally do not have provisions for voluntary termination.

Mortality.   There are several elements of mortality risk in the annuity business.   Perhaps the highest degree of risk arises from the mortality associated with life contingent benefits of structured settlement annuities.   Typically, reinsuring these contracts using either coinsurance or mod-co will transfer the mortality exposure. Similarly, terminal funding annuities include both mortality risks associated with pension funding: more individuals living to collect benefits than assumed and beneficiaries living longer than expected.

Most accumulation products also have exposure to mortality risks.   In many annuities surrender charges do not apply in the event of death.   Higher than assumed mortality leads to fewer assets under management and higher cash pay outs.   On the other hand, improving mortality can make annuity purchase rate guarantees inadequate for the insurer and reinsurer.

Annuitization.   The long term guarantees of annuity purchase rates and benefits are risks to insurers.   As mentioned previously, if mortality improves significantly or interest rates drop significantly, these guarantees can cause losses to the insurer or its reinsurer.

Reinsurance agreements usually provide for the reinsurer to participate in the business after annuitization.   Many agreements, however, allow the reinsurer to settle its participation in annuitizations by payment of a lump sum.   These agreements may call for the payment of an amount related to the reserve or the accumulated value in lieu of a string of annuity payments.   The ceding company is then solely responsible for the annuity benefits.

This is similar in concept to the life reinsurance situation where the beneficiary elects to receive a settlement option pay out other than cash, but the reinsurance is settled as a lump sum payment by the reinsurer to the ceding company.   This treatment is also equivalent to recapture upon annuitization.

Depending on the annuity purchase rates and the profit expected during the pay out period, the payment by the reinsurer may be equal to the full fund or some percentage thereof, either smaller or larger.   Some treaties allow the reinsurer the option to select a lump sum settlement upon annuitization if the annuity purchase rate actually used is more favorable than that guaranteed in the annuity contract.

If the reinsurer participates in the benefit pay out, it will change its reserves to reflect the new liabilities.   Statutory reserves often increase when a contract annuitizes because the reserves must now reflect the present value of the future benefits;   during the accumulation phase, reserves reflected only the accumulation and cash values.

Administration

Reinsurance of annuities is nearly always done on a quota share basis with self administration or simplified accounting if the volume of contracts reinsured is significant. Listings or other forms of notification are sometimes provided to the reinsurer showing contractholder names and pertinent data if the reinsurer is concerned about limits on amounts issued to single individuals.

If coinsurance is used, the reinsurer would be wise to request information regarding the liabilities which will enable it to select investments of appropriate maturity and yield. As mentioned previously, asset management is perhaps the single most important element of profitability for annuity writers or reinsurers.

STRUCTURING REINSURANCE

Clarity of asset management and of crediting strategies are the most important elements to consider in structuring an annuity reinsurance treaty. Care must be taken to define each party's responsibilities and rights. If coinsurance is chosen, the treaty should be constructed to ensure that the ceding company will be able to take reserve credits. This might mean that the reinsurer yields all rights to set crediting rates to the ceding company, regardless of the investment performance of the reinsurer. The treaty also should be clear regarding the reinsurer's participation in future premiums, expenses, and annuitizations.

Since relatively large sums of money are involved with annuities, it is perhaps even more important to be comfortable with the integrity of the reinsurance partner than it is for the reinsurance of other types of business. Trust is important because all elements of crediting strategy and investments cannot be defined in advance for all future years. New regulations, changing economic conditions, or new investment vehicles may arise which will have to be addressed by both parties. In spirit, reinsurance of annuities, especially those in the accumulation phase, is more of a partnership than an indemnity arrangement.

21 | Reinsurance of Other Lines and Products

The earlier chapters of this book have dealt with general issues regarding individual life, health, and annuity reinsurance. This chapter addresses special considerations which are unique to selected life insurance products or provisions.

Some of the products and problems discussed in this chapter are no longer current. Other products are new in concept and reinsurance procedures are still evolving. This discussion is not intended to be complete, as reinsurance is a dynamic tool, but to serve as a guide in responding to new reinsurance needs and opportunities.

CREDIT INSURANCE

Credit life and credit disability insurance are generally reinsured as a package. That is, a reinsurer will usually receive both the credit life and credit disability reinsurance from a particular company. While reinsurers may share the reinsurance ceded from a company, it would be uncommon for one reinsurer to receive only credit life, with another reinsurer receiving only the credit disability. However, it is not unusual for the reinsurer's share of the life insurance to be different than its share of the disability insurance.

Historically, most credit insurance has been issued on a single premium basis. However, monthly premium credit insurance currently is often issued in conjunction revolving credit loans or for loans of large amounts.

Credit insurance may be purchased on a single life or on a joint life basis. Credit insurance may be issued on an individual or group basis. Underwriting is generally limited in either event. The premiums usually are not age distinct. Joint life premiums are generally 50% higher than single life rates.

Credit reinsurance is generally administered by the ceding company, using bulk or simplified accounting procedures. Reinsurance may be ceded on either an excess or a quota share basis. The quota share method would be used to simplify administration or to relieve a surplus strain problem. It is not uncommon for the reinsurer to be a captive reinsurer of the distribution system.[1]

Credit reinsurance is almost always ceded on a coinsurance basis. The use of mod-co is fairly rare, but coinsurance using funds withheld by the ceding company or assets deposited in trust are common. This is largely the result of ceding to reinsurers that are licensed in only one state, usually not the ceding company's state of domicile.

Credit life insurance and credit disability insurance have differing degrees of complexity, reserving requirements, premium limitations, and profit levels and emergence patterns. Consequently, each is reinsured differently, as discussed below.

Credit Life

Of the two forms of credit insurance, credit life is usually the simplest and more profitable form. Because the gross premium is usually in excess of the initial mortality reserves required on credit life, the surplus drain is much less than for credit disability insurance. In some cases, the commissions may be structured so that there is no surplus strain. Accordingly, reinsurers frequently insist on a share of the life insurance if they are requested to provide credit disability reinsurance.

Credit life insurance is generally purchased to cover the full amount of the loan. Such coverage is usually purchased on a single premium basis. If the insured pays the loan off early or decides to cancel the insurance, he is entitled to refund of his unearned premium.

---

[1]See Chapter 17, Captive Reinsurance.

Critical period coverage has become more common recently as loan amounts have increased. This provides protection for a period of time less than the amortization period of the loan. This limitation is utilized to reduce costs to the consumer while providing protection during the period where the outstanding balance of the loan is at its highest. This coverage is more likely to be sold on a monthly premium basis.

Credit insurance is also solicited with most credit card or revolving credit accounts. The premiums for this coverage are added to the monthly billings of the creditor and vary with the loan balance. The benefit each month is the credit balance for that month.

In addition to mortality risk sharing, there are several reasons for a company to reinsure credit life insurance risks. These reasons include the need to offset the surplus strain resulting from morality reserves and acquisition expenses and the specific business purposes discussed in Chapter 17, Captive Reinsurance.

Credit Disability

Credit disability insurance is the more volatile of the two forms of credit insurance, and usually involves more surplus strain due to the unearned gross premium reserve requirements. Commissions on credit insurance are quite high, so the cash left to the insurer after paying commissions is inadequate to cover the unearned premium reserve.

If surplus strain is a problem for the reinsurer, as may be the case with a captive reinsurance company, credit disability reinsurance may be ceded on an earned premium basis so that the reinsurer will not be required to establish any active life reserves. The earned premium for each period is developed as the reinsurer's share of the corresponding reduction in the gross unearned premium reserve for the covered policies. Expense allowances are usually expressed as a percentage of the earned premiums. Each period, the ceding company remits to the reinsurer the earned premiums less earned expense allowances and less the reinsurer's share of paid claims. The ceding company also reports the information necessary for the reinsurer to establish the necessary claim reserves and liabilities so that it can report claims on an incurred basis. If the sum of allowances and paid claims exceeds the earned premium for a given reporting period, the reinsurer must pay the deficit to the ceding company.

Experience Rating

In the world of credit reinsurance, the term *experience rating* can refer to either of two calculations. In the first, the direct insurer may pay an experience based commission or profit sharing amount to the distribution source based on that account's experience. In the second, the reinsurer may pay an experience refund to the ceding company based on the experience of the reinsured block.

If the credit insurance program includes a provision for an experience commission or profit sharing to be paid to the agency or sponsoring company, the reinsurance agreement may include provision for the reinsurer to participate in the distribution. If not, the ceding company may find it has to share profits it does not have. Alternatively, the experience rating calculation may provide that reinsurance premiums and claims are netted out of the gross results in determining any refunds.

If the ceding company administers the business, it usually charges a fee to cover its administrative costs and to produce a profit. This fee is commonly known as the retention, not to be confused with the ceding company's retention of risk or retention limit. The retention charge is normally deducted in the experience refund formula.

Credit reinsurance can also be subject to experience rating like any other reinsurance contract. However, in some credit reinsurance contracts, the experience rating provision can act in reverse of the normal procedure. If the experience on the reinsurance falls below an agreed upon level, the reinsurer can demand refund of part of the ceding commission. This provision is known as a contingent or sliding commission or a claw-back.

For example, if the reinsurer grants a 60% allowance and the business develops losses of 38%, the reinsurer could recover enough allowance to cover its agreed upon retention, say 6%. There is usually a cap on the recoverable amount of the allowance, such as 15% of the original premium. Ceding companies do not usually reserve for this contingent cost; the cause of the payment is the same as that which would cause excess claim losses if the company had retained all the business.

Special Considerations

Credit insurance normally involves small amounts of short-term coverage. Therefore, if credit insurance is ceded on an excess basis, the volume of reinsurance ceded is normally quite low. The amount of underwriting information received is usually quite limited. Credit insurance is generally issued on a simplified underwriting basis using a two to four question application. Because of this, the mortality and morbidity experience will be significantly worse than individually underwritten life insurance.

Because competition in the credit insurance marketplace is at the distribution source level, rather than at the consumer level, a "reverse competition" situation exists. In short, the higher the premiums and commissions, the more likely that a company will sell through a given source.

To provide some protection to the consumer, state regulators have placed limits on the premium and commission levels allowed. Credit insurance premiums may not exceed these maximum legislated premiums, called the *prima facie rates*, unless it can be demonstrated that a company's experience exceeds that level.

Some states employ mandated loss ratios, causing larger credit insurance groups to develop premium rates based on the experience of that group alone, even if that experience produces rates lower than the legislated maximum rates.

The reinsurer should be aware of any maximum premium or commission rates or mandated loss ratios which apply to the risks that it will reinsure.

The reinsurance pricing actuary will use the same techniques as the ceding company actuary. While mortality, morbidity, and persistency experience may vary by the purpose of the loan, generalized assumptions are commonly used. Prior experience on the ceding company's credit business and on the specific block offered for reinsurance should be analyzed before establishing pricing assumptions.

Pricing techniques are usually fairly simple, often involving only the anticipated loss ratios and expenses. If the arrangement is to be conducted on an experience rated basis, a larger gross profit objective may be included in the assumptions. The credit reinsurance market is very competitive, and profit margins may be small.

Credit insurance is subject to an unusual risk in that it is not uncommon for a third party sponsor, such as a credit card issuer, to switch the insurance to a new carrier. Most coverage is group insurance and the group contract holder can move coverage at its will. The reinsurer must be aware of this possibility when setting its rates and allowance, especially if early losses are expected. It should examine the direct insurance contract and discuss the third party sponsor with the ceding company to determine its exposure to such switching.

GROUP LIFE AND AD&D INSURANCE

The demand for group life and accidental death and dismemberment (AD&D) reinsurance has grown as the demand for higher issue limits has grown. The demand for guaranteed issue or limited underwriting has also increased. Issue limits without evidence of $500,000 or even $1,000,000 are not uncommon. In order to provide such coverage, many companies have turned to reinsurers.

Group life and AD&D insurance can be reinsured on an excess or on a quota share basis. When using an excess basis, the ceding company reinsures amounts on lives in excess of the retention limit. Generally, the reinsurer will assume 100% of all risks in excess of the ceding company's group life retention limit, but if that retention is small, the reinsurer may require the ceding company to retain a percentage of the excess in order to maintain an interest in properly insuring large risks without any underwriting evidence.

Excess reinsurance is sometimes further divided into excess risks and high limit or catastrophic risks. A working excess retention refers to a retention level set to produce a reasonable number of claims. A high limit, or catastrophic excess, refers to an excess situation where the retention limit is at a high level so that few reinsurance claims are anticipated. Pricing and the assessment of fluctuation should recognize the actual conditions of the situation.

Excess life reinsurance agreements are usually on a YRT basis, often with an experience refund provision. The typical requirements imposed by the reinsurer for a refunding arrangement include a minimum amount of premium, the use of a working excess type retention, and a cap on the maximum amount of insurance per life which may be included in the calculation of the refund. Amounts in excess of this limit are reinsured on a non-refunding basis, usually with a different premium per unit.

The quota share method closely resembles the quota share method used for individual life reinsurance. The ceding company cedes a percentage of each risk. The reinsurer pays the ceding company an allowance to cover the ceding company's commissions and expenses. Under a quota share arrangement, the reinsurer may actually control the premium rates of the ceding company or at least participate in the rate setting process. While quota share reinsurance of group life is usually on a coinsurance basis, YRT may also be used. Group AD&D is usually reinsured on a YRT basis and is nearly always employs simplified administration.

Group insurance is usually term insurance, but group permanent insurance is also available. Reinsurance of group permanent is usually done on a YRT plan, based on the net amount at risk. Traditional coinsurance, applying allowances to the ceding company's premiums rates, is feasible, but the volume may not justify the effort.

The term *coinsurance* used in the group reinsurance field normally refers to a variation of quota share reinsurance. Under a coinsurance approach, the ceding company sets its own premium rates and the amount which the reinsurer pays to the ceding company is called the commission rather than a ceding allowance. Coinsurance arrangements are usually managed on a refunding basis.

Catastrophic reinsurance[2] (cat cover) refers to coverage of claims on the occurrence of a specified event. A cat cover usually requires a minimum number of deaths to occur in a single catastrophic event for a claim to be incurred and may provide for a deductible of three or more maximum retentions. The reinsurer then pays all or a percentage of excess claims, subject to a per event maximum.

Group life and AD&D retention limits are generally lower than individual life limits because of limited underwriting and lower total premiums in the group line.

Companies reinsure group life and AD&D coverages for largely the same reasons that they reinsure individual life. Examples of this include claim fluctuation protection, surplus relief, and service[3]. Other reasons for reinsuring group life and AD&D business include the need or desire to increase the limits for guaranteed or simplified underwriting issues, to minimize the negative effect of claims from a few large groups, and to minimize the fluctuations of a small line of business.

When pricing group life and AD&D reinsurance, the reinsurance actuary must consider underwriting guidelines, waiver of premium and other disability provisions, guaranteed issue limits, benefit structure, and optional amounts of insurance. The reinsur-

---

[2]See Chapter 15, Nonproportional Reinsurance.

[3]See Chapter 1, Introduction.

ance actuary uses the same pricing techniques as the ceding
company actuary. When pricing catastrophe coverage, the pricing
actuary should consider the concentration of risks at any particular
geographic location and any special hazards inherent to the group.

SELECT AND ULTIMATE TERM INSURANCE

Select and ultimate term and graded premium whole life (GPWL)
products captured the lion's share of the term insurance market in
the early 1980's. These products feature a premium scale which is
dependent on the insured's original issue age and current duration.
Select and ultimate products nearly always contain a "re-entry"
provision allowing the insured to reenter, or receive rates similar to
those for a new policy every few years. The premium rates of the
reentered policy are based on the insured's current age and are
normally substantially lower than the premiums based on the
insured's original issue age and current duration.

For those who reenter, these products will result in
substantial cost savings along with more commission income for
the agent. The major problem with these products is that the
group that does not qualify for re-entry will experience very
substandard mortality. This poor mortality coupled with poor
persistency inherent in the product's structure caused the
experience to be much worse than originally anticipated. This, in
turn, caused several reinsurers to cease reinsuring such products.
Most of the reinsurers that remained in this market became much
more cautious in their pricing.

Coinsurance has always been the favored method of
reinsuring these term products. In many respects, developing
coinsurance allowances is like developing a YRT rate scale for each
product. Rules for medical and other underwriting evidence and
overall underwriting practices vary significantly between the issuers
of re-entry products. The major pricing consideration in reinsuring
these products is for the reinsurance actuary to understand the
rules for re-entry and the way in which the products are marketed.
This knowledge will influence assumptions for both mortality and
persistency. The treaty must be very clear on topics such as re-
entry underwriting and allowances. Policy continuation and
change procedures are also very important[4].

---

[4]See Chapter 22, Selected Additional Reinsurance Topics.

NONGUARANTEED ELEMENTS IN LIFE INSURANCE CONTRACTS

The introduction of universal life and excess interest whole life in the early 1980's changed the face of the life insurance market. The unique design of these products also changed reinsurance pricing and administration. These products featured somewhat modest interest rate guarantees and relatively high mortality charge guarantees with actual interest rates and mortality charges being redetermined periodically.

Setting credited interest rates is somewhat of an art. An insurer and its reinsurer can easily have different investment portfolios and reasons to credit different rates. The interest element in these products is very important from a marketing viewpoint. The ceding company has a direct relationship with the insured and needs to be able to set rates independently.

Reinsurance of non-guaranteed elements can be difficult because the interest credits to the policyholder and the mortality charges are not set in advance. The ceding company wants to be unrestricted by reinsurance considerations in setting the credited interest rate. While coinsurance is possible, it requires detailed cooperation and agreement between the ceding company and the reinsurer in establishing credited rates and investments. The considerations are essentially the same as those described for interest sensitive annuities in Chapter 20.

Mod-co allows the ceding company to retain control of the assets and, therefore, control over the credited interest rate. Even so, the reinsurer could still be vulnerable to aggressive, nonprofitable interest crediting strategies used by the direct insurer. Difficulties in developing mutually agreeable interest crediting strategies and profit objectives have prevented the extensive use of mod-co for interest sensitive product reinsurance.

While coinsurance and modified coinsurance treaties involving interest sensitive products have been infrequent, some do exist. When used, they have required careful discussion, negotiation, and documentation of mutually acceptable investment and interest crediting strategies.

Most reinsurance of interest sensitive products has involved YRT reinsurance or the "coinsurance" of the mortality element of the policy. The YRT scales used for reinsurance purposes on these products are generally made specifically for each product and are usually expressed in coinsurance terms, based on allowances applied to the cost of insurance rates used in the policy. In fact, because the mortality premiums in an interest sensitive product are normally expressed as ART premiums, there is no economic or cash flow difference between YRT and coinsurance of the cost of insurance rates. The difference lies largely in the choice of terminology.

The three primary classes of life insurance products which feature non-guaranteed elements are interest sensitive whole life, universal life, and variable life. In addition, most term insurance plans and many ordinary life insurance plans feature indeterminate premiums, which are not guaranteed to remain at the initial level. These four general classes of products and some of the reinsurance considerations regarding them are discussed in this section.

Interest Sensitive Whole Life

Interest sensitive whole life is a fixed, level premium form of permanent life insurance. Like any level premium whole life product, it has guaranteed cash values to comply with the Standard Nonforfeiture Law. However, this product also has an accumulation element using insurer declared interest rates which are usually higher than the policy guaranteed rate. The actual cash surrender value is the greater of the accumulation fund and the guaranteed cash value. The products generally contains either front-end loads or surrender charges.

As with all interest sensitive life products, this level premium product is generally reinsured on a YRT basis. Most often, it is reinsured on a self-administered basis with the reinsurance premium calculation coinciding with the normal fund calculation, such as once a month. Because continued premium payment is required to keep the product from going on nonforfeiture status, the net amount at risk can be projected more accurately. Because of this, it is possible to use an individual cession approach or an annual premium approach.

Universal Life

Universal life products have flexible premiums which can be paid at any time and in any amount. Projections of future cash values are very difficult and largely futile, making normal individual cession accounting difficult. Accumulation amounts vary monthly and the projection of net amounts at risk is uncertain. Most universal life products are administered by the ceding company with monthly premiums based on the costs of insurance rates and individual notification of issues and terminations so the reinsurer can arrange for retrocession if needed.

The above discussion assumes that the ceding company wants to reinsure the exact amounts at risk. It is possible to use projected cash values and reinsure the resulting net amount at risk. Both reinsurance premiums and claims are then based on this predetermined net amount at risk. While not precisely matching the insurer's exposure, this method allows more simple and less costly administration.

Variable Life

Variable life insurance creates problems of administration and in projection of net amounts at risk similar to those of universal life. The solution is usually the same, utilizing self-administration and YRT premiums. Variable life has asset based fees for mortality, not cost of insurance rates, so regular YRT rates are used. Administration can be on an individual cession basis with approximate net amounts at risk or the ceding company may use exact calculations on a self administration basis.

Indeterminate Premium Policies

Many individual insurance products today do not guarantee gross premiums for future years, or may guarantee only that the future premium will not exceed a certain level. This level is usually at or above the statutory net valuation premium. This allows the insurer to avoid having to establish deficiency reserves as it would have to do if it guaranteed rates at the initial level. The practice also provides the insurer some protection in that it can increase premiums if projected experience falls below that assumed in the initial pricing or the last repricing of the product. It may also reduce rates if anticipated experience and competition so indicate.

The use of indeterminate premiums provides some complications for the reinsurance agreement, however. Specifically, there are complications of establishing new allowances for coinsurance or modified coinsurance if the insurer changes rates, either up or down. If the reinsurer guarantees to always accept the same net cost, it could be held responsible for deficiency reserves the ceding company does not have to hold. If the reinsurer has an independent right to change premiums, then the ceding company could find itself in a position where its reinsurance premiums will exceed its gross premiums.

Some reinsurance agreements have addressed this concern by stating that the reinsurer will participate in the new rates with the original allowances. Other agreements give the reinsurer the right to change allowances in a manner that leaves the net amount of premium less allowance the same. In any event, it is advised that any reinsurance treaty covering indeterminate premium plans address this issue.

DEPOSIT TERM

Deposit term products present a unique reinsurance problem. These products feature an additional premium in the first year. This premium is several times larger than the basic term premium. The underlying term policy may be an ART, five year renewable term, or most common historically, a ten year renewable term product followed by a whole life policy or a decreasing term policy to age 100. The excess of the initial premium over the basic first year term premium is referred to as the "deposit."

In most products, the deposit normally "grows at interest" to two to three times its original size and is returned at the end of ten to twelve years. The deposit feature was created to improve persistency. In some cases, persistency did improve, but the profit improvement which would be expected was often negated by high first year commissions and agency financing costs.

The original deposit term policy did not develop cash values until near the end of the deposit period, but modifications in the Standard Nonforfeiture Law changed this situation and cash values are now required at early durations. Before the introduction of cash values, it was more profitable for the insurer if the insured lapsed before the end of the term period. Coinsurance was commonly used because the high commissions created considerable surplus strain. It was not unusual for the ceding company to request first year coinsurance allowances which exceeded the total first year premium including the deposit. In some instances, to avoid the risk of loss from lapse, the reinsurer would offer to coinsure the underlying term product and not participate in the deposit or investment element of the policy.

Reinsurance premiums may be paid either on the actual modal basis or annually, and may include or exclude the deposit. Allowances are usually annualized, at least in the first year. Frequently, allowances are calculated as a combination of percent of premium and an amount per policy issued or in force. When expressed as percentages of the basic first year premium, excluding the deposit, the allowance may be a much as 400% of the term premium. In this case, a chargeback is often required. The chargeback feature provides that if a policy terminates prior to a certain period or prior to the point where reinsurance premiums received exceed reinsurance allowances paid, the ceding company will return the excess of allowances paid over premiums collected[5].

INCREASING BENEFITS

Products with increasing benefits can present special problems for the determination of reinsurance. One problem concerns policies which fall within the ceding companies retention limit at issue, but may in later years exceed the retention limit because of the increasing benefits. Since experience under benefit increases has demonstrated antiselection, reinsurers prefer to participate in a broad cross-section of business, not just in the increases. Unless special arrangements are made when the policy is issued, it is unlikely that a reinsurer would accept reinsurance arising from the increases.

The two principle types of increasing benefits are guaranteed insurability option (GIO) and cost of living adjustment (COLA), usually issued as riders. Both benefits allow the insured to increase the death benefit without any underwriting or evidence of insurability, regardless of any change in underwriting class, under specified conditions or at specific intervals.

A GIO rider provides the policyholder with options to purchase additional policies at certain specified intervals or at the occurrence of certain specified events, such as marriage or the birth of a child. The maximum amount of each benefit increase is defined in advance. The policyholder pays premiums for a standard issue at his then current age.

A COLA rider provides for death benefits on a policy to increase annually at the same rate as the change in a prescribed cost of living index, subject to some maximum limit. Normally, if the policyholder declines the increase in any year, he forfeits the right to exercise any future increases. Premiums on the policy are

---

[5]For further discussion of chargeback mechanics, see Chapter 9, Managing Assumed Reinsurance.

increased to reflect the new death benefits, usually treating these amounts as term insurance.

The simplest method for reinsuring increases is to employ YRT using point-in-scale rates. Coinsurance is also feasible, depending on policy design and rate structure. The presence of cash values may complicate administration.

The most important reinsurance consideration regarding such riders is that the agreement be clear as to the treatment of the future increases. At the outset of the treaty, it is necessary to determine how the increases will be apportioned between the ceding company and the reinsurer. The reinsurer may be willing to absorb all the increases, but many prefer that the ceding company share the increases on a quota share basis.

The quota share method is used to ensure that the ceding company maintains an interest in the policy and has designed the benefits in a reasonable manner. For example, if the reinsurer has 35% of the initial risk, it will agree to assume 35% of all future increases in risk. It is common for a ceding company to reduce its initial retention to a point that its future share, if all options are exercised, will not exceed its maximum retention at issue of the policy. Others will assume their retention will increase in the future and keep a somewhat larger portion of the initial risk.

On occasion, the reinsurer will agree to assume future increases with no participation in the initial risk. This procedure requires the ceding company to notify its reinsurer of any guaranteed insurability options issued. The reinsurer then indexes this information and treats its business as though it had a current risk, arranging retrocession for any other business it might receive on that life. Since the reinsurer guarantees future coverage, it charges a premium to the ceding company. This premium may be a single premium, an annual premium developed like that of a YRT scale, or coinsurance premiums based on the ceding company's premium for the option with coinsurance allowances.

LIVING BENEFIT RIDERS

In the late 1980's, life insurance companies introduced a new group of benefits broadly classified as living benefits. The provisions allow the policyholder to collect some portion of the death benefit prior to death. The terms vary by insurer. In some situations the policyholder must be diagnosed as suffering from one of several specifically designated fatal diseases. In others, he must meet certain criteria regarding illness or medical expense.

Some of these benefits are an advance on cash values. Others, however, are a prepayment of death benefits. The reinsurance agreement should be clear as to the responsibility of the reinsurer relative to these payments. Extra premiums are charged for most of these benefits, and the reinsurer needs to share in this income if it is to participate in the benefits. These benefits are usually coinsured, but YRT can be used.

22 | Selected Additional Reinsurance Topics

The earlier chapters of this book have dealt with general issues regarding individual life, health, and annuity reinsurance. This chapter covers some special considerations which are unique to certain product features or to certain underwriting and issue programs. In addition, some of the special uses and concerns of reinsurance with affiliated companies are addressed.

DEFICIENCY RESERVES

Deficiency reserves can be a major source of surplus strain. At times, the strain is so great that reinsurance is sought simply because of the need for surplus to cover the deficiency reserves.

In order to transfer deficiency reserves, coinsurance or modified coinsurance must be used. The use of YRT reinsurance will not transfer deficiency reserves. Mod-co can be used to fund the ceding company's deficiency reserve liability if the deficiency reserves are included in the mod-co reserves. Alternatively, a mod-co agreement can transfer deficiency reserves if the agreement specifies mod-co treatment of the basic plan, but coinsurance for the deficiency reserves. In the latter case, the reinsurer must be admitted in the ceding company's state of domicile or some acceptable form of security must be employed.

Although it has been attempted, it is a basic tenet of reinsurance that it is not possible to reinsure deficiency reserves alone. The related policy benefits must also be reinsured.

In the past, insurance products which had deficiency reserves were coinsured with companies located in jurisdictions, foreign or domestic, which had less stringent reserve requirements. In such transactions, the deficiency reserves sometimes vanished[1] as neither company held them.

If the reinsurer was an admitted reinsurer, the ceding company normally would take credit in its statement for all reserves, including deficiency reserves. However, some reinsurers would not hold the deficiency reserves if they were not required by their state of domicile. If the reinsurer was not admitted, it would purchase a letter of credit to cover the total reserves, including deficiency reserves, but only establish those reserves required by its domestic regulators. In either situation, the ceding company would take credit for reserves which the reinsurer did not hold.

Some regulators have expressed concern about these transactions and such treaties may be subject to increased scrutiny. These regulators regard the regulatory reserve requirements as being designed to ensure that certain minimum reserves are established and that premiums are adequate to maintain reserves at that level. Vanishing reserves are believed to circumvent that system.

As a result of these concerns and some blatant exploitations of the system, regulators have pursued concepts such as mirror reserving[2] in an attempt to guarantee that total reserves of all insurers and reinsurers for a given policy are at least equal to the required minimum reserves.

DIVIDEND OPTIONS

Insurers have developed many different and creative dividend options. Some of these are used to purchase additional death benefits which may increase both gross death benefits and net amounts at risk. These increases in turn will affect the need for

---

[1]See Chapter 10, Reinsurance Regulations.

[2]*Ibid.*

reinsurance. The considerations for reinsuring these benefits are similar to those for increasing benefits.[3]

Most frequently, reinsurance of these benefits is on a YRT basis. Participation by the reinsurer is proportionate to its participation in the base policy. Since most dividend options used to increase death benefits are applied as single premiums, coinsurance is a logical method for purchasing any needed reinsurance. However, applying YRT reinsurance to the net amount at risk is also simple and reasonable. The primary concern is to address the treatment of dividend purchases in the treaty so confusion or disagreement does not arise later.

CONVERSION, REISSUE, AND CHANGE

As noted in Chapter 6, the reinsurance treaty usually spells out specific rules concerning conversions, reissues, and other changes including reductions, terminations, and reinstatements.

The most common type of conversion involves the replacement of term insurance coverage with a whole life plan of insurance. The new policy's premiums and values are based on the insured's attained age at the time of conversion. In essence, this is a new issue which has no evidence of insurability. Any reinsurance would continue with the original reinsurer using point-in-scale YRT rates.

Conversions may also be made based on the insured's original issue age and date. In this case, the policyholder will make up any deficiency in cash value or reserve between the old policy and the new one. The plan of reinsurance will depend on the original plan of reinsurance and the terms of the reinsurance treaty. Most commonly, reinsurance is on a YRT basis, with the net amount at risk based on the new reserve and point-in-scale rates.

Reissues usually involve treating the reinsurance in the same manner as would have applied to the new issue from inception. Both reissues and other policy changes usually involve adjusting both parties' shares of the risk proportionately.

---

[3]See Chapter 21, Reinsurance of Other Lines and Products.

REPLACEMENT PROGRAMS

Replacement programs, both internal and external, are sometimes major sources of business for insurers. Reinsurance for these programs can be complicated and should be clarified before the insurer initiates the programs. Otherwise, the insurer may find that its reinsurance on the policies involved is more costly than expected or even that it does not have reinsurance coverage. Reinsurance administration has also been complicated by replacement programs.

Internal Replacements

Some insurers have offered their policyholders the opportunity to exchange an existing policy for a new one based on a new policy form. Reasons insurance companies adopt such programs are to provide increased policyholder benefits, improve the company's tax position, and prevent replacement by other companies.

Typically, the insurer issues the new policy with a current issue date and issue age. Before initiating the internal replacement program, the insurer will normally do an analysis of the net costs involved to determine the program's feasibility. This involves, among other things, repricing the replacement product to reflect its use in the replacement program. The mortality assumptions are different from those that entered into the original pricing of the replacement product since the insureds are not being reunderwritten. The increased mortality costs are sometimes offset by the payment of lower commissions than were originally provided. The cost of reinsurance, if based on a point-in-scale approach, will also be greater than originally assumed. Depending on the amount of the reinsurance involved, the program may prove to be economically infeasible using this reinsurance cost basis.

It is important that the insurer reach an agreement with the original reinsurer as to the basis for the reinsurance rates to be used for these programs before they are initiated. The reinsurer is likely to refuse to accept the replacement program issues, at least without modification in its rates, and the insurer could find itself with no reinsurance coverage.

External Replacements

External replacements may create even more problems for reinsurance. External replacement, in this discussion, refers to a company's program to replace the policy of another insurer with a new policy of its own without new underwriting.

The ceding company's current automatic reinsurer is likely to deny coverage under its normal agreement because normal underwriting has not been followed. Unless the insurer negotiates reinsurance terms in advance, it likely will find that it has no reinsurance. The insurer may try to negotiate a special arrangement with the current reinsurer to cover the program and, if unsuccessful, may have to seek a new reinsurance carrier.

General Practices

Most reinsurers have evolved practices with respect to replacement programs which allow reinsurance coverage to be granted. While not firmly established, the following guidelines are contained in many reinsurance agreements:

(1) Internal replacements are treated as continuations or conversions, with reinsurance being continued with the original reinsurer at point-in-scale costs. Other terms may be negotiated between that reinsurer and the ceding company.
(2) Internal replacements may be reinsured with a new reinsurer if the original reinsurer gives its permission.
(3) External replacements can be reinsured with any reinsurer that will take the business. They are not covered by an agreement intended for new issues subject to normal underwriting unless the replacement program requires such underwriting or the reinsurer specifically agrees to terms and underwriting for the replacement program.

REINSURANCE WITH AFFILIATES

Reinsurance between affiliated companies follows the same basic principles as reinsurance between unrelated parties. There are some special aspects to consider. This section addresses selected topics involving reinsurance from one affiliated insurance company to another. Neither party need be a professional reinsurer.

Uses

Reinsurance can provide strategic or tactical opportunities for company to better manage two or more life insurance subsidiaries.

For example, reinsurance may provide an easy way to move capital from one insurance company to another using coinsurance with large initial allowances. No stock or debt instruments need to be involved, and movement of funds across state or national borders can be accomplished with relative ease. The surplus repayment comes from statutory earnings, not dividends, and may receive more favorable tax treatment than would dividends.

Reinsurance can assist with capital needs in several ways. Allowances can be constructed so as to permit the financially stronger company to incur the acquisition expenses of the company in need of relief. Risks can also be transferred, reducing the need for surplus.

Reinsurance may be a tax preferred way to move surplus and risks, especially internationally. Capital contributions typically would be earned and taxed in one company, paid in dividends to another, taxed again, and contributed to the carrier needing surplus. On repayment, the whole process would be reversed.

On another level, reinsurance between affiliates can be used to maximize the retention of a commonly held group of companies, reducing the volume of reinsurance ceded outside the group. Presumably this will increase total profits by reducing the cost of reinsurance.

Other opportunities are available in which reinsurance may be creatively and legitimately used between affiliates. The key is to define the problem to be addressed and then apply the principles of unrelated party reinsurance to design an acceptable program.

Concerns

There are, naturally, some additional concerns to be addressed when dealing with reinsurance between affiliates. Many agreements between affiliates have developed serious problems because the treaties received inadequate attention at the time of drafting. It is advisable to devote at least the same time and attention to affiliated party reinsurance as to unrelated party agreements. Failure to do so may undermine tax strategies or corporate financial planning, especially with respect to statutory reporting.

One rule of thumb frequently used is whether or not the agreement meets the "arm's length" test. In other words, would each party enter into a similar agreement with an unrelated party with terms negotiated at arm's length. While it is not a guarantee, if the answer is affirmative, the agreement will likely meet most tests. If the answer is negative, the agreement may need to be reexamined to ensure that it meets all needs and will stand the test of time.

Another reason to devote as much time and effort to related party transactions as to others is that one or both companies may be sold and the parties might become unrelated. Several related party transactions have ended in arbitration or in court following the sale of one or both parties.

For the same reasons, administration of related party reinsurance should be just as fastidious and thorough as that for any other agreement. Lack of attention to items such as regulation, financial reporting, and taxation has caused some affiliated reinsurance agreements to fail to meet their objectives.

Regulation. Regulation of affiliated reinsurance is not very different than that of any other reinsurance. The terms should be those of an arm's length transaction. The reinsurance treaty provisions must be clear and the reinsurer must honor all commitments related to claims, benefits, and reserves.

The Model Holding Company Act developed by the NAIC contains provisions regarding reinsurance between affiliated companies. Most states have adopted modifications of this act or apply its guidelines in some manner. Companies considering an affiliated reinsurance transaction are advised to review this and other applicable laws before finalizing any agreement.

In particular, some states have adopted more stringent rules about accepting letters of credit for reserve credits if a related party is involved as either a reinsurer, a retrocessionaire, or the bank granting the letter of credit.

GAAP Reporting. GAAP accounting is usually on a consolidated basis for companies with common ownership. The effect of consolidated GAAP treatment of related party transactions should be that no net gain or loss from the transaction is reflected. If one company reports a GAAP gain, the other should show a corresponding GAAP loss. If ownership is not identical, say, for example, there is only partial overlap of ownership, then GAAP results may differ from those described.

The GAAP provisions for taxes may not cancel out, however, since the ceding company and the reinsurer may be in different tax positions and taxed at different rates. Also, one party may be in an alternative minimum tax position and the other not, leading to tax results which may not offset each other.

Taxation. The IRS has tended to give careful scrutiny to related party reinsurance. Section 845(a) of the Internal Revenue Code specifically grants the IRS broad authority to reverse or reallocate the effects of reinsurance transactions between related parties. A arm's length argument may not be suffi-cient protection from IRS action.

The tax effects of consolidation must be considered when designing related party reinsurance. Expected benefits in one company could be more than offset by the tax effects on the other or in the consolidation. Internal allocations of taxes may be affected by reinsurance. The effects of the transaction on alternative minimum taxes should be anticipated.

REINSURANCE INTERMEDIARIES

In the property and casualty market, the majority of reinsurance is placed through reinsurance intermediaries, also referred to as brokers, because few property and casualty reinsurers employ a sales staff. In the traditional life reinsurance market, most professional reinsurers have sales staffs and the ceding companies' reinsurance needs are fairly straightforward, so intermediaries are infrequently encountered. However, reinsurance intermediaries are sometimes used for situations involving unusual or large trans-actions, such as financial or nonproportional reinsurance, where special expertise or market access is needed. Brokerage involve-ment is common for accident and health reinsurance.

In a typical transaction involving intermediaries, the intermediary does not represent a specific reinsurer, but purports to search the market for the best quote. He works with the ceding company to put together a package to fill its reinsurance needs, then approaches reinsurers with the package, and negotiates terms and fees. The intermediary is generally paid on a contingent fee basis. This fee is normally included in the cost of reinsurance and paid by the reinsurer. The ceding company is usually aware of the fee and, in some instances, may pay it directly to the intermediary.

In the life reinsurance market, any funds transferred for any reason generally flow directly between the reinsurer and the ceding company.   However, for property and casualty reinsurance, funds typically pass through the intermediary.   Because of this, the NAIC has recommended the Reinsurance Intermediary Model Act. This act provides for the licensing of reinsurance intermediaries and is designed to protect the ceding company against misappropriation of funds by the intermediary.   The intermediary is required to have written authorization from the ceding company specifying the responsibilities of each party.

The act requires the intermediary to provide the ceding company with reports detailing all material transactions including commissions and fees.   The act also requires the intermediary to keep a complete record of each transaction for at least ten years after the expiration of the contract.   The records must include contract terms, reinsurance premium rates, commissions, records of financial transactions, names and addresses of all reinsurers, and proof of placement.   The intermediary must also provide the ceding company with access to, and the right to copy and audit, all accounts and records.   Conditions are also placed on the intermediary's handling of funds and bank accounts.

If the intermediary is allowed to settle claims on behalf of the reinsurer, the act provides that the intermediary must report all claims to the reinsurer on a timely basis and provide the reinsurer with a copy of the claim file in certain circumstances. These circumstances include, for example, claims that exceed the intermediary's settlement authority, involve coverage disputes, or have been open for more than six months.

Some intermediaries also serve as managers who have authority to perform underwriting services for the reinsurer and bind the reinsurer to risks.   Depending upon their type of responsibilities and the independence of action, intermediaries may be required to have a bond and provide proof of errors and omissions insurance coverage.

New York is currently the most active state in requiring the licensing of intermediaries, but it is expected that other states will soon follow.

Appendix A

REINSURANCE AGREEMENT

between

ABC Life Insurance Company

of

Cederville, U.S.A.

hereinafter referred to as the *"Reinsured,"*

and

XYZ Reinsurance Company

of

Assumption GAAP, U.S.A.

hereinafter referred to as the *"Reinsurer."*

---

[1]This reinsurance treaty is provided to give an example of an indemnity agreement for YRT reinsurance coverage. It has been graciously provided by Lincoln National Life Insurance Company of Fort Wayne, Indiana.

This sample treaty is provided for reference purposes to enhance the reader's understanding. The authors do not endorse this particular treaty or any particular terms; each reinsurance treaty should be designed to reflect the agreement it covers and the requirements of the parties involved.

I.   REINSURANCE COVERAGE
      A. On the basis hereinafter stated, the *reinsured's* excess
         as specified in the subject Reinsurance Schedule of
         individual ordinary life, waiver of premium disability,
         and accidental death insurance issued by the *reinsured*
         on the policy forms listed in the Subject Reinsurance
         Schedule shall be reinsured with the *reinsurer*
         automatically, shall be submitted to the *reinsurer* on a
         facultative basis, or shall be reinsured with the
         reinsurer as continuations; a continuation is a new
         policy replacing a policy issued earlier by the *reinsured*
         ("original policy") or a change in an existing policy
         issued or made either (1) in compliance with the terms
         of the original policy or (2) without the same new
         underwriting information the *reinsured* would obtain in
         the absence of the original policy, without a suicide
         exclusion period or a contestable period as long as those
         contained in new issued by the *reinsured*, or without
         the payment of the same commissions in the first year
         that the *reinsured* would have paid in the absence of
         the original policy.
      B. Subject to the *"Conditional Receipt Reinsurance"*
         article and, in the case of facultative submissions for
         reinsurance, to the *reinsured's* accepting the *reinsurer's*
         offer to reinsure, the liability of the *reinsurer* shall
         begin simultaneously with that of the *reinsured*. In no
         event shall the reinsurance be in force and binding
         unless the insurance issued directly by the *reinsured* is
         in force and unless the issuance and delivery of such
         insurance constituted the doing of business in a
         jurisdiction in which the *reinsured* was properly
         licensed.
      C. Life reinsurance under this Agreement shall be term
         insurance for the amount at risk on the portion of the
         insurance of the original insurance which is reinsured
         with the *reinsurer*. The amount of reinsurance shall be
         the death benefit provided by the portion of the original
         insurance which is reinsured with the *reinsurer*. The
         amount at risk on such a policy shall be the death
         benefit of the policy less the cash value under the
         policy. This amount at risk shall be determined at the
         beginning of each policy year and shall be amended

during that year only if there is a change in the amount of reinsurance on the life arising from a change in the specified amount under the policy reinsured hereunder. For the second and subsequent years, the *reinsured* shall notify the *reinsurer* of the amount at risk for that policy year at least fifteen days before the beginning of that policy year. The portion reinsured shall be the amount at risk on the policy less the *reinsured's* retention on the policy. The basis for determining the amount at risk may be changed for new reinsurance by agreement between the *reinsured* and the *reinsurer.*

D. If the face amount of the policy changes, the portion reinsured hereunder shall continue to be determined as described in section C of this article. If the face amount increases subject to the approval of the *reinsured,* provisions of the *"reinsurance limits"* article hereof shall apply to the increase in reinsurance hereunder. If the face amount increases and such increase is not subject to the *reinsured's* approval, the *reinsurer* shall accept automatically increases in reinsurance arising from such increases in the face amount.

E. Reinsurance of Disability insurance shall follow the original forms of the *reinsured.*

F. Accidental Death reinsurance in amounts less than $_____ or Life reinsurance in amounts less than the amount at risk upon $_____ of insurance shall not be placed in effect under this Agreement.

G. If the *reinsured* issues a policy as a continuation of a policy reinsured under this Agreement, reinsurance of the continuation shall continue with the *reinsurer.* Such reinsurance shall be in effect under the reinsurance agreement between the *reinsured* and the *reinsurer* which provides reinsurance of the policy form issued as a continuation if there is such an agreement in effect on the effective date of the continuation; otherwise, reinsurance shall be in effect under the terms of this Agreement.

H. The amount of reinsurance under this Agreement shall be maintained in force without reduction so long as the amount of insurance carried by the *reinsured* on the life remains in force without reduction, except as provided in the *"Payment of Reinsurance Premiums"* and *"Increase in Limit of Retention"* articles.

II.   REINSURANCE LIMITS

A. If the following requirements are met, reinsurance may be ceded automatically under this Agreement in amounts not to exceed those specified in the Limits Schedule.

(1) The *reinsured* shall retain its limit of retention.

(2) The sum of the amount of insurance already in force on that life in the *reinsured* and the amount applied for from the *reinsured* on the current application shall not exceed the sum of the appropriate automatic limit shown in the Limits Schedule, and the *reinsured's* maximum limit of retention for the mortality class, plan of insurance, and age at issue on the current application.

(3) The sum of the amount of insurance already in force on the life and the amount applied for currently, in all companies, shall not exceed the following amounts.

Ages	Waiver of Premium	Accidental Death
----	------	-----
----	------	-----

(4) The *reinsured* has not made facultative application for reinsurance of the current application.

(5) The policy was issued in accordance with the *reinsured's* normal individual ordinary life underwriting rules and practices.

(6) The policy is not a continuation.

B. If the requirements in section A of this article are not met or if the *reinsured* prefers to do so, it shall make an application for reinsurance under this Agreement on a facultative basis for all issues specified in the Subject Reinsurance Schedule other than continuations; the *reinsured* may, at its option, make application for reinsurance under this Agreement on a facultative basis for other issues.

C. The *reinsurer* shall have no liability under facultative applications for reinsurance unless the *reinsured* has accepted the *reinsurer's* offer to reinsure.

   D. Continuations shall be reinsured under this Agreement only if the original policy was reinsured with the *reinsurer;* the amount of the reinsurance under this Agreement shall not exceed the amount of reinsurance of the original policy with the *reinsurer* immediately prior to the new issue or change.

III.   **PLACING REINSURANCE IN EFFECT**

   A. When the *reinsured* submits a risk to the *reinsurer* for reinsurance upon a facultative basis, a facultative application for such reinsurance shall be made on a form in substantial accord with the appropriate part of the Administrative Forms Schedule. Copies of the original applications, all medical examinations, microscopical reports, inspection reports, and all other information which the *reinsured* may have pertaining to the insurability of the risk shall accompany the application. Upon receipt of such application, the *reinsurer* shall immediately examine the papers and shall notify the *reinsured* of its underwriting action as soon as possible.

   B. To effect reinsurance, the *reinsured* shall, within thirty working days after the original policy has been reported delivered and paid for, mail to the *reinsurer* a reinsurance cession in substantial accord with the appropriate part of the Administrative Forms Schedule. The *reinsurer* shall send the *reinsured* a record of reinsurance ceded in substantial accord with the appropriate part of the Administrative Forms Schedule. Upon request, the *reinsured* shall furnish the *reinsurer* with copies of any underwriting information in he *reinsured's* files.

   C. To effect Accidental Death reinsurance apart from life reinsurance, the *reinsured* shall mail to the *reinsurer* consecutively numbered cards in substantial accord with the appropriate form of the Administrative Forms Schedule. The *reinsured* shall send the cards within thirty working days after the original policy has been reported delivered and paid for.

   D. All offers of reinsurance made by the *reinsurer* under this Agreement shall, unless otherwise terminated by the *reinsurer*, automatically terminate on the earlier of

(1) the date the *reinsurer* receives notice from the *reinsured* of its withdrawal of its application and (2) the later of (i) the date 120 days after the date the offer was made by the *reinsurer* and (ii) the date specified in the *reinsurer's* approval of a written request from the *reinsured* to grant an extension of the offer.

IV. COMPUTATION OF REINSURANCE PREMIUMS
A. The premium to be paid to the *reinsurer* for Life reinsurance shall be the sum of:
(1) the appropriate premium rate from the schedule of premiums in the Premium Schedule applied to the appropriate amount at risk reinsured; plus
(2) any flat extra premium charged the insured on the face amount initially reinsured less total allowances in the amount of 75% of any first year permanent flat extra premium and 10% of any renewal flat extra premium.
B. The portions of the reinsurance premiums described in the subparagraphs of the preceding section shall hereinafter be referred to as the basic premium.
C. The premium charged the *reinsured* for increases in reinsurance hereunder described in section D of the "*reinsurance coverage*" article hereof shall be computed using the age and date of issue of the policy if the increase in face amount is not subject to approval of the *reinsured* and using the age at and date of the increase if the increase in face amount is subject to the *reinsured's* approval.
D. The premium to be paid the *reinsurer* for reinsurance of Supplemental Benefits shall be as shown in the Premium Schedule.
E. For technical reasons relating to the uncertain status of deficiency reserve requirements by the various state insurance departments, the Life reinsurance rates cannot be guaranteed for more than one year. On all reinsurance ceded at these rates, however, the *reinsurer* anticipates continuing to accept premiums on the basis of the rates shown in the Premium Schedule.

V.   PAYMENT OF REINSURANCE PREMIUMS

A. The *reinsurer* shall send the *reinsured* each month a statement in duplicate showing all outstanding first-year policies for which the *reinsurer's* records have been completed and a statement in duplicate showing all renewal reinsurance premiums on reinsurance policies having anniversaries in the preceding month.

B. One copy of each statement received from the *reinsurer* shall be returned to the *reinsurer* not later than fifteen days after the statement was received with notice of any adjustments made necessary by changes in reinsurance during such month.   The *reinsured* shall remit with such statement the premiums due the *reinsurer* as adjusted.   Premiums for reinsurance hereunder are payable at the Home Office of the *reinsurer* or any other location specified by the *reinsurer* and shall be paid on an annual basis without regard to the manner of payment stipulated in the policy issued by the *reinsured.*

C. The payment of reinsurance premiums in accordance with the provisions of the preceding section shall be a condition precedent to the liability of the *reinsurer* under reinsurance covered by this Agreement.   In the event that reinsurance premiums are not paid as provided in the preceding section, the *reinsurer* shall have the right to terminate the reinsurance under all policies having reinsurance premiums in arrears.   If the *reinsurer* elects to exercise its right of termination, it shall give the *reinsured* thirty days' notice of its intention to terminate such reinsurance.   If all reinsurance premiums in arrears, including any which may become in arrears during the thirty-day period, are not paid before the expiration of such period, the *reinsurer* shall thereupon be relieved of future liability under all reinsurance for which premiums remain unpaid.   Policies on which reinsurance premiums subsequently fall due will automatically terminate if reinsurance premiums are not paid when due as provided in section B of this article.   The reinsurance so terminated may be reinstated at any time within sixty days of the date of termination upon payment of all reinsurance premiums in arrears; but, in the event of such reinstatement, the *reinsurer* shall have no liability in connection with any claims incurred between the date of termination and the date of reinstatement of the reinsurance. The *reinsurer's* right to terminate reinsurance as herein provided shall be without prejudice to its right to collect premiums for the period reinsurance was in force prior to the expiration of the thirty-day notice period.

D. Any payment which either the *reinsured* or the *reinsurer* shall be obligated to pay to the other may be paid net of any amount which is then due and unpaid under this Agreement.

VI.   SETTLEMENT OF CLAIMS

A. The *reinsured* shall give the *reinsurer* prompt notice of any claim submitted on a policy reinsured hereunder and prompt notice of the instigation of any legal proceedings in connection therewith. Copies of proofs or other documents bearing on such claim or proceeding shall be furnished to the *reinsurer* when requested.

B. The *reinsurer* shall accept the good faith decision of the *reinsured* in settling any claim or suit and shall pay, at its Home Office, its share of net reinsurance liability upon receiving proper evidence of the *reinsured's* having settled with the claimant. Payment of net reinsurance liability on account of death or dismemberment shall be made in one lump sum. In settlement of reinsurance liability for Waiver of Premium Disability benefits, the *reinsurer* shall pay to the *reinsured* its proportionate share of the gross premium waived.

C. If the *reinsured* should contest of compromise any claim or proceeding and the amount of net liability thereby be reduced, or if at any time the *reinsured* should recover monies from any third party in connection with or arising out of any claim reinsured by the *reinsurer*, the *reinsurer's* reinsurance liability shall be reduced or the *reinsurer* shall share in the recovery, as the case may be, in the proportion that the net liability of the *reinsurer* bore to the total net liability existing as of the occurrence of the claim. As used in this section, "recovery" shall include, but not be limited to settlements, judgments, awards and insurance payments of any kind.

D. Any unusual expenses incurred by the *reinsured* in defining or investigating a claim for policy liability or in taking up or rescinding a policy reinsured hereunder shall be participated in by the *reinsurer* in the same proportion as described in section C, above.

E. In no event shall the following categories of expenses of liabilities be considered, for purposes of this Agreement, as "unusual expenses" or items of "net reinsurance liability":

(1) routine investigative or administrative expenses;

(2) expenses incurred in connection with a dispute or contest arising out of conflicting claims of entitlement to policy proceeds or benefits which the *reinsured* admits are payable;

(3) expenses, fees, settlements, or judgments arising out of or in connection with claims against the *reinsured* for punitive or exemplary damages;

(4) expenses, fees, settlements, or judgments arising out of or in connection with claims made against the *reinsured* and based on alleged or actual bad faith, failure to exercise good faith, or tortuous conduct.

F. For purposes of this Agreement, penalties, attorney's fees, and interest imposed automatically by statute against the *reinsured* and arising solely out of a judgment being rendered against the *reinsured* in a suit for policy benefits reinsured hereunder shall be considered "unusual expenses."

G. In the event that the amount of insurance provided by a policy or policies reinsured hereunder is increased or reduced because of a misstatement of age or sex established after the death of the insured, the net reinsurance liability of the *reinsurer* shall increase or reduce in the proportion that the net reinsurance liability of the *reinsurer* bore to the sum of the net retained liability of the *reinsured* and the net liability of other *reinsurers* immediately prior to the discovery of such misstatement of age or sex. Reinsurance policies in force with the *reinsurer* shall be reformed on the basis of the adjusted amounts, using premiums and reserves applicable to the correct age and sex. Any adjustment in reinsurance premiums shall be made without interest.

H. The *reinsurer* shall refund to the *reinsured* any reinsurance premiums, without interest, unearned as of the date of death of the life reinsured hereunder.

I. If the *reinsured* pays interest from a specified date, such as the date of death of the insured, on the contractual benefit of a policy reinsured under this Agreement, the *reinsurer* shall indemnify the *reinsured* for the *reinsurer's* share of such interest. Interest paid by the *reinsurer* under this section shall be computed at the same rate and commencing as of the same date as that paid by the *reinsured.* The computation or interest paid by the *reinsurer* under this section shall cease as of the earlier of (1) the date of payment of the *reinsurer's* share of reinsurance liability and (2) the date of termination of the period for which the *reinsured* has paid such interest.

VII.   CONDITIONAL RECEIPT REINSURANCE
reinsurer shall not be liable for any claim made against the *reinsured* as a result of the *reinsured* having issued a conditional receipt or a temporary insurance agreement.

VIII.   EXPERIENCE REFUNDS
Reinsurance hereunder shall not be considered for experience refunds.

IX.   PREMIUM TAX REIMBURSEMENT
The *reinsurer* shall not reimburse the *reinsured* for any taxes the latter may be required to pay with respect to reinsurance hereunder.

X.   POLICY CHANGES
If a change is made in the policy issued by the *reinsured* to the insured which affects reinsurance hereunder, the *reinsured* shall immediately notify the *reinsurer* of such change.

XI.   REINSTATEMENTS
If a policy reinsured hereunder lapses for nonpayment of premium and is reinstated in accordance with its terms and the rules of the *reinsured,* the *reinsurer* shall automatically reinstate its reinsurance under such policy. The *reinsured*

shall mail notice of the reinstatement to the *reinsurer* not later than the tenth working day after the reinstatement of the original policy. The *reinsured* shall pay the *reinsurer* all reinsurance premiums in arrears in connection with the reinstatement with interest at the same rate and in the same manner as the *reinsured* received under its policy.

XII. EXPENSES

The *reinsured* shall bear the expense of all medical examinations, inspection fees, and other charges incurred in connection with the original policy.

XIII. REDUCTIONS

A. Except as provided in section C of the "*Reinsurance Coverage*" article hereof, if a portion of the insurance issued by the *reinsured* on a life reinsured hereunder is terminated, reinsurance on that life hereunder shall be reduced as hereinafter provided to restore, as far as possible, the retention level of the *reinsured* on the risk, provided, however, that the *reinsured* shall not assume on any policy being adjusted as provided in this article an amount of insurance in excess of the higher of, for the retention category of that policy, (1) its retention limit at the time of the issue of that policy and (2) the retention limit of that policy as already adjusted by the provisions of the "*Increase in Limit of Retention*" article. The reduction in reinsurance shall first be applied to the reinsurance, if any, of the specific policy under which insurance terminated. The reinsurance of the *reinsurer* shall be reduced by an amount which is the same proportion of the amount of reduction so applied as the reinsurance of the *reinsurer* on the policy bore to the total reinsurance of the policy. The balance, if any, of the reduction shall be applied to reinsurance of other policies on the life, the further reduction, if any, in the reinsurance of the *reinsurer* again being determined on a proportional basis.

B. The *reinsurer* shall return to the *reinsured* and basic life reinsurance premiums and any reinsurance premiums for Supplemental Benefits, without interest thereon, paid to the *reinsurer* for any period beyond the date of reduction of reinsurance hereunder.

XIV.   INSPECTION OF RECORDS

The *reinsurer* shall have the right at any reasonable time to inspect, at the office of the *reinsured*, all books and documents relating to the reinsurance under this Agreement.

XV.   INCREASED IN LIMIT OF RETENTION

A. The *reinsured* may increase its limit of retention and may elect, subject to the other provisions of this article, to (1) continue unchanged reinsurance then in force under this Agreement, (2) make reductions in both standard and substandard reinsurance then in force under this Agreement, or (3) make reductions in standard reinsurance then in force under this Agreement. The increased limit of retention shall be effective with respect to new reinsurance on the date specified by the *reinsured* subsequent to written notice to the *reinsurer*. Such written notice shall specify the new limit of retention, the effective date thereof, and the election permitted by the first sentence of this section. If the *reinsured* makes election (2) or (3), the amount of reinsurance shall be reduced, except as hereinafter provided, to the excess, if any, over the *reinsured's* new limit of retention.

B. No reduction shall be made in the amount of any reinsurance policy unless the *reinsured* retained its maximum limit of retention for the plan, age, and mortality classification at the time the policy was issued, nor shall reductions be made unless held by the *reinsured* at its own risk without benefit of any proportional or nonproportional reinsurance other than catastrophe accident reinsurance. In the case of Life and Disability reinsurance, no reduction shall be made in any class of reinsurance fully reinsured; Accidental Death Benefits fully reinsured because the *reinsured* retains Life insurance first and then Accidental Death Benefits may be reduced as herein provided, but other fully reinsured Accidental Death Benefits may not. No reduction shall be made in any Supplemental Benefits reinsured on a Life reinsurance cession unless the Life reinsurance is also being reduced as described hereunder. The plan, age, and mortality classification

at issue shall be used to determine the *reinsured's* new
retention an any life on which reinsurance policies are
reduced in accordance with the provisions of this article.

C. The reduction in each reinsurance policy shall be
effective upon the reinsurance renewal date of that
policy first following the effective date of the increased
limit of retention or upon the tenth reinsurance renewal
date of the reinsurance policy, if later.   If there is
reinsurance in other *reinsurers* on a life on whom a
reinsurance policy will be reduced hereunder, the
reinsurer shall share in the reduction in the proportion
that the amount of reinsurance of the *reinsurer* on the
life bore to the amount of reinsurance of other
reinsurers on the life.

D. In the even the *reinsured* overlooks any reduction in the
amount of a reinsurance policy which should have been
made on account of an increase in the *reinsured's* limit
of retention, the acceptance by the *reinsurer* of
reinsurance premiums under such circumstances and
after the effective date of the reduction shall not
constitute or determine a liability on the part of the
reinsurer for such reinsurance.   The *reinsurer* shall be
liable only for a refund of premiums so received,
without interest.

XVI.   ERRORS

If either the *reinsured* or the *reinsurer* shall fail to perform
an obligation under this Agreement and such failure shall
be the result of an error on the part of the *reinsured* or the
reinsurer, such error shall be corrected by restoring both
the *reinsured* and the *reinsurer* to the positions they would
have occupied had no such error occurred; an "error" is a
clerical mistake made inadvertently and excludes errors of
judgment and all other forms of error.

XVII.   ARBITRATION

A. It is the intention of the *reinsured* and the *reinsurer*
that the customs and practices of the insurance and
reinsurance industry shall be given full effect in the
operation and interpretation of this Agreement.   The
parties agree to act in all things with the highest good
faith.   If the *reinsured* and the *reinsurer* cannot

mutually resolve a dispute which arises out of or relates to this Agreement, however, the dispute shall be decided through arbitration as set forth in the Arbitration Schedule. The arbitrators shall base their decision on the terms and conditions of this Agreement plus, as necessary, on the customs and practices of the insurance and reinsurance industry rather than solely on a strict interpretation of the applicable law. There shall be no appeal from their decision, except that either party may petition a court having jurisdiction over the parties and the subject matter to reduce the arbitrator's decision to judgment.

B. The parties intend this article to be enforceable in accordance with the Federal Arbitration Act (9 U.S.C. Section 1 et seq.) including any amendments to that Act which are subsequently adopted. In the event that either party refuses to submit to arbitration as required by section A, the other party may request a United States Federal District Court to compel arbitration in accordance with the Federal Arbitration Act. Both parties consent to the jurisdiction of such court to enforce this article and to confirm and enforce the performance of any award of the arbitrators.

XVIII. INSOLVENCY

A. In the event of the insolvency of the *reinsured*, all reinsurance shall be payable directly to the liquidator, receiver, or statutory successor of said *reinsured*, without diminution because of the insolvency of the *reinsured*.

B. In the event of the insolvency of the *reinsured*, the liquidator, receiver, or statutory successor shall give the *reinsurer* written notice of the pendency of a claim on a policy reinsured within a reasonable time after such claim is filed in the insolvency proceeding. During the pendency of any such claim, the *reinsurer* may investigate such claim and interpose, in the name of the *reinsured* (its liquidator, receiver, or statutory successor), but at its own expense, in the proceeding where such claim is to be adjudicated, any defense or defenses which the *reinsurer* may deem available to the *reinsured* or its liquidator, receiver, or statutory successor.

C. The expense thus incurred by the *reinsurer* shall be chargeable, subject to court approval, against the *reinsured* as part of the expense of liquidation to the extent of a proportionate share of the benefit which may accrue to the *reinsured* solely as a result of the defense undertaken by the *reinsurer*. Where two or more *reinsurers* are participating in the same claim and a majority in interest elect to interpose a defense or defenses to any such claim, the expense shall be apportioned in accordance with the terms of the reinsurance agreement as though such expense had been incurred by the *reinsured*.

D. Any debts or credits, matured or unmatured, liquidated or unliquidated, regardless of when they arose or were incurred, in favor of or against either the *reinsured* or the *reinsurer* with respect to this Agreement or with respect to any other claim of one party against the other are deemed mutual debts or credits, as the case may be, and shall be set off, and only the balance shall be allowed or paid.

XIX. **PARTIES TO AGREEMENT**

This is an agreement for indemnity reinsurance solely between the *reinsured* and the *reinsurer*. The acceptance of reinsurance hereunder shall not create any right or legal relation whatever between the *reinsurer* and the insured or the beneficiary under any policy reinsured hereunder.

XX. **AGREEMENT**

This Agreement represents the entire contract between the *reinsured* and the *reinsurer* and supersedes, with respect to its subject, any prior oral or written agreements.

XXI. **EXECUTION AND DURATION OF AGREEMENT**

The provisions of this reinsurance agreement shall be effective with respect to policies for which the date on which application was first made to the *reinsured* is on or after the day of _____, 19___, but in no event shall this Agreement become effective unless and until it has been duly executed by two officers of the *reinsurer* and its Home Office. This Agreement shall be unlimited as to its duration but may be terminated at any time, insofar as its pertains to the handling of new reinsurance thereafter, by either party giving three months' notice of termination in writing. The *reinsurer* shall continue to accept reinsurance during the three months aforesaid and shall remain liable on all reinsurance granted under this Agreement until the termination or expiry of the insurance reinsured.

IN WITNESS WHEREOF

the said

ABC Life Insurance Company

of

Cederville, U.S.A.

and the said

XYZ Reinsurance Company

of

Assumption GAAP, U.S.A.

have by their respective officers executed and delivered these presents in duplicate on the dates shown below.

Signed at _____

By _____   By _____

Title _____   Title _____

Date _____   Date _____

Signed at _____

By _____   By _____

Title _____   Title _____

Date _____   Date _____

SUBJECT REINSURANCE SCHEDULE

Insurance Subject to Reinsurance under this Agreement

A. One hundred percent of the *reinsured's* entire excess of its issues of the following plans bearing register dates in the range shown below to insureds having surnames beginning with the letters of the alphabet shown below.

| | Dates | | Letters | |
Plan	From	Through	From	Through
M	---	-----	A	K
N	---	-----	L	Z

B. Continuations of the *reinsured's* issues to any of the plans listed above, provided the original policy was reinsured with the *reinsurer* under this or another reinsurance agreement.

RETENTION SCHEDULE

Retention Limits of the *reinsured*

Life

| Issue Age | Table Rating or Equivalent | | |
	0 - 200%	225% - 400%	Above 400%
0-65	-----	--------	-------
66-80	-----	--------	-------

Waiver of Premium Disability

Same as Life

Accidental Death

None

LIMITS SCHEDULE

Maximum Amounts which the *reinsured* may
Cede Automatically

<u>Life</u>

M times retention, but not more than $_____.

<u>Waiver of Premium Disability</u>

The *reinsured* may cede automatically Waiver of Premium
Disability reinsurance in amounts applicable to the amount of Life
reinsurance ceded automatically, not to exceed the following limits:

<u>Issue Ages</u>	<u>Standard-Table 6</u>	<u>Over Table 6</u>
---	---------	------
---	---------	------

<u>Accidental Death Benefits</u>

<u>Issue Ages</u>	<u>Standard-Table 6</u>	<u>Over Table 6</u>
---	---------	------
---	---------	------

ADMINISTRATIVE FORMS SCHEDULE

Facultative Application

Reinsurance Cession

Record of Reinsurance Ceded

Cession Card

PREMIUM SCHEDULE, PART I

Reinsurance Premium Rates

Fully Underwritten Issues
Standard Risks
The annual reinsurance premium for reinsurance not in excess of $5,000,000 on any one life shall be the attached cost of insurance rates charged the insured per thousand of the net amount at risk times the following percentages:

Substandard Risks
The substandard table extra premiums shall be the number of tables assessed the risk times 25% of the attached appropriate standard rates times the above percentages.

Continuations to Issues Reinsured Hereunder
The reinsurance premium for policies reinsured under this Agreement as continuations shall be the appropriate premium described in this Agreement; unless the reinsurance agreement under which the original policy was reinsured specifies otherwise, the policy duration and attained age of the insured for purposes of calculating such premiums, shall be determined as though the continuations were issued on the same date and at the same issue age as the original policy.

Continuations from Issues Reinsured Hereunder
The reinsurance premium for continuations of policies reinsured under this Agreement shall be as described in the agreement which covers the new policy; unless that agreement specifies otherwise, the policy duration and attained age of the insured, for purposes of calculating such premiums, shall be determined as though the continuations were issued on the same date and at the same issue age as the original policy. If no such agreement is in effect between the *reinsurer* and the *reinsured*, reinsurance shall continue hereunder.

Continuation Policy Fee

If the premium scale applicable to a continuation contains a policy fee, a continuation shall, for purposes of determining the policy fee only and notwithstanding the method prescribed for calculating the basic premium, be considered a renewal if the *reinsured* has paid the *reinsurer* a first-year policy fee on reinsurance of the original policy and as a new issue if the *reinsured* has not paid the *reinsurer* a policy fee on reinsurance of the original policy.

Waiver of Premium Disability

Accidental Death Benefits

PREMIUM SCHEDULE, PART II

Reinsurance Premium Rates

The reinsurance premium rates for reinsurance in excess of $5,000,000 on any one life shall be the rates labeled "*nonsmoker*," "*smoker*," "*aggregate*," and "*substandard-extra*," nonrefunding and age nearest birthday.

ARBITRATION SCHEDULE

To initiate arbitration, either the *reinsured* or the *reinsurer* shall notify the other party in writing of its desire to arbitrate, stating the nature of its dispute and the remedy sought. The party to which the notice is sent shall respond to the notification in writing within ten (10) days of its receipt.

The arbitration hearing shall be before a panel of three arbitrators, each of whom must be a present or former officer of a life insurance company. An arbitrator may not be a present or former officer, attorney, or consultant of the *reinsured* or the *reinsurer* or either's affiliates.

The *reinsured* and the *reinsurer* shall each name five (5) candidates to serve as an arbitrator. The *reinsured* and the *reinsurer* shall each choose one candidate from the other party's list, and these two candidates shall serve as the first two arbitrators. If one or more candidates so chosen shall decline to serve as an arbitrator, the party which named such candidate shall add an additional candidate to its list, and the other party shall again choose one candidate from the list. This process shall continue until two arbitrators have been chosen and have accepted. The *reinsured* and the *reinsurer* shall each present their initial lists of five (5) candidates by written notification to the other party within twenty-five (25) days of the date of the mailing of the notification initiating the arbitration. Any subsequent additions to the list which are required shall be presented within ten (10) days of the date the naming party receives notice that a candidate that has been chosen declines to serve.

The two arbitrators shall then select the third arbitrator from the eight (8) candidates remaining on the lists of the *reinsured* and the *reinsurer* within fourteen (14) days of the acceptance of their positions as arbitrators. If the two arbitrators cannot agree on the choice of a third, then this choice shall be referred back to the *reinsured* and the *reinsurer*. The *reinsured* and the *reinsurer* shall take turns striking the name of one of the remaining candidates from the initial eight (8) candidates until only one candidate remains. If the candidate so chosen shall decline to serve as the third arbitrator, the candidate whose name was stricken last shall be nominated as the third arbitrator. This process shall continue until a candidate has been chosen and has accepted. This candidate shall serve as the third arbitrator. The first turn at striking the name of a candidate shall belong to the party that is responding to the other party's initiation of the arbitration. Once chosen, the arbitrators are empowered to decide all substantive and procedural issues by a majority of votes.

It is agreed that each of the three arbitrators should be impartial regarding the dispute and should resolve the dispute on the basis described in the "*arbitration*" article. Therefore, at no time will either the *reinsured* or the *reinsurer* contact or otherwise communicate with any person who is to be or has been designated as a candidate to serve as an arbitrator concerning the dispute, except upon the basis of jointly drafted communications provided by both the *reinsured* and the *reinsurer* to inform those candidates actually chosen as arbitrators of the nature and facts of the dispute. Likewise, any written or oral arguments provided to the arbitrators concerning the dispute shall be coordinated with the other party and shall be provided simultaneously to the other party or shall take place in the presence of the other party. Further, at no time shall any arbitrator be informed that the arbitrator has been named or chosen by one party or the other.

The arbitration hearing shall be held on the date fixed by the arbitrators. In no event shall this date be later than six (6) months after the appointment of the third arbitrator. As soon as possible, the arbitrators shall establish prearbitration procedures as warranted by the facts and issues of the particular case. At least ten (10) days prior to the arbitration hearing, each party shall provide the other party and the arbitrators with a detailed statement of the facts and arguments it will present at the arbitration hearing. The arbitrators may consider any relevant evidence; they shall give the evidence such weight as they deem it entitled after consideration of any objections raised concerning it. The party initiating the arbitration shall have the burden of proving its case by a preponderance of the evidence. Each party may examine any witnesses who testify at the arbitration hearing. Within twenty (20) days after the end of the arbitration hearing, the arbitrators shall issue a written decision that sets forth their findings and any award to be paid as a result of the arbitration, except that the arbitrators may not award punitive or exemplary damages. In their decision, the arbitrators shall also apportion the costs of arbitration, which shall include, but not be limited to, their own fees and expenses.

Appendix B

INTRODUCTION

Reinsurance treaties are negotiated agreements. For many years the primary area of negotiation for most companies was price. Reinsurers traditionally performed the administrative functions associated with the business based on information transmitted on individual cession forms.

Times have changed. There has been a great development of self-administered reinsurance in recent years. These self-administered arrangements have generally resulted in lower costs for reinsurers, and consequently in lower reinsurance rates. For ceding companies, increased administrative costs have tended to offset the reinsurance rate decrease. Self-administering companies have gained a significant amount of control over reinsurance processing, but they have also assumed a greater responsibility for its accuracy and timeliness.

With the advent of self-administered agreements, the range of negotiated items has expanded to include the question of what shall be reported to the reinsurer. The primary purpose of this

---

[1]The guidelines also include sample report forms, which have not been reproduced in this appendix.

441

document is to provide guidance to ceding companies and reinsurers alike on the information which should be reported through a self-administered arrangement.

Since there is a great deal of variation in the abilities of ceding companies, the needs of reinsurers, and the purposes for reinsurance, there is a correspondingly great variation in the terms of self-administered agreements. For example, there are certain arrangements which are reported on a "pure bulk" basis where only summary information is transferred. These arrangements frequently are used for financial planning reinsurance and are outside the scope of this document.

The agreements to which this document applies are those designed to replace individual cession reinsurer-administered agreements. These are frequently referred to as bordereau or listed-based reinsurance agreements. While the focus is on life insurance, the discussion can be generalized to other forms of insurance.

It is important to remember that self-administration is a two-way street. Ceding companies considering that option should weigh the savings generated by lower reinsurance rates and the additional control over handling against the higher self-administration costs and the added responsibility. For reinsurers, the reduced administration expenses must be weighed against the loss of direct control of the reinsurance processing and the reduced reinsurance rates.

The negotiated reporting requirements of an agreement can play a large role in its ultimate cost to both ceding companies and reinsurers.

CONSIDERING SELF-ADMINISTATION: THOUGHTS ON SYSTEMS DEVELOPMENT

A ceding company which has never self-administered before or which is considering a revision of an existing self-administered agreement should consider many details in the course of developing the new self-administration system. Naturally, no single list of considerations can be completely comprehensive, particularly when products are evolving as rapidly as today, but the following list is presented to indicate the scope of matters that should be addressed before a ceding company decides to self-administer.

Responsibility

In cession basis reinsurance, the ceding company is responsible for the determination of facts regarding the reinsured policy (such as policy status and premium payments) and the transmission of these facts to the reinsurer. Self-administration requires the ceding company to assume some or all of the reinsurance support functions from the reinsurer (such as billing reports and annual statement information). The ceding company therefore becomes responsible for the timely and accurate reporting of the agreed items. Year-end timing can be especially critical.

EDP Resource Allocation

Developing and maintaining any reinsurance system will require a significant investment of EDP time and money. Many ceding companies find it difficult to assign a high priority to reinsurance systems work. If a company cannot devote sufficient EDP resources to the reinsurance system, it should not be self-administering. This source of expenses should be carefully examined by any ceding company which is considering self-administration. Some ceding companies reduce their EDP requirements by doing extensive systems work on local microcomputers instead of the company main frame. In this case, audit systems or procedures should be developed for the separate microcomputer systems to insure their accuracy.

Development Approach

A system might be more easily developed in piecemeal fashion than by attempting to handle the entire reinsurance process at once. Top priority would normally be given to major blocks of business currently being issued which require reinsurance. The piecemeal approach may be necessary if EDP resources are limited.

System Design

System design should be as flexible as possible in order to adapt to new situations without an inordinate amount of new programming. Adaptability could be required for new types of policies, new coinsurance allowances or YRT rates, and variations in the treatment of factors such as sex-distinct vs. unisex treatment, smoker/nonsmoker vs. composite rates or varying select periods.

Similarly, certain transactions may vary from agreement to agreement in the manner in which they are calculated. The optimal approach is to anticipate as much future variability as possible when building the system without encumbering it with overcomplexity.

Manual Processing

Most systems still require some degree of manual processing. It may not be realistic or cost effective to expect to program every-thing. Attempting to build too ambitious a system can result in delays and cost overruns.

External Constraints

Reinsurance is not governed solely by an agreement between ceding company and reinsurer. State regulations, tax rules and auditing requirements can all constrain a reinsurance arrangement.

Furthermore, such constraints are largely beyond the control of the ceding company and reinsurer and may change with little or no warning which may force changes in the self-administration system. A recent example is the development of the AICPA Statement of Position on Auditing Life Reinsurance.

Detail Reporting

In addition to the obvious reporting situations such as those described in later sections of this document, there are many ancillary issues which must be addressed. For example, how will the system handle the following:

(1) Multiple inforce policies on the same life with different reinsurers.
(2) Multiple inforce policies on the same life with the same reinsurer.
(3) Multiple reinsurers on the same policy.
(4) Replacements and continuations (such as select term pro-ducts).
(5) Automatic versus facultative treatment.
(6) The reinsurer's retrocession arrangements, particularly where additional information or different timing is a factor.
(7) Recapture and small amount cancellation rules.

(8) ADB retention (added to or included in basic life retention).

(9) Waiver of premium reinsurance which is frequently coinsured even though the other risks use a different form of reinsurance such as YRT.

(10) Coordination of ceded business with business being assumed from the same reinsurer.

(11) Changes in the retention level.

Errors and Omissions

The errors and omissions clause of a reinsurance contract is designed to address instances where a case has been processed incorrectly by accident. It is not intended to cover situations where a system is known to be deficient when it is put into production. A self-administration system should not be put into production until it is fully checked. The tendency of some ceding companies and reinsurers to negotiate an agreement first and worry about the self-administration later can put a great deal of pressure on the company to rush a system into production.

File Management

Some ceding companies have found that the best course is to build all necessary reinsurance information into a trailer on the policy master file. Others have preferred to set up a separate reinsurance master file which is coordinated with the policy master file. This decision is a fundamental one that should precede any systems work.

The advantage of using the policy master file itself is that handling problems caused by two separate systems can be eliminated. On the other hand, modifying the policy master file and its associated programs can be a more difficult and time-consuming task than creating an independent database. The advantage of setting up a separate reinsurance master is the complete control the reinsurance area has over its structure and operation. A disadvantage is the extra handling required to keep the reinsurance file in agreement with the policy master file.

There is another related consideration. User friendly languages and modern database management techniques may not be readily adaptable to the existing policy master file and programs. In order to take advantage of these advances, it may be necessary to build a separate reinsurance file.

Safeguards

Any production system should have documentation, backup files, hard copy records and security procedures to cope with accidental of intentional damage to the system.

Special Products

Products such as Universal and Variable Life can create different self-administration problems than traditional products. For example, how will the system handle the following:

(1) Varying risk amounts as they affect retention. Options include level retention, proportional retention or a combination of the two.

(2) Varying risk amounts as they affect the net amount at risk. Options include a fixed annual amount, monthly updating or exact adjustment. Reinsurance benefits can be paid for either the amount purchased or the actual amount of loss.

(3) Varying risk amounts that float above and below fixed retention limits.

(4) Varying risk amounts on other policies on the same life whether retained or reinsured.

(5) Varying risk amounts as they affect the establishment of future waiver of premium disability reserves.

(6) An alternate set of reinsurance premiums required for increasing benefit policies (*e.g.*, with a cost of living adjustment).

Report Formats

There are many options, once the above considerations are settled, as to how the information should be presented. The desired form of presentation may in some cases suggest or dictate other parts of the system.

Multiple benefits (*e.g.*, basic life, ADB, waiver of premium, other insured lives) can be reported together on one form or separately. Various transactions (*e.g.*, new issues, renewals, lapses, reduction, conversions) may require different information and different report formats.

Uniform Reporting

When a ceding company works with several reinsurers, it can be very helpful to have all of the reinsurers agree to a uniform reporting format. While this may take some initial work to negotiate, it will be very beneficial to the ceding company in the long run.

Management Reporting

Management reports can be produced relatively efficiently and inexpensively if they are designed as part of the overall self-administration system. They are likely to be neglected by the ceding company if they are not specified as part of the initial system. One useful report, particularly for YRT reinsurance arrangements, is a simple cash flow summary.

Summary

It is not possible to define one approach to the above considerations which is right for all companies. Nevertheless, in setting up a self-administration system, they must all be addressed to the satisfaction of both ceding company and reinsurer.

TRANSMISSION OF INFORMATION

When considering the transmission of information between ceding company and reinsurer, it is clear that a great many options are available to get the job done. This document does not recommend any particular approach. Each ceding company and reinsurer should consider its alternatives before negotiating the methods in which information will be transmitted. The areas which should be addressed include the following.

Mode of Transmission

Although historically information has been transferred almost exclusively by paper, in recent years ceding companies and reinsurers have been exploring other options such as the use of computer tapes, floppy disks and direct computer interfacing over telephone lines.

If one of the more sophisticated methods is contemplated, it must be carefully coordinated with the company which is to receive the data.   Many ceding companies and reinsurers are not yet prepared to use or currently discourage the use of these methods.

Frequency and Timing

With the exception of some reporting such as Annual Statement work whose timing requirements are imposed by state regulators, there is room for ceding companies and reinsurers to negotiate whatever terms are appropriate. A typical provision might provide for the monthly or quarterly transfer of reports with a stated deadline (*e.g.*, 30 days after the end of the reporting period).

Format

No generally accepted standard format for reports currently exists, nor is one proposed. In many cases, the selection of the information to be transferred will have a lot to do with the report format. To the extent that electronic data transfer is contemplated, both parties must have a complete understanding of the format used in order for the transfer to be successful.

Summary vs. Detail

In self-administered reinsurance, much reporting is of summary information (*e.g.*, aggregate reserves, total premium due). One of the advantages of self-administration for the reinsurer is the greatly reduced amount of information that it is required to handle.

Under certain circumstances, however, significant amounts of detailed backup may be transferred between ceding company and reinsurer.   New issues would normally be listed individually along with any information which the reinsurer needs to handle new issues according to the agreement.

A few general statements may provide some guidance to ceding companies and reinsurers in negotiating an agreement.

First, summary information such as statutory reserves that the ceding company has to calculate whether the business is reinsured or not should normally be reported to the reinsurer. Summary information that would not normally be calculated by the ceding company should be negotiated. An example of this might be a smaller company which does not have to calculate separate tax reserves while its reinsurer does.   Obviously, if the ceding company must take on extra tasks, this tends to undermine the cost justification for self-administration.

Second, both detail and backup information should be provided to reinsurers when necessary for reinsurance support. Typical situations where detailed information might be required are new issue listings, premium reports (including new issues, renewals, adjustments and lapses) and audits. Such detailed information should be kept to a minimum and is generally required to support summary information.

Third, whether transmitted or not, the ceding company should maintain sufficiently detailed backup information in its office to provide documentation for claims and reinsurer audits.

Fourth, some reinsurers prefer to calculate certain summary items themselves. In particular, the reinsurer may need to value its statutory reserves on a different basis than the ceding company. In these cases, it is usually sufficient for the ceding company to provide the reinsurer with appropriate policy master file (or reinsurance file) information.

Summary

When developing a self-administration system, major decisions must be made in the transmission of information that are not as clearcut as in the past. The resolution of these questions can significantly affect the cost and ease of administration.

It is preferable to consider these questions openly between ceding company and reinsurer before entering into a self-administered agreement. Otherwise, there is the risk that the ceding company and reinsurer may have significantly different perceptions of how the information will be transferred.

PURPOSES OF SELF-ADMINISTERED REPORTS

Under the traditional individual reporting of cessions the reinsurer would maintain its own records as to policies in force, policy movements and reserves, would generate appropriate premium billings, and thus would usually be in a position to satisfy a wide range of reporting requirements including internal management reports as well as statutory and other external reports. Self-administered reports have to provide essentially the same information.

Statutory Reporting Requirements

Most life reinsurers doing business in the United States have to file
an Annual Statement (Convention Blank) with one or more State
Insurance Departments. As a minimum, they must have the information necessary to complete the following Annual Statement
Schedules and Exhibits.

Exhibit 1:   Premiums and Annuity Considerations
Premiums and commissions, split by first year (other than single),
single and renewal, must be reported.

Exhibit 8: Aggregate Reserve for Life Policies and Contracts
Some reinsurers also are required to make quarterly reports of
certain Annual Statement items such as reserves.

Exhibit 11: Policy and Contract Claims
This is still reported on an individual claim basis by most ceding
companies.

Exhibit of Life Insurance: Policy Exhibit
This summary includes the annual transactions on assumed reinsurance business.

Schedule S - Part 3C
This schedule gives data on reinsurance assumed as of December 31.
For life reinsurance, amounts in force at end of year, reserves,
premiums, and reinsurance payable on paid and unpaid losses must
be shown.

Corresponding items will be used by the ceding company in
its Annual Statement. These items may not be equal to the items
in the reinsurer's statement if there are differences in timing,
reserve basis, or valuation method.

Other Reporting Requirements

In addition to providing for statutory reporting requirements as set
out above, many reinsurers find it necessary or desirable to obtain
basic policy information for other purposes. The uses of such basic
data include the following:

(1)   Indexing (*e.g.*, alphabetic) policies to identity accumula-
      tions of coverage on a given life.

(2) Determining retrocession needs and producing retrocessions.

(3) Verifying the accuracy of self-administered reports (usually on a sampling basis), particularly with respect to premium calculations.

(4) Verifying that automatic binding requirements such as proper retention and treaty coverage are satisfied.

(5) Determining the disposition of facultative cases on file (*i.e.*, the reinsurer needs to close out pending case files).

(6) Verifying the inforce status and any preliminary claim amounts on death claim reimbursement requests from the ceding company.

(7) Developing statistics for internal management purposes such as projections of premiums, inforce, reserves, etc.

(8) Developing comparisons of actual versus expected mortality and persistency.

(9) Developing the reinsurer's GAAP reserves and tax reserves.

ADMINISTRATIVE REPORTING GUIDELINES

This section presents information that is transferred periodically (*e.g.*, monthly or quarterly) from ceding company to reinsurer in order to provide for the basic administration of the reinsurance. Uses of this information include those listed in the previous section under Other Reporting Requirements, items 1-6.

Although reinsurance agreements vary considerably in the specific information transferred, these guidelines list those items commonly reported. The details listed here are developed from list-based or bordereau reinsurance agreements. This is the most common form of self-administration in the amount of information provided.

Significant departures from this approach which transfer less information can be negotiated with reinsurers depending on factors such as the purpose of the agreement, the past experience of the ceding company with self-administration, and the ease of reinsurer audits.

Policy Details Generally Required

The following details are commonly required to be reported in self-administered reinsurance agreements. Where appropriate, items should be split by life, ADB, waiver of premium, and other ancillary benefits.

(1) Policy number of other cession identification. There is some interest in using social security numbers as identification.
(2) Name of insured (last name, first name and middle initial).
(3) Sex.
(4) Date of birth.
(5) Issue age.
(6) Attained age (or policy duration).
(7) Policy date.
(8) The following transactions (with the appropriate details on the number of policies, amount and premium) plus a transaction code or other means to identify them:
(a) First year or renewal premiums.
(b) New business not previously reported (required when modal first year reinsurance premiums are used).
(c) Policies resulting from a continuation of coverage.
(d) Policy movements or changes such as
    (i)   Not taken
    (ii)   Surrender
    (iii)   Lapse
    (iv)   Reinstatement
    (v)   Conversion
    (vi)   Increase in amount
    (vii) Decrease in amount
    (viii) Cancellation of reinsurance
    (ix)   Recapture
    (x)   Death
    (xi)   Expiry
    (xii) Other changes.
(9) Effective date of transaction.
(10) Table rating.
(11) Flat extra amount and term in years. If multiple flat extras are a possibility, the system should allow for it.
(12) Plan name or plan code.
(13) Underwriting or premium class (*e.g.*, smoker/nonsmoker/preferred or special underwriting).
(14) Amount issued.
(15) Death benefit option (especially for Universal Life or similar plans).

(16) Reinsurance amount (separately for Life, ADB or WP if applicable). An alternative is to show the net amount at risk and the percent reinsured.
(17) Reinsurance premium due (separately for Life, ADB or WP).
(18) Reinsurance commission or allowance.
(19) Net amount due reinsurer or ceding company.
(20) Automatic or facultative indicator.

Additional Policy Details Not Always Required

Some ceding companies and reinsurers find it desirable to provide or obtain certain additional policy details not included in the above list.

(1) Retention indicator (*e.g.*, F = Full retention, P = Partial retention, N = Nothing retained). Provide either an indicator or actual amounts retained for both previous and new issues. This information is required both on a per cession and a per life basis.
(2) Large volume indicator (or a separate listing) where total reinsurance on an insured equals or exceeds a specified amount.
(3) Policy fee.
(4) Currency code.
(5) Amount reinsured at issue.
(6) Premium taxes to be reimbursed.
(7) Cash value to be reimbursed.
(8) Dividend to be reimbursed.
(9) Special risk class (*e.g.*, aviation, military, foreign).
(10) Joint life information.
(11) Policy duration and an indication of whether the duration is based on a previous policy.

One report that is not always required but which many reinsurers find useful is a list of pending facultative cessions.

Form of Administrative Reports

Some self-administered agreements specify separate listings for new issues, renewals, lapses and other adjustments. Others allow for the intermingling of various transactions on fewer listings.

From the reinsurer's point of view, it is usually more convenient to work with separate listings. For example, a new issue listing can be used to add policies to the reinsurer's database or to set up retrocessions. A separate lapse listing can be used to terminate retrocessions.

Another approach is to have only a couple of listings, but provide various subtotals. In general, a minimum of two listing is required:

(1) List of Risks Reinsured (including new issue and renewal information).
(2) List of Adjustments or Changes.

Each report should include appropriate subtotals and totals so that the reinsurer can readily record premiums and commissions in the proper categories (*e.g.*, First Year/Renewal/Single). In addition, subtotals split by new issue and renewal for each transaction type should be provided for policy movements (number of policies and amount).

In addition to the individual policy details set out above, a policy exhibit summary and a premium summary should be provided with each periodic listing. These summaries include totals of all transactions being reported with appropriate subtotals as required for the completing of Annual Statement Exhibit 1 and Exhibit of Life Insurance. Where applicable, corresponding totals for items such as expense allowances, dividends or cash values should be included.

Some method of transmitting information that does not affect premiums (*e.g.*, a name change) should also be included in the discussions between ceding company and reinsurer.

GUIDELINES FOR STATEMENT REPORTING

As was discussed earlier, one of the reinsurance support activities that is assumed to some degree by a self-administering ceding company is that of calculating statutory Annual Statement information for the reinsurer. In addition, there may be quarterly statements or GAAP statements prepared by the reinsurer for which it requires information.

In general, the ceding company has a clear responsibility to provide accurate and timely information for statutory statements. To the extent that reinsurers desire additional information for non-statutory purposes (*i.e.*, GAAP statements or internal management reports), these additional requests should be specifically discussed by the ceding company and reinsurer as a part of the negotiation process.

In some instances, reinsurers are willing to work from inforce files or other sources to generate some or all of the GAAP and statutory reports that are required.

A further question that should be agreed upon by the ceding company and reinsurer is how the various due and unpaid items listed below will be treated. In many cases, the emphasis is placed on "unusual" situations where the transactions are significantly past due. The more typical situations where there are simply timing differences between the ceding company and the reinsurer are not reported as due and unpaid.

Operating Statement Items

For the most part, the information necessary to complete Operating Statement items is available from the transactions made throughout the year. Exhibit 1 shows premiums, dividends, reinsurance expense allowances and reinsurance commissions. Exhibit 11 shows claims. Except where affected by due and unpaid items, this information is obtained directly from the paid entries to the reinsurer's accounting system. The ceding company normally does not do any special report of these items at year end.

Balance Sheet Items

These items represent the bulk of the extra statement reporting required. They can be grouped into two categories: the reinsurer's share of ceding company assets and liabilities, and due and unpaid adjustments to the reinsurer's paid accounts.

Reinsurer's Share of Assets of Assets and Liabilities

(1) *Reserves (Exhibit 8).* The reinsurer's share of any ceding company Exhibit 8 reserve is reported here. In addition to statutory reserves, some agreements may require the transfer of tax and/or GAAP reserves. It is also possible that some sort of detailed master file information is required in addition to, or in lieu of, summary information. This should all be negotiated between the ceding company and reinsurer.

(2) *Dividend Liability.* This is usually reported if the reinsurer participates in dividends.

(3) *Policy Loan Asset.* This is reported if the reinsurer participates in policy loans.

(4) *Deferred Premium Asset.* This is reported if the reinsurer participates in modal premiums.

Due and Unpaid Adjustments

(1) *Due and Unpaid Reinsurance Premiums.* As with the other due and unpaid items, the ceding company and reinsurer should agree on standards for declaring a premium payment due and unpaid.

(2) *Due and Unpaid Reinsurance Allowances or Commissions.*

(3) *Due and Unpaid Mean Reserve Transfer.* This is applicable to modified coinsurance reserve transfers.

(4) *Amounts Recoverable on Paid or Unpaid Losses.* This represents those claims that the ceding company has identified as payable by the reinsurer. The amount is split into claims paid by the ceding company and claims not yet paid (including claims in course of settlement).

(5) *Due and Unpaid Experience Refund.* Normally the reinsurer would perform this calculation and report the result to the ceding company.

Exhibit of Life Insurance (Policy Exhibit)

If this type of statement is prepared with every periodic statement as discussed previously, there will be little reporting required other than adding together the routine reports. If not, then some agreements provide for such an exhibit to be transferred at year end.

Some additional Policy Exhibit information may be requested by the reinsurer, specifically a split of Industrial and Ordinary insurance for dividend and other paid up additions, a split of term and whole life, a split of participating and non-participating insurance, and breakdowns of Credit and Group policies in several categories.

Statement of Ceding Company Actuarial Review

Any use of these statements should be discussed and agreed to by both the ceding company and the reinsurer. Their is no required use of this type of statement by any regulatory or professional body.

The Statement of Ceding Company Actuarial Review provides the reinsurer with a source of documentation to satisfy its auditors. Furthermore, it assures the reinsurer of appropriate ceding company review of the reported numbers.

From the ceding company point of view, completion of the Statement of Ceding Company Actuarial Review should not be a problem if the ceding company's numbers are reasonable. If not, the need to sign it might provide some incentive to the ceding company to improve its method of calculation.

The purpose of the Statement of Ceding Company Actuarial Review is not to cause second guessing and professional review of the actuaries completing the form. Actual professional standards on self-administered reinsurance have not been proposed, nor is there any expectation that they will be. Reinsurers simply want to rely on the normal professional competence and standards of an actuary who has reviewed the reported numbers.

GAAP Breakdowns of InForce

Many reinsurers report on a GAAP as well as statutory basis. Those that do have developed a variety of approaches to obtaining inforce breakdowns for calculating deferred acquisition costs and related items. The three most common approaches are for the reinsurer to (a) calculate inforce breakdowns from the reinsurer's own inforce file, (b) ask the ceding company to calculate such a breakdown on the ceding company files, and (c) obtain an inforce file from the ceding company upon which the reinsurer can do its own breakdowns. The reinsurer might request additional information such as annual gross premium with the inforce breakdowns.

The three options result in varying degrees of timeliness, accuracy and control for the reinsurer as well as a varying amount of work for both parties. All three should be considered in entering a self-administration arrangement.

Auditing Requirements

Auditors are more concerned about reinsurance transactions today than has been the case in past years. A set of reporting and record-keeping requirements can be imposed on any reinsurance agreement by the auditing environment as it changes over time. The guidelines discussed in this document regarding all three types of reporting will be affected over time by changes in auditing standards.

A document that should be reviewed carefully by all ceding companies and reinsurers is the AICPA Statement of Position on Auditing Life Reinsurance which was published in November 1984.

GUIDELINES FOR STATISTICAL REPORTING

This section outlines the policy-level data needed by a reinsurer of self-administered life reinsurance business in other to conduct basic experience studies and analyses. This includes small scale studies of individual ceding companies by individual reinsurers and also large scale studies such as those sponsored by the Society of Actuaries. Topics often studied include lapse experience, mortality experience and overall financial results. Most of the data items needed for experience studies and statistical reporting are also needed for basic administrative and annual statement reporting. A few additional data items allow the reinsurer to perform additional analyses that have great potential value to both the reinsurer and the ceding company.

Although self-administered reinsurance business offers a number of advantages, one unfortunate disadvantage is that it has been difficult, if not impossible, to conduct experience studies on such business. This is because the reinsurer has not had sufficient data to perform such studies. Even in situations where the reinsurer has had sufficient data, often it has not been in a particularly usable form so that the studies would have had to be performed manually at a prohibitively high expense.

Ceding companies benefit in a number of ways if reinsurers are able to conduct experience studies. For example, some companies are unable to do their own experience studies. Analysis of their experience by a reinsurer, even if the analysis applies only to reinsured business, can provide helpful insights. In addition, industry risk classification practices seem to be under increasing scrutiny from regulators. Only reinsurers and very large direct writing companies have enough experience on various impaired lives to help support underwriting practices. But industry impairment mortality studies can be done on self-administered reinsurance business only if ceding companies are able to provide the necessary data.

Finally, and perhaps most important, experience studies enable reinsurers to establish more accurate pricing assumptions. In the long run, the use of more accurate pricing assumptions by reinsurers will mean lower reinsurance rates for ceding companies, since uncertainty in pricing assumptions requires larger contingency margins (or more conservative assumptions).

It is important to note that a reinsurer wishing to conduct experience studies on self-administered business faces two obstacles. First, the reinsurer must obtain the necessary data from the ceding company. Second, the reinsurer must obtain the data in a form compatible with its automated file maintenance and study systems. As mentioned earlier, the cost of conducting manual experience studies is probably prohibitive. The same is true of manually inputting all of the information from paper reports. All this points to the necessity of retransmitting administrative data in a different format suitable for studies.

A uniform format for reporting data on self-administered business would greatly facilitate the transmission process; however, no such format currently exists. The same considerations apply on an even larger scale when considering industry studies.

The types of data that are needed for statistical studies include the following:

(1) Identification information which allows for a clear description of the business being studied. This data is also useful in audit situations.

(2) Experience information (*e.g.*, deaths, lapses, amounts at risk) which is necessary for the study itself.

(3) Segmentation information (*e.g.*, impairment, line of business, smoker/nonsmoker) which allows the study results to be broken down by various factors.

(4) Special characteristics of the ceding company or the business which allow results to be specifically tailored to the business and which allow for the meaningful comparison and combination of results of various ceding companies and blocks of business.

(5) Policy change information which allows for the calculation of exposure data. Depending on the accuracy desired for the study, this type of information might be used very extensively or not at all.

(6) Expected results which enable actual vs. expected calculations to be made.

Normally information which is being collected for studies is collected on a current year basis. For this reason, a reinsurer and ceding company might agree to regularly transfer only certain basic information for routine reinsurer studies. In special situations more substantial data might be transferred to do more extensive studies or to participate in a Society of Actuaries study.

The following data items are needed for statistical studies.

A. Summary Information
    (1) Client identification
    (2) Age basis
    (3) Type of reinsurance
    (4) Reinsurance agreement number

B. Information also Required for Administrative or Statement Reporting
    (1) Policy number
    (2) Primary insured's name
    (3) Primary insured's date of birth
    (4) Primary insured's sex
    (5) Primary insured's issue age
    (6) Issue date
    (7) Amount issued by ceding company
    (8) Amount reinsured*
    (9) Plan of insurance*
    (10) Death benefit option
    (11) Automatic or facultative indicator
    (12) Retention indicator (full, reduced, or none)
    (13) Risk classification (preferred, nonsmoker, smoker, standard, table rating, etc.)*
    (14) Flat extra per thousand,* and term in years
    (15) Policy status (premium paying, paid up, nonforfeiture option, terminated, etc.) and effective date
    (16) Termination type (cancellation, not taken, conversion, lapse, surrender, death, recapture, expiry, maturity) and effective date
    (17) Amount of accidental death benefit reinsured*
    (18) Amount of waiver of premium reinsured*
    (19) Source (replacement, conversion, rollover, new business, etc.)
    (20) Activity type (reinstatement, change in issue dage, age, rating, plan, amount, or status) and effective date
    (21) Currency code

C. Information Required only for Experience Analysis
   (1) Underwriting basis (guaranteed issue, simplified issue, nonmedical, paramedical, or medical)
   (2) Primary impairment code

*Include effective date if different from issue date (line 6)

A striking feature of the list of data items is that only two of them are needed strictly for experience studies. All other items are already needed for another reason. Thus supporting experience studies requires very little additional data from the ceding company.

Unfortunately, many ceding companies do not keep this information on any existing database. This should be considered as yet another matter for negotiation between ceding company and reinsurer when self-administration is being contemplated.

One point that cannot be overemphasized is that the reinsurer needs data in a form (disk or tape) compatible with its file maintenance and study systems. With the information in the proper form, the reinsurer is able to build automated records with historical information that can be used to analyze activity for a variety of time periods. Without the information, the industry, both ceding companies and reinsurers, risks running short of supporting data when it seems to be needed more than ever before.

With good planning and cooperation between ceding companies and reinsurers, it appears quite possible to improve the effectiveness of self-administered reinsurance without taking away the ability to perform valuable experience studies.

Appendix C

Guidelines for the Auditing of Administration and Reporting of Individual Life Reinsurance Assumed

INTRODUCTION

This paper is a sequel to the *Guidelines for the Reporting of Self-Administered Reinsurance* dated January 1, 1986, and includes guidelines which are intended to apply to the administration and reporting of individual life reinsurance which is covered by a treaty or other written agreement between the ceding company and reinsurer. In the absence of a written agreement setting out the terms and conditions of reinsurance, the rights and responsibilities of the parties to the reinsurance may be so unclear that an audit as considered in this paper might be inappropriate.

Prior to the 1980's it was very rare for reinsurers to perform on-site audits of the records of ceding companies. For a variety of reasons, it is becoming increasingly common for such audits to be performed.

This paper includes a brief review of some of the developments which led to the need to conduct on-site audits. In addition, some suggestions as to the scope of audit are included along with some ideas on how to make the process efficient for both the ceding company and audit team.

Reviews of surplus relief or other financial reinsurance arrangements are outside the scope of this paper. Likewise, audits of activities such as underwriting which require special expertise and techniques not applicable to audits of administration and reporting are not covered by this paper.

A properly conducted audit should be beneficial to both the ceding company and the reinsurer(s) conducting the audit. Through such a process, each of the parties should become more familiar with the needs of the other and the problems encountered in trying to meet those needs. One anticipated result is a strengthening of the once traditional "gentlemen's agreement" nature of the reinsured/reinsurer relationship.

TRADITIONAL METHOD OF ADMINISTRATION

Until recently, most ordinary life reinsurance in North America was administered under a traditional individual cession basis. The ceding company sent the reinsurer an individual "formal cession" or "application for reinsurance" documenting the details of each risk for which reinsurance was sought. In turn, the reinsurer created a "reinsurance guarantee" or "reinsurance certificate" which was sent to the ceding company as written evidence of acceptance of the risk by the reinsurer.

The reinsurer maintained its own records as to risks reinsured based on the details contained in the formal cessions received from ceding companies. With this basis of administration, reinsurers rarely found it necessary to inspect the records of ceding companies for a variety of reasons including the following:

(1) The reinsurer sent monthly premium statements which were expected to be reviewed by the ceding company to identify any cases which had lapsed or been amended;

(2) Annual inforce and reserve listings would typically be sent to each ceding company for comparison with its records to assure that the reinsurer was carrying appropriate cessions in force;

(3) Except for certain requirements, such as jumbo limits, formal cession details normally permitted the reinsurer to verify that treaty provisions were being met as to qualification for automatic cession, etc. (*e.g.*, letter of alphabet, amount retained, plan of insurance, mortality classification); and

(4) Facultative cessions were documented by a formal exchange of documents to support the reinsurer's acceptance of risk.

Reinsurers' concerns about ceding companies' internal controls over reinsurance ceded are minimal under the traditional individual cession basis of administration for reasons set out above. They are not, however, nonexistent.

It may well be that a ceding company whose reinsurance is administered solely on an individual cession basis will require an audit. The need for such an audit may become evident in a variety of ways (*e.g.*, from late-reported transactions or details of a claim). Specialized audits such as claims or underwriting audits which are not considered in this paper may be little affected by the basis of administration.

DEVELOPMENT OF THE NEED OF AUDITS

Self-Administration

Self-administration of reinsurance ceded has become very common in recent years. Several reinsurers have reported that over 50% of their business in force is self-administered by ceding companies, and the proportion seems to be increasing. Some of the factors influencing the shift to self-administration are as follows:

(1) The development of flexible-premium, variable-benefit products resulted in reinsurance administration by traditional methods becoming unwieldy;

(2) The development of interest-sensitive products led to more sophisticated data processing systems for policy administration, with increased capabilities to provide reinsurance reporting as a by-product of routine processing;

(3) Premium rate levels have continually declined in recent years, putting pressure on insurers and reinsurers to price for ever lower per-unit expenses; and

(4) Reinsurers sometimes provided more attractive allowances to ceding companies who agreed to self-administer their reinsured business. This is becoming less common, largely because both ceding companies and reinsurers are finding that self-administration may not be as efficient and cost-effective as it was once thought to be.

The widespread shift to self-administration of reinsurance resulted in the transfer of considerable control over various reporting activities from reinsurers to ceding companies. The reinsurer may not maintain a database for individual risks reported on a self-administered basis. Ceding companies find that they are not always able to provide information on individual risks in a format consistent with the reinsurer's needs. The result is that reinsurers typically have somewhat limited access to the details of individual risks.

Another effect of the changes in administration is that reinsurers have lost some control over the timeliness of their own reporting because they may have to wait until reports are received from ceding companies before their own reports can be prepared.

Other Factors

Naturally, reinsurers have always been interested in the timeliness, completeness, and accuracy of the details of reinsurance assumed. Prudent business judgment dictates that a reinsurer take reasonable steps to assure that adequate information is received from ceding companies or other responsible parties such as brokers and intermediaries.

Besides the shift to self-administration, other factors have led reinsurers to expand their activities to assure that the internal controls of ceding companies (as they affect reinsurance ceded) are adequate. One of the main factors has been the increase in complexity of placing reinsurance; some of the reasons for this are as follows:

(1) Reinsurers may differ by plan and/or pricing classification;
(2) Reinsurers may change over time for a given plan as treaties are renegotiated;
(3) Exchange or replacement programs have led to confusion about how to reinsure replacement polices;
(4) Extreme price competition among reinsurers has led some companies to reduce their retention limits on selected (typically term) plans; and
(5) Rapid development of new products (*e.g.*, interest-sensitive plans, cost-of-living adjustments, flexible- or indeterminate-premium plans or variable life plans) has outstripped the ability of ceding companies to get administrative systems in place to support these products so that, in many cases, reinsurance administration has received little or no support.

Because of the complexity of placing reinsurance, the subject of controls over reinsurance ceded or assumed has attracted attention from auditors, regulators, and shareholders. This has resulted in actions by the following groups:

(1) The American Institute of Certified Public Accountants (AICPA) issued in November 1984, a *Statement of Position* (SOP) on *Auditing Life Reinsurance*;

(2) The National Association of Insurance Commissioners (NAIC) became increasingly interested in various aspects of reinsurance and established a Reinsurance and Antifraud Task Force which developed a Model Law on Credit for Reinsurance. In addition, the NAIC has developed a model regulation on surplus relief agreements and has formed a Study Group on Life Reinsurance that reports to the Accounting Practices and Procedures Task Force; and

(3) The Foreign Corrupt Practices Act of 1977 amended the Securities Exchange Act of 1934 to require all publicly held companies to maintain accurate records and adequate systems of internal control. This places an added burden on the management of those publicly traded insurance companies who engage in significant reinsurance activities. Those insurers who assume business from a ceding company under self-administration arrangements appear to have an added obligation to ensure that the controls used by the cedant in preparation of the reports are adequate.

The AICPA's SOP on *Auditing Life Reinsurance*, in conjunction with the other factors discussed above, focuses considerable attention on reinsurance arrangements and seems to make it almost mandatory for a reinsurer to perform on-site audits of some ceding companies. For example, paragraph 22 of the SOP states that "The absence of adequate procedures by the assuming company to obtain assurance regarding the accuracy and reliability of data received from the ceding company, or the lack of reasonable assurance that such procedures are in use and operating as planned, may constitute a material weakness in the assuming company's system of internal accounting control."

Typically, a reinsurer's large accounts, especially those which are self-administering reinsurance ceded, will most likely be candidates for on-site audits based on SOP. Other reasons to audit may include recent adoption of self-administration by a particular company, prior audit experience, system changes, or changes in management or staff.

TERMINOLOGY: AUDIT OR REVIEW

The public accountant views the terms 'audit' and 'review' very specifically. An audit is an examination of financial statements in accordance with generally accepted auditing standards for the express purpose of giving an opinion of the fair and consistent presentation of those statements. A review has been defined by the Auditing Standards Division of the AICPA in their *Statement of Standards for Accounting and Review Services* issued in December 1978, and is significantly narrower in scope.

The procedures discussed in the writing of this paper are designed so that they may be performed by the staffs of the insurance companies involved and as such are not a true audit. Auditing techniques, however, are useful for helping to determine that all parties are properly complying with the terms of the reinsurance agreement.

A ceding company being audited should discuss any concerns it may have about terminology with the reinsurer conducting the audit. Naturally, the parties involved may agree upon whatever terminology convention they find most acceptable. Nevertheless, for convenience, the term "audit" is used in this paper to refer to the overall process of inspecting a company's reinsurance procedures, controls, and records.

PURPOSE OF AUDIT

So far, we have described the general concerns which led to an increased interest in having reinsurers perform on-site audits of ceding companies. Each reinsurer wants to be sure that it is receiving all the reinsurance it is supposed to be getting, but *only* that which it should receive, that the reinsurance received is proper, that the correct premiums and allowances are paid, and that claims are paid only on valid, in force cases. Some specific goals for the audits are set out in this section.

(1) Ascertain that all transactions are accurately recorded, properly valued, and reported in a timely manner;

(2) Verify that both the ceding company and the reinsurer have a mutual understanding of the terms and conditions of the applicable treaty covering the reinsured policy;

(3) Educate the reinsurer as to the day-to-day problems encountered by the ceding company in attempting to comply with treaty terms and conditions;

(4) Review the ceding company's internal controls to assure that treaty terms and conditions are being followed;

(5) Where confusion exists, clarify the ceding company's interpretation of treaty terms by reviewing the application to specific cases;

(6) Assist the ceding company by providing a relatively objective review of systems and procedures by an interested party;

(7) Establish a dialogue between ceding company and reinsurer to provide a framework for resolving misunderstandings which may arise from time to time;

(8) Satisfy the management needs of both the ceding company and reinsurer to gain reasonable assurance that appropriate systems, procedures, and controls governing reinsurance administration are in place; and

(9) Satisfy external auditors and regulators that the reinsurance relationship is functioning as intended, with appropriate controls to identify and correct administrative problems in a timely fashion. These controls should be of both a detective and a preventive nature.

Most reinsurer audits will pertain to reinsurance administration and will be general in nature. Occasionally, it may be necessary for the reinsurer to conduct a special purpose audit not covered by the guidelines in this paper. The scope of audit and audit procedures employed should be tailored to the particular purpose of such an audit.

SCOPE OF AUDIT

The reinsurer's audit is designed to permit a reasonable evaluation of a ceding company's internal controls over the receipt and initial set up of cases, including changes, and the related determination of the need for reinsurance. Although the audit will normally be restricted to an examination of ceding company records, systems and procedures which have a direct impact on the administration of reinsurance ceded, this may involve almost every aspect of the ceding company's policy issue and administration systems as well as claims administration. Where transactions affecting reinsurance involve processing with an EDP system, testing of input, processing, and output may be necessary.

Because of the potential exposure of the reinsurer due to actions or inactions of the ceding company's agency force, some reinsurers will want to review the ceding company's agency operations. The reinsurer will have an interest in the ceding company's attitude toward an agent that makes significant mistakes or intentionally takes positions adverse to the company and whether agents are required to maintain errors and omissions coverages.

It has to be appreciated that not all ceding companies and reinsurers will agree upon the interpretations to be given to specific treaty wordings. Similarly, there is not yet universal agreement in the life insurance/reinsurance industry as to how certain transactions are to be administered.

Because of the differing practices adopted by ceding companies and reinsurers, the scope of audit set out below may need to be modified in some respects to suit a particular situation. For example, the criteria for distinguishing new business from continuation policies may need to be worked out between the ceding company and reinsurer.

Most reinsurers do not want their audit teams to be put in the position of negotiating terms or conditions of reinsurance. Thus, the auditors typically are not authorized to make final decisions as to how particular transactions should be handled or how treaty terms are to be interpreted.

Accordingly, if a finding involves a financial adjustment or a significant question as to interpretation of treaty terms, the audit team will be expected to defer to its management to evaluate the situation and discuss the matter with the appropriate members of the management of the ceding company.

Specific items to be reviewed will typically include the following:

Reinsurance Agreements
(1) Provisions are maintained on a current basis

(2) Ceding company's and reinsurer's agreement files are consistent

(3) Essential details are disseminated fully and in a timely fashion to employees responsible for reinsurance administration;

New Business Policies Requiring Reinsurance
(1) Issued only in accordance with written company guidelines
  (a) Issued per underwriting classification (including any required Aviation Exclusion or other endorsement)
  (b) Issued in accordance with the proposed insured's signed Application for Insurance
  (c) Initial premium received
  (d) Appropriate nonsmoker or other declarations signed by proposed insured
  (e) Conditional receipt rules being followed
(2) Allocated appropriately to each reinsurer
  (a) Routed to appropriate person or department for processing
  (b) Identified whether or not overall retention is exceeded on the current policy
  (c) Confirmed that proper retention amount is kept (*e.g.*, for automatic reinsurance requirements)
  (d) Recorded properly in reinsurance in force, premium billing, and valuation files
  (e) Followed facultative submission requirements (and any additional requirements of the reinsurer)
  (f) Followed automatic and jumbo limits
  (g) Reported to correct reinsurer in a timely manner

Changes to Policies In Force
(1) Reinsurer notified in a timely manner
(2) Conversions, exchanges, reissues, rollovers, reinstatements, reentries, or other changes reported in accordance with the reinsurance treaty. Such changes are commonly categorized as either
  (a) *Continuation* to be reported to the original reinsurer even if that reinsurer is not a reinsurer for current new business; or
  (b) *New business* to be reported to the current reinsurer for the plan of insurance.

Questions which may be involved in deciding whether a particular policy qualifies as new business for reinsurance purposes are as follows:

(i) Was appropriate underwriting performed?

(ii) Is the new policy unmodified as to suicide and incontestability?

(iii) Was a full first year commission paid to the agent?

(iv) Was any required nonsmoker declaration or other preferred risk documentation obtained?

(3) Appropriate reinsurer approvals obtained (*e.g.*, the reinsurer may need to underwrite reentries, reinstatements, or increases in amount)

(4) Appropriate endorsements included in continuation policies are

(a) Suicide provision

(b) Incontestability provision

(c) Other (*e.g.*, Aviation Exclusion)

(5) Policy changes supported by appropriate forms signed by policyowner

(6) Terminations documented

(7) Changes to Extended Term Insurance (ETI) or Reduced Paid Up (RPU) properly reported to the reinsurer, and consistent with policy form and any policy loans outstanding (the needs here will vary by type of treaty and whether or not the reinsurer participates in policy loans or surrender values)

(8) Contractual increases or decreases, such as COL adjustments, applied correctly

(9) Recaptures made according to the treaty

Claims (may be evaluated prior to audit)

(1) Prompt notification given to the reinsurer

(2) Appropriate details supplied to reinsurer

(3) Reinsurer's approval obtained (if required) before claim is settled

Valuation Reports

(1) All inforce reinsured cessions are included in the reserve listing

(2) Totals agree with reports to reinsurer

(3) Valuation factors and methods are appropriate (different factors of methods may apply to reinsurer)

Reinsurance Billings
(1) Proper calculation of premiums, allowances, etc.
(2) Proper payment of renewal premiums of allowances
(3) Timely payments to reinsurers
(4) Adequate controls on cash payments to assure that payments are consistent with amounts reported as due
(5) Adequate control of accounts receivable or payable items.

Although Financial or Management Control Reports may be outside the scope of an administrative audit, some reinsurers will find it convenient and appropriate to obtain and review such documents as part of the audit. The reports to be reviewed might include any or all of the following:

(1) Insurance Department Examination Report
(2) Independent Auditor's Report
(3) Internal Audit Reports
(4) Letter relating to the adequacy of internal accounting controls filed with regulatory authorities
(5) Annual Statement (Convention Blank)
(6) NAIC Early Warning Test
(7) GAAP Financial Statement

PREPARATION FOR AUDIT

Many steps can be taken by both the ceding company and reinsurer prior to the on-site audit to help minimize the amount of time spent in the offices of the ceding company. By performing as many of the required steps as possible in advance, the disruption of the ceding company's routine and staff can be kept to a minimum.

Setting the Audit Date

The date and duration of the audit should be set well in advance. For the convenience of both the ceding company and reinsurer, a lead time of as much as two or three months could be desirable.

It is important to time the audit so that appropriate ceding company personnel will be present. To the extent possible, the timing of the audit should be at the convenience of the ceding company. Factors for which allowances must be made include valuation periods, the extent of the audit, and vacations.

Reinsurers may find it desirable to establish an audit date by informal discussions between the reinsurer's marketing representative and appropriate personnel at the ceding company. Once the date has been set, reinsurer personnel involved in the audit may then take over and follow up with various details involved in conducting the audit.

Audit Preparations by the Ceding Company and the Reinsurer

The reinsurer's audit team will need to be selected. Some reinsurers have staff permanently assigned to do reinsurance audits as part of the internal audit function (typically including CPA's under the direction of the President, Treasurer, Controller, or possibly the Board of Directors). Such staff may need to be augmented by personnel drawn from other areas of the company.

For example, it is common to include individuals from the Reinsurance Administration and Actuarial staff. Depending upon the nature of the audit and any special problems encountered or anticipated, it may be appropriate to include Claims or Underwriting staff on the audit team.

It is also important that the reinsurer send in writing to the ceding company the audit objectives as well as the items and procedures they will want to review. This type of communication should minimize the confusion and discomfort the ceding company may have about being audited.

The reinsurer may find it helpful to prepare a summary of the basic details of the treaties covering the business to be audited. It could be helpful to send a copy of such a summary to the ceding company for their review. Not only is this a possibly helpful tool for the ceding company, it may facilitate early identification of any areas of misunderstanding of treaty terms.

The audit process can be further facilitated if the ceding company will send the audit team any written documentation setting out the general procedures, work flow and controls of the ceding company applicable to reinsurance administration. This will permit the team to focus more quickly on details and take up less of the coordinator's or other ceding company staff's time in becoming familiar with the administration system.

It is also helpful to have the ceding company send any necessary Financial and Management Control Reports to the audit team for its review prior to the on-site audit.

Some of the audit steps are best performed in the offices of the reinsurer prior to the on-site audit. For example, it may be possible for the reinsurer to verify most calculations of amounts at risk, premiums, allowances, bonuses, and chargebacks from the reports submitted by the ceding company.

Such a review should identify any systematic errors (EDP, or otherwise) that may be occurring. This early identification of calculation or other systematic problems will enable the audit team to quickly focus on problem areas during the on-site audit.

Another way to speed up the actual audit process is for the ceding company to give the audit team a set of sample forms identifying the fields which are relevant to reinsurance. The set could include, for example, various forms likely to be encountered in the policy files such as policy status sheets (showing status of policy according to the computer records) or underwriting worksheets showing the status of prior policies and the allocation of reinsurance on a current policy.

Depending on audit objectives, a sample of policy files to be reviewed should be made by the reinsurer prior to the audit. Such a sample would typically be drawn from self-administered reports submitted by the ceding company and might include the following information.

(1)   A variety of plans of insurance
(2)   Different years of issue
(3)   Different transaction types such as (a) new business, (b) terminations, (c) reissues, reinstatements, exchanges, conversions, etc., (d) increases and decreases in amount, and (e) claims (Life, WPD, ADB, etc.)

Most reinsurers make some effort to select the sample on a random basis. In addition, the sample size may be determined statistically based upon the amount of business covered by the treaty(ies) according to the ceding company reports. Naturally, if particular problems have been noted in the self-administered reports or on individual cessions, the sample selection may include more of the transactions in question than would arise from a purely random selection process.

Working exclusively from reports submitted by the ceding company may permit confirmation that reported cases are administered properly but cannot establish whether or not all cases are being properly reported. Accordingly, most audits will involve further samples selected on-site, possibly including a sample of cases drawn from the direct insurance master records of the ceding company.

If possible, the samples should be available in both alphabetical and numerical (by policy number) order. Some companies find it more convenient to access their files alphabetically while others prefer to utilize policy number.

The policy sample should be sent to the ceding company at least one or two weeks in advance of the audit. This gives the ceding company adequate time to pull the policy files requested (or any associated policy files which might affect the placement of reinsurance) without significantly disrupting normal operations.

Logistical Considerations

Audit Team. It is convenient for both the ceding company and reinsurer to know who will be involved in the audit. Where possible, the reinsurer should give the ceding company advance notice of who will be on the audit team and identify the team manager for purposes of coordination between the ceding company and the audit team.

Ceding Company Coordinator. Similarly, the audit team needs to know with whom it will be working at the ceding company. It is expected that contacts with ceding company personnel will be coordinated through one individual assigned as coordinator and who would also provide access to policy registers (*e.g.*, new issues, terminations, changes, claims) or other records as needed.

The audit team should make it a point to know the name, location, and telephone number of the ceding company's coordinator and respect the wishes of the ceding company which may require that all staff contact be made through the coordinator. Ideally there should be a deputy coordinator to be contacted in case the principal coordinator is unavailable (*e.g.*, due to sickness or other business).

Access to Office. It will be necessary for the team members to know the usual office routine. For example, they will probably want to try to adhere to normal office hours. It may, however, be necessary for them to work before or after hours in order to get the job done. Accordingly, they need to know if work outside normal hours is acceptable to the ceding company and, if so, what special arrangements need to be made.

If there are special security procedures to be followed, the team will need to be informed. There may be a need for security passes or for the team to have someone accompany them while on the ceding company premises (either at all times of outside normal office hours).

Access to Records/Files. It is important for the audit team to know the forms in which the ceding company records are kept (*e.g.*, microfilm, microfiche, paper file, on-line computer record) land to have appropriate means of accessing those records (*e.g.*, microfilm reader, microfiche reader, video display terminal). If required access devices are not available, the audit team will have to provide its own.

The ceding company may wish to limit the degree to which the audit team has access to records. There may also be some concerns about the audit team making hard copies of ceding company records. These issues should be resolved early on, preferable long before the audit commences, so that there will be no misunderstanding about these important activities.

Other Items. Other minor points ideally should be addressed in advance of the audit. Most audit teams expect to provide their own (usually portable) calculators; however, desk calculators are most convenient to use and some ceding companies choose to make them available to the audit team.

The audit team will have frequent need to contact the coordinator. For this reason it would be most convenient to have access to at least one telephone.

Naturally, the audit team will expect to make its own arrangements as to accommodations, meals, and travel. In special circumstances, the ceding company may find it desirable to advise the audit team.

PERFORMANCE OF THE AUDIT

Initial On-Site Meeting

It is important for the on-site audit process to begin with a meeting of the audit team with ceding company personnel who will be involved with the review process so they can get to know each other. In addition, a discussion about how the audit will proceed in line with the audit objectives sent earlier and the basic steps to be taken will help to alleviate any misgivings about the review process.

At this time, the logistical considerations can be reviewed and the team will be assigned to a work space. In order to acquaint the audit team with the environment in which they will be working, some ceding company coordinators may find it worthwhile to give the team a brief guided tour of their offices or other facilities.

This initial meeting is probably a good time to set up a closing conference to be held at the end of the on-site audit. Naturally, the duration of the audit may not be fixed, so the meeting time may have to be revised as circumstances warrant.

Interviews with Ceding Company Personnel

Interviews with ceding company reinsurance administrative personnel will help the audit team gain an understanding of the general nature of the reinsurance administration and document flow. In addition, it may be helpful to interview selected key personnel involved in overall reinsurance administration to help gain an understanding of the way the company administers its direct business and evaluates that business for reinsurance administration purposes. These interviews should be controlled by the company coordinator.

Overview of Administrative System

A good starting point for the audit itself is to trace the physical flow of paperwork associated with underwriting and issue of new business. This may be accomplished by reviewing the written workflow provided by the ceding company prior to the audit. Another possibility is to have a "walk-through" of the path followed by various transactions as they relate to ceded reinsurance.

This will usually give the team a good overall picture of how the administration system works in general, and will help them to know where to look for appropriate controls. Some audit teams find it helpful to create a simplified flowchart of the administrative system and have this reviewed by ceding company staff to assure that the audit team's understanding of the system flow is essentially correct. The extent to which such a flowchart is needed depends in part upon the documentation provided by the ceding company.

The basic steps involved in policy issue can be observed in brief. For example, the usage of an alpha index or similar controls for verifying previous inforce will be seen in the walk-through should this take place.

Further Sample Selection

Depending upon audit objectives, audit teams may want to select additional samples on-site to supplement those previously selected from the reports submitted by the ceding company. This may include samples drawn from a recent verifiable inforce or reserve listing, a new business register, a claims register, or a terminations/changes register.

By making these sample selections early in the audit process, the ceding company staff can be assured of having adequate time to retrieve the appropriate policy files or other documentation.

Specific Review Assignments

In order to speed up the review process, audit team members may be assigned specific tasks to be undertaken concurrently. For example, one member may review treaty documentation while others are working on the system flowchart or selecting samples of new business or terminations/changes. The review of claims may also proceed separately from the review of individual policy files from the initial samples.

Peer Review

Insurance/reinsurance transactions have become very complicated in recent years. Some reinsurers have found it helpful to have audit members cross-check each other, at least on a number of cases, to make sure that they agree on their interpretation of the documentation and the application of treaty terms to specific cases and to assure that all recorded notes are both legible and intelligible.

Noting Discrepancies

It is recommended that detailed notes made of any apparent discrepancies that are found. These will be helpful for further research or for discussion with the company coordinator.

The audit team should review and summarize the types of discrepancies found. This summary will be needed for discussion with the company coordinator, both in the course of the audit and in the closing conference to be held later.

It is desirable for the audit team to thoroughly review its findings in time to permit follow-up of any loose ends before the closing conference begins. It is helpful to have any audit findings summarized in approximately the same order as the scope of audit which itself may be taken as a rough guide for both the closing conference and the audit report.

Closing Conference

It is important to have a "wrap-up" session or closing conference so that the audit team can discuss its findings with the ceding company. It is strongly recommended that the company coordinator arrange to have as many as possible of the people involved in the audit attend the conference which will help minimize the likelihood that the ceding company will be surprised by any of the findings reported in the audit report.

In addition, it may be that the audit team has misunderstood some documentation or procedure. By reporting and discussing what it perceived as "discrepancies," the audit team assures the ceding company staff of having an opportunity to correct any such misperceptions in a timely fashion.

The conference may also cover any plans the ceding company may have for correcting any discrepancies found or for strengthening internal controls where necessary.

If not already arranged it may, at this time, be decided to whom the audit report or summary letter will be submitted (original or copies). Normally, someone at the ceding company (typically the company coordinator) will want to review a draft audit report or summary letter before a final document is submitted to avoid unnecessary surprises. The final document is typically addressed to the ceding company management.

Other Audit Procedures

Other actions might be taken by some reinsurers. For example, it might be arranged for the reinsurer to obtain information from the ceding company's external auditor about steps taken by the auditor to confirm directly with policyholders information in the ceding company's inforce policy files. This could save considerable duplication of work and effort.   This information would be obtained through the company coordinator.

If suitable arrangements cannot be made to obtain assurances that the policy files have been adequately confirmed, some reinsurers may want to undertake an independent verification of policyholder information contained in the ceding company files and used as a basis for self-administered reinsurance.   Such a measure would be somewhat unusual because the treaty is between the ceding company and the reinsurer who has no direct relationship with the policyholders, and could normally be undertaken only with appropriate ceding company permission and cooperation.

It may also be desirable for the reinsurer's audit team to meet with the ceding company's internal auditors to review the steps they have taken to confirm the adequacy of reinsurance systems and procedures and the reliability of information in the policy files.

AUDIT REPORT

The draft report should be prepared as quickly as possible after the audit.   Invariably, some important points found or discussed will not have been reduced to writing; therefore, timely preparation of the audit report will maximize the likelihood that all important findings will be reflected in the report.

Some reinsurers prefer to address the audit report to their own management.   They may send a copy of the formal report to the ceding company or, instead, they may send a letter summarizing the findings of the audit.

The draft report or summary letter should be submitted to the coordinator of the ceding company for review and comments. There should be some agreement on the time frame for reviewing the draft report.

Once the comments of the ceding company have been reviewed and considered, the audit report can be put in final form. The report should then be submitted as agreed.   The distribution of the report needs to be done with the approval of the ceding company.

As a rule, the audit report will stress the findings of the audit and should at least be copied to someone at a senior management level in the ceding company.   In some cases, however, it may be appropriate to include reasons why certain things were done so as to avoid unnecessary questions and to put findings in the proper context.

The final audit report will probably contain a disclaimer to clarify that the audit may not necessarily disclose any or all material weaknesses in the ceding company's reinsurance administration systems and that the identification of, or failure to identify, specific problems or errors in any of the policies included in the review does not alter any of the terms or conditions of the governing reinsurance agreements.

FOLLOW-UP TO AUDIT

If the audit is to be of the greatest possible value to both the ceding company and reinsurer, there should be a definite plan for following up the findings and recommendations of the audit. This might involve having the reinsurer's marketing representative keep in touch on a regular basis with the ceding company to ascertain that appropriate steps are being taken to correct any deficiencies, strengthen internal controls, and so on.

Sometimes, audits lead to a need to revise treaty terms or conditions. For example, it may be found that it is not feasible for the ceding company to meet some treaty requirements. If that is the case, it may be possible to change the arrangement to put it on a more workable basis with requirements that the ceding company will be able to fulfill.

ALTERNATIVES TO ON-SITE AUDITS

Ceding companies frequently ask if there is anything they can do to eliminate or minimize the need for audits by reinsurers. For some companies, especially those which reinsure large volumes of reinsurance on a self-administered basis, there will be an ongoing need for reinsurer audits.

The frequency of such audits may, however, be reduced if current audits indicate that the ceding company has adequate procedures and controls to assure that policies requiring or involving reinsurance are properly identified and reported to the reinsurer in a complete, accurate, and timely manner. Obviously, if the company is seen to be doing a very responsible and thorough job in its reinsurance administration, the reinsurer will be inclined to spend its resources auditing other companies where the track record may not be as good. Such a demonstration might be made by sharing a copy of the audit report made by another reinsurer.

Audit Reports

Some reinsurers would be willing to have ceding companies conduct "self-audits" or quality control reviews and report the results to the reinsurer. Another method of supplying this information is through actuarial certification of reserves and inforce. These reports would not replace reinsurer audits entirely, but could help reduce the frequency or extent of reinsurer audits by providing assurance that the ceding company has an ongoing program for reviewing its reinsurance administration.

A ceding company might find it helpful to obtain special letters or reports from its external auditors or state examiners covering the ceding company's reinsurance administration. If such letters or reports indicate that the ceding company has adequate internal controls over reinsurance ceded, the reinsurer may be able to defer or even forego an on-site audit.

Each of these sources must be reviewed in light of the purpose served and the expertise with which each was executed. In any case these audits should not be relied upon solely.

Electronic Data Transfer

At least one reinsurer utilizes a procedure whereby the ceding company supplies the reinsurer with an abbreviated copy (*e.g.*, on magnetic tape) of their entire policy master file. The reinsurer then combines all policies on the same insured, based on name and birth date, and compares the total face amount to the retention of the ceding company as of each policy date.

If the sum of policy amounts is greater than the ceding company's retention and there is no reinsurance indicator, a listing of these policies is then printed out to be checked by the ceding company. If jumbo polices are involved they should be checked to make sure they were submitted facultatively.

If the sum of policy amounts is within the ceding company's retention but there is a reinsurance indicator, this information is also listed and reported to the ceding company. These cases should be checked to reconcile the apparent inconsistency.

If the ceding company denotes reinsurance by reinsurer, it is possible to compare all the policies that are reinsured against the reinsure's records. The comparison is based on the ceding company's policy number. The reinsurer checks to make sure that each policy shown as reinsured with them is on its reinsurance master file, and any policy on its master file is also shown as an active policy on the ceding company's file. The reinsurer indicates discrepancies for the amount issued by the ceding company, birth date, policy date, and name of insured and reports this information to the ceding company for further investigation and appropriate corrective action.

JOINT-REINSURER OR SHARED AUDITS

There may be situations in which consideration should be given to the possibility of reinsurers sharing in an audit of a ceding company. The most common situation involves reinsurance pools. The audit can take the form of either two or more reinsurers providing personnel to make up a single audit team (joint-reinsurer audit), or one reinsurer undertaking the audit of a ceding company on behalf of all interested reinsurers and supplying the results directly to them (shared audit).

Some of the advantages of joint-reinsurer or shared audits include the following.

(1) Convenience to the ceding company (by reducing the number of on-site audits)
(2) Expense savings, primarily for the reinsurers but, to some extent, for the ceding company as well
(3) Increased likelihood that the several reinsurers will adopt consistent interpretations of treaty wordings which may not have originated with any one of them.

There can be distinct disadvantages to joint-reinsurer or shared audits; some of them are as follows.

(1) There may be issues regarding impermissible sharing of information between competitors (this is probably not significant if the only connections among the reinsurers and the ceding company relate to a common reinsurance pool)

(2) Some reinsurers may not wish to rely upon the standards and care used by another reinsurer conducting an audit

(3) If the lead (or other appointed) reinsurer performs an audit and reports to other reinsurers, there may be issues of (a) liability as to any problem not identified, and (b) disputes with the ceding company as to any negative comments communicated to third parties.

In many cases, the reinsurers may have agreements with the ceding company other than a pool agreement. If so, the reinsurers may have very different points of view about the significance of specific findings. For example, one reinsurer may have an ongoing relationship for reinsuring new business while other reinsurers may have only "runoff" agreements. In addition, some reinsurers may be reluctant to have the specific terms and conditions of their agreements, including various exchanges of correspondence, shared freely with other reinsurers.

Given the potentially serious concerns associated with joint-reinsurer or shared audits, such an undertaking should be approached very carefully. Good communication among all the parties involved in such an audit is a must.

The subject of joint-reinsurer or shared audits may, if sufficient interest is identified, be the subject of a separate paper.

Glossary[1]

Acquisition Costs
Expenses incurred by an insurer or *reinsurer* in the process of writing new or renewal business, including producer commissions.

Admitted Assets
Cash and investments that meet criteria for liquidity and safety set by the National Association of Insurance Commissioners and by individual state commissioners. Only *admitted assets* are used in measuring the *capacity* and soundness of an insurer. Non-*admitted assets*, such as overdue receivables, are excluded from statutory assets and *surplus*.

Admitted Reinsurance
Reinsurance that is provided by a *reinsurer* licensed or authorized in the jurisdiction in question. *Ceding companies* may automatically take credit in that jurisdiction for *admitted reinsurance*. A

---

[1]An important contribution to this glossary was made by Robert Kaufman, Ardian Gill, and Kirk Roeser, in the form of an earlier glossary of reinsurance terms which they prepared for Gill and Roeser, Inc., 535 Fifth Avenue, New York, NY 10017. We gratefully acknowledge their permission to incorporate that work into this glossary.

ceding company may take credit for non-*admitted reinsurance* only if it is secured by a *letter of credit,* a *trust agreement* or *funds withheld* in a form acceptable to the regulators.

Aggregate Limit
The maximum sum of recoveries payable under those reinsurance agreements that provide an overall maximum loss limitation.

Aggregate Retention
An additional *retention* kept net by the *ceding company* of losses otherwise recoverable from the *reinsurer.* Only after the *aggregate retention* is exceeded can the *ceding company* recover from the *reinsurer.*

Alien Reinsurer
A non-U.S. domiciled *reinsurer* writing reinsurance in the U.S.

Alphabet Split
A method of allocating automatic reinsurance among several *reinsurers.* Using this method, each *reinsurer* is assigned a series of letters, and reinsurance is *ceded* based on the first letter of the insured's surname.

Arbitration Clause
A provision in reinsurance agreements that provides for nonjudicial settlement of disputes between parties. Generally, each party chooses an arbiter, the arbiters agree on an umpire and these three agree on a resolution of the dispute. Under some clauses, an unsatisfied party may have the option to seek judicial relief following an arbitration finding.

Assume
To accept or take over a risk, the converse of *cede.*

Assumption Reinsurance
A form of reinsurance under which policy administration and the contractual relationship with the insured, as well as all liabilities, pass to the *reinsurer;* the novation of liability is evidenced by an assumption certificate issued to the insured who, in some jurisdictions, has the right to refuse the change in insurers. See *Indemnity Reinsurance.*

Attachment Basis

A provision in many *stop loss* reinsurance agreements that determines whether, and in what manner, a reinsurance agreement covers a specific loss.

Automatic Reinsurance

A reinsurance agreement under which the *reinsurer* is obligated to accept or *assume* risks which meet certain specific criteria based on the *ceding company*'s underwriting.

Binding Limit

The amount of risk over the *ceding company*'s *retention* which can be automatically *ceded* if all other conditions are met.

Bordereau

A written schedule of insureds, premiums and losses submitted to *reinsurers* under certain types of reinsurance agreements. See *Self-Administration*.

Brokerage Market

Reinsurers who write business through reinsurance *intermediaries* or brokers. *Reinsurers* who do not generally accept such business are referred to as professional or direct *reinsurers*.

Calendar Year YRT

A *YRT* scale where the annual premium is due and payable on January 1 of each calendar year.

Capacity

The amount of *exposure* that a *reinsurer* is willing to accept on a risk, program, line of business or entire book of business.

Captive

An insurance or reinsurance subsidiary of an agent, group of agents, industrial company, trade association, or not-for-profit organization. *Captives* insure or reinsure parent-related business, non-parent business, or both. Though the number of domestic *captives* is increasing, most *captives* are still located in offshore domiciles such as Barbados, Bermuda or the U.K.'s Channel Islands.

Carryover Provisions

A multi-year rating device found in some reinsurance agreements which provides that a loss to *reinsurers* in a given time period may be applied to the results of a previous period (loss carryback) or may be applied to a future period (loss carryforward).

Catastrophe

A disaster involving multiple insureds and/or locations. Hurricanes, tornadoes, explosions and earthquakes are the most common *catastrophe* examples. *Catastrophe* is also sometimes used to designate a single large loss-generally $5,000,000 or more, or an event affecting a minimum number of lives, *e.g.*, three. *Catastrophe* reinsurance indemnifies the *ceding company* for such losses, subject to an agreed *retention, coinsurance,* and maximum limit.

Cede

To transfer an insurance risk from the company originally issuing the policy to another insurance company known as the *reinsurer.*

Ceding Commission

The amount paid by the *reinsurer* to the *ceding company* to cover the *ceding company's acquisition costs* and overhead expenses, taxes, licenses and fees, and, perhaps, a share of expected profits, usually expressed as a percentage of the gross reinsurance premium.

Ceding Company

A ceding insurer or a ceding *reinsurer*. A ceding insurer is an insurer which underwrites and issues an original, primary policy to an insured and contractually transfers (*cedes*) a portion of the risk to a *reinsurer*. A *ceding reinsurer* is *reinsurer* which transfers (*cedes*) a portion of the underlying reinsurance to a *retrocessionnaire*.

Chargeback

A specified portion of the excess of reinsurance allowances paid over *ceded* premium which the *ceding* company returns to the *reinsurer* in the event of a lapse during a defined period. *Chargebacks* are used to protect the *reinsurer* in the event of early lapse.

Coinsurance

Indemnity life reinsurance under which the reserves as well as the risk are transferred to the *reinsurer;* the *ceding company* retains its liability to the contractual relationship with the insured.   See *Modified Coinsurance* and *Assumption Reinsurance.*

Commutation

The *termination* of all obligations between the parties to a reinsurance agreement, normally accompanied by a final cash settlement.   *Commutation* may be required by the reinsurance agreement or may be effected by mutual agreement.

Co Mod-co

See *Partially Modified Coinsurance.*

Conditional Automatic

A reinsurance arrangement where the *reinsurer* underwrites all cessions. Conditional *automatic reinsurance* is generally used only if the *ceding* company does not have underwriters or MIB facilities.

Conditional Receipt

A provision included in some life insurance policies providing coverage from the date of the application to the date at which the policy is either issued or declined.

Convention Blank

A summary of an insurance company's financial operations for a particular calendar year, supported by detailed exhibits and schedules, and filed with the state insurance department in each jurisdiction where the insurance company is licensed. It is also referred to as the annual statement. The *convention blank* is developed by the National Association of Insurance Commissioners (NAIC).

Cover Note

Confirmation by the *intermediary* to the *ceding company* of terms and conditions and percentage placed with each *reinsurer.*

Credibility

A statistical measure of the reliability of experience data, based on the size of the sample.

Cut Through Endorsement

An endorsement to a reinsurance agreement which requires that, in the event of the *ceding company's* insolvency, any loss covered under the reinsurance agreement be paid by the *reinsurer* directly to the insured (or a third party beneficiary). Also called assumption endorsement or assumption of liability endorsement (ALE).

Direct Premium Written

An insurer's premium income calculated before reflecting reinsurance inward or outward.

Errors and Omissions Clause

A provision in reinsurance agreements which is intended to neutralize any change in liability or benefits as a result of an inadvertent error by either party.

Escrow Account

An instrument used to segregate assets of one company for the benefit of another company.

Excess Reinsurance

A form of reinsurance under which recoveries are available when a given loss exceeds the *ceding company's retention* defined in the agreement. Also called excess of loss reinsurance.

Experience Rated

A reinsurance arrangement which allows the *ceding company* to share in a portion of any profits realized on the reinsurance.

Experience Refund

Under a reinsurance agreement, that part of the profits which is returned to the *ceding company* after recognition of contingency reserves, loss carryforward and loss carryback provisions. See *Carryover Provision.*

Experience Refund Reinsurance

A form of reinsurance, typically *yearly renewable term,* under which the premium *rates* are subject to an *experience refund* as opposed to being fixed (non-refund).

Exposure
Measure of vulnerability to loss, usually expressed in dollars or units.

Extra Contractual Obligations (ECO)
A generic term that, when used in reinsurance agreement, refers to damages awarded by a court against an insurer which are outside the provisions of the insurance policy, due to the insurer bad faith, fraud or gross negligence in the handling of a claim. Examples are *punitive damages* and *losses in excess of policy limits.*

Facultative
Reinsurance under which the *ceding company* has the option (faculty) of submitting and the *reinsurer* has the option of accepting or declining individual risks.

Facultative Obligatory
A form of life reinsurance which is a hybrid between *facultative* and *automatic.* A risk *ceded* is submitted to the *reinsurer* which has limited rights to decline individual risks.

FEGLI
A reinsurance *pool* established for the Federal Employees Group Life Insurance

Financial Reinsurance
A form of reinsurance which considers the time value of money and has loss containment provisions. Its primary objective is typically the enhancement of the *ceding company's* financial statements or operating ratios.

Flip-flop
A method of allocating *automatic reinsurance* among several *reinsurers* used in conjunction with *layering.* Under this method, each *reinsurer* is assigned a portion of the alphabet and receives the first *layer* of reinsurance on all insureds with surnames falling in its portion of the alphabet. It will receive the second *layer* of reinsurance on a different portion of the alphabet, and so on depending on the number of *layers.*

Follow the Fortunes
A provision in some reinsurance agreements, not always specifically identified as such, in which it is agreed that the *reinsurer* is bound to the same fate as the *ceding company* with respect to risks covered.

Foreign Reinsurer
A *reinsurer* chartered (domiciled) in one state writing business in another state is considered to be foreign in the non-domiciliary state. In its own state, the *reinsurer* is considered to be domestic.

Fronting
A situation where one insurance company issued policies to specified applicants and reinsures all or substantially all of the risks on the insurance to another insurance company for a fee or portion of the profits. *Fronting* typically is used in jurisdictions where the reinsuring company is not licensed to do business.

Funds Withheld
Assets that would normally be paid over to a *reinsurer* but are withheld by the *ceding company* to permit statutory credit for non-*admitted reinsurance*, to reduce a potential credit risk or to retain control over investments. Under certain conditions, the *reinsurer* may withhold funds from the *ceding company*.

Funds Withheld Mod-co
A form of modified *coinsurance* where the initial allowance which is normally paid to the *ceding company* is withheld by the *reinsurer* to lessen the *reinsurer's exposure* to risk.

Generally Accepted Accounting Principles (GAAP)
A method of reporting financial results in accordance with a going concern basis.

Gentlemen's Agreement
A concept formerly applied to reinsurance agreements which emphasized the reliance upon the mutual integrity and good will of the parties to the agreement in order to solve disputes.

Guaranteed Cost Reinsurance
A form of reinsurance which has no adjustable or *experience refund* features. The final premium *rate* for the coverage is exactly as set forth *ab initio* in the contract.

Honorable Undertaking

A phrase in some older reinsurance agreements, usually in the following context: "This agreement is considered by the parties hereto as an *honorable undertaking*, the purpose of which is not to be defeated by a strict or narrow interpretation of the language thereof."

Incurred But Not Reported (IBNR)

The actuarial estimate or reserves required to pay *ultimate net losses* (*UNL*) after netting out existing reserves on reported but unpaid claims. This estimate includes an allowance for potential changes in such existing reserves as well as additional reserves for claims that have already occurred but are yet to be reported.

Indemnity Reinsurance

A form of reinsurance under which the risk but not the administration is passed to the *reinsurer* which indemnifies the *ceding company* for losses covered by the reinsurance agreement of *treaty*. The *ceding company* retains its liability to and its contractual relationship with the insured.

Indexing, Indexation

The adjustment of a *ceding company's retention* and the reinsurance limit by a measure of inflation such as the Consumer Price Index. Under *indexation*, the *ceding company's* original *retention* and the reinsurance limit are multiplied by the result of dividing the index on the settlement date by the index as of the effective date of the reinsurance agreement.

Individual Cession Administration

A reinsurance arrangement where the *reinsurer* sets up individual records for each cession and calculates the reinsurance premium, inforce, and reserve information for its financial reports.

Insolvency Clause

A provision in reinsurance agreements that provides for the continuance of payments of the obligations of the *reinsurer* as though no insolvency had occurred, with appropriate recognition of additional expenses of the *reinsurer* caused by the insolvency. Required in most states.

Intermediary

A third party in the design, negotiation and administration of a reinsurance agreement. Intermediaries recommend to *ceding companies* the type and amount of reinsurance to be purchased and negotiate the placement of coverage with *reinsurers*. Also called a broker. See *Brokerage Market.*

Intermediary Clause

A provision in reinsurance agreements which identifies the *intermediary* negotiating the agreement. Most *intermediary* clauses shift all credit risk to *reinsurers* by providing that (1) the *ceding company's* payments to the *intermediary* are deemed payments to the *reinsurer*, (2) the *reinsurer's* payments to the *intermediary* are not payments to the *ceding company* until actually received by the *ceding company*. This clause is mandatory in some states.

Jumbo Limit

A limit placed on the amount of coverage that may be inforce or applied for on an individual life for *automatic reinsurance* purposes. If such insurance exceeds the limit, the risk must be submitted for *facultative* review.

Layer

A horizontal segment of the liability insured, *e.g.*, the second $100,000 of a $500,000 liability is the first *layer* if the *ceding company* retains $100,000, but a higher *layer* if it retains a lesser amount. See *Pro Rata.*

Layering

A method of allocating *automatic reinsurance* among several *reinsurers*. Using this method, reinsurance is *ceded* in *layers*. The *layers* are defined in terms of amounts of insurance. One *reinsurer* will receive all reinsurance up to the limit of the first *layer*. A second *reinsurer* will receive all reinsurance in excess of the first *layer* up to the limit of the second *layer*, and so forth, depending on the number of *layers*.

Lead Reinsurer

The *reinsurer* who negotiates the terms, conditions and premium *rates* and first signs on to the *agreements*; *reinsurers* who subsequently accept those terms and conditions are considered following *reinsurers*. Uncommon in life reinsurance.

Letter of Credit

A financial guaranty issued by a bank that permits the party to which it is issued to draw funds from the bank in the event of a valid unpaid claim against the other party; in reinsurance, typically used to permit reserve credit to be taken with respect to non-*admitted reinsurance*; an alternative to *funds withheld* and *modified coinsurance*. Also referred to as a LOC.

Lloyds

An insurance or reinsurance organization in which individuals or groups of individuals, called syndicates, rather than corporations, are at risk.

Loss Event

Any trigger for a recovery under an insurance of reinsurance agreement. Examples include *occurrence*, claims made, death or disability.

Losses in Excess of Policy Limits

A term that, when used in reinsurance agreements, refers to damages awarded by a court against an insurer in favor of the insured, due to the insurer's having failed to settle a third party claim against the insured within the policy limits by reason of bad faith, fraud or gross negligence. See *Extra Contractual Obligations* and *Punitive Damages*,

Losses Portfolio Transfer

A form of *financial reinsurance* for property and liability insurers involving the transfer of loss obligations already incurred which, when ultimately paid, will exceed the consideration paid to the *reinsurer* for undertaking such obligations. The amount by which the transferred obligations exceed the consideration paid is the resultant increase to the *ceding company's* statutory *surplus*.

Loss Ratio

Incurred losses (including applicable (*IBNR*) dividend by *earned premium* for an accounting or *treaty* period. *Loss ratios* can be calculated on an accident year, calendar year, or underwriting year basis.

Loss Ratio Coverage
A form of *stop loss* reinsurance under which the *reinsurer* pays a portion of the claims represented by a *loss ratio* in excess of a specified *loss ratio*. For example, "20% on excess of 110%" will result in claims between 100$ and 130% of premium being paid by the *reinsurer*.

Medical Information Bureau
A service bureau which compiles underwriting information. Member companies submit coded underwriting information on applicants to the MIB and receive coded information concerning impairments on new applicants from the bureau based on information compiled by other insurance company members. The company receiving information regarding an impairment must independently verify the information.

Minimum Cession
The smallest cession that a *reinsurer* will accept automatically. The minimum size is set to avoid the expenses associated with small cessions.

Mod-co Adjustment Interest Rate
In *modified coinsurance*, the interest rate used to calculate the amount payable by the *ceding company* in consideration of the reserves being transferred back by the *reinsurer*. See *Mod-co reserve Adjustment*.

Mod-co Interest Rate
The interest rate used to determine the interest credited on the beginning reserves in a mod-co transaction.

Mod-co Reserve Adjustment
The net of two *modified coinsurance* items: the interest on reserves (payable by the *ceding company* to the *reinsurer*) and the increase in the reserve (payable by the *reinsurer* to the *ceding company*).

Modified Coinsurance
Indemnity life reinsurance that differs from *coinsurance* only in that the reserves are returned to the *ceding company* while the risk remains with the *reinsurer;* the *ceding company* is required to pay interest to replace that which would have been earned by the

reinsurer if it had held the assets corresponding to the reserves in its own investment portfolio. Used to permit reserve credit to be taken with respect to a non-*admitted reinsurer*, to secure credit, and to retain control of investments. See *Funds Withheld, Coinsurance* and *Assumption.*

Net Amount at Risk

The excess of the death benefit of a policy over the policy reserve.

Non-experience Rated

A reinsurance arrangement which does not allow the *ceding company* to share in any profits realized on the reinsurance. Premiums for *non-experience rated* reinsurance generally have smaller loads than premiums for *experience rated* reinsurance.

Nonproportional

A form of reinsurance where the *reinsurer's* liability is not fixed in advance, but is dependent on the number or amount of claims incurred in a given period.

Normal Underwriting

One of the conditions for *automatic reinsurance.* The definition of what is normal for the plan is set at the inception of the agreement.

Occurrence

An adverse contingent accident or event neither expected nor intended from the point of view of the insured. With regard to limits on *occurrences,* catastrophe reinsurance agreements frequently define adverse events having a common cause and sometimes within a specified time frame, (for example, seventy-two hours) as being one *occurrence.* This definition prevents multiple *retentions* and reinsurance limits from being exposed in a single *catastrophe* loss.

Offset Clause

A provision in reinsurance agreements which permits each party to net amounts due against those payable before making payment; especially important in the event of insolvency of one party which ceases to remit amounts due to the other. This clause is often challenged by state insurance departments, creditors and others interested in maximizing the assets of the insolvent party. Also know as *set off.*

Outstanding Surplus Account
A record kept by the *reinsurer* of the amount of *surplus* that it is carrying in a *financial reinsurance* arrangement.

Partially Modified Coinsurance (Part-co)
A combination of *coinsurance* and modified *coinsurance*. In most situations a portion of the initial reserves equal to the initial allowance are held on a mod-co basis, while the remaining reserves are held on a *coinsurance* basis, eliminating any initial cash transfer. Also known as Co/Mod-co.

Participation Limit
A limit place on the absolute amount of coverage that may be inforce or applied for on an individual life for reinsurance purposes. If the insurance exceeds the limit, the *reinsurer* will decline to *assume* any of the risk. This is most commonly applied to supplementary benefits such as accidental death coverage.

Persistency Bonus
An amount paid to the *ceding company* by the *reinsurer* if the reinsurance *ceded* in a given period meets certain persistency standards. *Persistency bonuses* are used to encourage the writing of persistent business.

Placement Ratio
The ratio of paid *facultative* cessions to number of *facultative* submissions. The *placement ratio* can be used to determine the effectiveness of the *reinsurer's facultative* underwriting and the cost per cession.

Point-in-Scale YRT
A term used in conjunction with a select and ultimate *YRT* scale. It refers to the premium rate appropriate for the insured's original issue age and duration.

Policy Expense Allowance
An amount payable to the *ceding company* by the *reinsurer* in lieu of actual commissions and expenses incurred by the *ceding company*.

Pool
A method of allocating reinsurance among several *reinsurers*. Using this method, each *reinsurer* receives a specified percentage of each risk *ceded* into the *pool*. Percentages may vary by *reinsurer*.

Premium (Written/Unearned/Earned)

Written premium is premium registered on the books of an insurer of *reinsurer* at the time a policy is issued and paid. Premium for a future *exposure* period is said to be *unearned premium*. For an individual policy, *written premium* minus *unearned premium* equals *earned premium*. *Earned* premium is income for the accounting period while *unearned premium* will be income in a future accounting period.

Production Bonus

An amount paid to the *ceding company* by the *reinsurer* if the amount of reinsurance *ceded* in a given period exceeds a specified amount. *Production bonuses* are used to encourage a *ceding company* to place reinsurance with a certain carrier.

Professional Reinsurers

Reinsurers that deal with the *ceding company* through their account executives, rather than through *intermediaries*. Also known as direct *reinsurers*. See *Brokerage Market*.

Profit Commission

A provision found in some reinsurance agreements which provides for profit sharing. Parties agree to a formula for calculating profit, an allowance for the *reinsurer's* expenses, and the *ceding company's* share of such profit after expenses. See *Adjustable Features, Risk Charge* and *Experience Refund*.

Proportional

A form of reinsurance where the amount *ceded* is defined at the time of cession, although the amount of the cession may vary with time by formula.

Pro Rata

See *Quota Share*.

Punitive Damages

A term that, when used in reinsurance agreements, refers to damages awarded by a court against an insured or against an insurer in addition to compensatory damages. *Punitive damages* are intended to punish the insured or the insurer for willful and wanton misconduct and to serve as a deterrent. when the award is against an insurer, it is usually related to the conduct of the insurer in the handling of a claim, and can arise in both first party and third party coverage situations. See *Extra Contractual Obligations* and *Losses in Excess of Policy Limits.*

Quota Share
A form of reinsurance in which premiums and losses are shared proportionately between *ceding company* and *reinsurer.* One such reinsurance agreement is *quota share,* in which the same percentage applies to all policies reinsured. Another is surplus share, in which the percentage may vary from policy to policy and usually increases as policy limits increase.

Rate
The premium *rate* is the amount of premium charged per *exposure* unit, *e.g.,* per $1,000.

Recapture
The process by which the *ceding company* recovers the liabilities transferred to a *reinsurer.*

Reinsurance Pool
A multi-*reinsurer* agreement under which each *reinsurer* in the group or *pool* assumes a specified portion of each risk *ceded* to the *pool.* Contrast with *Reinsurance Wheel.*

Reinsurance Wheel
A procedure for retroceding individual life insurance risks in excess of a *reinsurer's* own *retention* to a group of *retrocessionnaires* (up to their subscribed limits) in rotation, the order being determined by their positions as spokes on an imaginary wheel. The spokes need not be of the same length, *i.e.,* limit, and a company may have more than one spoke. Contrast with *Reinsurance Pool.*

Reinsurer
A *reinsurer* contractually accepts a portion of the *ceding company's* risk.

Retention
The dollar amount or percentage of each loss retained by the *ceding company* under a reinsurance agreement.

Retrocede
To transfer a reinsurance risk *assumed* by the *reinsurer* to another insurance company.

Retrocessionnaire
A *reinsurer* that contractually accepts from another *reinsurer* a portion of the *ceding company's* underlying reinsurance risk. The transfer is known as a retrocession.

Risk Charge
An amount identified in some reinsurance agreements as specifically to be retained by the *reinsurer* for assuming the risk under the policies reinsured; a share of the profits in excess of the *risk charge* is returned to the *ceding company* as an *experience refund.* Also known as profit and expense charge, risk and profit charge, or risk and expense charge.

Risk Premium Reinsurance (RPR)
Another name for *YRT* reinsurance.

Self-Administration
A reinsurance arrangement where the *ceding company* provides the *reinsurer* with periodic reports for reinsurance *ceded* giving premium, inforce, reserve, and any other information required by the *reinsurer* for its financial reports. Also known as Bulk or *Bordereau.*

SGLI
A reinsurance *pool* established for the Servicemen's Group Life Insurance.

Sliding Scale Commission
A *ceding commission* which varies inversely with the *loss ratio* under the reinsurance agreement. The scales are not always one-to-one: for example, as the *loss ratio* decreases by 1%, the *ceding commission* might increase only $\frac{1}{2}$%. Sometimes used in reinsurance of credit insurance plans.

Spread Loss
A form of reinsurance under which premiums are paid during good years to build up a fund from which losses are recovered in bad years. This reinsurance has the effect of stabilizing a *ceding company's loss ratio* over an extended period of time.

Stop Loss
A form of reinsurance under which the *reinsurer* pays some of all of a *ceding company* aggregate retained losses in excess of a predetermined dollar amount or in excess of a percentage of premium. See *Loss Ratio Coverage*.

Surplus
The excess of assets over liabilities.   Statutory *surplus* is an insurer's or *reinsurer's* capital as determined under statutory accounting rules.   *Surplus* determines an insurer's or *reinsurer's capacity* to write business.

Surplus Relief
An increase in the *ceding company's surplus* through *financial reinsurance*.   *Ceding companies* are able to use the increase in *surplus* to write more business while retaining reasonable operating ratios.

Termination
The formal ending of a reinsurance agreement by its natural expiry, cancellation or *commutation* by the parties.   *Terminations* can be either on a cutoff or runoff basis.   Undercutoff provisions, the parties' obligations are fixed as of the agreed cutoff date. Otherwise, obligations incurred while the agreement was in force are run off to their natural extinction.

Traditional Reinsurance Market
A reinsurance arrangement where risk sharing is the primary purpose.

Treaty
The legal contract defining the *reinsurance* agreement.   A *treaty* contains common contract terms, such as a specific risk definition, data on limit and *retention*, and provisions for premium and duration, and is signed by representatives of both parties.

Trust Agreement
An agreement under which certain assets are deposited by one party (the grantor), for the sole benefit of another party (the beneficiary), into an account managed by a third party (the trustee).   In reinsurance, such an agreement is most frequently used to permit a *ceding company* to take credit for non-*admitted reinsurance* up to the value of the assets in trust.

Unusual Expenses

In life reinsurance, non-routine expenses of the *ceding company* for claims investigation, legal defense or rescission actions. The *reinsurer* typically agrees to pay such expenses as distinct from *punitive,* exemplary or other noncontractual expenses which it does not agree to pay.

Yearly Renewable Term (YRT)

A form of life reinsurance under which the risks, but not the permanent plan reserves, are transferred to the *reinsurer* for a premium that varies each year with the amount at risk and the ages of the insureds.

Zero First Year YRT

A *YRT* scale with no premium in the first year.

Bibliography

1. Bowers, N.R., et al., *Actuarial Mathematics*. Itasca: Society of Actuaries, 1984.

2. Bunner, Bruce, "Will Setoffs be Set Aside?" Best's Review, December 1989.

3. Coopers & Lybrand, *International Reinsurance Industry Guide*. London: Lloyds of London Press, LTD., 1985.

4. Ernst & Ernst, *GAAP/Stock Life Insurance Companies*. Cleveland: Ernst & Ernst, 1974.

5. Grossman, Eli, *Life Reinsurance*. Atlanta: Life Office Management Association, 1981.

6. Kempe, D.P., "Insolvency of Offshore Insurance Companies-Bermuda," Proceedings of ABA National Institute on Insurer Insolvency, June 7-8, 1986.

7. Patterson, W.S., "The New Life and Health Insurance Guaranty Association Model Act-Changes and Implications," Proceedings of ABA National Institute on Insurer Insolvency, June 7-8, 1986

8. Peat, Marwick, Mitchell, *International Reinsurance.* New York: Peat, Marwick, Mitchell and Company, 1985.

9. Pentikäinen, T., "On the Net Retention and Solvency of Insurance Companies," Skand. Aktur. J., XXV (1952). 71.

10. Robertson, R.S., "GAAP Accounting for Reinsurance Accepted" and "GAAP Accounting for Reinsurance Ceded," TSA XXVII (1975), 375.

11. Rosenthal, I., "Limits of Retention for Ordinary Life Insurance," RAIA, XXXVI (1947), 6.

12. Schibley, J.V., "A Sampler of Legal and Regulatory Issues Concerning Life Reinsurance," The Reinsurance Reporter (Lincoln National Life Insurance Company), First Quarter, 1990.

13. _____, "The Life Reinsurance Contract," unpublished presentation to the American Bar Association, August 10, 1987.

14. Semple, T.D. and R.M. Hall, "The Reinsurer's Liability," Proceedings of ABA National Institute on Insurer Insolvency, June 7-8, 1986.

15. Strain, R.W., *Reinsurance.* New York: College of Insurance, 1980.

16. Tiller, J.E., "Reinsurance - Current Financial Reporting Topics," RSA 11, No. 2 (1985). 1019.

17. Tract, H.M., "The Effect of the Insolvency of Reinsurer on Letters of Credit," Proceedings of ABA National Institute on Insurer Insolvency, June 7-8, 1986.

18. VanMieghem, D.P. and T.M. Brown, *Federal Taxation of Insurance Companies.* Paramus: Prentice-Hall Information Services, 1986.

Index

About the Authors

DENISE FAGERBERG (AKA Mrs. Tiller) is a graduate of the University of Nebraska-Lincoln. She is a Fellow of the Society of Actuaries, a member of the American Academy of Actuaries, and a Fellow of the Life Office Management Association.

Ms. Fagerberg began her actuarial career with CNA and worked at Maccabees Mutual Life Insurance Company prior to joining Transamerica Occidental Life Insurance Company as Manager of Reinsurance Pricing in 1980. In 1983, she joined Tillinghast, Nelson, and Warren, Inc. where she focused her consulting services on individual life insurance product development and reinsurance.

Ms. Fagerberg has served on the Reinsurance Section Council and as chairman of the Committee on Professional Development of the Society of Actuaries. She was a faculty member for the 1988 Society of Actuaries Seminars on Financial Reinsurance, and has participated in a number of panels and workshops at Society meetings. Ms. Fagerberg also has served as president of the Los Angeles Actuarial Club.

Since 1983 she has been married to her coauthor. Other Tiller collaborations include daughters Elizabeth Elaine (1985) and Victoria Jo (1990). Since 1987 she has been employed as full-time chef, chauffeur, banker, social director, housekeeper, bookkeeper, zookeeper, wife, and mother of the Tiller family. In her spare time, she writes reinsurance books and runs to maintain her sanity.

JOHN E. TILLER, JR. (AKA Tex) is a graduate of Harvey Mudd College in Claremont, California. He is a Fellow of the Society of Actuaries and a Member of the American Academy of Actuaries.

Mr. Tiller began his insurance career as a part-time insurance agent while in college. After pursuing an agency career for some fifteen months following college graduation, he "saw the light" and joined the actuarial student corp at Transamerica Occidental Life Insurance Company. After three years in the actuarial systems department, he transferred to Transamerica's reinsurance line of business where he eventually became Vice-President and Actuary. During his reinsurance career at Transamerica, Mr. Tiller was responsible for product development and pricing, valuation and financial reporting, underwriting, contracts, sales and marketing, and strategic planning. He also was involved in corporate efforts and planning regarding surplus management and taxes.

In 1984 Mr. Tiller joined Tillinghast, Nelson, and Warren, Inc., now Tillinghast, a division of Towers Perrin, where he became a principle shareholder and manager of the life insurance consulting practice in Irvine, California. While Mr. Tiller has been engaged in a broad range of consulting assignments, a large portion of his time has continued to be devoted to reinsurance activities.

Mr. Tiller was on the original Reinsurance Section Council of the Society of Actuaries and served as secretary of that body. He is currently on the Nontraditional Marketing Section Council, serving as vice-chairman and chairman-elect. He has been chairman of the Society's Program Committee and has served on many other committees of the Society, including those for Services to Members, Research Policy, Continuing Education, and Professional Development. Mr. Tiller also served as chairman of the ACLI group for taxation of reinsurance transactions in 1981 and has served on an Academy task force on risk classification.

Mr. Tiller was a faculty member for the Society's seminars on reinsurance in 1981 and 1988. He is a frequent speaker or discussion leader at industry meetings, including both actuarial and non-actuarial groups.

A Texas native, Mr. Tiller recently transferred to Tillinghast's Dallas office in order to be closer to his roots and to focus even more on reinsurance and related activities. Married to his coauthor since 1983, he spends his spare time trying to cope with an "actuarial housewife," four daughters, and two golden retrievers.